ADVERTISING
SIN <u>AND</u> SICKNESS

DRUGS AND ALCOHOL

Contested Histories

ADVERTISING
SIN AND SICKNESS

THE POLITICS OF ALCOHOL AND TOBACCO MARKETING 1950–1990

Pamela E. Pennock

Northern
Illinois
University
Press

DeKalb

© 2007, 2009 by Northern Illinois University Press

Published by the Northern Illinois University Press, DeKalb, Illinois   60115

Manufactured in the United States using acid-free paper

First printing in paperback, 2009

ISBN-13: 978-0-87580-625-9 (paperback : alk. paper)

All Rights Reserved

Design by Shaun Allshouse

Library of Congress Cataloging-in-Publication Data

Pennock, Pamela E.

Advertising sin and sickness: the politics of alcohol and tobacco marketing,
1950–1990 / Pamela E. Pennock.

    p. cm.

Includes bibliographical references and index.

ISBN-13: 978-0-87580-368-5 (clothbound : alk. paper)

ISBN-10: 0-87580-368-7 (clothbound : alk. paper)

1. Advertising—Alcoholic beverages—United States—History—20th century.

2. Advertising—Cigarettes—United States—History—20th century.

3. Corporate speech—United States. I. Title.

HF6161.L46P46 2007

659.19′66310973—dc22

2006016679

CONTENTS

ACKNOWLEDGMENTS

The best part is expressing my gratitude to the many considerate and knowledgeable people who have assisted me along the way. My graduate adviser at Ohio State, K. Austin Kerr, planted the seed for what grew into this project when he, an expert on the politics of Prohibition, mused about the paucity of historical research on temperance after World War II. Already fascinated by the politics and culture of the postwar period, I did some quick digging and discovered the 1950s congressional hearings on alcohol advertising, revealing to me a movement about which I could find almost no scholarly literature, further piquing my curiosity. Reading what were, to me at least, the engrossing transcripts of those hearings, I saw many connections to the modern antismoking movement. Austin helped me articulate my ideas and encouraged me to take my subjects, antismoking and antidrinking activists, seriously in their roles as historical and political actors.

Professors Susan Hartmann and David Steigerwald also provided constructive guidance and feedback when this project was at dissertation stage. The Ohio State Graduate School funded two of my vital research trips, and the John F. Kennedy Presidential Library and the Hagley Museum and Library generously provided funds for my research at their impressive and welcoming facilities. At the University of Michigan—Dearborn, the Women's Studies program awarded me a grant to support research at the Bentley Library in Ann Arbor, the Library of Congress, and the National Archives.

As all researchers acutely realize, the assistance of librarians and archivists is invaluable, and I have been fortunate to benefit from the diligence of many experts in that field. In particular, Marge McNinch helped me navigate the Seagram's collection at the Hagley Library, and Katherine Mollan at the National Archives took the time to help me process and think about the enormous antialcohol petition collection I encountered in the congressional records. The friendly assistance provided by the archivists at the University of Utah's Marriott Library made my time there enjoyable. Marla Schlaffer at the Center for Science in the Public Interest graciously fulfilled my perhaps unprecedented request for documentation going back to the organization's inception.

I hope that my book does justice to the knowledge and support many scholars have shared with me over the years. David Courtwright, John Burnham, Ron Roizen, and Jack Blocker helped me think about the politics of alcohol and usually led me to revise my perceptions. Fellow participants at American Studies, American Historical Association, and Church History conferences provided me with much needed encouragement and confidence that the postwar drys were worth studying and that I was on the right track in my exploration of religious history. John D'Elia and Aaron Haberman especially proved helpful in this regard. Many thanks to Trevor Thrall for helping me develop quantitative methods for approaching the petitions.

Thanks go to colleagues Charlotte Weber, Marty Hershock, Georgina Hickey, and Liz Rohan, and to my dedicated student Jenny Huff for volunteering their time and expertise to read and comment on parts or the whole manuscript; I am certain their valuable input has improved its argument and style. The reviewers who read the manuscript for Northern Illinois University Press offered perceptive suggestions, and I have tried to incorporate many of them. I'm especially grateful to the readers of my work at either book or article stage who pointed out biases I did not hold nor intended to convey. My editor, Melody Herr, has given me careful guidance and helped me to streamline the text and much of its scholarly apparatus. I wish to thank the editors of the following journals for permission to redevelop and use the essays I first published with them: *Social History of Alcohol and Drugs* 20 (2005) and *Historical Journal of Film, Radio, and Television* 25:4 (October 2005).

I could not have sustained the energy and effort to research and write this book while I was having children and teaching if not for the moral support and relief provided by many friends and, most important, my extended family. Thank you to Peg and Dwight Steen, Julie Carpenter, and Laura Yoder DeCoste for housing and looking after me during my research trips. Victoria Clement, Charlotte Weber, Molly Wilkinson Johnson, Julie Phillips, and Colleen Kennedy Hotz are old and good friends on whom I have often relied for comfort and fun. Special thanks to Marty Hershock for his selfless friendship and willingness to take time to listen to and advise me. Gerry Moran, Cam Amin, Georgina Hickey, and Liz Rohan have also helped sustain and mentor me in my pursuits as a teacher and scholar. My Aunt Pat and Uncle Jim White have frequently helped me with my work and family life, and I appreciate their generous interest in my work.

My deepest appreciation is for my husband, Bob, and our sons, Isaac and Sam, for the love and joy they give me and for hanging in there through this long process; it has encompassed most of our marriage and all of the boys' lives. I am sorry for all the times that it has taken me away from you. Thank you for your sacrifices. Finally, my parents, Ron and Donna Ehresman, who are the smartest and coolest people I know, provided me with an exceptional foundation for living and learning, and they have nurtured and supported me in countless ways emotionally, intellectually, and financially. I dedicate this book to them.

ADVERTISING
SIN <u>AND</u> SICKNESS

INTRODUCTION

Health, Morality, and Free Speech

In 1952 Methodist Bishop Wilbur Hammaker pronounced to the House and Senate Committees on Commerce that it was against "the interest of the public welfare for the manhood, the womanhood, and the youth of the land to be teased in almost unbelievably enticing ways to use liquor and use more and more of it."[1] Joined by tens of thousands of church-affiliated supporters, he demanded the abolishment of alcohol advertising from all media, particularly the virulent broadcast media. From 1947 to 1958, congressional committees held nine hearings on proposals to outlaw the marketing of alcohol. Composed primarily of Protestant reformers armed with religious-moral arguments, the movement to ban alcohol ads had strong ideological, tactical, and personal ties to the historic temperance movement. Their allies in Congress generally were identified as conservatives. The alcohol industries and their supporters in the advertising and media industries raised constitutional objections to the ad ban proposal and declared that the purpose of advertising was to nurture brand loyalty in adult drinkers. The "drys" lost: no government restrictions on alcohol advertising were implemented during the decade-long campaign.

Just a few years later, in 1964 and 1965, scientists and public officials, allied with a handful of liberal politicians, declared before the same congressional committees that cigarette smoking was harmful to the nation's health, particularly to the well-being of the nation's youth. Leaders of the emerging antismoking movement insisted that the federal government needed to take action by requiring warning labels on cigarette packaging and advertisements. In 1969 antismoking activists returned to Congress to demand that cigarette ads be banned from the airwaves, if not from all media. The tobacco industry responded by declaring constitutional objections, emphasizing the industry's economic contributions to the nation, and averring that its marketing was aimed not at hooking kids but at convincing adult smokers to switch brands. The antismokers won partial victories: tepid warning label laws and the banishment of cigarette commercials from radio and television.

Fast forward to 1985, when a coalition of public interest groups, scientists, and government officials descended upon the same congressional committees to demand tough restrictions on alcohol marketing —including warning labels and the ban of beer and wine ads from broadcast media—to protect the health of the nation and the values of children. This new temperance movement emulated the public health approach of the antismoking campaign and disavowed the religious political culture of the old temperance movement. An American Medical Association spokesman, for example, defended the warning label proposal by insisting, "We're not out fighting sin. We're fighting disease."[2] Yet, despite its secular cast, the movement, like past campaigns for temperance, sought to inhibit alcohol consumption in society. Significantly, the movement's congressional supporters came from both sides of the aisle. In response, the affected industries raised the same objections that the tobacco, alcohol, advertising, and media industries had raised since the 1950s. In the end, the advocates of alcohol marketing restrictions could claim only one small victory: the requirement of a warning label on alcohol packaging, passed in 1988.

These three episodes reveal both change and continuity in repeated policy debates over alcohol and cigarette marketing and tell us much about Americans' cultural values and policy process. Operating under the shadow of Prohibition and its repeal, Americans in the second half of the twentieth century questioned anew the consumption of alcohol and tobacco, but the questioning at the national level had largely shifted from issues of manufacture and sale to the realm of marketing. Although leaders also used a patchwork of other policy approaches such as taxation and age limitations in attempts to restrict consumption, heightened attention to advertising and labeling was evident in the national political arena after World War II. The recurring disputes over alcohol and cigarette marketing engaged a number of cultural and political issues, primarily morality, youth, science and health, commercial free speech, and federal government regulation. These regulatory efforts sparked ongoing controversy that revealed how deeply divided Americans were over the extent to which government can and should control business behaviors, public health, and individuals' values and choices.

The central question posed by the three marketing control debates was whether the principle of free expression could be held inviolate when a legal consumer product could harm human health and, as some argued, morality. Senator Strom Thurmond, a leader of the new temperance movement, raised the point of ideological conflict when he declared, "I am fully cognizant of the free speech rights of the alcohol beverage industry. But what is the cost to society of this freedom to advocate unlawful teenage drinking?"[3] Could government permit a product to be sold yet prohibit it from being advertised? Was advertising a "right" of American free enterprise? Did the federal government possess the authority to intervene in a private company's ability to advertise and in the content of its advertisements? Should the righteousness of self-restraint, the authority of science, and the ideology of wellness triumph over commercial free speech? Americans and their policymakers tried to balance the protection of health and the preservation of moral values against both their libertarian tradition and their enjoyment of consumer culture as they sought solutions to these dilemmas, encapsulated in the alcohol and cigarette marketing controversies.

All three of the marketing control movements employed comparable and sometimes identical arguments, pronounced similar policy goals, and encountered related industry and ideological opposition. At the same time, many of their tactics and constituencies differed, both because of the particular period in which each movement operated and because of the different nature and politics of the drugs they sought to regulate. The similarities speak to the ongoing contradictions inherent in America's consumer culture and constitutional polity, but the differences between the movements are just as significant, for they illustrate changes in America's political culture over the second half of the twentieth century and show how Americans have reacted differently to alcohol when compared with tobacco. Teasing out the changes and continuities among the alcohol and tobacco marketing control debates—examining them in light of one another—illuminates significant themes and problems in recent American politics and culture.

AMERICAN VALUES IN TENSION

In American consumer culture, tension is continually created because, while the economy ceaselessly manufactures objects of desire, for other cultural reasons Americans have found it necessary to control desires. Often this tension between desire and control has manifested itself in parental panics about the influence of consumer culture, specifically the mass media, on their children.[4] These cultural struggles were brought into sharp relief in the post–World War II period when certain groups of Americans, in the face of formidable economic and political opposition, attempted to impose government restrictions on the advertising of two of the most popular yet controversial consumer products, cigarettes and alcoholic beverages. For many reformers, the advertisement of alcohol and cigarettes showcased the worst of America's consumer culture: manipulation, profligacy, hedonism, and corruption of innocent youth.

Mass consumer culture did not truly arrive in America until the mid-twentieth century, when the economy's burgeoning cornucopia of goods, the rise of mass media, and the growth of ever more sophisticated advertising campaigns together fueled its expansion. And this mass consumption culture and economy was arguably the predominant shaper of post–World War II American society. The mid-twentieth century also witnessed heated criticism of mass consumption, as well as the mobilization of social-political movements that sought government control over what some critics viewed as the increasingly obtrusive marketing of alcohol and tobacco products.[5]

Since the 1920s, smoking and drinking have been emblematic behaviors of consumer culture, typifying the cosmopolitan, pleasurable, and superfluous lifestyle encouraged by consuming desires. To challenge the marketing of cigarettes and alcohol, then, was to challenge fundamental elements of American consumer society: confronting not only the "bad habits" of smoking and drinking but also the pervasiveness of commercial behavior and expression.[6] Thus, we see the efforts to control the promotion of alcohol and cigarettes arising at the same time that Americans confronted this alluring but troubling new consumer culture, a culture that played a greater part in their lives than ever before and that was largely delivered by the mass media. To borrow Peter Stearns's phrase, America's "battleground of desire" was epitomized by disputes over cigarette and alcohol marketing during the second half of the century.[7]

The three marketing control movements embody key critiques of consumerism by emphasizing public health concerns, consumer safety issues, and the protection of youth.[8] As Americans confronted their consumer culture, they struggled to sort out three often-competing value systems: liberty, morality, and health. The alcohol and tobacco marketing controversies pitted liberty and pleasure against traditional Protestant morality and self-restraint, and increasingly, as the twentieth century progressed, against a new secular morality that valued physical and psychological health.[9]

Whether for religious or secular reasons, many Americans in the second half of the twentieth century disapproved of alcohol consumption and cigarette smoking, although Americans have possessed greater consensus in their attitudes toward smoking than toward drinking. But for both substances, Americans were more troubled by their promotion in advertisements, particularly in campaigns that reached children, than by their consumption. On the other hand, Americans were wedded to ideals of freedom and individuality that they believed, despite anxieties and fears, were expressed in consumer culture and mass media.[10] The ongoing tension between these two impulses meant that, at the end of the century, Americans' position on government's right to control cigarette and alcohol advertising remained ambivalent and unresolved. This ambivalence was reflected in the policy process.

ILLUMINATING THE POLICY PROCESS

Because I examine political coalitions and concentrate on evidence from congressional hearings and debates, this is a political history. The main actors are government officials and the religious, scientific, and business leaders who pressured them, and the main narrative follows the progression of policy proposals through federal government channels and examines the reasons for their political failure or success. Determining political failure or success requires attention not only to whether proposed legislation and administrative rulings were passed and in what form, but also to how the policies were enforced, to how new policies altered the political landscape, and to whether policies produced the expected outcomes.

I concentrate on the federal arena because the three marketing control movements focused their efforts at the national government level. As the twentieth century progressed, the alcoholic beverage and tobacco industries became highly concentrated, and most firms became national and even multinational. As the media, too, increasingly became nationalized, the vast majority of cigarette and alcohol marketing was beamed across the country, projecting the same messages about drinking and smoking into every community. While at various times marketing control movements existed at state and local levels, activists understood that only the federal government—particularly Congress, the Federal Trade Commission (FTC), and the Federal Communications Commission (FCC)—possessed the jurisdiction to regulate this part of the economy effectively.

In terms of the federal policy process, these marketing control debates offer many lessons. Corresponding to the American public's conflicting values, the federal government's role in cigarette and alcohol advertising policy has also been ambivalent. National legislators and administrators—influenced by control advocates and their powerful industrial opponents, by scientific evidence and by moral claims, and by the shifting political climate regarding federal government activism—sought compromise solutions to address what they considered the most egregious problems in marketing but would leave private enterprise, profits, and constitutional freedoms intact. Although some important policy changes were enacted, for the most part federal policymaking has been characterized by hesitant measures that leave the commercial promotion of alcohol and cigarettes prominent in America's marketplace.

The three case studies are significant for showing how the political culture of marketing control movements changed over the second half of the twentieth century. The major shift I chronicle has been from a religious-moral basis of policymaking to a secular morality still founded upon values but drawing on scientific evidence to combat industry, consumerism, and illness. Although many important policy debates, such as over abortion, have not become secularized, alcohol and cigarette issues provide clear examples of the "secularization of American public life" over the course of the twentieth century.[11] A related change in political culture involves the different ways that the movements used leadership and mobilized constituencies. The first alcohol marketing control movement employed strategies similar to those of Protestant activists in the late nineteenth and early twentieth centuries; the 1960s campaign to restrict cigarette marketing used technocratic leadership and did not reach much beyond secular elites; and the second movement against alcohol marketing operated in a public interest vein characteristic of many contemporary social causes such as consumer rights and environmentalism.

We also learn from these policy contests that blanket political ideologies, encapsulated in the terms "conservative" and "liberal," do not apply neatly to alcohol and cigarette politics or to consumer culture debates in general. Liberals committed to government protection of consumers and youth often found themselves aligned with moral conservatives in advocacy of intervention, whereas liberal civil libertarians tended to form an uneasy alliance with free-market conservatives and the industries against regulating commercial speech. The debates also shed light on the subjectivity of science in the policy process and how science sometimes competes with and sometimes augments moral or ethical claims. Furthermore, the policy episodes demonstrate the role of national politicians and administrators as policy initiators in social-political movements, instead of merely operating as brokers among various interests. We also see the political mobilization of big businesses within and across industries as they confronted public attack.[12]

Integrating these stories into the established literature on postwar policymaking improves our understanding of how policy discussions about thorny personal and cultural issues proceeded as well as stalled in the late twentieth century. It also furthers our understanding of how Americans, at least from the perspective of the policy arena, have tried to hold the line against the encroachment of consumerism and mass media on values and behaviors, and how those efforts to establish principles for all of society were framed as movements to protect vulnerable children.[13]

LOOKING AT ALCOHOL AND CIGARETTES TOGETHER

In each of the three periods of policy debate, the federal government considered whether to control the marketing of a legal, widely used, and extensively marketed consumer product. Because public policy responses to alcohol and tobacco were linked throughout the twentieth century, studying policies and attitudes toward both substances provides greater insights than concentrating on only one. During the successive policy debates, participants constantly referred to policies and attitudes toward the other substance: cigarettes were frequently mentioned during discussions of alcohol marketing policy, and vice versa. Indeed, the degree to which the participants in these separate policy episodes grappled with the implications of the other substance is remarkable. Because of the way the restrictionists and their opponents themselves addressed the two substances, a thorough history of alcohol marketing policy must take into account the history of policies regulating the marketing of cigarettes. I do not examine illegal drugs, because they were almost never mentioned by the participants and did not significantly impinge on the discussions of widely advertised products. Many of the common characteristics of alcohol and cigarettes can be extended to many illegal drugs, but I concentrate on the two most advertised licit drugs to explore debates over legal marketing practices.

Americans have often thought about cigarettes and alcoholic beverages together and in the same terms, morally and politically.[14] Curiously, although the substances' physiological effects are widely different, many—if not most—Americans *perceive* tobacco and alcohol as somehow equivalent because of their historical association as "bad habits." Antidrinking and antismoking movements have been intertwined since at least the early twentieth century in the United States.[15] Other reasons for the common perception of their equivalence are that consumers ingest both products, many people consider them pleasurable, and many people consume them in similar social settings. Meanwhile, by pointing to phenomena such as secondhand smoke, harm to a fetus, and drunk driving, antismokers and antidrinkers alike claim that the legal substance in question is most insidious when it harms innocents. The similarities between alcohol and cigarettes extend to the way they are marketed. The alcoholic beverage and cigarette industries have enjoyed tremendous power in American society and economy. Both have been leading national advertisers and often engaged in comparable marketing strategies such as sponsoring rock concerts and sporting events. One advertising executive reflected that alcohol and cigarettes possessed "similar product attributes" and that both industries worked to create the same mood in their ads: "entertainment and enjoyment."[16] Indeed, alcohol and cigarette advertising have become two of the best examples of the main thrust of consumer culture in the twentieth century: the therapeutic ethos. Through abundant use of lifestyle symbols, advertisers focus on selling not merely the product, but a total lifestyle that promises pleasure, sexual attractiveness, adventure, and sophistication, among other desirable attributes.[17]

The differences between alcoholic beverages and tobacco, however, are undeniably significant, as participants on both sides of the marketing control debates have sometimes found it politically advantageous to emphasize. Although some restrictionists have argued that the two are similar in that they are the only addictive substances widely advertised on the consumer market—a claim that ignores caffeine and sugar—their habit-forming properties, effects on the body, and costs to society differ. Yet the dominant perception among Americans and policymakers has been that alcohol and tobacco are analogous and even interrelated. As a consequence, policy approaches toward these distinct drugs have been surprisingly similar. To one senator speaking in 1969, "the distinction between alcohol and cigarettes" in terms of policymaking was only "one of timing."[18] Although the political movements against alcohol and cigarette marketing have been largely separate and involved mainly different constituencies, anticigarette and antialcohol activists have used many of the same arguments, borrowed tactics, and learned lessons from one another. Leaders of all three movements argued that the advertising in question was dangerous because it glamorized the product, which was an unquestionable threat to public health and even moral and social well-being. To turn this argument into a rationale for government action, restrictionists in each movement insisted that advertisements were inherently false and misleading because they failed to disclose the "other side of the story"—the hazards caused by consumption.

Although the ideological foundation of the marketing control movements shifted from preserving religious morality to protecting public health, the desired policy outcomes and, for most participants, the underlying values did not change significantly.[19] Leaders of each marketing control movement asserted that the product in question was "unhealthful," a word that carries negative cultural connotations. Some religions and persons equate unhealthful behaviors (that is, behaviors that could harm physical health) with immorality because they pollute the temple of the body. Even if the moral condemnation of cigarettes and alcohol were not taken that far, discussions that indicted the products from a scientific standpoint easily slid into discussions that revolved around the propriety of the product. Although the marketing restrictionists, especially those who participated in the second two movements, were not the moral zealots and raving prohibitionists that the industries painted them as, they also were not unprejudiced.

Just as the movements to restrict alcohol and cigarette marketing shared critical ideological and political impulses, the defensive strategies used by the alcohol and tobacco industries were markedly similar to one another. Among American industries in the twentieth century, the alcoholic beverage and tobacco industries shared the distinction of having been most threatened by hostile public opinion. The manufacturers, organized in trade associations, established self-policing codes of advertising, as did the broadcast industry. All of these codes included comparable rules, and both the tobacco and the distilled spirits industries have, at various times, refrained from advertising on broadcast media. In addition to their marketing decisions, the industries' rhetorical strategies displayed considerable similarities to one another. They charged that any curb on the marketing of a legal product would result in the eventual regulation and possible ban of all advertising, a dire threat to American free enterprise. Related to this theme was the industries' charge of paternalism—that government would in effect act as Big Brother (or National Nanny) if it enacted the proposed cigarette and alcohol marketing controls.[20] Yet, because of the often acknowledged distinctions between alcohol and cigarettes, as well as the differences in how the public has perceived these substances over time, the alcohol and tobacco industries' responses to public criticism also have differed from one another. This difference mainly derives from the reality that the intoxicating effects of alcohol cannot be denied, but the health hazards of tobacco have been more readily concealed.

Further connecting the three marketing control movements and the responses of the affected industries was the shared experience of being overshadowed, or haunted, by the legacy of Prohibition. The Victorian era temperance movement culminated in the passage of the Eighteenth Amendment in 1919, but fewer than fifteen years later the movement suffered a terrible blow when Prohibition was repealed. The prevailing view—which has been firmly held by opponents of alcohol and cigarette marketing controls—has been that Prohibition was an ill-conceived and failed experiment in federal government authority to dictate unpopular moral values to the American public and devastate a private industry by overstepping boundaries of freedom and choice in a democratic society. During Prohibition, it was held, the federal government, swayed by a minority group of zealots, turned into Big Brother—with disastrous results. Prohibition, then, became a lesson in guarding against government intervention in our private lives and enterprise.

Alcoholic beverage manufacturers, not surprisingly, were highly sensitive to criticism of their products and to encroachment on their "rights" in the years (which extended into decades) after repeal. As damaging health reports about cigarettes began to surface in the 1950s, tobacco companies shared their anxiety. Both industries painted any move to restrict their manufacturing, sales, and marketing as a step back toward Prohibition: the dreaded slippery slope. Industry representatives in all three debates often argued that the marketing control advocates were closet prohibitionists whose real aim was to impose their moral strictures onto everyone else. A significant number of policymakers thought that the industries' slippery slope and "backdoor prohibition" arguments had merit, for government intervention in marketing might prove as injurious to the nation as prohibition of manufacture and sale, especially in an era of high consumerism when marketing was so instrumental in people's daily lives and fueled America's economy and culture.

As I trace the attempts to control and ban cigarette and alcohol marketing—initiatives that, if successful, promised to reshape Americans' definitions of and relationships to the consumer market—I explore the dialogue between politics and cultural values. Federal politics was the arena in which profound cultural dilemmas about morality, health, consumerism, free expression, and the authority of science were encountered and contested. The policy movements explored here represent a continuation of many Americans' historic demands for public policies to ameliorate the health problems and perceived moral corruption caused by tobacco and alcohol consumption. At the same time, they reflect a changing society as modern America moved into an age of science, mass consumerism, new media, and changing regulatory climates. The campaigns against cigarettes and alcohol and their marketing are prime examples of an affluent society's rising assessment of the value of public health, as well as its anxiety about marketing's influence on personal behaviors, both of which demonstrate how the scientific assessment of risk became entangled with moral condemnation.

PART I

The Failed Fight to
Ban Alcohol Advertising,
1947–1958

TEMPERANCE AND MASS SOCIETY

In mid-January 1950, a standing-room-only crowd flocked to a Senate hearing room to show its support for a bill before the Committee on Commerce that would ban all interstate advertisement of alcoholic beverages. The national press, which dedicated very limited coverage to the affair, found the size, composition, and behavior of the hearing's audience worthy of curiosity and comment. Not only were there so many vociferous elderly women, but they also had brought box lunches and ate them while sitting on the steps leading up to the building. Box lunches, apparently, were an oddity in Washington, D.C., and, to the reporters at least, they demonstrated how out-of-touch and old-fashioned these "old ladies" were.[1]

This was the fourth time this scene had been repeated in a hearing room in the nation's capital since 1939, and it would occur six more times during the 1950s, for a total of ten congressional hearings devoted to antialcohol advertising proposals. Almost twenty years after the repeal of Prohibition, these women (and men) had not abandoned their intense commitment to achieving a temperate, if not abstinent, America. The vast majority of them belonged to Protestant denominations and affiliated nondenominational organizations that had supported temperance for more than a century. By the late 1940s their chief strategy for attaining a moral, pure, temperate America was to persuade Congress to ban interstate alcohol advertising. Though they did sometimes discuss alcohol's harm to health, they operated mainly from a religious-moral perspective, not from a secular-scientific or public health orientation. Alcohol advertising offended their enduring Protestant sensibilities of righteousness and self-restraint, the preservation of home and family, and the protection of innocent youth.

Such a proposal—to completely ban the advertising of an entire class of legal consumer goods from all media—was radical and significant. If successful, it would have set an important precedent not only for the alcoholic beverage industries but also for the field of advertising and for the whole of American consumer society. Even in its failure, the movement against alcohol advertising is instructive because it demonstrates how a coalition of Americans attempted to reduce the consumption of a potentially harmful and widely used consumer product by targeting its marketing for government regulation. Although such a proposal side-stepped the difficult constitutional and political questions raised by the prohibition of manufacture and sale, advertising restrictions raised a whole host of other issues that revolved around the questions of commercial free speech, acceptable advertising, and the power of mass media. Alcohol advertising was the front chosen by tens of thousands of Americans, impelled by the organized drys, to challenge society's expanding consumer desires.

The postwar temperance movement was largely out of step with the advancing trends of America's mass society, for the acceptance of alcoholic beverages was an important part of the invigorated consumerism of the late 1940s and 1950s. Contributing to this increasing acceptance of alcohol was the rise during the postwar period of a new school of thought among those who studied and treated alcohol problems—often called the alcoholism movement—that attempted to insert scientific neutrality and remove morality from alcohol concerns. The alcoholism movement's indifference, if not opposition, to restrictions on alcohol advertising demonstrated that scientists were at odds with the advocates of advertising controls, a relationship that would nearly reverse during the antismoking and the new temperance movements.

PARTICIPANTS IN THE MOVEMENT AGAINST ALCOHOL ADVERTISING

Church-affiliated temperance groups ran an organized and compelling campaign against alcohol advertising, strikingly reminiscent of the campaign for prohibition earlier in the century. Led by a core of activist drys, yet attracting many types of white Protestants, the new campaign reached Protestant churches across the country, and tens of thousands of people signed letters and petitions in support of regulatory legislation. The level of interest and support among certain pockets of the American population was extremely high. Reading the thousands of alarmed and passionate letters to members of Congress in support of the proposed ban might leave one to guess that alcohol advertising, rather than the atomic bomb and communism, was the major evil that threatened to destroy American society. This movement to ban alcohol ads relied on a strong, committed base of support that extended from U.S. senators to churchwomen in the heartland, but it could never muster enough strength to get its bill passed, let alone get it reported out of committee. The political and cultural context within which dry reformers agitated had transformed significantly since the repeal of Prohibition.

The surviving temperance movement of the 1950s was a continuation of the Christian lobby that was active on Capitol Hill in the nineteenth and early twentieth centuries. At its height, this lobby spearheaded a specific agenda to "establish the religious authority of the state" by promoting the insertion of Christ and the Bible in the Constitution as well as laws against breaking the sabbath, polygamy, obscenity, prostitution, divorce, and the liquor traffic.[2] Although the Christian lobby cannot be conflated with the temperance movement of the same period, for not all drys supported the full agenda of the Christian lobby, the lobby's activist style, minority status, and evangelical Protestant ties mark it as a predecessor to what the temperance movement became after repeal. The groups at the core of the movement carried into the second half of the twentieth century the Christian lobby's commitment to achieving moral reform through federal legislation. Some organizations' names had changed, some leaders had passed on, and some objectives were altered, but the postrepeal movement drew from the same constituency and largely maintained the same values as it had since the nineteenth century. Often, leaders of the movement to ban alcohol advertising were the very same people who had been active before and during Prohibition and were, by the 1950s, elderly. The movement mobilized mainly Protestant churches and affiliated organizations from every region of the country, but churches and organizations from the South and West, along with groups centered in and near the nation's capital, were best represented at the congressional hearings.

Methodists and Baptists were particularly committed to temperance, as they had been throughout American history, and after World War II they devoted considerable resources to this political movement. The Methodist Church's commitment was represented by its Board of Temperance, which was based in Washington, D.C., and enjoyed substantial institutional support from the larger church structure.[3] Temperance themes and coverage of alcohol advertising politics were prominent in the Board of Temperance's publication, *The Voice,* as well as in the Methodist Church's official organ, *The Christian Advocate,* that reached hundreds of thousands of members. In addition to the Board of Temperance, other Methodist divisions and organizations sent representatives to testify in favor of the antialcohol advertising bill, including the Woman's Division of Christian Service (which at the time was becoming active in the movement for

African American civil rights),[4] the National Conference of Methodist Youth, and the Council of Bishops of the Methodist Church. In 1947, the General Board of Methodism called upon all members to sign an abstinence pledge on the first Sunday in Lent and proclaimed the establishment of that Sunday as an annual Commitment Day. At the Methodist Citizenship Convocation in Washington, D.C., in 1953, national church leaders pledged to "wage unceasing war upon the liquor traffic." In that same year, the church reported that 3.5 million of the nation's 9 million Methodists had signed the Commitment Day pledge.[5]

The Baptist churches had not established a division specifically to address temperance, but the Southern Baptist Convention's Social Service Commission and the Northern Baptist Council on Christian Progress, as well as numerous pastors of Baptist churches from around the country, were active in the movement and testified multiple times at the congressional hearings. Also testifying were representatives of the Southern Baptist Convention Sunday School Board, the Woman's Missionary Union to the Southern Baptist Convention, and the Executive Committee of the Southern Baptist Convention. Many other mainstream and evangelical Christian denominations testified or sent statements of support to the congressional committees responsible for the antialcohol ad bills. Presbyterians (United and Reformed), Quakers, Evangelical Lutherans, Congregationalists, Church of the Brethren, Evangelical United Brethren Church, Seventh Day Adventists, Church of the Nazarene, the Assemblies of God, Mormons, and Christian Scientists all participated in this extensive Christian coalition against the marketing of alcohol.

Although numerous temperance and religious organizations sustained the movement, the Woman's Christian Temperance Union (WCTU) was at the helm, and its national leaders worked closely with the Methodist Board of Temperance to orchestrate the political campaign against alcohol advertising. Founded in 1874, the WCTU became the nineteenth century's largest women's organization. In its heyday, its reform aims were wide ranging and included prison reform, labor reform, aid to indigent women and children, woman's suffrage, censorship of "immoral" media and entertainment, and of course its main cause, the fight against the liquor traffic. In the late nineteenth and early twentieth centuries the WCTU was in the forefront of progressive reform. Though it continued its campaigns for censorship through the 1930s, by the 1910s the Union's principal aim was achieving national prohibition and, once won, maintaining its enforcement. Through the Prohibition period, Union membership reached 350,000. Membership declined to just over 250,000 in the early 1950s and down to 200,000 by 1961. Its publication, *The Union Signal,* had a circulation averaging 27,000 in the postwar years. Though in decline, the WCTU maintained its well-organized national network, featuring thousands of local unions, and relied on dedicated state and national leaders.[6]

A remarkable array of interdenominational, temperance, and other church-affiliated organizations appeared at or sent formal statements to the series of congressional hearings on alcohol advertising. These groups included the Federal Council of Churches, National Council of Churches, National Association of Evangelicals, United Christian Brotherhood of America, National City Youth for Christ, Christian Life Commission, National Sunday School Association, United Christian Missionary Society, International Reform Federation, National Civil League, Salvation Army, National Grange, American Temperance Society, Temperance League of America, World Prohibition Federation, National Temperance and Prohibition Council, Catholic Total Abstinence Union of America, National Temperance League, National Temperance Movement, International Order of Good Templars, Interdenominational Committee on Alcohol Problems, and a multitude of state and local temperance organizations from all parts of the nation. Norman Vincent Peale, the popular religious figure of the fifties, also participated in the movement, sending statements of support for almost every hearing and turning up to testify at the hearings in 1952 and 1958.

THE CULTURAL SETTING

Why were these religious Americans so committed to, perhaps fixated on, this advertising ban? Why was the rest of America opposed to, or simply not interested in, this cause? To generalize, the drys in the postwar period held values consistent with the old Protestant middle class of the nineteenth century: self-restraint, thrift, and sobriety. Temperance had been a significant component of the value system of most American Protestants in the nineteenth and early twentieth centuries. Originally, "temperance" had connoted restraint and moderation, but through the nineteenth century, in what was a uniquely Protestant formulation, drys increasingly equated the word with total abstinence. Abstaining from alcohol was thought to be symbolic of deeper marks of character such as self-restraint and industriousness, qualities considered necessary for success in commercial and industrial economies. For more than a century, abstinence had been the quintessential visible way to demonstrate to society that one was "respectable."[7] By the early twentieth century, at the height of Progressivism, Protestant values, with temperance at the forefront, had penetrated national political culture.

The 1920s stand as a watershed era when groups of Americans who clung to old values clashed with those who raced forward with new, modern values. One symbol for this clash is the Scopes Trial of 1925, an event that in popular accounts was supposed to have sealed the victory for secular modernity.[8] Another manifestation of value conflict during the twenties, of course, was the debate over and eventual repeal of Prohibition.

America's underlying economic transformation from an industrial, producer-oriented society into a postindustrial, consumer-oriented society meant that values associated with temperance, such as discipline and diligence, were less prized. Instead, sociability, easiness, and tolerance were embraced.[9] Moreover, the specific political event of repeal in 1933 proved highly critical in changing attitudes toward alcoholic beverages. The skillful campaign conducted by repeal advocates such as the Association Against the Prohibition Amendment convinced many who had been dedicated to abstinence as a mark of their middle-class status that drinking alcoholic beverages would make them sophisticated and, in enhancing their personal liberty, somehow more American. Newspapers and highbrow magazines in large metropolitan centers ridiculed old-fashioned prudery, and the fashionable film industry glamorized smoking and drinking.[10]

Cultural changes were accompanied by changes in political culture. During the New Deal era, the pragmatic impulse of Progressive reformers prevailed over what had been the equally influential religious-moral impulse. Reformers in the thirties spoke less of duty, shame, and sin than they did of needs, skills, and results. American society was still predominately Protestant, but the cultural milieu that had been receptive to the religious-moral discourse of the drys was fast receding.[11]

Postwar scholars such as David Riesman and William Whyte probed the cultural transformations of the last few decades. Whyte's terminology in *The Organization Man* was especially apt, labeling the shift as from a Protestant ethic to a social ethic.[12] The first part of the twentieth century saw the rise of a new middle class that embraced this social ethic, which encompassed cosmopolitanism and secularism. When this new class with its modern values attained a position of cultural dominance after World War II, the traditional values of the old middle class seemed quaint and obsolete. They were increasingly associated with rural and small-town America, even when those who adhered to them lived in cities, and these were areas that had been declining both in population and in cultural authority over the course of the century. More than ever before, rural and small-town America found itself overwhelmed in the 1950s by the relentless penetration of urban, and increasingly suburban, values spread by an ever-expanding mass culture. The choice to drink alcoholic beverages was a marker of this cultural divide in postwar America.

Although the repeal of Prohibition and the growing secular cultural and political style damaged their credibility, the drys survived—albeit with diminished cultural authority and in smaller numbers.[13] The fight to ban alcohol advertising provides a glimpse of the clash of values persisting through the 1950s. It demonstrates a part of America that the dominant culture ignored then and that continues to be overlooked today. Many Americans who held values at odds with modern, urban America had not ducked their heads and surrendered to the onslaught. Many protested what they saw as alarming trends in postwar mass society and fought for the restoration of traditional—what by then had been signified as rural— values in American life. The movement to ban alcohol advertising in part emerged from this situation. Supporters of an alcohol advertising ban were a subculture of conservative, grassroots opposition to the dominant postwar mass consumer society. They saw themselves as guardians of the nineteenth-century Protestant evangelical tradition.[14] Their movement combined a long-standing Protestant commitment to abstinence with a suspicion of mass media—particularly the new medium of television—and the techniques of modern advertising.

IDEOLOGY AND STRATEGY AFTER REPEAL

While fears of atomic disaster and pressures of conformity surely touched them, many discussions in mainline Protestant churches still focused on fears of moral decay in American society. They continued to worry about gambling, prostitution, crime, juvenile delinquency, and what for many remained the root evil, alcoholic beverages.[15] Furthermore, many church-going Americans continued to express their concerns in the form of organized political pressure on legislators, one of the most notable examples of which was the national political campaign against alcohol advertising.

The drys persisted in situating their concern about alcohol in the language of home protection, which increasingly centered on the protection of innocent youth. As had the WCTU women who campaigned for censorship of immoral literature and films earlier in the century, their rhetoric emphasized the necessity of reasserting moral control over youth, yet the activists learned to use language from political and social science arenas to express their concerns to public audiences.[16] Most other groups that were concerned about alcohol consumption in the postrepeal period, such as Alcoholics Anonymous and the Yale Center of Alcohol Studies, focused mainly on private or medical solutions, but the traditional drys continued to press for public policies targeting the alcohol industries' practices (the "liquor traffic") for regulatory action. They maintained their moral conception of law and their belief in the vital role of the state in effecting moral reform.[17]

Evidence from the drys' writings, speeches, and congressional testimony does not indicate that they sustained the nativist motivations of some reformers who participated in the earlier temperance movement, nor does it any longer evince an overt anti-Catholicism. Nevertheless, these impulses may have been implicit in the continuation of a Protestant-dominated campaign against alcohol after World War II.

Temperance organizations enjoyed a surprising amount of political power in the immediate postwar years, in light of the overall unpopularity of their cause.[18] Drys had controlled Congress in the 1920s, and some of that influence remained as late as the 1950s. Their lobbying tactics were essentially unchanged from the late nineteenth and early twentieth centuries. Drys relied heavily on mass petition and letter-writing campaigns, and their arena of mobilization remained the national Protestant organizations and local churches across the nation.[19] The Methodist Board of Temperance and the WCTU maintained offices just steps from the Capitol, employed skilled lobbyists who cultivated close contacts with key congressional members, and sometimes wrote the legislation themselves. Elizabeth Smart of the WCTU's legislative committee was also secretary of the National Temperance and Prohibition Council, an umbrella organization created by the major temperance groups to provide organizational consensus on the antiadvertising proposal. In Smart's frequent correspondence with members of Congress, she was bold in urging that hearings be held, indicating when she would like them to be held, and asking the congressional committees to discuss and vote on the bills in executive session. Methodist Board of Temperance leader Bishop Wilbur Hammaker also performed the duties of a lobbyist and essentially ran the first few congressional hearings on the alcohol ad ban proposal in the late 1940s and early 1950s.[20]

The most significant adjustment made by the postrepeal movement at the national level was its concentration on alcohol marketing controls. The movement before repeal had not completely neglected alcohol advertising, and, in fact, in the 1917 Reed Bone Dry Amendment to the Postal Act, Congress banned liquor ads from the mail. By the time the Prohibition amendment was ratified, eighteen states had passed laws restricting alcohol advertising. Moreover, an interest in marketing restrictions was a natural extension of the WCTU's long-standing agitation for censorship of various cultural forms.[21] A movement-wide focus on a national antiadvertising campaign, though, did not emerge until after World War II, and it did not really gain steam until the advent of television.

In the decade following repeal, the vanquished temperance movement concentrated on licking its wounds at the local level. Participants remained involved in temperance education and distributed temperance lessons to schools and churches.[22] Its main political strategy was to pass local option laws and dry up as many counties as possible. In fact, this strategy was moderately successful, but mainly in traditionally dry regions such as the South. After seeing steady wet gains through the 1930s, the temperance movement enjoyed an increase in dry areas during the war years. In 1946, 19.1 percent of the nation's population, or 25 million Americans, lived in areas that prohibited the manufacture and sale of liquor, including the three states (Kansas, Mississippi, and Oklahoma) that remained dry. The next few years saw increases in wet territory, and Kansas repealed state prohibition. Nationwide, the percentage of the population residing in dry areas dropped to 16.2 percent by 1951. By 1960, Mississippi was the only state under statewide prohibition, and local option elections had dampened many traditionally dry counties and towns across the country. The percentage of Americans living in dry areas dropped further to 12.7 percent.[23]

At the national level, the drys tried to take advantage of World War II by advocating measures to protect men in the armed services from alcoholic beverages, but these attempts to link the temperance cause with patriotism were unpopular and failed.[24] In the mid-1950s the temperance movement also initiated a campaign to pass national legislation to prohibit alcoholic beverages on commercial aircraft.[25] Although it tried to maintain a national presence, the movement was most active in states and localities that had opposed repeal.

Perhaps in reaction to the burgeoning mass consumer culture and concomitant acceleration of national consumer advertising after the war, by the late 1940s a ban on alcohol advertising had risen to the top of the temperance movement's national agenda. It was this issue that united the fragmented and locally oriented movement, reinvigorated it at the national level, and attracted Protestants who were not steadfast drys. Temperance groups did try to win advertising restrictions at the state level. For example, proposals for alcohol advertising bans or restrictions went before voters in Idaho, Oregon, and Washington in 1946, 1950, and 1954, respectively. All failed.[26] But temperance leaders realized that state and local regulation was inadequate. Like most advertised products in the nationalizing American marketplace of the postwar years, the most influential alcohol advertising increasingly became national in scope.[27] Drys therefore reasoned that federal regulation was needed to counter it. They began to reorganize nationally and meet with national legislators.

Striking at advertising seemed a more attainable goal than other means of reducing consumption of alcohol. In a consumer-oriented and mass media–dominated age, national advertising seemed to be the lifeblood of the business. Thus, controlling and restricting advertising would severely restrict the prosperity of the industries that supplied drink. Proponents of the ban, even though they often defined themselves as outside of the mass consumer society, shared the assumption with consumer industries and advertising men that advertising fueled business. In a publication devoted to temperance, one activist argued in 1947, "Alcoholic beverage propaganda and advertising hold the number one place among the contributors to the country's liquor problem. The liquor industries have grown steadily since repeal. . . . Without liquor advertising and propaganda this growth would not have been possible."[28] The drys assumed that a ban on advertising would seriously handicap the alcohol industries by debilitating their means of expansion, which drys believed was the use of advertising to reach new (youthful) drinkers.

Certainly, a pragmatic motive also impelled the movement to shift its focus from the control of manufacture and distribution of alcohol to the regulation of advertising. Many temperance activists remained dedicated to achieving an abstinent society, but the legacy of repeal made them careful about their politicking. It was dangerous to admit advocacy of prohibition; it left one open to the charge of being a zealot and could get a dry laughed right out of congressional chambers. In this important respect, then, the organized drys did adapt to their changed surroundings. In response to their hostile environment, postrepeal temperance activists set a less ambitious agenda for realizing a temperate America. It is important, though, to note that they still turned to national legislation as an instrument for attaining moral improvement.

Many, perhaps most, dedicated drys ultimately advocated a return to national prohibition. Accordingly, their opponents would dub their attempt to ban alcohol advertising "backdoor prohibition." Public opinion polls taken in the 1930s through the mid-1950s showed that one-third of Americans said they favored the restoration of Prohibition. By the late 1950s, this figure had dropped to one-fourth of Americans and continued to fall throughout the next few years. A survey of Methodists in 1959 revealed that 63 percent advocated prohibition. These numbers challenged the common wisdom of the "failure" of Prohibition, exposing the persistence of sharply conflicting views about the role of the state in regulating popular drugs. These polls also demonstrated that proponents of prohibition were more likely to be women than men, older Americans than younger, residents of farms and small towns than city dwellers, and Southerners than citizens from any other region.[29]

More moderate participants in the movement, however, came to believe that national policy of Prohibition had been misguided. They fought for an advertising ban because they believed, as future antismokers would, that advertising a potentially harmful product in a seductive way without warning of its deleterious effects was wrong and that the law should reflect that judgment. They accepted alcohol's legality but were intensely offended by what they saw as the blatant promotion of a commodity that they continued to view as morally and socially malevolent. Sell it, they conceded, but do not encourage it.[30]

Whatever the motive, the antiadvertising campaign excited and energized longtime temperance activists and reminded them of the heady days right before the passage of the Eighteenth Amendment. To the drys as well as their opponents it seemed that temperance strength was increasing as the ad ban campaign gained momentum. Both this excitement and the fervent belief in the righteousness of their cause led temperance leaders to exaggerate their following. For instance, Mamie Colvin, president of the WCTU, proclaimed in 1947 that "organizations having members equal to more than half of the country's voters are aligned" to support the antialcohol advertising bill. Bishop Hammaker went even further, pronouncing that 75 to 80 percent of Americans would support the bill. Several key drys grew overly optimistic about their chances, not only for the achievement of the national ban but also, for some of them, for the next step—a return to national Prohibition.[31]

MAINSTREAM AMERICA'S ACCEPTANCE OF
ALCOHOLIC BEVERAGES

Neither the advertising ban nor any government regulations of alcohol advertising, and certainly not the restoration of Prohibition, was achieved in the postwar years. Mainstream America, or the "tastemakers"—the new middle class, most media and marketers, scientists and the intelligentsia—accepted the moderate consumption of alcohol, which was typically called "social drinking," and rejected the religious political style of the bearers of the Christian lobby tradition. While it was able to hold on to some power on the national level and in major Protestant denominations, the temperance movement never approached its historic levels of popularity. The alcoholic beverage and media industries were correct in calling their opponents a minority pressure group. Most Americans were not concerned with the offensiveness of alcohol advertising. Consuming alcoholic beverages became an accepted component of the new value system that, with the rise of postwar affluence and mass society, had come to dominate America.[32]

When advertisers depicted the typical new middle-class couple sharing a cocktail in the evening or beer on the weekend while they socialized with friends, they were reflecting—and shaping—reality. Drinking alcoholic beverages—"cocktail culture"—was part of the complex of behaviors and consumption patterns that made one cosmopolitan in the postwar era, and alcoholic beverage advertisers took care to depict their products in that context. The industries were acutely aware of the social and economic trends in their favor and frequently promoted studies that heralded them.[33] Their aggressive marketing and public relations campaigns in the years after repeal were part of a strategic effort to, as historian Lori Rotskoff argues, "normalize and domesticate drinking."[34] The greater acceptance of alcoholic beverages among the middle class was one of the measures of the shift in the postwar era from traditional or rural values to new or urban values.

Yet, although drys and drinkers reflected a significant divergence in values, the advocates of an alcohol ad ban were not entirely separated from mainstream American culture. Many Americans, not just drys, were troubled by the ascendancy of mass culture, and they directed their anxieties into a wide-ranging debate over mass media's influence on youth. The mass culture debate of the 1950s, however, was populated by principally secular figures, and they had little interest in, or awareness of, the alcohol advertising controversy that was occurring simultaneously and in neighboring congressional hearing rooms. Many factors marked the antialcohol advertising movement off from the more mainstream deliberation over the effects of mass media, not the least of which was the drys' appeal to nineteenth-century evangelical traditions. Nevertheless, the antialcohol advertising movement fits into the larger anxiety over youth and mass culture in the 1950s.

THE ALCOHOLISM MOVEMENT

Another major shift that both contributed to and was influenced by Americans' increasing acceptance of alcoholic beverages after repeal was the emerging attitude of the academic and professional health communities toward the consumption of alcohol. The new attitude encompassed two components: scholarly research, represented by institutions such as the Yale Center of Alcohol Studies, and grassroots activism, represented by Alcoholics Anonymous. The antagonistic relationship between the alcoholism movement and the temperance movement sheds light on the dynamic between science and morality in the mid-twentieth century. The scientific and social scientific communities were indifferent, if not opposed, to the antialcohol advertising proposal and other temperance initiatives in this period.

During the 1930s and 1940s, the groups of people involved in the alcoholism movement progressively narrowed the definition of alcohol problems until the sole focus was on alcoholism and the alcoholic. A medical model of alcohol problems, best represented by the disease theory of alcoholism, was revived from nineteenth-century attempts and popularized in the 1940s and 1950s. Most proponents of medicalization viewed alcoholism as a progressive disease, starting as a psychological addiction and leading to a physical addiction to alcohol. Some adherents expanded on the theory and argued further that the abuse of alcoholism was not a choice or moral failing, but rather an inborn, physiological defect, sometimes referred to as an allergy to alcohol. Therefore, in its shift from sin to sickness, the ultimate implication of the disease theory was to remove moral stigma from alcohol abuse. In this way, proponents considered it a more compassionate and enlightened approach to alcoholism.[35]

This stance toward problems of alcohol was successfully promoted by a number of organizations, including the Yale Center of Alcohol Studies, the Research Council on Problems of Alcohol, and especially the National Council on Alcoholism (formerly the National Committee for Education on Alcoholism). Alcoholics Anonymous (AA), which was formed in 1935 as an organization to promote the self-reform of alcoholics, by the 1950s had seen its chapters spread through communities across the nation. AA played a major role in publicizing the disease concept of alcoholism, and a principal component of AA's philosophy was that alcoholics were constitutionally different from "normal" drinkers. Reflecting the cultural transformations since the 1920s and the repeal of Prohibition, most Americans, as well as the mainstream media, were responsive to a medicalized model and largely accepted this new paradigm for thinking about alcohol consumption and alcohol problems.[36]

The alcohol industries, after a period of uneasiness and skepticism, came to wholeheartedly support the alcoholism movement. Because the movement located the problem of alcoholism not in the bottle but in the minority of drinkers with physiological defects, it in effect removed the old stigma from alcohol suppliers. Industry members and their trade associations financially supported alcoholism research programs, and organizations such as the Research Council on Problems of Alcohol courted their support. Added to their own advertising themes and public relations campaigns, the industries' promotion of the alcoholism movement and its medical model was an important component of their campaign to normalize drinking.[37]

The new paradigm and its acceptance by tastemakers and policymakers deeply influenced public policy toward alcoholic beverages for decades. According to proponents of the alcoholism movement, moderate, or social, drinking was the norm and perfectly acceptable. Only a minority of the population was afflicted with the disease of alcoholism, so the rest of the public could drink alcoholic beverages with few problems. The movement did not recognize the gray area of the occasional "problem drinker." One was either an alcoholic or not. This perspective, then, removed the need for strict regulations on alcoholic beverages because the majority of Americans could enjoy them without bad result. For instance, in 1945 Howard Haggard, editor of the *Quarterly Journal of Studies on Alcohol*, published an editorial that disparaged a proposal in the state of Massachusetts to attach warning labels to liquor containers. He argued that, because all drinkers will read the label, "it has not separated by a sharp line the moderate drinker from the excessive. It has tried to embrace all drinkers in whatever amount and has got more than its arms will hold." The proposed label, in effect, "cried wolf" because only a very few of the many who drink were in danger. The label, Haggard concluded, would lead to "indifference and disregard." He believed that any initiative to control alcohol abuse should be directed at the small minority of alcoholics instead of forcing "the 41.5 million [normal drinkers] into an unwilling alliance with the excessive drinkers."[38] Haggard's piece stands as a prime example of the scientific community's rejection of the comprehensive public policy solutions of the temperance movement. The alcoholism movement also influenced public policy through its focus on treatment instead of prevention of alcoholism. Public funding for alcohol abuse was almost exclusively channeled into treatment centers that were springing up around the nation during the 1950s and 1960s.[39]

The alcoholism movement and the temperance movement thus comprised two groups of Americans who were both concerned with alcohol problems, even though they defined those problems very differently. At an early point some drys were intrigued by the alcohol studies programs and even participated in the Yale Alcohol Studies summer school programs in the 1940s, but by the late 1940s the two movements had reached loggerheads. The alcoholism movement consciously tried to separate itself from the drys, partly so that it could attract financial support from the alcoholic beverage industries and partly because it believed that the traditional temperance stance was not humanitarian.[40] Its members smirked at dry propaganda and ignored or opposed most of the temperance movement's public policy initiatives. The alcohol studies field certainly did not support the proposal to ban alcoholic beverage advertising, and its adherents were conspicuously absent from the multiple congressional hearings.

As for the drys, once the moral and political implications of the alcoholism movement's positions became apparent, the temperance movement responded with animosity. Although some of the mainline, more liberal denominations such as the Episcopalians accepted the new orientation toward drink, steadfast drys interpreted the alcoholism movement's statements that social drinking was normal as condoning a proven social evil. A 1955 article in a temperance publication criticized the "neutralist" stance and asked "those whose primary concern is for rehabilitation of the alcoholic to step outside of their alcoholic neutralism long enough to recognize the liquor traffic's large responsibility for today's four or five million alcoholics." To express its opposition to the disease theory, the National Temperance League's publication adopted as its slogan "Alcohol makes Alcoholics." Drys also criticized the alcoholism movement's treatment orientation, which clashed directly with the temperance movement's focus on prevention. They came to view the alcoholism movement as wet—a suspicion confirmed for them by the fact that the industries supported the research.[41]

Participants in the alcoholism movement denied that they were wet. In fact, they denied that they held any political stance on alcohol at all. In their discourse, proponents of the alcoholism movement generally equated science with moral detachment and with truth. They constantly stressed their neutral, scientific stance toward the problems of alcohol consumption. By medicalizing alcohol problems, they sought to demoralize and thereby depoliticize the issue of alcohol abuse. They said they wanted to avoid the emotional and propaganda-flooded wet-dry axis.[42]

This approach and associated rhetoric about objectivity resonated with mainstream, new middle-class Americans for three main reasons. First, these Americans were tired of the wet-dry battle that was supposed to have been settled by repeal. They were attracted to an approach that promised to move forward, and the alcoholism movement's proponents promoted it in those terms. Second, mainstream Americans put great faith in science and revered its modernity, which they associated with its claims of objectivity and progress. Third, the alcoholism movement both reflected and endorsed the recent shift in middle-class drinking behavior. The disease theory, and the larger movement that supported it, was just as much a product of its time as the earlier temperance movement was of its. Americans who engaged in backlash against Prohibition and dry sentiment eagerly embraced an authoritative scientific theory that validated their new lifestyle. Although the alcoholism movement's proponents claimed to be neutral, they were undoubtedly, and perhaps blatantly, creatures of culture and politics.[43]

In contrast to the alcoholism movement's professions of scientific neutrality, the temperance movement was firmly rooted in religious values, even when it used secular language. In public discourse the drys represented bias and subjectivity—the polar opposite of the rational scientists and the humanitarian AA members. Viewed in this fashion, most Americans would choose the scientists' approach over the drys'. Still, the alcoholism movement could not claim complete victory over American thought. Mainstream Americans highly respected scientific expertise and scorned old-time religious zealots, yet they retained an ingrained moral disapproval of drunkards. Alcohol could not be demoralized in American society, even during the height of science's cultural dominion.[44]

Nevertheless, if we view these two movements as competing for ownership of alcohol problems in postwar America, then the alcoholism movement clearly won the match. Although both movements were value-laden, the alcoholism movement's cultural and political orientation was generally shared by an increasingly secular mainstream America, while the temperance movement's, by that time, was not. The temperance movement, with its attachment to old middle-class values, could gain the legitimacy of support from neither the scientific community nor the larger community of the new middle class. The ascent of the alcoholism movement, under the aegis of science, helps to explain the waning cultural influence of the temperance movement and the increasing tolerance of alcoholic beverage consumption in the postwar period.

THE MEDIA AND ALCOHOL ADVERTISING

Another measure of the greater acceptance of alcoholic beverages in mainstream culture was the increasingly "wet" attitude of the mainstream media. If the major media outlets reported on controversies over alcoholic beverages, which was rare, they nearly always presented the temperance advocates in a negative light, usually mocking them for their old-fashioned ways.[45] Most newspapers, magazines, television networks, and radio stations cultivated a close relationship with the alcoholic beverage industries for the simple reason that they provided valuable advertising dollars. For example, in a speech before the U.S. Brewers Foundation convention in 1955, the president of the American Broadcasting Company declared that ABC was "a willing servant of the beer industry" and "not only actively solicit[ed]" beer advertising but would "cut the pattern to fit your cloth." For the drys, the ABC speech further confirmed what they knew to be true: the mainstream media and the alcohol industries had formed a close partnership, the result of which was the overpowering promotion of alcoholic beverages everywhere one looked.[46]

After repeal, a surprising number of newspapers and periodicals refused to accept alcohol advertising. In 1938, *The Voice* of the Methodist Board of Temperance reported that 552 daily newspapers banned hard liquor ads, and 178 of those even refused beer ads. Several years later, in 1951, a spirits industry spokesman lamented that 418 daily newspapers still refused hard liquor advertising. Many popular magazines, especially women's magazines, also prohibited the advertising of alcoholic beverages in their pages. As late as 1958, *Reader's Digest, TV Guide, Good Housekeeping, Better Homes and Gardens, Ladies Home Journal,* and *Woman's Day* were among the several magazines with circulation of more than two million that continued to refuse alcohol advertising.[47]

During the 1950s, however, several major periodicals dropped their bans. Most significant was when the *Saturday Evening Post,* one of the nation's most popular magazines, began to accept spirits advertising in 1958. More than any other magazine that made this change, the *Post*'s move seemed to signal a major shift in attitudes toward liquor. The publisher of the *Post* defended the new policy as "appropriate at this time and compatible with the viewpoint of the vast majority of [the magazine's] present and potential audience." At the end of the decade, a spirits company spokesman approvingly considered several recent developments in alcohol advertising, including the move by more publications to accept alcohol ads, the rising interest of radio and television broadcasters in accepting hard liquor advertising, and a recent decision by the spirits industry to lift its ban on portraying women in its ads. He concluded, "We are now in a new age, and what may have been decided some 25 years ago as right and proper is now outmoded."[48] As did the alcoholism movement, the mainstream media both mirrored and encouraged a widespread cultural endorsement of social drinking in America's growing mass consumer culture.

DRYS AND THE MASS CULTURE DEBATE

Mass consumer society epitomized the prevailing lifestyle of this "new age." The times were characterized by acquisitiveness, affluence, and abundance as pent-up demand for consumer goods exploded in the late 1940s and early 1950s. Advertising was a crucial component and driver of mass consumer culture, and televised advertising was the most influential medium promoting domesticity grounded in consumption and leisure.[49]

Many observers remarked on—and were often horrified by—the homogenizing force of mass media. Americans seemed to have a love-hate relationship with the accelerating mass consumer culture and its henchmen, television and advertising. At the same time that the postwar suburban lifestyle was becoming the "American Way," it attracted plenty of criticism, both from the right and the left. Leftist critics of postwar mass society often wrote from a cosmopolitan, secular perspective and generally were concerned with aesthetics and the preservation of high culture.[50] Conservative opponents, which included the drys, recognized the homogenizing influence of mass culture and realized that it threatened their own value systems. Increasingly in the postwar period, when close-knit communities and family networks began to disintegrate, and juvenile delinquency, crime, and other pernicious behaviors seemed to increase, Americans of all stripes pointed the finger of blame outward, in the direction of mass media and advertising. Not only were these media transmitting cosmopolitan values, but many opponents believed they were also projecting lower-class and perhaps criminal values.[51]

Because it constituted a key component of this dominating, homogenizing mass culture, opponents on the left and right often aimed their attacks at advertising. Although they are generally remembered as the golden years of consumerism, widespread antagonism toward advertising intensified in the 1950s. After a depression and a world war, Americans and their corporations became intensely oriented toward consumption, and they feared a lapse into another overproduction-underconsumption predicament such as had struck the country in the late 1920s. Businesses became obsessed with selling and consumers with consuming, and this, in some critics' view, produced an "anything goes" marketing atmosphere that was offensive and potentially dangerous. The "hard sell," or "puffery," was characteristic of over-the-top advertising in the years after World War II, and it grated on many nerves. As they had since at least the 1920s, ads emphasized products' "attributes" and appealed to consumers' needs to be accepted in society and their fears of being shunned. But the marketing research and psychological tactics of advertising firms intensified in the 1950s. In his 1957 best-selling exposé on the advertising industry, *The Hidden Persuaders,* Vance Packard showcased how ad men used "motivational behavior" theories and other psychological knowledge about their consumers to influence them. Packard called it a "depth approach" and "probing and manipulation."[52]

Some critics found advertising annoying and base, others considered it degrading and in bad taste, while still others charged it with being downright offensive and pernicious. This last sentiment was usually reserved for alcohol and cigarette advertising, as well as for advertising specifically targeted to children. Furthermore, the medium of television made advertising more obvious and arguably more obnoxious and intrusive. Universally, television was viewed as the most powerful selling medium because of its entrancing combination of sight and sound and its ubiquity as a constant companion in American homes.[53]

Alcohol advertising provides a prime example of the bigger and brasher advertising trends of the 1950s. Almost every year, some alcoholic beverage producer would set a new industry record with the size and cost of its advertising campaign. For instance, National Distillers made news when it ran an eight-page advertisement in *Coronet* in 1954—the largest liquor advertisement ever placed in a national magazine.[54] The Bureau of Advertising of the American Newspapers and Publishers Association reported that advertising by distillers increased by 118 percent in newspapers and 33 percent in magazines over the period 1948 to 1955. By 1955, spirits companies were spending more than $41 million on newspaper advertising and in excess of $27 million on magazine advertising. In 1952, brewers spent $52 million on advertising in all media while the wine industry's advertising expenditures came in a distant third at $5 million. In 1953, the National Association of Radio and Television Broadcasters estimated that beer and wine producers spent $34 million on radio and television advertising alone. Also in 1953, drys lamented that three distillers were among the top ten newspaper advertisers. In 1957, alcoholic beverage advertising constituted 10.1 percent of advertising revenues at *Life* magazine and 13.3 percent at *Look* magazine.[55] Alcohol advertisers enjoyed a great measure of financial clout over the media.

Further demonstrating alcohol's participation in new advertising trends, Dr. Ernest Dichter, president of the Institute for Motivational Research, served as a consultant to the spirits industry. In *Hidden Persuaders,* Dichter and his institute served as one of Packard's prime examples of unethical manipulations of consumer psychology in postwar advertising. Dichter warned distillers that Americans still associated drinking alcohol with "guilt feelings." To combat this "sin complex," spirits advertising should assure consumers of the brand's quality and the company's respectability, and endeavor to change Americans' backwards attitudes toward drink.[56] In essence, Dichter articulated the normalization strategy characteristic of nearly all alcoholic beverage advertising.

Public opinion polls in the 1950s demonstrated widespread consumer dislike and distrust of advertising in general. Much grumbling was heard from cultural conservatives. Colston E. Warne, president of the Consumers Union in 1949, presented a list of his complaints against advertising and added, "Such opinions as these are not alone mine. They represent the attitudes felt by millions of Americans who resent being pestered to death by advertising twaddle. . . . We welcome many of the innovations it heralds. Yet we are increasingly wondering whether the enormous force of advertising is not engulfing human values. . . . Ordinary standards of value and choice crumble under the onslaught." Figures such as Margaret Mead and Herbert Hoover spoke out against advertising during the 1950s. At the annual Advertising Federation Association convention in 1952, advertising men listened to James McCarthy, the dean of Notre Dame's College of Commerce, berate them for the "bad taste" of advertising. He singled out "the seductive claims of whisky makers" for his strongest criticism, warning the advertisers that their critics were not "professional scolds, the reformers, the do-gooders," but were "a segment of the population that is conservative, . . . people who are steeped in American tradition." As a result of mounting criticism and scrutiny, many advertisers felt under siege. In 1954 *Advertising Age* griped, "[I]t is beginning to look as if advertising has become one of the nation's 'most investigated' businesses."[57] The drys' specific campaign to ban alcohol advertising added to the atmosphere of antipathy and made not just alcoholic beverage producers but the advertising and media industries in general fearful for their future.

Worries about the outside forces of mass culture often were linked with the fear of communism. Both were viewed as agents of social disintegration because they invaded and undermined local institutions and values. More than ever before, it seemed, mass culture was inserting itself between parent and child and thereby disrupting social order.[58] Americans were uniquely concerned about youthful disaffection in the decade after World War II, in part because of the disruption that wartime caused in families, but also because of the consumer culture's creation of a consumer niche for youth. This was the era of young children demanding Howdy Doody toys and sugary cereals they saw advertised on TV; of affluent adolescents spending untold amounts of money on rock-and-roll records, comic books, clothes, and cars; of young adults engaged in a serious dating game, dancing close, and cruising in their cars; and of teenagers idolizing worrisome figures such as the restless, rebellious James Dean and the sexual, race-and-class-transgressing Elvis Presley. In an era of rapid demographic, social, and economic changes, to many puzzled adults youth culture and delinquent culture seemed identical.

Exacerbating the anxiety surrounding the containment of youth was the rise of television. Upon its earliest arrival in their living rooms, many Americans hoped that TV would bring families together and encourage youth to spend leisure time at home. Yet many Americans were ambivalent about the television set that, in many homes, had become the center of family life. Many adults worried about the impact of television on the family and on their children because it represented, in Leo Bogart's words, the "intrusion of the impersonal influences of the mass media into the intimate circle of family life." Some considered the potential socializing power of this machine worrisome if not dangerous. Many Americans, particularly "old-fashioned" Americans of a temperance bent, believed that domestic space and children should be shielded from the marketplace. They were afraid that TV would teach their children the wrong values and encourage passive and even addictive behavior.[59] The temperance movement's alarm at alcohol advertising, especially that shown on television, and the movement's focus on the harm it caused to impressionable youth was part of this larger atmosphere of anxiety about mass culture in the 1950s.

In Congress, these general concerns about the bewildering influence of mass media took shape when it held a hearing on television and radio programming in 1952, followed by a series of hearings on juvenile

delinquency in the mid-1950s. The 1952 hearing, held by the House in accordance with resolutions introduced by Representative Ezekiel Gathings
to study radio and television programs, heard much discussion of the
problems of alcohol advertising. Temperance leaders took advantage of
the hearing to publicize their concerns—even though that was not Gathings's purpose or concern. Of the thirty-two witnesses at the hearing, nine
were drys, such as Bishop Hammaker and the WCTU's Elizabeth Smart,
who used their allotted time to publicize the harm done by a particular aspect of mass media: alcohol ads. Brewers accused the drys of "virtually
monopolizing" the hearing.[60]

To a lesser extent, the issue of alcoholic beverages in the media was also
aired at Senator Estes Kefauver's hearings on juvenile delinquency. The
drys linked their specific concerns about alcohol advertising to the central
inquiry of the hearings: how the media contributed to the perceived increase in juvenile delinquency. Following a long-standing dry tradition,
they reduced the cause for social problems to liquor and its promotion.
For example, Sam Morris, a prominent dry personality who had his own
radio program on temperance and who was a leader in the fight to ban alcohol advertising, testified at the 1955 hearings that young people's alcohol consumption was the cause of juvenile delinquency.[61]

Congressional hearings on alcohol advertising were occurring at the
same time as the juvenile delinquency and mass media hearings, but it appears that only activist drys connected the two debates and saw their
agenda as a subset of a broader concern. Otherwise, the two issues were
kept completely separate, and none of the social scientists, leaders of secular citizens' groups, or government officials who dominated the Gathings
and Kefauver hearings appeared at the alcohol advertising hearings nor
evinced any interest in that concern. Perhaps they did not want to be associated with those whom they viewed as backward evangelicals because
that might delegitimize their own agendas. Although drys were desperately trying to place it on the radar, the alcohol advertising controversy
was screened out of mainstream America's consciousness.

In terms of its place in postwar culture and politics, the drys' movement against alcohol advertising was paradoxical: it was situated in a
broader societal debate about morality and culture that engaged mainstream Americans, yet at the same time the drys were marginalized in the
postwar era. Like other deeply religious Americans, these drys experienced
tension between the realities of modern life on the one hand and their religious convictions and associated moral values on the other. They were
patriotic, capitalist Americans, and probably enjoyed shopping for the latest models and styles at the new Sears and Roebuck as much as the next
American. They were dispersed and diverse, and they did not withdraw
from the modern world into isolated sects. Yet the participants in the
movement to ban alcohol advertising presented two fundamental chal-

lenges to the American culture and economy. First, they advocated what to many businessmen seemed a fundamental change in—and challenge to—America's capitalist practices: the prohibition of the advertising of a legal product. Judging from the reaction of the alcohol and media industries, the drys clearly posed a threat to at least some American businesses. Second, if we view alcohol consumption as a crucial feature of new middle-class social rituals and as a symbol of the values associated with mass consumer culture,[62] the drys functioned as cultural critics confronting that dominant culture and trying to craft a middle-class culture that included both consumerism and traditional Protestant values.

2

THE INDUSTRIES'
REGULATORY RESPONSE

Adding to the sociocultural changes and shifting scientific paradigms of the mid-twentieth century, existing regulation of the alcohol industries proved critical in conquering the movement to ban alcohol advertising. Federal, state, and local government policies formed part of the regulatory apparatus, but even more important for the political battle over advertising were the regulation and promotion strategies put in place by the industries themselves. In the two decades after the repeal of Prohibition, the major trade associations for the beer, wine, and distilled spirits industries established codes or guidelines for the advertisement of their respective products. The trade associations designated certain themes, such as the depiction of Santa Claus, and practices, such as endorsement by celebrities, as inappropriate. The distillers went the farthest in regulating their advertising by banning its broadcast on radio and television. In addition to restricting their own advertising practices, all three industries designed public relations campaigns that endeavored to improve their reputations with the American public. Through this two-pronged strategy—marketing self-regulation and public relations campaigns—the alcohol industries hoped to undercut public criticism, derail the antialcohol advertising movement, and preclude further government regulation. Negotiating America's enduring cultural conflict between controlling desire and expressing freedom, the industries tried to secure commercial freedoms by accepting limits on awakening desires.

Integral to their battle against the drys were the industries' campaigns to persuade Americans that moderate alcohol consumption in the home was normal and benign. The normalization and domestication themes were common to all three alcohol industries, but the industries did diverge in other marketing practices and themes, owing mainly to the different characteristics—along with varying public perceptions—of beer, wine, and spirits. Moreover, as they competed for a growing yet limited market, they sometimes experienced interindustry disputes. Largely successful in their marketing and public relations strategies, and profiting from their connections to powerful media and other interests, the industries were able to present enough of a united front to inhibit most policymakers' willingness to enact restrictions on alcohol ads, even when some of those policymakers admitted to finding such advertisements of questionable taste.

Yet, in spite of their seeming boldness and apparently successful normalization campaigns, the industries were worried. At the heart of their self-regulation efforts was timidity and even fear. Since the nineteenth century the embattled industries had fought public opinion that vilified them, and they had suffered through the Prohibition decade. After repeal the industries clambered to get back on their feet, but they were shell-shocked and wary of further attacks. In 1953 an *Advertising Age* reporter tried to explain why the industries continued to behave cautiously so long after Prohibition had ended: "In the beginning, industry leaders felt they were on probation and were exceedingly circumspect in their efforts; it is now a matter of habit in the industry, and anything else would be met with suspicion to hostility by regulatory bodies." An attorney for the spirits industry acknowledged, "[I]f [the industries] did not impose the restriction the Government probably would."[1] Intensifying their anxieties, in the 1930s and 1940s the industries experienced disappointing market conditions. Because government regulation, especially tax policies, restricted the industries' ability to lower their prices in order to stimulate demand, they relied on carefully crafted marketing campaigns to win not only the spending money, but also the goodwill of American consumers. When the drys organized a national movement against the industries' vital marketing campaigns and were able to publicize their views at a series of congressional hearings, the alcohol industries found these developments highly threatening and tended to overestimate them.

The alcohol industries were so alarmed by continuing dry sentiment, the prospect of bad publicity, and the threat of stricter government regulation—even a return to national prohibition—that they chose to deny themselves the use of powerful advertising strategies in an effort to attain respectability and undercut criticism. Although mainstream Americans' attitudes toward alcoholic beverages were clearly changing, and the industries wanted to promote and reinforce this change, industry leaders also believed that the public retained powerful associations between alcohol and impropriety. To avoid reactivating attacks, trade association leaders drew lines around industry marketing practices and insisted that affiliated companies not cross them. These self-restrictive policies were in some respects surprising because the industries, especially the distilled spirits industry, faced low demand for their overstocked product. Some industry members believed that the best solution to their market predicament was more aggressive marketing, and indeed the industries' expenditures for advertising showed a steady increase through the postwar years.[2] The industries' position toward marketing, therefore, was conflicted: they embraced and relied on advertising for their continued advancement at the same time that they restricted their advertising, also to ensure their progress.

FEDERAL GOVERNMENT REGULATION OF ALCOHOL ADVERTISING

After the government legalized the manufacture and sale of alcoholic beverages in 1933, it had little interest in regulating the marketing of these products. Significantly, the Twenty-first Amendment gave the states the power to determine their own alcoholic beverage policies. President Franklin Roosevelt did create the Federal Alcohol Control Administration (FACA) to oversee the reestablishment of the alcoholic beverage industries, but his administration, exhausted by the wet-dry debate and consumed by other national crises, wanted to avoid involvement in regulation of the industries. Headed by Joseph Choate, Jr., the FACA's mission was to foster the industries' growth, mainly by helping them develop trade associations. A key reason for this assistance was to bring the industries under the auspices of the National Recovery Administration, which in 1933 asked every industry's trade association to draw up a code of fair competition.[3]

With the termination of the National Industrial Recovery Act in 1935, the FACA also ended. Later that year, Congress passed the Federal Alcohol Administration Act, which created the Federal Alcohol Administration (FAA). Much the same as its predecessor, the FAA was not interested in public health or temperance concerns. Instead, the agency's interest lay in reestablishing the alcoholic beverage industries in an orderly manner, without much attention to the social consequences. In 1936, despite the protests of both agency administrators and Treasury Department officials, Congress placed the FAA in the Treasury Department, an action that served to emphasize the agency's revenue-collecting function. When the Treasury Department reorganized in 1940, the Bureau of Internal Revenue's Alcohol Tax Unit took over the responsibility of administering the Federal Alcohol Administration Act. After another Treasury Department reorganization in 1952, federal oversight of alcohol policy was placed in the Alcohol and Tobacco Tax Division (ATTD) of the Bureau of Internal Revenue.[4] The FAA Act did allow for protection of consumers, but the Treasury rarely concerned itself with this purpose. Instead of showing concern for public health or fairness to consumers, it used the regulations mostly to resolve problems of product identification related to revenue-collection issues.[5]

After holding extensive hearings in the mid-1930s, from which temperance activists were expressly excluded, the FAA established a series of regulations on the labeling and advertising of alcoholic beverages. Most of the rules concerned the inclusion of proper information on product labels, including disclosure of certain ingredients and geographical designation to prohibition of bootlegging and impurities. These provisions also applied to advertising but were usually less detailed. FAA rules on advertising and labeling tried to ensure fairness by prohibiting

> statements which are false or untrue or which by ambiguity, omission, or inference tend to create a misleading impression; disparaging statements; obscene or indecent statements; the use of names such as of athletes or celebrities which would falsely indicate endorsement or sponsorship; any simulation of government stamps; or any other indication of government approval or endorsement of the product; any statements relating to analyses, standards or tests which might mislead the consumer; misleading statements with respect to guarantees; and any statements with respect to curative or therapeutic effects.[6]

Except for the restriction on statements of curative or therapeutic effects, the FAA's advertising rules were similar to the FTC's fairness guidelines for most commercially advertised products. Alcoholic beverage companies were required to have their product labels, but not their ad copy, approved by the agency before production, yet the agency did spot check print and broadcast ads.

In 1939 temperance leaders persuaded the Senate Commerce Committee to hold what would be the first hearing on an alcohol ad ban bill. The head of the FAA, Wilford Alexander, testified in support of the bill. Alexander professed concern about the character and excessiveness of alcohol advertisements, and he opposed their appearance in Sunday newspapers or on the radio, the depiction of women, children, or religious themes, and any reference to healthful or food qualities of an alcoholic beverage. His testimony marked the only time that the federal government agency in charge of alcohol regulation has forthrightly supported a goal of the temperance movement—and Alexander lost his job soon afterward.[7]

The federal government's attention to monitoring alcohol ads declined drastically after the Bureau of Internal Revenue took over authority of the

FAA Act in 1940. The Treasury's Alcohol and Tobacco Tax Division did take action against the alcohol industries a few times during the 1950s when the ads explicitly made health or therapeutic claims. In 1954 the ATTD asked brewers to terminate advertising with "low calorie" claims, and in 1957 the agency told distillers they could not state that whiskey soothed nerves. Finally, in 1959 the agency clamped down on the United States Brewers' Foundation's "Good for You" campaign. Although the decisions annoyed industry members, they complied.[8]

The industries appreciated the ATTD's efforts at developing universal regulations on labeling and other forms of marketing and at tackling illegal production and distribution. The spirits industry in particular recognized that it could use the sympathetic agency to achieve stability and growth. Stanley Cohen, a fair-minded reporter for *Advertising Age* who closely followed the alcohol advertising controversy, declared that the relationship between the brewers and the ATTD was "less cordial" than that between the distillers and the agency. Friction probably developed because the brewers were less dependent than distillers on the federal government for setting standards and establishing legitimacy. Nevertheless, according to Cohen, the brewing industry always followed the ATTD's suggestions when the agency questioned brewers' practices, even though the companies were under no legal obligation to comply. Cohen observed, "Despite the fact that [ATTD] is unquestionably the most powerful agency ever created by this government to supervise an industry dealing with millions of consumers, it has continued to enjoy the support of the industry it regulates."[9] For the most part, then, the Treasury's ATTD and the alcohol industries cultivated good relations with each other. The industries' leaders did not feel much threatened by the ATTD and felt assured that the agency was on their side on the question of an advertising ban.

Generally, restrictive policies rested with the states, not the federal government. In time, every state implemented a system to regulate the alcoholic beverage trade. All established control agencies, but policies and their administration varied considerably from state to state.[10] Forty-five of the forty-six states that allowed the sale of liquor in the mid-1950s had laws to regulate alcoholic beverage advertising. Most states banned advertising matter that included family scenes with children present, religious holidays, famous athletes, public and historical figures, and appeals to children. Fifteen states banned billboard advertising of alcohol, and thirteen states banned radio advertising of alcohol. There were also confusing and widely varying policies on listing prices in alcohol advertisements.[11] Though generally more stringent than federal government guidelines, the patchwork system of state regulations pertained only to advertising within each state's borders and therefore was ineffective and awkward when confronting the accelerated trend toward national alcohol advertising campaigns by large corporations.

INDUSTRY MARKETING AND SELF-REGULATION

Enthused by the rhetoric and success of the movement for repeal, the alcohol industries anticipated a great revival in sales. They soon discovered that they had been overly optimistic, and it was not long before they faced problems of overproduction. Industry leaders, especially distillers, were dismayed by market conditions and preoccupied with fighting excise taxes and bootleggers, both of which they blamed for the disappointingly low consumption level. In a 1953 feature issue that marked the twentieth anniversary of repeal, *Advertising Age* characterized the 1947–1953 period as marked by high taxes, disappointing sales, high inventory, and bitter interindustry disputes. In one article in the issue, a Seagram executive expressed bafflement as to why liquor sales had declined three years in a row while the country's prosperity was rising. Americans simply were not drinking as much as the repealers said they would.[12] Although the industries would never acknowledge it, the temperance message, or at least temperance habits, seemed to have influenced a significant number of Americans and remained with them even after repeal, depression, and war, and into prosperous times. It took decades before consumption reached pre-Prohibition levels.[13]

In this market context, industry leaders felt acutely threatened by temperance activism. Still, they desperately tried to discount the movement, often publicly referring to it as a fringe group of fanatics who should not be taken seriously. The calculated depiction of drys as absurd and out of touch, however, was to some extent false bravado. While industry members imposed the fringe label, they were warning one another about the political power of the drys. Each time Congress held hearings on the proposal to ban alcohol advertising, industry leaders declared that the bill's chances for passage were very good—when never once was the bill even reported out of committee.[14] At a liquor industry conference in 1950, industry executives fretted over the spread of dry propaganda, which they termed a "step-by-step plan to bring prohibition back." One called the 1950s "Prohibition" movement "the most threatening since repeal," and the head of a distilling trade association thought the American public needed to be mobilized against the temperance movement.[15] The editors of *Modern Brewery Age,* the brewing industry's leading trade publication, warned brewers not to become complacent in the face of the dry threat:

> And yet the drys are more dangerous today than at any time since 1933 and, accordingly, bear closer watching. . . . They are more dangerous now because they have adopted smoother, subtler tactics, their leaders are less wild-eyed and fanatical and, while they still resort to half-truths and plain distortions, they make them sound plausible instead of ridiculous even to the uninformed man on the fence. Wise in the ways of mass psychology and persuasion, their

> chieftains hold up a calming, reassuring hand that they are not after national prohibition—they are merely looking for restraints and controls against excessive drinking. . . . Informed industry people know that they dare not be lulled into a sense of security, that the new dry strategy is the backdoor approach, the inching along to national prohibition.[16]

The editor's language paralleled the inflated rhetoric used by his dry opponents. Informed by an era when communist spies were purportedly lurking everywhere and anxiety over thought control was as its height, each side accused the other of manipulating the masses in a duplicitous quest for power. Indeed, the perceived threat from dry sentiment and political power caused the industries to adopt a type of self-regulation unique for its time.

Although each industry—spirits, beer, and wine—faced diverse market conditions and differed in some marketing tactics and controls, their experiences and efforts during the 1950s shared much in common. All three industries, particularly spirits, experienced concentration into fewer but larger firms. All saw increases in home consumption of their beverages, encouraged by packaging innovations, improvements in refrigeration, advertising campaigns that featured the home and family, and government licensing policies that allowed for beer, wine, and in some states, spirits sales at grocery stores.[17] During an era when Americans emphasized domesticity, all of the industries understood that normalization of alcohol consumption meant that it must be integrated into everyday home and private life.

Normalization also meant that women, viewed by the industries as the chief consumers for the household, must be appealed to with inventive marketing tactics. Plagued by problems of overstock, the industries were searching for ways to expand their markets, and many companies decided to defy a long-standing taboo against marketing liquor to women. Reaching out to women as consumers of alcoholic beverages was vital to the industries' efforts to change attitudes about drink because historically women drank less than men, and women's drinking was viewed by many Americans as further outside cultural norms than drinking by men. Industry public relations releases emphasized the role of the postwar American woman who played "an increasingly larger role in the purchase, serving, and consumption of cocktails." Persuading the wife and mother to add alcoholic beverages to her weekly grocery list and integrate the beverages into meals and entertaining was thought to be the key to bringing alcohol into the home and increasing the number of social drinkers. Some companies also introduced marketing strategies thought to entice women, such as a slimmer beer can and more colorful ads.[18] Using female models in liquor advertising, something that probably would have upset even committed wets earlier in the century, had, by the late 1950s, become good business sense. For the most part, this appeal to women was nonchalantly accepted by most Americans, though limited protest came from temperance groups and even some nontemperance organizations such as the General Federation of Women's Clubs.[19]

Advertising by each of the alcohol industries aimed to construct positive and respectable associations with their products, emphasizing enjoyable yet relatively staid environments and effects, with certainly no suggestion of inebriation or other consequences that might appear troublesome or disrespectable. They seized upon "moderation" as the watchword of their marketing vocabulary, and each industry vied to present its product as the true "beverage of moderation." The rhetoric of moderation became a shrewd public relations tactic because it undercut drys' attempts to portray them as irresponsible drug pushers. By issuing nebulous advice to drink "responsibly" and "moderately," they could promote the purchase and consumption of their products at the same time that they assuaged Americans' continuing anxieties about alcohol problems.

The spirits industry, which for decades had been facing declines in sales relative to beer, worked the hardest in its advertising to connect its products with refined and dignified living and sever any association with a sordid past. Beer, which maintained a common-man association, was largely marketed to middle- and working-class markets. Wine, whose market share and advertising expenditures lagged far behind beer and spirits, had not yet become a popular beverage for American sophisticates. Despite these differences, they all practiced similar tactics of promotion and self-regulation. Because they were all under continual attack by the drys, all three—probably more than most American industries at the time—developed a keen sense of public relations.

The Distilled Spirits Industry

Historically, distilled spirits have been viewed as the most objectionable of alcoholic beverages because of their high alcohol content, and this traditionally stronger association of spirits with disrespectability and alcohol problems plagued the industry through the postwar era. As the most embattled of the alcoholic beverage industries, the spirits manufacturers were the most stringent in their self-regulation. Right after repeal, the manufacturers established a trade association, the Distilled Spirits Institute (DSI), which took as a major responsibility the establishment and enforcement of marketing policies. In 1936, the DSI wrote an advertising code for the industry, a main component of which was the prohibition of advertising on the radio. Later in the 1930s, the DSI added more regulations to the code, including prohibitions on the depiction of women in their advertising, advertising in Sunday newspapers, and advertising in religious publications. In 1948, the DSI pledged not to advertise on television. Following the distillers' lead, the National Association of Broadcasters likewise forbade the advertisement of hard liquor on radio or television. According to their own regulations, then, spirits companies were not permitted to offer their advertising to radio and television, and radio and television stations were not allowed to accept it.[20]

Distillers, even more than brewers and vintners, felt beleaguered and defensive in the postwar years. One observer argued that "the liquor man" was "infinitely more sensitive to public opinion than his prototypes in other kinds of businesses."[21] The sensitivity was understandable. Even though spirits consumption was a popular component of the new middle-class lifestyle after World War II, the market for spirits was suffering more than that for beer. A 1953 *Advertising Age* article ominously reported that "sales of distilled spirits have fallen close to a ten-year low in many states."[22] Contributing to their market woes, spirits were taxed at higher rates than beer and wine, by both federal and state governments. Distillers were smarting from a 1951 increase in the federal excise tax on spirits—the purpose of which was to raise revenue and not to encourage temperance—from $9.00 per proof gallon to $10.50, at which rate it stayed, despite inflation, until 1985. Brewers, too, experienced a federal tax increase in 1951, from $8.00 to $9.00, but their rate was leveraged on a per-barrel, not proof gallon, basis. During the postwar period the federal government taxed spirits at nineteen cents per ounce, wine at six cents per ounce, and beer at one cent per ounce. Adding to the inequality in tax policy, many local communities in the United States had voted themselves dry for spirits but continued to allow wine and beer sales.[23] The drys' antiadvertising campaign, too, fell heaviest on the spirits trade. Although most of the proposals applied to all alcoholic beverages, some singled out spirits advertising for restriction.

Distillers used both brand advertising and public relations campaigns in an attempt to improve their image and fend off attacks. As far as the producers and advertisers were concerned, distilled spirits henceforth were to be associated solely with sophistication, wealth, and respectability, and pre-Prohibition associations with the saloon and the skid row alcoholic had to be erased. Cocktail culture had become a symbol of the suburban age. Along with purchasing the best, newest, and most expensive cars, appliances, and clothes, many in the new middle class felt it was imperative to keep and serve the finest brands of distilled spirits in their homes. By design, the distillers' product advertising appealed to the social-climbing and status-seeking behavior of many Americans in the postwar years. Industry leaders called the movement to costlier brands of spirits "trading up." They believed that an inclination to "trade up" was characteristic of the entire postwar consumer culture and that spirits, even the standard brands, must be marketed as "deluxe" if they were to benefit from the trend toward conspicuous consumption.[24]

Most spirits advertising therefore appealed to snobbery and portrayed the beverages as the preferred choice of the sporting, upper-class white man. Ads typically featured the bottle and glass in the foreground, with perhaps a gentleman's library, a hunting horse, or an elegant meal in the background. Rich reds and browns dominated the color schemes. If the ad depicted people—which was true in only about half of liquor advertisements during this period—they were always men (before a policy change in 1959) and always appeared to be very wealthy. The "Men of Distinction" advertising campaign for Calvert Whiskey featured a different wealthy, often well-known, businessman in each advertisement. Walker's Bourbon ran a campaign that featured an African American butler offering the viewer of the ad an elegant tray of drinks. Another common theme was American tradition and heritage, often evoked by a sketch of an historic scene, such as Philadelphia Whiskey's "Committee Examining the Liberty Bell in 1753," or the prevalent image of a genteel man riding in a horse-drawn carriage. Canadian Club took a different approach from most whiskey campaigns when it ran a series that featured photos of wealthy young men on adventurous vacations, such as climbing a pyramid or deep-sea diving, and then ending their adventures by relaxing with highballs. A few campaigns employed more juvenile themes. For years Black and White Scotch used drawings of talking black and white Scottie dogs that engaged in silly banter to sell the drink. A campaign for PM Blended Whisky featured cartoonish Bambi-like, big-eyed creatures such as raccoons and ponies. Most spirits ads before the 1960s, though, were somber and stuffy.[25]

Copy in liquor ads stressed the drink's refined quality, age, "lightness," "smoothness," and appeal to the best, "most knowledgeable" men. Some ads went so far as to emphasize the relaxing qualities associated with the drink, and these campaigns were always pitched at the busy, professional man. For instance, a 1957 advertisement for Old Forester whiskey presented a photograph of a professional man at work with the copy: "You've earned it." Below appeared a picture of the same man at home, barbequeing chicken and drinking whiskey with a male friend, and here the copy advises: "Live a Little! When it's time to relax, don't you feel entitled to something a little special?"

The tenor of spirits advertisements changed noticeably after 1958, the year that the DSI dropped its prohibition against depicting women in spirits advertising. The new rule stated that the women must be dressed tastefully and, until another rule change in 1963, could not be pictured holding or consuming the drink. DSI representatives said it had lifted the ban because "the social evolution of the last 25 years had made the ban . . . unrealistic." *Advertising Age* applauded the move, calling the new policy "realistic," and praised the DSI for "facing up to the facts of life"—namely, that many women drank liquor, and even if they did not, very few would be offended by women in spirits ads.[26] These changes were a measure of the extent of the inversion of values associated with drink and abstinence in the postwar period.

De Luxe:
*specially
elegant...
uncommon.*
WEBSTER

WALKER'S DE LUXE *is a straight Bourbon whiskey, 6 years old;*
elegant in taste, uncommonly good—a Hiram Walker whiskey.

Emphasizing the word "De Luxe," and featuring a distinguished-looking African American servant, this Walker's Bourbon ad is meant to impart a sensibility of elitist privilege and luxury. *Life*, 26 May 1947.

Even before the industry took the momentous step of showing women in their ads, distillers had been appealing to women customers throughout the postwar years. The industry's trade association Licensed Beverage Industries (LBI) had a division specifically to address women consumers. Women working in the industry had also formed their own association, the Women's Association of Allied Beverage Industries, to promote women's involvement in the liquor trade, often to the consternation of the male-directed LBI.[27] Schenley Distillers hired five women to travel around the country and talk to retailers about how to appeal to women customers. They also addressed women's groups on the topic of serving alcohol when entertaining. Some spirits ads were designed to teach the hostess how to prepare mixed drinks using the company's products and featured cocktail recipes.[28]

With the inclusion of women, an element of sexuality was introduced into spirits advertising. For example, Calvert Whiskey began using the slogan "Calvert has the Power to Please" and showed beautiful, bejeweled women serving liquor to handsome, tuxedoed men, "to make the most of the evening's pleasure." An ad for Arrow Vodka showed an attractive man and woman sitting close to one another, she holding a bouquet of flowers that he had just given to her. The copy states, "Your breath never tells." Presumably, this ad meant that a man could loosen up by drinking vodka, but his date would not be able to detect that he had been drinking. This ad is curious because it admits that spirits consumption still demanded concealment and therefore was not fully "normalized." It also depicted drinking as a male custom, not shared by the woman. On the whole, spirits advertisements after 1958 were looser, sexier, and less focused on images of the bottle and glass, though the people and settings still appeared refined.

But because the decision to allow women occurred so late, the same year as the last congressional hearing held on the alcohol ad ban proposal, it does not account for the drys' long-standing objections to alcohol advertising. During the height of the antiadvertising movement, most spirits ads were rather dignified and strove to maintain good taste. The thematic restrictions that distillers placed on themselves were in their own best interest as they endeavored to remove associations with vice, immorality, and damaging inebriation. But even these subdued themes would instigate the drys' ire because just the fact that spirits, viewed by drys as a powerfully damaging drug, were being promoted in a positive manner in major media was objectionable to them. And worse, the ads glamorized spirits as part of fine living and respectability instead of a contributor to poverty and failure—as something to aspire to instead of to renounce as harmful to morality, social relations, and health. Indeed, it probably did not matter what the spirits companies showed in their ads. Their very existence invited attack from the drys, who asked not for alterations in the advertising but for a complete ban.

You've earned it...

LIVE A LITTLE!

Pretty demanding, today's pace. And today's rewards, more abundant than ever. When it's time to relax, don't you feel entitled to something a little special? Then just add famous bonded Old Forester to your pleasures. You'll soon learn what a wonderful difference in rich, hearty flavor Old Forester offers...at only pennies more. Every bottle registered to assure your satisfaction.

"There is nothing better in the market"

KENTUCKY STRAIGHT BOURBON WHISKY • BOTTLED IN BOND • 100 PROOF
BROWN-FORMAN DISTILLERS CORPORATION • AT LOUISVILLE IN KENTUCKY

This Old Forester advertisement depicts its whiskey as the pleasurable reward for the hard-working Organization Man. *Life,* 28 January 1957.

In addition to their brand advertising, distillers simultaneously used public relations campaigns to construct a benign impression and fight their opponents. Licensed Beverage Industries hired the preeminent public relations firm Hill & Knowlton to help them run an overtly defensive and political PR campaign to enhance the image of the hard liquor business.

Hill & Knowlton advisers saw "research" as the "fountainhead" of any effective PR effort, which meant establishing a division that churned out data about alcohol consumption, market trends, economic contributions of the industry, and any other subject in ways that benefited the industry's reputation, and then feeding this "background material" to the media and public officials. Hill & Knowlton also helped LBI carefully design an advertising campaign that ran in major magazines.[29] One typical ad boasted of the contributions the industry had made to the U.S. economy by listing the number of jobs, the annual payroll, dividends, and tax revenues the industry had provided, as well as contributions the industry had made to other important U.S. industries, such as agriculture, railroads, and glass and can manufacturers. The ad—printed seventeen years after repeal—repeatedly emphasized that the industry was legal. In an additional effort to associate the industry with respectability, it featured headshots of about twenty-five spirits company executives and explained that these men "have come into the industry from virtually every other business and profession. They have brought to it the experience and abilities which earned recognition and respect in other endeavors. They have made the *legal* sale of alcoholic beverages mean these things to the American people today."[30] Another LBI ad featured the owner of a small liquor package store who was incensed about high taxes on distilled spirits. The ad's copy had him worrying about the "professional drys" who threatened to "end our dream of security." The LBI ads listed three goals that the liquor companies aimed to promote: "the encouragement of moderation by word and by example," "the licensing of only orderly places of business," and "the strict observance and enforcement of the law." Finally, the LBI proclaimed, "We do not want the patronage of the few who *abuse* the right to drink."[31]

Similarly, the Distilled Spirits Institute regularly produced booklets entitled "Repeal Facts" that defended the legalization of alcohol sales and reiterated the case against prohibition. The 1952 edition listed several arguments made by "Prohibitionists," refuting them one by one. Another edition publicized the industry's efforts at self-regulation. "Did you know?" the booklet declared, "that the members of the Distilled Spirits Institute follow self-imposed advertising restrictions. That these distillers do not advertise over radio or television. That they do not show women in their advertisements. That they do not advertise in Sunday publications. That these voluntary restrictions have been in effect during almost the entire period since repeal of prohibition."[32] The spirits trade associations and companies not only felt they needed to enact self-regulations; they also believed they needed to constantly remind the public of their sacrificial efforts—for what good were the restrictions in winning Americans' favor if consumers were unaware of them?

Less-strident public relations campaigns came from various spirits companies, most notably from Seagram, one of the leaders in an increasingly concentrated industry. The hallmark of its campaign was the promotion of moderation, and like the DSI with its booklets, Seagram not only promoted moderation but also incessantly reminded its audience that it was promoting moderation. The moderation campaign was the company's form of philanthropy and penance, and by all accounts it succeeded in winning many Americans' goodwill. The company was enormously proud of its public relations efforts and annually distributed booklets of its moderation messages to ensure others knew of its efforts.[33]

Although uneasy and constantly fighting to establish their legitimacy, some distillers asserted that the industry had succeeded in changing its image by convincing mainstream Americans of its respectability. An advertising man who wrote a book on the spirits trade declared in 1955, "Through federal and state control, and through the self-policing activities of the industry itself, liquors have at last become respectable members in the family of American products. No longer do the drys have the same sort of targets which they shot at before Prohibition."[34] In the face of the drys' campaign, one hopeful DSI leader elucidated the industry's outlook: "We realize there is a strong organized minority fundamentally opposed to our industry, but through proper appreciation of the public relations involved, we also have gained the good-will of the majority of the public. That good-will we consider our most valuable asset. We definitely are opposed to any move that will unquestionably stir up controversies . . . and upset the mutual relationship we have established."[35] As the statement indicates, even when distillers were feeling confident, they were insecure. As they balanced these two outlooks, distillers also maintained a precarious balance between currying the public's favor and aggressively pushing their products. Under the direction of their trade associations, they remained cautious.

The Brewing Industry

The brewing and wine industries also practiced advertising self-regulation, though their rules were generally more lenient than those imposed by the spirits industry. Because they benefited from the long-standing notion in America that wine and beer were more benign beverages than spirits, brewers and vintners advertisers, along with the media that accepted their advertising, allowed two practices that distillers had forbidden: depicting women and advertising on broadcast media.[36] Nevertheless, wine and beer manufacturers knew they had to be careful and were aware of the need for good public relations to overcome Americans' suspicions.

The brewers' main trade association, the United States Brewers' Foundation (USBF), did not establish a formal advertising code after repeal, but it communicated to its members several advertising guidelines. The brewing industry's chief tactic was to distinguish its product from hard liquor. One of the foundation's early public relations campaigns pushed beer as a cure for "the evil of too much alcohol."[37] Its pamphlet entitled "Do's and Don't's for Beer Advertising" stated as its first "Do" that beer should be portrayed as a beverage of moderation. "Moderation," it declared, "may well be the basic article in the creed of every beer advertiser."[38] The pamphlet also suggested placing beer in "wholesome surroundings" and in the context of traditional American values. Over and over, the trade association stressed that most beer consumers were law-abiding, settled, married persons.

A main objective of beer producers and marketers was to make beer as accepted and consumed as any nonalcoholic beverage. The USBF pamphlet advised, "Beer goes with food on the shopping list of more and more housewives. Not only at the tavern, but for picnics, parties, home get-togethers and the noon-day or evening meal, beer is a delicious accompaniment to good food." To achieve this acceptance, women, as the household's chief consumer, had to be persuaded of beer's wholesome goodness and dissuaded from temperance ideas: "When women know beer better and recognize its relation to other food, they will place less credence in exaggerated claims of beer's enemies." Yet the industry recognized that it occupied an awkward position on the consumer market because its products were not, of course, as harmless as the nonalcoholic items on the housewife's shopping list. Thus, the trade association warned beer marketers not to "play up alcoholic content," "appeal to children or minors," or "give ammunition to fanatics."[39] Beer wanted to belong, yet it had to play by some different rules.

Brewers, like distillers, clearly recognized the importance of the woman consumer to the growth of sales. Less stigmatized than distillers, they sought the female market even more aggressively. In the early 1950s many brewers emphasized the low caloric content of their beers in an attempt to appeal to women consumers and implemented labeling and merchandising alterations with an eye on the female market. The USBF started an advertising campaign in 1956 that featured tips for women on how to pour and serve beer because, according to the USBF president, women were "largely responsible for deciding what goes on the table and into the refrigerator." In addition, he proclaimed that the "acceptance of beer by women has given the beverage a new prestige and social acceptance."[40]

"Beer Belongs," another USBF public relations campaign, reflected the principles urged in its "Do's and Don't's" pamphlet. Each of the ads in this series, which ran in mass-circulation magazines, featured a different painting of a scene of adults enjoying themselves, and their beer, in "everyday" activities in white middle-class homes. Examples include "No. 3: New Beau," which shows a young woman introducing her boyfriend to her parents while her mother is serving beer, and "No. 40: Indoor Golf Clinic," which depicts two men practicing their putting in the living room while their wives look on—and, of course, beer is part of the scene. Most of the ads connected drinking beer at home with postwar domesticity and the

American dream, which it associated with personal liberty, sociability, and tolerance. For example, the copy of the "Golf Clinic" ad states, "In this home-loving land of ours . . . in this America of kindliness, of friendship, of good-humored tolerance . . . perhaps no beverages are more 'at home' on more occasions than good American beer and ale." It further claims that beer and ale "belong—to pleasant living, to good fellowship, to sensible moderation. And our right to enjoy them, this too belongs—to our own American heritage of personal freedom." In capital letters, the words "AMERICA'S BEVERAGE OF MODERATION" appear at the bottom of the eighty or so advertisements in the "Beer Belongs" series.[41]

Beer brand print advertising often used family scenes similar to the USBF's campaign. A Budweiser campaign in 1950 featured the slogan "Budweiser is right at home" and stressed that beer did not have to be saved for special events but was appropriate for ordinary occasions such as painting Easter eggs or building a model of a new home. Beer ads in the 1950s differed from spirits ads because they generally depicted middle-class, rather than upper-class, and family, as opposed to male-only, settings. Brewers were less concerned about establishing their products as sophisticated and "deluxe." Moreover, they had allowed themselves to include women in their advertising from the beginning. Brewers often played up gender issues and sexual attraction in their ads. For instance, a notable Schlitz ad showed a new wife who, sadly, had just burned dinner on the stove, and her husband seated at the kitchen table looking sympathetic. The ad's copy does its best to comfort her: "Anyway, you didn't burn the Schlitz! There's hope for any young bride who knows her man well enough to serve him Schlitz Beer. For what man (or woman) can resist the taste of Schlitz Beer." Budweiser ads in the late 1950s featured close-up photographs of attractive men and women serving each other beer, displaying unmistakable sex appeal.

Another significant way that beer advertising differed from spirits advertising was that brewers allowed themselves to take advantage of the more powerful broadcast media and could employ catchy jingles and moving pictures to entice consumers. Some of the best-remembered jingles from the 1950s came from beer commercials, such as Duquesne's "Have a Duke" and Rheingold's "Banana Boat Song."[42] Many televised beer ads used animation to sell the product. Rheingold's popular commercials showed a parade of beer bottles and cans marching to the Rheingold song. Hamm's Beer featured a cartoon of a silly bear floating down a log on a river, with Indian tom-toms beating in the background and women singing that it was the beer "from the land of sky blue waters." A humorous animated commercial for Carling's Black Label beer showed a man coming home from work to relax in his hammock while his wife ("the little woman"), who was doing heaps of housework, stops to serve him his favorite beer, and a catchy tune narrates the lives of this cartoon couple.[43]

"NEW BEAU" by Douglass Crockwell. Number 3 in the series "Home Life in America," by noted American illustrators.

Beer belongs...enjoy it

In this home-loving land of ours ... in this America of kindliness, of friendship, of good-humored tolerance ... perhaps no beverages are more "at home" on more occasions than good American beer and ale,

For beer is the kind of beverage Americans like. It belongs—to pleasant living, to good fellowship, to sensible moderation. And our right to enjoy it, this too belongs — to our own American heritage of personal freedom.

AMERICA'S BEVERAGE OF MODERATION

"No. 3: New Beau," in the United States Brewers' Foundation's "Beer Belongs" public relations campaign for the brewing industry. Depicting beer as the social beverage in such a Norman Rockwell–like family setting would have been disgraceful earlier in the century. *Life*, 5 May 1947.

Characteristic of the "normalization" effort of beer marketing in the years after World War II, this Schlitz ad portrays white, young adult couples socializing and enjoying beer with their suburban backyard barbeque. *Life,* 7 July 1947.

The Wine Industry

The wine industry's main trade association established its advertising guidelines in 1949, right when the antiadvertising movement was shifting into high gear. The Wine Conference of America's "Statement of Principles for Advertising in the Wine Industry" allowed holiday parties to be depicted (except Memorial and Armistice Days) and permitted drinking scenes with children present, though the guidelines prohibited the depiction of children drinking or of characters that appealed to children, such as Santa Claus or fairy-tale characters. The advertising guidelines also did not permit endorsement by celebrities or the suggestion that wine and athletic ability were linked, but wine advertising was permitted to show "friendly and recreational activities."[44]

Like the brewers, the wine industry endeavored to differentiate itself from distilled spirits. Marketers mainly portrayed wine as an upscale beverage to be consumed—in moderation, of course—with dinner. Wine manufacturers advertised much less than did their beer and spirits cousins and were virtually absent from TV before 1960, but typical of their print advertisements was an ad for Valliant wine that featured a couple at dinner and stressed the "romantic meal with Valliant California Burgundy." One brand of wine, Virginia Dare, however, tended to be more "daring" than most alcoholic beverages in its advertising themes. A frequent advertiser in *Life* magazine, its early ads featured the drawing of a pretty woman, presumably Virginia herself, serving wine on a tray and asking the ad's viewer to "make a date for tonight." Another ad pictures Virginia, again serving wine, but this time to two young men and a woman who are listening to blues records. Virginia tells the young people, "It's Bye-Bye blues whenever you serve the only wine of its kind in the world!"

Also like beer and spirits, vintners promoted sales to women. One 1950 ad by an industry trade association, the Wine Advisory Board, combined its moderation message with education for hostesses on entertaining with wine. The ad features the testimony of experts on etiquette and homemaking, as well as guidelines on which wines should be served with which foods. One "young matron" declares, "I've discovered more and more people like a chance to choose a moderate beverage like wine," and a Chicago homemaker agrees, "many folks believe wine has won its new popularity *because* it is a moderate drink." The ad implies that wine should be viewed as a sophisticated alternative to serving spirits and that women were instrumental in making that decision.[45]

INTERINDUSTRY CONFLICT

Despite the similarities in overall marketing approaches, the frustrating market conditions, exacerbated by the threat of more government restrictions,

Also indicative of the "normalization" theme, this ad, sponsored by the California vintner's trade association, the Wine Advisory Board, was directed toward women and emphasized wine as an "easy, economical, and versatile" accompaniment for "everyday meals" and entertaining. The copy at the bottom asks the consumer to write for free wine recipes and a booklet entitled "Home Fun with California Wines."

often provoked clashes among the industries as they faced dry attacks. For example, the members of the USBF and the United States Brewers Association (USBA), both of which represented large brewers, suspected that the Small Brewers' Association (SBA) thought that the elimination of interstate alcohol advertising would work to the advantage of small, local brewers. USBF officials were dismayed and mistrustful when the SBA would not agree to meet to coordinate testimony before the 1950 congressional hearing.[46]

More important, the brewers and the distillers were suspicious of one another as they confronted the antiadvertising movement. Most divisive was the question of whether advertising raised sales and consumption. This question proved fundamental in this and all subsequent inquiries into the social effects of advertising and the media: could exposure to commercial media alter a person's behavior? In the early 1950s, the brewers' trade associations took the stance that advertising did influence consumers' purchasing behavior and increase overall sales. Leading distillers, on the other hand, contended that advertising did not increase overall sales and consumption; rather, advertising's sole purpose was to provoke consumers to switch brands. Underlying the debate about the purpose and power of advertising was tension caused by uneven market conditions. Beer sales were rising at a faster rate than spirits sales, causing distillers to be even more anxious and suspicious of a competing industry they viewed as stealing their market.

Instead of attempting to smooth over the rift in the interest of presenting a united front against the drys, the brewers could not restrain themselves from publicly taking on the distillers. In 1950, *Modern Brewery Age* published an editorial questioning the distillers' motives and threatening a severe split: "Some [brewers] are convinced that the distillers want a law banning beer from the air and pictures of women. . . . Apparently, some brewers say, the distillers are jealous—and desperate. If the distillers are taking sly shots at brewers, they'd better watch out. The brewing industry could pull away from them and work only for beer in Washington and state capitols and in local option campaigns."[47] Just as distillers suspected that brewers wanted to turn the advertising ban proposal to their advantage by limiting it to spirits, brewers suspected the same tactics of the distillers and were determined to fight back.

SELF-REGULATION—RESISTANCE AND CAPITULATION

Industry members also experienced conflict over whether self-regulation of marketing was the right method to win customers and assuage enemies. Considering, on the one hand, their victory in repealing Prohibition and, on the other, their current market problems, it is not surprising that several alcohol company executives were displeased with the cautious, defensive, and, to them, cowardly stance of the trade associations.[48]

Undoubtedly, most manufacturers and broadcasters chafed under these self-imposed regulations. Every so often, a maverick company spokesman would argue that the industries should act as would any other legitimate industry in America and advertise where, when, and how they wished. Spirits companies, especially, resisted their industry's strict restrictions on marketing. In an address to fellow industry men in 1951 the outspoken W. W. Wachtel, president of Calvert Distillers Corporation, fantasized about what it would be like to market hard liquor without restrictions: "But if we were able to use the methods to increase the consumption of alcohol that I used to increase the sale of crackers, I would guarantee to double the consumption. . . . If we were permitted to really go out and sell our industry's goods the way the radio and television people sell, what an industry we would have! One hundred seventy, 180, 350 million gallons would be a pushover." Coming back to earth, Wachtel exhibited the self-flagellating attitude of many liquor men and spoke, probably through gritted teeth, as if he were trying to convince himself and his audience of the truth to these statements: "We do not use those tactics. We do not think we should. We do not want to. We do not believe in increasing the consumption of alcoholic beverages. The beer and wine people do it. We in distilled spirits do not do it. We are just nice guys. I only wish we could do something to see to it that we got credit for being nice guys."[49]

In 1949 Schenley Distillers, one of the biggest distilling firms and at that point not a member of DSI, announced its intention to procure an advertising contract with a radio or television station. *Newsweek* reported that Schenley representatives had been in discussions with ABC, CBS, and NBC but that "on all sides the conversations were cautious, so volatile was the subject." None of the networks would bite, so controversial was the thought of spirits advertising on the air.[50] Later in the 1950s other distilling firms would periodically send out feelers about the possibility of broadcast advertising. In isolated cases liquor advertisements were broadcast, but none lasted long.[51]

By the late 1950s, *Broadcasting,* the leading periodical for that industry, had grown disgusted with the National Association of Broadcasters' (NAB) ban on hard liquor ads and printed three widely noted editorials that strongly advocated radio and television spirits advertising. The editors likened the broadcast ban to "taboos of primitive tribes" that were "cultivated by fear," and proceeded to mock broadcasters' and distillers' "unrealistic estimate of prohibitionist power." A year later, *Broadcasting* proclaimed that the "heretofore almost solid front against hard liquor advertising is beginning to crumble" and wondered whether "the much-advertised advertising ban is no ban at all, but merely a no-man's-land into which neither side is anxious to venture."[52] Nevertheless, the conservative counsel of the powerful trade associations suppressed these attempts at defiance. The DSI remained steadfast in its opposition to broadcast advertising, and it strong-armed association members that tried to get on the air. The NAB also strongly opposed the acceptance of hard liquor advertising contracts. NAB president Harold Fellows became irate when he read *Broadcasting*'s editorials and learned of radio stations that had accepted spirits advertising. At an NAB conference in 1958, Fellows excoriated those broadcasters who "upset traditional broadcasting policy" by seeking spirits advertising dollars, charging them with "selling [their] birthright for a $20 bill."[53]

The system of self-regulation not only was maintained but, except for the distillers' inclusion of women in their ads, was strengthened over the 1950s, primarily in response to the continuing activism of the drys. In 1954, the broadcasting, brewing, and wine industries complied with a House Commerce Committee suggestion to prohibit the actual consumption of beer and wine in television advertising. Also in that year, the DSI implemented a ban on paid testimonials. In 1955, brewers established an Advertising Review Panel as another guard against offensive advertising. As late as 1960, the NAB added strictures to its advertising code by banning "products that induce the use of hard liquor," such as cocktail mixes.[54] All of these measures were taken to assuage activist drys and, more important, their potential allies in Congress.

Pointing to their advertising codes was an impressive tactic used by industry representatives to counter the proposals for an advertising ban. It was no secret that staving off increased government regulation was the chief reason for the industries' self-regulatory efforts. Temperance leaders, of course, disparaged the industries' attempts at self-regulation and cast a cynical eye on moderation and other ostensibly altruistic industry public relations campaigns. Furthermore, many congressional members, even some who were not whole-heartedly in the dry camp, were persuaded that the industries' regulations did not go far enough and were not well enforced. Nevertheless, for legislators who sought nonstatist solutions, as was increasingly the case in the politically moderate to conservative 1950s, the fact that the industries were at least trying to be responsible about their marketing efforts was a strong reason to oppose a legislated ban on alcohol advertising. The Treasury's ATTD clearly favored industry self-regulation over government regulation, and so did Congress. After holding hearings in 1954 on the alcohol advertising matter, the House Commerce Committee found that "the potential evils inherent in government controls might be even greater than the evils that such controls might be designed to remedy," and "[s]elf-regulation is making substantial progress in this field and so long as public interest is served, is preferable to government-imposed regulation."[55] Thus, the key legislative body with jurisdiction over advertising, whose members claimed to sympathize with drys' concerns and whose report agreed that most alcohol ads were in poor taste, favored voluntary solutions to the moral and commercial speech dilemmas presented by the alcohol advertising controversy.

Although emphasizing self-regulatory efforts proved a compelling argument, it tended to undercut the industries' other main defensive tactic. Out of one side of their mouths, industry representatives claimed that the drys were an insignificant minority and that the vast majority of Americans liked to drink in moderation and made no objections to alcohol advertising. Out of the other side of their mouths, though, the same industry spokesmen publicized their attempts to be very careful about how they advertised their products—in effect acknowledging that alcoholic beverages were still controversial in American society and that their opponents did wield real power. The industries' double rhetoric demonstrated that they were in the awkward position of constituting an important part of the new middle-class consumer culture yet remained the object of condemnation by a fading, yet still fairly politically influential, minority of religious Americans.

The industries' efforts to establish limits on their marketing themes and outlets, as well as their construction of defensive public relations campaigns, revealed the extent to which they were unnerved by continuing dry sentiment. Yet, although they suffered from interindustry disputes and were operating under restrictions—and at the same time *because* they were operating under restrictions—the alcohol industries prevailed in the wet-dry battle that carried on into the postwar years.

3

LEGISLATIVE BATTLES

Politics and Rhetoric

As the national temperance movement shifted its battle against alcohol to the realm of advertising, it engaged a wider postwar debate about mass society and youth. Drys were able to tap into broader fears about consumer culture and a decline in morals that were shared by many Americans, including members of Congress who were not entirely sold on the "dry line." Advocates of the ban argued that alcohol advertising posed a threat to morality and social relationships and emphasized the ads' harmful influence on young people. The alcohol industries and their powerful allies, however, used constitutional objections to advertising controls as an effective way to shape the legislative debates and deflect the ethical issues that their opponents wished to raise. At the series of congressional committee hearings on the proposal to ban alcohol advertising held from 1947 to 1958, the industries concentrated on raising First, Fifth, and Twenty-first Amendment objections and employed related arguments, such as "the slippery slope" and the sufficiency of current regulation, to counter the legislative proposals and moral arguments of the drys. The industries' strategy forced the drys to respond with constitutional arguments of their own. Furthermore, the industries' strategy caused many policymakers who had seemed sympathetic with the case against alcohol advertising to grow ambivalent and ultimately refuse to enact controls. A close examination of the long and rugged journey of the alcohol ad ban proposal in the 1940s and 1950s, including the failure of alternative policy solutions, provides necessary context for understanding the later clashes over federal government regulation of cigarette and alcohol marketing.

PLAYERS AND POLITICS

The Drys and Their Congressional Supporters

The drys approached the ad ban movement with a command of political skills acquired in the Prohibition movement decades earlier. Their overall strategy was to place continual and unrelenting pressure on Congress to consider their proposal. They persuaded sympathetic congressmen to introduce their bill year after year and publicized their movement by pressuring the Senate and House Committees of Commerce, under whose jurisdiction the bill fell, to hold frequent hearings. These hearings gave the movement an opportunity to dominate a national forum, and drys hoped the publicity would aid the temperance movement in all of its endeavors, including local option contests and temperance education in the schools. Furthermore, they believed that the more times the committees held hearings, the likelier they were to pass the bill. Drys viewed each hearing as a chink in the armor of wet rule.[1]

The antiadvertising campaign in Washington was, by necessity, managed by a handful of leaders, but the drys' chief strategy was to display massive and widespread support for their cause. Portraying their cause as a mass movement of God-fearing Americans was crucial to combat the industries' potent argument that only a very small and fanatical minority was bothered by alcohol ads. Furthermore, this majority-rights argument was meant to carry a great deal of moral force.[2] The temperance organizations' main tactic was to conduct ambitious letter-writing and petition campaigns. In their speeches and publications, dry leaders frequently beseeched their followers to write to Congress in support of pending legislation to ban alcohol advertising. For instance, in 1950 WCTU national president Mamie Colvin asked for 500,000 letters to be sent to the Senate Commerce Committee imploring it to report favorably on the bill. Sympathizers heeded these calls and sent tens of thousands of letters, telegrams, and postcards to national policymakers throughout the 1940s and 1950s. At the 1954 hearing, the House committee chairman announced that, to his amazement, the committee had received between 20,000 and 25,000 letters and telegrams in recent weeks. At several of the hearings, dry leaders quite impressively presented enormous petitions in the form of long scrolls tied with white ribbons, the traditional symbol of the temperance cause.[3]

To further demonstrate a massive outpouring of support, temperance groups flooded the hearing rooms with applauding supporters, who often were asked to be quiet by presiding members of Congress, and packed the docket of witnesses with dry activists, sometimes forcing the hearings into extra days so that everyone could be heard. The audience at the 1950 hearing, for example, was much larger than that of the average congressional committee hearing. *Time* reported that all 555 seats in the hearing room were taken, and many more people "spilled out into the aisles and perched on the window ledges." *Modern Brewery Age* estimated that the hearing drew as many as 800 people. As late as 1958 attendance at the hearings was still unusually high, with the *New York Times* comparing it to "that of a Broadway hit."[4]

Because the movement mobilized its forces and flocked to Washington about every other year, and sometimes twice a year, for more than a decade, by the late 1950s these tactics were no longer remarkable. In 1958 *Advertising Age* yawned, "The usual hundreds of thousands of letters had been directed to committee members and other legislators in advance of the hearings." Overall, though, as a result of the drys' savvy political tactics, the alcohol industries and their allies viewed them with a mixture of awe, fear, and distaste. *Broadcasting* magazine went so far as to call the drys "one of Washington's most powerful lobbies."[5]

Support for the temperance movement came from cultural conservatives in both parties. Though much smaller and less influential than it had been in the 1910s and 1920s, a bipartisan congressional dry bloc persisted. Drys in the postwar period generally could count on the support of mainly rural and conservative southern Democrats and western Republicans, with Republicans dominating the dry bloc in the Senate and the Democrats providing leadership in the House. Senators who were most important in introducing and pressing for legislation to ban alcohol advertising included Arthur Capper (R-KS), William Langer (R-ND), and Edwin C. Johnson (D-CO). Senators Strom Thurmond (D-SC), Francis Case (R-SD), and Fredrick Payne (R-ME) also provided key support. In the House, Representatives Joseph Bryson (D-SC), James Davis (D-GA), and Eugene Siler (D-KY) proved most active on the dry front. Representatives Edward Rees (R-KS) and Brooks Hays (D-AK) also strongly advocated the ban.[6]

Senator Capper first introduced a bill that proposed a ban on all interstate alcoholic beverage advertising very soon after the adoption of the Twenty-first Amendment. Although he was most certainly a dry and had been an ardent prohibitionist, his relationship to temperance groups is unclear. In terms of his national reputation, he was not thought of as a dry leader; instead, he was well known as an isolationist Republican and individualist from Kansas. He embodied the values of a rural conservative and, because of his career of publishing magazines for farmers, was considered an important leader of the farm bloc. In fact, Capper had finally advocated the repeal of Prohibition because he believed it had caused economic destruction for the nation's farmers. Nevertheless, he agreed to be the temperance organizations' strategic legislator in the Senate on the issue of alcohol advertising.[7]

After Capper left Congress in 1948, Senator William Langer took over as sponsor of the alcohol ad ban bill. Like Capper, Langer drew attention for his maverick qualities and his isolationist stance on foreign policy, while his commitment to temperance was rarely noted. In the same year that he first sponsored the advertising ban, Langer was included on *Time* magazine's list of "most expendable" senators, and the article added that he had "probably introduced more trivial bills than any other Senator."[8] Although Langer and Capper were important in maintaining dry visibility in Congress during these years—and indeed, the bill to ban all alcoholic beverage advertising was first dubbed the "Capper bill" and then the "Langer bill"—neither enjoyed a position on the Senate Commerce Committee, so their control over the bill's fate was limited.

Senator Edwin C. Johnson, a Democrat from Colorado, became much more important to the movement than Capper or Langer because of his membership, later chairmanship, on the Commerce Committee and because of his sense of political realism. Like other senators who actively supported dry legislation, Johnson was by and large conservative and an isolationist who had built a reputation for being controversial and idiosyncratic. While nominally a Democrat, it was rare that he stuck to the party line. He was concerned generally about the degradation of morals in American society and made a name for himself nationally when he called for an investigation of immorality in Hollywood films. The brewers' leading publication claimed that Johnson thought of himself as a moralist and that he was "one of the best publicity men the drys ever had."[9]

On the alcohol advertising issue, however, Johnson was not an extremist. In his words, he believed that "a great deal of present-day liquor advertising is of questionable taste"—a much more moderate statement than many dry leaders would make. Alcohol advertising most offended him when it depicted women and when it was aired over broadcast media, but he did not think that a wholesale ban on all alcohol advertising was practicable or necessary. Instead, he tried several alternate routes to the elimination of objectionable alcohol advertising, such as introducing less drastic bills and pressing for federal government agencies, instead of Congress, to take stronger regulatory action. He hoped that established laws and regulations would resolve advertising problems and make new legislation unnecessary.[10]

Johnson found himself in the difficult position of representing a movement with which he sympathized but from whose leaders he often differed, especially tactically. He was often frustrated with the extremism and stubbornness of the temperance leaders with whom he worked. At one point he had a falling out with the WCTU's Colvin, when she refused to support his more moderate bill that would, as a preventive measure, ban only broadcast spirits advertising.[11] Johnson was sometimes convinced that the dry leaders' unwillingness to compromise meant there was no hope for any federal government action on alcohol advertising. He vented these frustrations in a letter to a dry constituent who was pressing him for action against alcoholic beverages: "The cold facts are that there is practically no support in Congress for any 'dry' movement however moderate. That is due in part to the arbitrary attitude of many so-called 'drys.' They would tear their best friends to pieces and enjoy his [sic] discomfort unless they are given their way and have their views accepted without question." Despite the tension between them, drys relied on Johnson. One leading dry told Johnson he was "the last hope of the drys on the Democratic Aisle."[12] In 1952, Johnson ascended to the chairmanship of the Senate Commerce Committee, and from this position he was able to propel the antialcohol advertising cause into even more prominence. This was the best possible place for the drys to have a friend in power. Notwithstanding his ambivalence about the proposal, as well as his sometimes stormy relationship with fervent dry leaders, Johnson's activism and influence is an important reason why the bills to prohibit alcohol advertising received so much congressional attention in the postwar period.

While dry strength was better represented in the Senate, the House did harbor two steadfast temperance activists. Joseph Bryson, a conservative Christian from South Carolina, was well known for being an outspoken and extreme dry. In the early 1940s he used the exigencies of wartime as a rationale for proposing prohibitionist measures. As late as 1947 Bryson introduced a House resolution proposing the reinstitution of national prohibition. In 1953 Bryson sponsored the House version of the alcohol ad ban bill. When he unexpectedly died less than a year later, Representative Eugene Siler, a freshman Democrat from Kentucky, was dubbed the "new Bryson" and took over sponsorship of the antialcohol advertising bill.[13] To make any progress with their antiadvertising movement, it was crucial for drys to be able to count on this handful of congressional members, congressmen who were fighting for a cause viewed by many Americans, especially political sophisticates in Washington, as quaint and ill fated.

The Industries: Tactics, Disputes, and Allies

The alcohol manufacturers were able to mobilize numerous industry and labor groups to support their fight against the ad ban bill. Influential in making the case that the ad ban threatened American freedoms were the statements of the many representatives of the advertising, print media, and broadcast media trades who appeared at the hearings to add their considerable influence to the fight against what they viewed as censorship. Representatives of brewery and distillery workers' unions, as well as leaders of grocery, hotel, restaurant, and tavern trade associations, also appeared in significant numbers at the congressional committee hearings, and, although they also spoke to constitutional and ideological issues, their presence emphasized the economic importance of the alcoholic beverage trade. The Licensed Beverage Industries "solicit[ed] the active interest" of many of these supporters and prepared "speech material" for them to use at the hearings.[14]

Despite this show of support from affiliated interests, the industries' efforts to mobilize the masses, in the words of a *Modern Brewery Age* editor, were "dwarfed" by those of the drys. They did not conduct petition or letter-writing campaigns, pack the hearing rooms with their supporters, or engage in any of the mass pressure activities at which their opponents excelled.[15] Furthermore, the industries took longer to assemble themselves than did the drys. During the first couple of hearings, the industries were barely organized to counter the antiadvertising initiative. The *New York Times* observed that the industries "stay[ed] discreetly, if somewhat anxiously, in the background." Brewers started to come together in 1949 to discuss strategy for the next year's hearing and decided their main tactic would be to focus on constitutional questions. When the United States Brewers' Foundation counsel drew up an extensive legal brief of constitutional objections to the proposed advertising ban, brewers applauded themselves for at last taking the offensive.[16]

Although they were impeded by internal disputes, by 1956 the industries seemed to have joined common cause, at least temporarily. That year, as the House Commerce Committee prepared to hold another hearing on the ad ban bill, the industries seemed more nervous than usual and more determined than ever to apply coordinated pressure on Congress. Distilling and brewing trade association leaders asked everyone even remotely associated with the industries to contact their members of Congress, demand that the committee kill the bill, and, as an indication of their overestimation of the bill's chances, insist that the House Rules Committee reject the bill if it were to be reported to the House floor. *Modern Brewery Age* sounded the alarm: "The brewing industry appears to be faced with one of the most ominous threats in its post-Prohibition history—the threat that interstate advertising of its product may be drastically curtailed if not eliminated altogether." Big-city newspapers joined the industries' counterattack by running editorials that denounced the ad ban proposal. It is difficult to measure the impact of this lobbying effort, but many industry members believed it was consequential in pressing the committee not only to ignore the bill, which it did not make room for in its executive session, but also to abandon a rumored committee report unfavorable to the industries.[17]

Despite their success in mobilizing allied interests and patching over entrenched conflicts, the alcohol industries could count very few vocal congressional members in their camp. Although some senators on the Commerce Committee, both Democrat and Republican, exhibited sympathy for the industries during the hearings, none appeared as witnesses on their behalf. In the House, by contrast, the industries found a powerful spokesman in Representative Emanuel Celler, a Democrat from New York

City, who delivered hard-hitting speeches at the hearings and on the House floor against the antiadvertising campaign. Celler, however, did not limit his criticism to the drys. Although he was a friend to the alcohol industries, he frequently chided them for their "apologetic, fearful attitude." In his view, the industries were perfectly legitimate and therefore should not act any differently than other lawful businesses. For years he expressed his disgust with, in his words, the industries' "abominable 'hushhush—someone is looking' attitude." He also attacked as cowardly the broadcasters' and distillers' agreement to keep hard liquor advertising off the air.[18] Even though he was looking out for the industries' best interests by pressing them to become more aggressive, many industry leaders no doubt wished Celler would keep quiet because he was playing right into the drys' hands.

Congressional Members: Damp But Not Wet

Several members of Congress who were neither committed wets nor drys tended to be critical of alcohol advertising at the same time as they were highly skeptical of the feasibility of a total ban. In 1948, Senator Clyde Reed (R-KS) announced, "It might surprise you if you knew the number of senators who are not prohibitionists [or] drys . . . who have almost unreservedly condemned this false advertising and have told us if we can find a workable bill they intend to vote for it."[19] To some degree, Senator Johnson fit into this category, but, despite his moderation, he was firmly in the dry camp. More typical was Senator Homer Capehart (R-IN), another member of the Commerce Committee, who told a WCTU leader he agreed liquor advertising often went too far but, because of constitutional objections, he was "of the opinion that no legislation can be enacted which will prohibit the advertising." Thomas Pelly, a member of the House Commerce Committee, also doubted the bill's constitutionality and argued that it would never succeed in its present form. Still, Pelly believed that alcohol advertising was harmful to children, and in 1954 he introduced a bill to ban such advertising from radio and television between the hours of 5 and 7 in the evening. This bill, however, was never taken up by committee.[20]

The most important member of Congress who shared this ambivalent position was Senator Warren Magnuson. In 1956 Magnuson succeeded Johnson as chairman of the Commerce Committee and thus assumed a crucial position from which he could influence the fate of the ad ban bill. Although Magnuson, a liberal Democrat from Washington, was not a dry—and in fact was renowned for enjoying hard liquor, as well as gambling and keeping company with Hollywood starlets—he was sensitive to abuses in advertising in general. On the issue of alcohol advertising, however, he was lukewarm. His primary objective was to maintain the status quo in the industries' standards; in other words, he wished to prevent any further liberalization, such as women in spirits ads or spirits ads on the air. He never expressed interest in a rollback by adding more regulations to alcohol advertising, and he explicitly opposed banning alcohol advertising from newspapers.

Like Senator Johnson, Magnuson hoped that federal agencies could solve the problems of alcohol advertising without resorting to new federal legislation. When federal agencies refused to act, he relied on his own backroom powers of persuasion, on which he had built his successful political career. He was moved to action in 1957 when he learned of rum ads in Puerto Rico that featured women. Magnuson repeatedly wrote to the governor of Puerto Rico, requesting that something be done to eliminate such advertising. Magnuson found the matter politically important enough to publicize it, along with his efforts to curb it, by sending copies of his correspondence with the governor to several other senators and their staffs. Later, when some distillers sought broadcasting contracts, Magnuson worked behind the scenes to ensure that the trade associations maintained their self-imposed prohibitions against broadcast spirits advertising.[21]

Yet, unlike Johnson, Magnuson was not recognized by the drys as one of their own, probably because his liberal politics and playboy lifestyle were well known. Drys were wary of the new chairman, accusing him of purposefully bottling up their bill in committee. When the committee failed even to consider the bill in 1956, Magnuson calmly explained to distressed drys that there was a "rush of business during the closing days" and the bill had simply died. In other correspondence, though, he stated that the committee had not voted on the bill because so many senators believed that "this type of legislation may present a constitutional question." He implied that he, too, objected to the bill for this reason.[22]

Alternatives to a Ban and Disputes within the Movement

Although the drys' principal legislative proposal during the postwar years was a complete ban on all interstate alcohol advertising in all media, sympathetic legislators sometimes proposed alternative policies to curb alcohol advertising. These alternatives, all of which failed and none of which enjoyed the drys' full support, demonstrate the various ways that policymakers in the 1940s and 1950s thought about using government to solve ethical problems in advertising. The sponsors of the alternative bills were congressional members who generally shared the temperance movement's concerns about alcohol advertising but considered the antiadvertising campaign too idealistic and ambitious. For instance, in 1947 Senator Reed was clearly supportive of the drys and their concerns, but he was uneasy about their ban proposal, which he considered too "sweeping" and "drastic" of a measure, and most committee members agreed that a complete ban on all alcohol advertising was not "practicable." Still, the committee was persuaded that alcohol advertising did present a real problem and that it might be the responsibility of Congress to find a remedy.[23]

In response to Reed's concerns, the committee asked him and Senator Johnson to study the issue and develop a more reasonable policy solution. Reed and Johnson proposed two bills that would enable Congress to restrict alcohol advertising without enacting a ban. One bill was patterned on Virginia's alcohol advertising law, the strictest in the nation, and stipulated that alcohol ads could display only the bottle, container, and label of the beverage, the images could not be larger than life, and the ad could contain no more than three such images. In other words, no people, fancy houses, or any other kind of lifestyle imagery could be included. Their second bill would amend the Federal Trade Commission Act to state specifically that an alcohol ad would be considered misleading if it portrayed the beverage as beneficial to health, raising social or business standing, or traditional in family life or part of the home. The last stipulation, especially, would have meaningfully changed contemporary beer advertising. Either piece of legislation, the senators claimed, would go a long way toward remedying the menace caused by offensive alcohol advertising.[24]

In response to the second Reed-Johnson bill, the FTC plainly communicated that it did not wish to become involved in the matter. During the 1948 Senate hearings on this bill, Johnson accused the FTC of having "an attitude of passing the buck." Revealing his impression of the Commission's stance on alcohol advertising, Johnson pressed the issue: "What is the explanation for the FTC's being so dilatory in doing its duty in respect to the matter? . . . [Y]ou are supposed to protect the people. You do not have to wait for a complaint. . . . When you see a false advertisement of any kind, you are supposed to move in, are you not?" Assuming that the FTC singled out alcohol marketing for inaction, he continued, "You do move in on patent medicines and a great many of other fields. You are very active. Why are you so reluctant to act in the case of alcoholic beverages?"[25]

The FTC, represented by Director of the Bureau of Stipulations Pgad Morehouse, responded to Johnson's persistent questioning first with a jurisdictional rationale, explaining that the Treasury's Alcohol and Tax Unit (ATU), not the FTC, had been granted primary jurisdiction over alcohol advertising. According to Morehouse, the FTC tended to "soft-pedal investigations of such commodities" because it wished to "avoid duplication of effort and to prevent probable conflict between the actions of the two agencies." But Morehouse also admitted that even if it did have primary jurisdiction over alcohol advertising, the Commission probably would not intervene. In an instructive statement about ethics and government regulation, Morehouse argued that, although "there is no question" that some alcohol ads have "bad morals" as well as "the tendency to be deceptive," most of them "are not false within the meaning of our statute." In other words, the leadership of the FTC saw a limit to the government's power to remedy unethical and deceptive advertising.[26] The Commission claimed both not to possess the authority to act against these ads and not to think there was much call for action in any case.

The senators next heard the ATU representative, Arthur Lacy, confirm the FTC's opinion that it possessed primary responsibility over the commerce, including advertising, in alcoholic beverages. Senators immediately set upon Lacy, asking him why, if it possessed the authority, the ATU had not acted to remedy the problems in alcohol advertising. Lacy insisted that his agency was doing everything it thought necessary to prevent misleading advertising and maintained a policy of preapproving nearly all alcohol ads. This forced him to admit that the ATU had approved several ads that moments earlier dry leaders had displayed as examples of especially offensive alcohol advertising.[27]

On top of all the constitutional and moral questions that would be unearthed by the antialcohol advertising movement, this kind of jurisdictional squabbling complicated the matter of alcohol advertising regulation during these years. Although Johnson and later Magnuson thought that the FTC, the ATU, and the FCC possessed authority to regulate alcohol advertising and hoped that a bureaucratic solution could be found, these agencies were reluctant to act, and none claimed jurisdiction over misleading alcohol advertising.

Reed and Johnson's proposal of alternative measures split the drys into radical and moderate factions, with the most vocal leaders falling into the radical camp. When the Senate committee opened its 1948 hearing on the Reed-Johnson bills, Senator Capper immediately rose to voice his objections to the watered-down measures. "I think it would be a gesture of appeasement for me to support either of these other bills," he stated. His bill, he declared, was still the best option: "After all, the way to prohibit liquor advertising is to prohibit it."[28] Many other militant temperance leaders made it clear that they would prefer the Capper bill over the Reed-Johnson substitutes. If one of the objectives of the Senate committee was to satisfy the persistent and vocal temperance constituency that was drowning the legislators in letters and petitions, passing either of the Reed-Johnson bills was not the way to placate them. Most drys demanded extreme measures—instead of monkeying with themes and images, simply ban the whole class of advertising. As a result of such pressure, the Reed-Johnson proposals for more moderate ways to control alcohol advertising were dropped for the remainder of the campaign.

The Politics of Regulating Broadcast Advertising

Despite this defeat, Senator Johnson was still determined to find a way to curb alcohol advertising abuses that would address the constitutional and political concerns of many national policymakers. Provoked by recent reports that Schenley Distillers had been negotiating broadcasting contracts, Johnson seized upon the federal regulation of broadcast media as the next policy solution. Not only were radio and the fledgling medium of television more powerful communicators than print, but they also were already subject to more government regulation than were the print media. Johnson hoped that a legislative ban on only the broadcast advertising of alcohol, particularly spirits, would simultaneously mollify the drys, satisfy the concerns of potentially sympathetic legislators, and genuinely solve the problems created by widespread alcohol advertising, especially its influence on youth. Guided by Johnson, the alcohol advertising controversy in the early 1950s centered on the regulation of the broadcasting industry.

On learning that Schenley was not at the time a member of the Distilled Spirits Institute and thus did not consider itself subject to the trade association's rule against broadcast advertising, Johnson's first inclination was to report the matter to the FCC. He believed that the Commission could use its power over licensing to prevent the possibility of broadcast spirits advertising. Under its statute, the FCC was supposed to license only stations that broadcast in the public interest. Clearly, Johnson argued, as already acknowledged by the distillers and broadcasters themselves through their trade associations' prohibitions against broadcast spirits ads, spirits advertising was not in the public interest. Therefore, he reasoned, the FCC possessed every right to deny a license to a radio or television station that chose to broadcast a commercial for hard liquor.[29] The FCC, however, disagreed with Johnson's assessment of how it could use its licensing power to guarantee that spirits advertising would stay off the air. The FCC's chairman, who like the FTC leadership was reluctant to become mixed up in the alcohol advertising controversy, explained to Johnson that the Commission could not act "in the absence of specific Congressional legislation."[30]

Faced with intransigent federal agencies, Johnson abandoned the administrative approach and decided that Congress would have to legislate a ban on broadcast spirits advertising. He argued that because a public license was involved, Congress possessed more authority over radio and television advertising than over other forms of advertising. Johnson explained to federal legislators that his bill was preventive—that there may not be spirits advertising on the air now, but unless the federal government acted, he was certain there soon would be. He tried to make the bill more palatable to the industry by arguing that he was trying to assist the DSI in enforcing its praiseworthy advertising code. The industry, of course, did not want any government help, and, in the end, a majority of the Senate Commerce Committee agreed that it did not need any help. Although from a practical standpoint the broadcasting ban bill was more attainable than the Capper bill, it was destined for defeat because not only did the industries detest it but the drys were unenthusiastic about it as well. All three alcohol industries refused to countenance any federal government regulation of their advertising, even in this moderate measure. Temperance organizations refused to back down from their conviction that all alcoholic beverages advertised in any media were wicked and should be prohibited. Therefore, the groups that comprised the chief stakeholders in the debate over alcohol advertising, and that would form the crucial constituency for a highly contested bill, could not be counted on for their full support for Johnson's moderate measure. Reacting to the drys' lack of enthusiasm, the industries' vehement opposition, and their own reluctance to enact legislation that was merely preventive, Senate committee members decided not to favor the bill—which had seemed promising at the start—by a close vote of seven to six.[31]

After this defeat, the drys returned to their preferred approach, the bill to ban all alcohol advertising, and took it to the House in 1954, but the debate remained focused on broadcast advertising. Although the House committee decided not to report the bill to the floor that year, many committee members had become convinced that alcohol advertising, particularly on the radio and television, was troublesome. The committee issued a report that called on the broadcast and alcohol industries to clean up their acts and went even farther than Johnson by including beer and wine advertising as chief concerns. The report was most concerned with alcohol ads it judged to be in "poor taste," such as those depicting a family scene, persons preparing, serving, or consuming drinks, and ads appealing to children. The committee put most of the onus on the broadcast industry, requesting that it voluntarily curb or eliminate radio and television beer and wine advertising as it had for distilled spirits. Furthermore, it criticized broadcasters for failing to police themselves effectively.[32] Because the House committee was most concerned with extant broadcast alcohol advertising, for once the distillers were off the hook.

The committee's decision to issue a report rather than send the bill to the House floor demonstrated the members' ambivalence over this controversial issue. Most felt that they should take some action, either for the purely political reason that they wanted to placate the vociferous drys or because they truly had been persuaded that abuses existed in alcohol advertising and, furthermore, that many Americans were troubled by these abuses. Members of the committee had received enormous stacks of letters and telegrams in support of the bill and had listened to days of testimony exhorting the abuses of alcohol advertising. That amount of concentrated pressure was difficult to ignore. Yet, passing the ad ban bill seemed too drastic a step, too statist a solution for many of these legislators, especially when they had the memory of Prohibition hanging over their heads—and pushed down their throats by the bills' opponents. Temperance forces could not muster enough support in the committee to secure their bill's passage, but they could achieve the compromise measure of a report that was highly critical of the industries.

House committee members reasoned that, if the industries already had seen fit to restrict their advertising through self-regulation, then with some congressional pressure they would "voluntarily" restrict it even further. Voluntary self-regulation, they hoped, would provide a solution without resort to a legislative fiat that would surely be controversial, subject to constitutional questions, and probably harmful to their political reputations. Thus, a fault-finding report seemed to be the best answer: it might quiet the drys, curb some abuses, and avoid damaging political careers.

Although they escaped legislation, industry leaders were quite dismayed by the House committee's report. *Modern Brewery Age* interpreted it as a victory for its dry opponents and accused the committee of adopting the "Dry Line." The brewers' magazine was most distressed by the report's criticism of ads that depicted beer in the home and by the committee's statement that complaints about beer advertising were "widespread." Harold Fellows, president of the National Association of Broadcasters, also expressed great displeasure with the report and counseled broadcasters to resist the pressure to eliminate beer and wine advertising. In a long article entitled "Alarming Precedent," a *New York Times* reporter was troubled by the report's coerciveness, which he said raised the threat of congressional paternalism. The report, he pointed out in protest, asked the industries to do something for which there was not enough support to pass a law. "Wouldn't it be more logical," he asked, "to have the issues thrashed out on the floor of Congress before a committee charges off to inform broadcasters that their house is in need of revolutionary changes?" He considered it acceptable for the committee to issue a report expressing its concern over alcohol advertising but contended that its "suggestion that all such advertising be eliminated is a shocking way to open the discussion."[33]

Despite their unhappiness with the report, the industries tried to cooperate with its recommendations, which was not surprising considering that for decades they had been on guard lest they reawaken widespread support for prohibition. Though they did not go so far as to eliminate beer and wine broadcast advertising, the industries did agree to stop showing the actual consumption of beer and wine in television commercials, and the brewers took the additional step of establishing an advertising review panel.[34]

The Unpopular Warning Label Proposal

As another alternative measure to address the problems posed by alcohol advertising, a few drys broached the idea of requiring a warning label. The idea did not prove popular. In the absence of a consumer rights movement as would emerge in the mid-1960s and push for truth in advertising and truth in labeling, a warning label was not a prominent policy proposal in the 1940s and 1950s. In addition, in most drys' estimation,

warning labels would only be a halfhearted measure: they could not counteract the power of the ads' imagery. In 1951, the WCTU included in its
annual report a proposal for "the correct labeling of alcoholic beverages
under the Federal Food and Drug Act by including on such label in large
type the word POISON," but Union leaders did not present this demand
to national policymakers during the hearings. One temperance leader,
Clarence Hall, the editor of *The Christian Herald*, took the idea of a warning label seriously and argued before Congress that it might produce the
same effect as enacting a ban: "But can you imagine how long this industry would last if it were forced to state in all its advertising and on all its
labels the real truth, not only as to its product's ingredients but also its potential effect on the physical body and on the body politic?" Hall's sentiment notwithstanding, dry activists took the more extreme route, as they
had been accustomed to doing since the beginning of the century, and ignored the warning label idea in favor of the all-out ban.[35]

Although the drys ultimately stuck with the ill-fated proposal to ban all
interstate alcohol advertising, Congress had considered some alternative
measures to control the marketing of alcoholic beverages. As they participated in this debate, national policymakers were thereby compelled to
contemplate the difficult dilemmas surrounding the politics of advertising
control in America's consumer culture, a culture increasingly dominated
by the influence of television and aimed at the youth market. For all of
their consideration, concern, and searching, however, federal legislators
never reached a policy solution. The commerce committees would revisit
the same questions about administrative versus congressional jurisdiction,
regulating advertising content, and banning broadcast advertising during
subsequent marketing control debates.

ARGUMENTS AND RHETORIC

The hearings on the alcohol advertising bills were replete with rich
rhetoric and keen arguments, much of which would be reproduced in
the congressional hearings on cigarettes in the following decade.
Whereas the strongest cases made on both sides of the controversy were
of a legalistic bent, wets and drys also took time to explain their stances
on broader issues such as advertising and mass media in general, its impact on youth, paternalistic government, freedom, and morality in modern American society.

The drys' argument that alcohol advertising was of questionable taste
proved persuasive to many congressmen. Temperance forces, however,
could never convince enough committee members that the federal government had the right or the duty to step in and regulate, never mind outright ban, alcohol advertising. The legislators' most frequently articulated
reason for opposing regulation was "constitutional questions."

The First Amendment and the Right to Advertise

One of the most difficult and far-reaching questions raised by the alcohol advertising controversy was whether advertising was a constitutionally protected right of legal industries. As an astute way of shaping the legislative debate, the wets posed this question, forcing the proponents of advertising regulation to respond. All parties involved realized the significance of the dilemma for America's consumer economy, even if the general population was not paying attention.

The drys replied with a compelling argument that advertising, any advertising, was not protected by the First Amendment and was thus subject to government regulation. In their legal briefs, drys presented examples of previous legislation that curtailed and sometimes prohibited the advertising of alcoholic beverages and other products such as prescription and over-the-counter drugs and emphasized that the Supreme Court had upheld this legislation.[36] The drys' argument that a ban on the advertising of alcohol was unquestionably constitutional was predicated on the assumption that alcoholic beverages were the enemy of health and morality. Furthermore, prohibition of alcohol advertising was perfectly legal because, as intoxicants, alcoholic beverages were unique among legal consumer products. Local, state, and federal governments in America had recognized the uniqueness of alcoholic beverages and treated them differently for, in some cases, hundreds of years. One dry leader enjoyed pointing out that the 1952 Democratic and Republican National Conventions had, out of all products, rejected alcoholic beverage sponsorship. Clarence Hall wondered, "Can you think of any other widely advertised product which has such disastrous effect on its users? Can you name any other industry which, because of its potentially harmful nature, has been historically given a limited status, and yet in our day is permitted to ballyhoo itself so unrestrainedly?" Alcoholic beverages, proponents argued, should be subject to special regulation, as they always had been; prohibiting alcohol's interstate advertising represented simply another measure in a long American tradition of special regulation.[37]

Because of the harmfulness of their products, the alcohol industries did not and should not enjoy "inherent or inalienable rights," especially not the right to advertise, drys contended. Mamie Colvin forcefully stated, "[T]he industries exist only by sufferance, and by virtue of Government license and strict policing. Please remember that it is not their right." Charlotte Endrews, of the Christian Science Committee on Publications, testified that alcohol was a "habit-forming drug" and therefore was subject to special restrictions on the "communication and advertising for increasing the use of its product."[38] It seemed to the drys that ample precedent and justification had been established for federal legislation to ban interstate alcohol advertising.

Even the Federal Trade Commission, which had resisted involvement in the matter, agreed with the argument that advertising was immune from First Amendment protection, and the Commission offered its opinion that an alcohol advertising ban would be constitutional. In 1950 the FTC submitted a report to the Senate committee, stating that the ad ban would not abridge the freedom of speech or press because the Bill of Rights "does not go to the extent of affording immunity to newspapers or magazine publishers from public regulatory measures otherwise valid. Due process does not guarantee to such publishers the right to sell advertising space for advertisements inimical to the public interest." The report flatly stated, "In our opinion, it is within the province of Congress to declare it to be against public policy to transmit advertisements for intoxicating liquors through the channels of interstate commerce, as a valid and reasonable measure for the protection of the health, morals, and social welfare of the public."[39] Drys surely were gratified by the FTC's opinion, but the Commission continued to withhold active assistance from their cause.

In a further attempt to appeal to national policymakers, drys argued that the entire class of alcohol advertising—not just particular ads—was dishonest and misleading by its very nature. They astutely adopted terms such as "deceptive" and "misleading" that were already part of the bureaucratic vocabulary. Drys argued that, because alcohol ads did not warn of the possible deleterious effects of alcohol consumption, they were unmistakably and inherently deceptive. The ads did not "tell the whole story." They showed only elegant, attractive, and happy people and settings—never "the skid rows, the Bowyers, the flop houses, the 'lost weekends,' the dead end drinkers," never crime, impaired driving, violence, and disease. Referring to the FTC Act and other laws affecting commerce, Hall asserted that government long ago had established that it was a "criminal offense to misstate, *or fail to state,* a material fact about a product and its effect on the consumer." He continued, "Anyone who makes even a cursory examination of the industry's public relations program knows that its claims are deceptive, false, and misleading." Regardless of First Amendment objections, drys averred, the industries' advertising should be prohibited because it was unlawful according to established statutes.[40]

In making these arguments, the drys were attempting to counter the very assured assumption of their opponents that the practice of advertising was a protected right of all legal industries. Advertising controls, the alcohol, advertising, and media industries insisted, would violate the First Amendment. Industry representatives argued the proposed ban constituted censorship and denied the freedom of speech, a freedom they equated with the freedom to advertise. Considering how dearly the industries claimed to cherish this much-lauded freedom to advertise, it might as well have been stated in the First Amendment. Some witnesses depicted advertising as the "lifeblood" of American capitalism and predicted collapse and doom if this "suppression of natural rights" were permitted. Arthur Jenkins, of the National Editorial Association, asserted the maxim uttered by many industry representatives at the hearings: "If it is legal to sell it, it should be legal to advertise it." The American Federation of Labor's George Riley stated the point more forcefully: "Destroy the informational methods in any consumer industry and you destroy the industry and all the human beings deriving their livelihood in that industry."[41] Although opponents of the ad ban devised these statements out of self-interest, their arguments about advertising, freedom, and capitalist commerce revealed a particular concept of how the consumer economy functioned in mid-twentieth-century American society, an economy they viewed as dependent on mass marketing.

Several members of Congress were persuaded by the industries' claim of a constitutionally protected right to advertise and used it to justify their opposition to the ad ban proposal. For instance, at the House hearings in 1954, Representative Arthur Klein (D-NY) stated, "What is troubling me is that this is a legal industry, and being such, it carries with it the right to advertise." One of his colleagues across the aisle, Steven Derounian (R-NY), also spoke up: "We are supposed to be a country where there is freedom of the press and freedom of advertising."[42] Although these legislators and fellow opponents of the ad ban thought the question over the First Amendment and advertising was self-evident and easily settled, this clearly was not the case. The controversy continued to vex federal legislators and administrators throughout the remainder of the century as they were forced to consider the First Amendment implications of restrictions on cigarette and alcohol advertising as well as on other products deemed harmful to consumers and the environment.

The Twenty-First Amendment and the Threat of Prohibition

Throughout the hearings, the industries voiced other constitutional objections to a ban on alcohol advertising, including the claim that it would contradict the Twenty-first Amendment to the Constitution. The amendment, which repealed Prohibition and granted the states jurisdiction over commerce in alcoholic beverages, thereby preventing the federal government from taking action to prohibit alcoholic beverages, allowed the industries to proclaim proudly that they alone were specifically sanctioned by the U.S. Constitution. Once and for all, the American people and their government had decided in 1933 that the alcohol trade was legal and legitimate; therefore, legislation that attempted to circumvent the Twenty-first Amendment by harming the business through "subterfuge and indirection" should be shot down. The Magazine Advertising Bureau's Frank Braucher argued, "[T]o enact a special statute restricting, almost to the point of extinction, the national advertising of alcoholic beverages would be, in effect, a violation of the expressed will of a great majority of the people as recorded in the votes of their representatives in the twenty-first amendment." John O'Neill, of the Small Brewers Association, similarly stated, "To us it seems apparent that the bill is an attempt to circumvent the Twenty-first amendment and to usurp the police powers of the states to regulate and control the traffic in alcoholic beverages within state borders." Others associated with the industries argued that, according to the amendment, not only manufacturing and retail restrictions, but also advertising restrictions in the alcohol trade, were a matter for the states to decide.[43]

Most wets assumed that the ad ban was prohibition in disguise. Nearly every industry witness at the hearings lambasted the drys for attempting "backdoor prohibition," with the implication that their indirect means were mightily dishonest. Edward Flanigan of the Globe Brewing Company, a small Baltimore brewer, explained to the congressional committee, "I cannot help but feel that this is a prohibition measure. In order for my company to continue operating profitably, we must maintain and expand our market. The extent to which we are able to accomplish this depends largely upon the success of our advertising program." Others acknowledged that an advertising ban would hurt small companies more than large firms because a ban would increase barriers to entry and preserve the already strong market positions of the big brewers and distillers.[44]

Regardless of whether the advertising ban would achieve full-blown prohibition, most opponents agreed that it would seriously harm the alcohol as well as the media and advertising industries. Representatives of brewers and distillers labor unions from around the country testified that the ad ban threatened jobs. Some industry and labor representatives also felt it pertinent to point out that the government's tax revenue would decline, perhaps drastically, as a result of the ban.[45]

In response to this common and largely effective line of criticism, several drys tried their best to convince the congressional committees that their bill was not an attempt to revive prohibition. Not all drys adopted this strategy, however. Many activists, such as Colvin, openly advocated the return of prohibition, and the antiadvertising measure was, in their eyes, a significant step toward the termination of the liquor trade. It was, however, politically dangerous to admit this motive, especially during the congressional hearings. Prohibition was a forbidden word in postrepeal America, and few wanted to be associated with it. Some drys, either because they truly were not committed to the idea of prohibition or because they were willing to jettison their principles for political opportunism, declared they had no intent to put the liquor industries out of business. Clarence Hall epitomized this tactical approach when he testified, "We are not here angling, obliquely or otherwise, for the return of prohibition. Nor are we singing the song of any so-called special interest group. The opposition could make no more stupid mistake than to laugh off this part of the hearing as just another prohibition party."[46] To the drys who asserted that the antiadvertising bill had nothing to do with prohibition, the advertising of a product was a completely separate function from the manufacturing and sale of a product. Curiously, both extreme drys such as Colvin and their industry opponents adamantly disagreed with Hall's position because they viewed advertising as an integral component of a consumer industry.

Discrimination and the Fifth Amendment

The last major weapon in the industries' arsenal of constitutionally based arguments was the position that the ban was patently discriminatory. The legislation singled out a particular industry for regulatory abuse and thereby violated yet another amendment, the due-process clause of the Fifth Amendment. R. E. Joyce of the DSI scored the bill as "class legislation." Assuming as they did that advertising was a right, wets felt that the bill would unfairly deprive the alcohol industries of a right "enjoyed by every other lawful business" in America.[47] The drys' reply, of course, was that the alcohol industries *were* different from all other lawful businesses in America because they produced a harmful product, and they therefore *should* be targeted for advertising restrictions.

As an attempt to prove discrimination, alcohol industry representatives appeared to be most bothered that their businesses had been targeted by such legislation while the cigarette industry had not. Although it would be several more years before the Surgeon General's Report of 1964 would detail the health hazards, evidence about the health hazards of smoking had been publicized by the early 1950s, and the hearings' participants, both wet and dry, well understood that cigarettes were in the same class of products as alcoholic beverages: potentially harmful and morally suspect. For example, the industries' defender Representative Celler wondered aloud why the drys had not gone after the tobacco industry. In 1954, after listening to testimony that criticized the alcohol trade for its abundant advertisements, Celler rose to defend the industry by drawing attention to what he saw as its natural counterpart, the tobacco trade: "[B]ut I can indicate that the tobacco company ads have assumed just as large, or larger dimensions as have liquor ads. If liquor ads are to be prohibited, then tobacco ads should also be prohibited." Celler continued, "[M]uch discussion has been current on the possibility that cigarettes may cause cancer. We find no attempt on the part of those who are the protagonists of this bill to prohibit or even censor any cigarette ads."[48] Pointing fingers in the tobacco industry's direction seemed to work for the bill's opponents. During the first day of the 1954 House hearings, John Dingell (D-MI), a staunch ally of organized labor, introduced a bill that added tobacco advertising to the alcohol ad ban bill. Dingell's measure, obviously intended to kill the bill and expose the hypocrisy of the temperance movement, did manage to tongue-tie the drys.[49] It was understood by opponents and proponents alike that a cigarette advertising ban would be impossible to achieve. Despite disturbing health reports, the political and cultural climate in America had not yet moved against cigarettes.

When questioned on cigarettes, drys tried to make the point that, although they opposed tobacco use, their focus for this piece of legislation remained alcoholic beverages solely. This was a difficult position to maintain, as several congressional members made clear through pointed questioning of dry leaders. In later hearings, drys were better prepared for this line of questioning, and instead of getting drawn into legal debates, they simply replied that cigarette use did not have as negative of "social consequences" as the consumption of alcohol; in a ranking of evil substances, cigarettes were less "objectionable" than liquor.[50] Still, it is important to note that the connection between the two types of products and the possibility of regulating them with the same approach was manifest at the 1950s antialcohol hearings, though cigarettes were always employed as an argumentative counterpoint and never seriously considered as a subject for marketing regulation.

The alcohol industries were not alone in charging discrimination. When faced with proposals that regulated alcohol advertising only on television and radio, the broadcasting industry cried discrimination and asked why the bills did not include the print media. Broadcasters emphasized that no spirits advertising had been broadcast since the DSI had developed its regulations and further argued that, because no broadcast spirits advertising existed (conveniently ignoring a major distiller's attempts to make it exist), congressional legislation to ban it was pointless.[51]

As policymakers journeyed through this largely uncharted territory of advertising controls, their attempts to make distinctions—between the alcohol industries and other industries, between broadcast media and other media—were open to quick and vehement opposition from the industries that had the most to lose. Although the drys had made a strong case for the constitutionality of alcohol advertising regulations, the industries' constitutional objections were eagerly accepted by many congressional members who opposed the ban for purely political or personal reasons. The constitutional objections allowed these legislators to oppose the measure on more principled grounds.

The Slippery Slope

All of the industries' constitutional arguments culminated in their strongest and most frequently stated case: the "slippery slope" argument. It was the domino theory applied to consumer regulation. Wets argued that, if Congress were to pass the alcohol ad ban bill, then it would set a dangerous precedent. Any time an organized group objected to a consumer product, whether it be cigarettes, cosmetics, automobiles, or fatty foods, its advertising could be banned too, and the situation would quickly get out of hand.

Many industry spokesmen did not waste their time trying to argue that alcohol advertising was good or harmless, though some did contend this. Instead, they focused on trying to impress the congressional committees with the larger significance of the proposed ban—in their view, the ruin of America's consumer economy and the rise to power of special interest groups and zealots. E. J. Soucy, of the New Hampshire Wholesale Beverage Association, claimed, "To prohibit beer advertising would seem to open the way for pressure groups of professional reformers to limit advertising of products such as tobacco, certain kinds of soft drinks, movies, or any commodity which might be judged harmful." Extending the argument to freedom of the press, and no doubt trying to demonstrate shared interests with the powerful ally of the media, Soucy further argued, "Editors see the bill as a move which could lead to extensive Federal control of the press through the power to dictate what products may or may not be advertised." The Advertising Federation of America's John Dwight Sullivan agreed with Soucy's assessment and feared, "If this prohibition of advertising can be directed against the alcoholic beverage industry, then it can be directed against any other industry, products of which may not find favor with the Congress at a particular time. It strikes at the very heart of the advertising business." The National Editorial Association's Arthur Jenkins then predicted that the alcohol ad ban would spell the end of free speech by opening the way for the government to abolish advertisements used by political groups and labor unions to set forth their views, a development he declared would threaten the very foundation of the United States.[52]

Several industry witnesses attacked the bill for controverting the "American way." One industry representative went so far as to attack the "Russianlike principles involved in this bill" and avowed that, if it were to become law, "we would be living in an atmosphere of communism."[53] Overtones of cold war politics often could be detected when the bills' opponents protested against the extension of federal government power over the practices of private industry. Ironically, the drys were generally quite politically conservative and committed anticommunists themselves.

Public Health and Morality

Most drys believed that alcoholic beverages and their advertisement presented a threat to morality and health, threats they viewed as intertwined and nearly equivalent, for they did not conceive a clear division between physical well-being and moral or social strength. Their language is a clue to their orientation: they often used words such as "evil" and "menace" to describe the public health problems of alcoholism and drunk driving. Bishop Wilbur Hammaker called alcohol consumption a "danger" and "hurtful to life" but did not clarify whether he meant morally or physically. Drys' discussions of health nearly always were linked with concerns about respectability and social relationships. Although they did talk about alcoholism and associated problems such as drunk driving, they worried most about alcohol advertising's impact on Americans' character and morale.[54]

The bulk of the witnesses who testified in favor of the legislation to ban alcohol advertising were moral witnesses, defined here as concerned citizens who were involved in the temperance movement. Of the hundreds who testified, only a handful of "scientific" witnesses, mainly health professionals, appeared in support of the legislation. These scientists, however, were usually associated with temperance organizations and presented moralistic testimony. For instance, Dr. Andrew C. Ivy of the Department of Clinical Science at the University of Illinois spoke in favor of the ban at multiple hearings. Typical of his rhetoric is the following statement, delivered at the 1950 hearing: "It is difficult to acknowledge the rationality of a society which would allow ads to increase the use of a beverage which makes physically and mentally deteriorated slaves out of one in twenty of the users of the beverage." A history of the Prohibition Party reveals that Ivy financially contributed to the party for at least some time during the postwar period.[55]

Several drys appeared at the hearings simply to testify against alcoholic beverages and not specifically against alcohol advertising. Much of their testimony was identical to the morals-based campaign for prohibition earlier in the century. For example, E. W. Turner of the Methodist Laymen's Club of Nashville proclaimed, "Liquor drinking is the chief enemy of decency and morality. It should be curtailed rather than encouraged." Another dry leader linked alcohol to narcotics, gambling, prostitution, and "many other . . . vicious and demoralizing social habits." Perhaps the most extreme and emotionally alarmist rhetoric came from the Methodist Board of Temperance's Caradine Hooton, who declared, "We are convinced that by every proper means we must work together for the protection of motherhood and womanhood against the growing brazenness of ruthless advertisers who use home-invading media to hawk their harmful products. Have we not witnessed an American type of totalitarian brainwashing in the suggestive sales both of tobacco and alcoholic drugs, until women and children have become victimized by an unconscionable device of thought control?"[56] Hooton's statement is remarkable for its traditional and paternalistic temperance rhetoric about the protection of vulnerable women; its traditional emphasis on the wicked "traffic" invading the sacred space of the home, here given a new twist in accordance with cold war and consumer society anxieties characteristic of the 1950s; and its equation of tobacco, alcohol, and drugs. Most drys, however, were mindful of their audience at the congressional hearings and tried to present their arguments in such a way as to appeal to the legal and ethical concerns of national policymakers. Therefore, most of their statements were not dripping with strongly moralistic language or infused with explicit religious rhetoric.

As for the witnesses who spoke against the ad ban, nearly all had a financial stake in the alcohol industries, advertising industry, or the media. The wets, in other words, did not mobilize "neutral" or "scientific" witnesses either. No medical professional stood up to dispute the harmfulness of alcoholic beverages or the efficacy of an advertising ban. Members of the alcohol studies field, who by that time principally adhered to the disease concept of alcoholism, refrained from participation.

Many drys appeared to accept the theory that alcoholism was a disease and equated it with contagious and life-threatening diseases such as tuberculosis or polio. They did not, however, accept the full paradigm promoted by the alcoholism movement, which tended to remove blame, locate the problem in the drinker as opposed to the drink or the advertisement, and focus on treatment rather than prevention. Instead, drys sought to integrate the disease theory of alcoholism into their traditional temperance outlook and their antipathy toward advertising. They believed that alcoholism was a preventable disease and that abolishing alcohol advertising was a prime way to prevent it. To connect the drys' antiadvertising movement with the increasingly influential alcoholism movement and at the same time challenge that movement's concept of the disease, Clayton Wallace, of the Temperance League of America, argued, "Much is being said about the growing threat of alcoholism. . . . But no one hears . . . or sees liquor ads which warn men and women that the only way to become an alcoholic is by drinking alcoholic beverages." He then drove his point home: "Advertising is an important part of the social pressure which leads to alcoholism." In his testimony, a leader of the National Temperance League echoed these thoughts about advertising as a cause of the physical disease of alcoholism and, in the same breath, declared that alcohol advertising caused "antisocial effects."[57] To most drys, "antisocial" and physiological damage were inseparable.

Several ban advocates juxtaposed the government's negligent handling of alcohol and alcohol advertising with the concern it showed for other threats to public health. For example, H. H. Hobbs, pastor of the First Baptist Church of Oklahoma City, claimed, "It is unthinkable that the Government of the United States would permit advertising through the mails and over the radio of such disease germs as scarlet fever, tuberculosis, and the like, for human consumption. In the same category it is unthinkable that our Government and society would sanction the advertising of that which produced the disease of alcoholism." Hooton chimed in: "When communicable diseases have threatened the health of the public, proper steps have been taken to safeguard people from exposure. Yet alcohol kills more people than polio and tuberculosis combined. Is there any doubt that the Congress would move quickly against any ominous plague or preventable scourge that may otherwise destroy or weaken human life?"[58] Presenting alcoholism as a disease—though not in a way that experts at the Yale Center of Alcohol Studies would have endorsed—and furthermore equating alcoholism with communicable diseases that could be cured with government-funded vaccines was a powerful rhetorical tool, whether the drys in fact believed the connection or were more likely swept up by the metaphor. Their intention was to convince policymakers that the federal government could help "cure" the disease by using its authority to remove one of the chief causes: advertising.

Youth and the Impact of Media and Advertising

The drys' most effective and exploited line of moral argument was that alcohol ads targeted youth and new users. Their discussions of youth and advertising assumed that children were particularly vulnerable to the seduction of alcohol ads and that it was the federal government's duty to protect the nation's youth from such corruption. If freedoms must be weighed, then protecting "the freedom of the home from harmful influence," one dry declared, should take precedence over protecting "the freedom of the advertisement of narcotic drugs." Another argued that, if the government were going to allow alcohol to be sold and consumed, "the moral duty of curbing its ill effects on family life in America now devolves upon our lawmakers."[59] This charge seemed to resonate with many legislators. When confronted with arguments—all of which were anecdotal—about the damaging impact of alcohol ads on youth and family, congressional members tended to take notice and even become outraged, especially when several witnesses, including members of congress, told stories about children who enjoyed reciting jingles from beer commercials, showed unusual curiosity about alcoholic beverages after being exposed to these ads, or mimicked the behaviors in the ads.[60] In an era when problems of juvenile delinquency and the adjustment to a new youth culture were highly salient, discussions of the corruption of children proved particularly troubling to many policymakers.

Some drys claimed that their reason for advocating the ad ban was solely to protect children and that they had little or no concern for adult drinkers. For instance, a representative of the Georgia Temperance League testified, "The passage of this bill will have little or no effect upon [those who are already "hopeless drunks."] But I am pleading with you for the millions of young people who are marching year by year into maturity. This advertising is designed to attract them and to persuade them to join the army of drinkers." Senator Glen Taylor (D-ID), one of the witnesses for the drys, argued that the purpose of the ban was to "remove a growing source of bad influence which is hindering the character of thousands of our children."[61] It attracted youth with glamorous imagery along with its insinuations that alcohol consumption would foster and ease social relationships.

In their congressional testimony, several drys appeared to be alarmed by the power of modern advertising, especially broadcast advertising, to infiltrate people's minds. They used their limited time allotted at the witness table to discuss recent psychological studies on conditioning to expose how advertising worked. When this startling power to affect the subconscious was used to persuade fresh-faced youth to consume something as insidious as alcoholic beverages—a commodity that by law had been forbidden for use by minors—then something must be done to "protect our children," they fretted. Bishop Hammaker accused the brewers of purposely advertising on televised sports programs because they were popular with children, and the brewers knew they could "condition the minds in that plastic period of life of boy or girl favorably to the brewery." At one hearing, R. H. Sherwood, a physician, stated, "Ideas are slipped into his mind. Beer and liquor advertising has an insidious influence on the formulation of young people's opinions about the use of alcohol and provides them with powerful ammunition against parental influence." Representing the Friends Committee on National Legislation, Mrs. Albert Ashton declared that alcohol advertisers had "deliberately and cold-bloodedly set up a false scale of cultural and social values" and that, in the face of the relentless promotion of such immoral and antisocial value systems, parents were helpless to protect their children.[62]

Many drys further argued that broadcast advertising was even more menacingly effective than advertising in print. Radio and television advertising, they asserted, was particularly offensive because it aggressively invaded the sacred space of the home and made it more difficult for parents to protect their children from the influence of unwanted advertising. At an early hearing, H. B. Cross, a Baptist minister from Nashville, raised the practical point that "[i]t is practically impossible to cut off the radio at such times when these ads are brought on, since you do not know when they are coming until the harm has been done. With our children and young people listening to the radio as they do, I believe that such advertising, especially with the untruth which is implied in the advertisements, is certainly harmful to our young people and children." Along with this feeling of physical helplessness in not being able to turn off the radio or television in time to block offensive ads, some argued that it was the visual and auditory enticement of broadcast advertising that was particularly dangerous, especially to innocent children. Clayton Wallace contended that the "eye appeal and vocal appeal" of television were very persuasive to young people. In fact, Wallace claimed, it was the "tremendous growth we are witnessing in television" that provided the most compelling reason for enacting the antiadvertising bill. The bill must be passed "now before the liquor traffic invades too many American homes," he declared. Lloyd Halvorson, an economist for the National Grange, expressed his fear that radio and television alcohol ads were so powerful that the "forces of temperance" could not counteract the menace of alcoholic beverages as they could when alcohol ads had been confined to print and billboards. National broadcast advertising was the wets' ultimate weapon, and only federal legislation could thwart it.[63]

Although the drys spent much of their allotted time asserting that alcohol ads appealed to youth, their opponents quickly dismissed the charge, avowing that they never intended to attract children with their advertising. Some industry representatives expanded on their Fifth Amendment argument to include the point that many other products that children should not use employed images and themes similar to alcohol ads, but it was alcohol that was being singled out and maligned unfairly. Other industry spokesmen employed the rather facile argument that alcohol advertising's supposed appeal to children was not a problem because every state had laws that prohibited the sale of alcoholic beverages to minors. For example, Randolph Childs, an outspoken opponent of the temperance forces, reasoned, "[T]he advertising of alcoholic beverages does not urge minors to drink any more than automobile manufacturers urge children too young to get licenses to drive." A few wets responded to drys' claim that children were attracted to alcohol ads by arguing that it was the parents' responsibility—not the government's—to inculcate good values in their children and protect them from corruption. These wets in effect portrayed the ad ban bill as an example of big government paternalism.[64]

What, then, was the purpose of alcohol advertising if not to attract new and young users? The industries answered with the "brand-switching" explanation. When they presented their views on the methods and functions of modern advertising, industry representatives stressed the limits of the power of advertising and challenged the drys' assumption that advertising influenced behavior. In other words, they contested the assumption that exposure to an alcohol ad would cause someone to desire a drink. Instead, as Edward O'Brien of the DSI averred, all that an alcohol advertiser wished to do was "register the impression that he offers a quality product" and provide brand information to consumers who already had made the decision to imbibe. E. V. Lahey, of the USBF, reinforced the argument made by his spirits counterpart and further argued that, historically, alcohol consumption had been relatively high in periods when national advertising did not even exist. Drinking liquor, he argued, was a custom that one learned from family and peer groups, not from advertising. Industry representatives contended again and again as they looked in the faces of eye-rolling drys that their advertising did not aim to expand the market for alcoholic beverages by attracting new users; its sole purpose was to convince current users to switch brands.

Drys, however, had no doubt that the purpose of alcohol advertising was to seduce children into the habit of drinking. Samuel McCrea Cavert, of the Federal Council of the Churches of Christ in America, stated plainly, "The purpose of such advertising involving a huge expenditure is obviously to increase the consumption of alcohol far beyond the point which would be reached if there were no such deliberate and artificial stimulus. Unlike most advertising, it is less directed to showing the consumers the merits of a certain brand as compared with others than to building good will among those who are not yet consumers." Also in response to the industries' brand-switching argument, the president of the National Reform Association, a dry organization, pointed to the USBF's million-dollar "Beer Belongs in the Home" campaign to question the real purpose of alcohol advertising. Others wondered aloud why, if the purpose of alcohol advertising was to endorse certain brands, there were so many nonbrand industry marketing and public relations campaigns.[65] Introduced in this series of alcohol advertising hearings, the brand-switching argument, along with advertising restrictionists' objections, would prove an enduring feature of alcohol and cigarette marketing debates through the remainder of the century.

Over-Regulation and Self-Regulation

Another key debate at the hearings centered on how much regulation the alcohol industries should endure and from where that regulation should emanate: the government or the industries themselves. A favorite tactic of industry representatives was to painstakingly list for the congressional committees the plethora of local, state, and federal regulations under which the alcoholic beverage trade suffered. Please, no more regulation is necessary, they implored. Besides, alcohol ads were perfectly acceptable as they were; because of the commendable system of self-regulation that the industries had voluntarily established, they emphasized, their ads refrained from using many questionable advertising techniques that several other industries employed. Industry representatives also took much of their allotted time to proudly present examples of their public relations campaigns that advised moderation. During the hearings at the end of the 1950s, brewers stressed that they recently had introduced new self-regulations, such as the establishment of the Advertising Review Panel and the prohibition of the depiction of actual drinking in their ads, to ensure the acceptability of beer advertisements.[66]

Their opponents responded to these statements by disparaging the efforts at self-regulation, calling them ineffective and phony. Several drys expressed their outrage at the industries' moderation campaigns, which they viewed as completely disingenuous. Moreover, the drys continued, despite the industries' complaints, the current system of government regulation was also ridiculously inadequate considering the harmful nature of the product in question. Clayton Wallace argued that the patchwork of state laws and lack of oversight by federal authorities meant that government was "helpless" in the face of "false and misleading" alcohol advertising. More government regulation was needed, and the place to start, temperance leaders maintained, was with strict federal government regulation of the industries' marketing.[67]

CONCLUSION

Against a cultural backdrop of escalated social drinking, an expanding consumer culture, and an increasingly secular public arena along with a determined scientific approach to alcohol problems, the postwar movement to ban alcohol advertising failed and was largely ignored by mainstream Americans. Nevertheless, the movement is significant for revealing persistent constitutional and moral dilemmas about the authority of the federal government to place limits on consumerism through restricting commercial freedom of speech. The drys' troubles concerning broadcast media and the corruption of youth and the industries' professed concerns about the First Amendment and a regulatory "slippery slope" have proved particularly enduring, for they tap into the persistent cultural tensions between liberty and restraint.

Although the industries did not mobilize masses of Americans behind their opposition to the ad ban, they did put together an impressive coalition of industry and labor interests and were able to mend intraindustry differences enough to present fairly unified and compelling arguments to the congressional committees. Despite the vocal constituency, clever tactics, and significant congressional presence enjoyed by the drys, federal policymakers were not willing to place further controls on the industries that had once been subject to the failed experiment of prohibition; nor were policymakers ready to use federal government power to curtail the advertising of a legal product. Their willingness to take these actions would increase when the product in question was tobacco and when the policy solutions, such as a warning label, were less drastic.

PART II

*The Battle to Regulate
Cigarette Marketing, 1960s*

EMERGENCE OF THE POSTWAR
ANTISMOKING MOVEMENT

Asked by President Kennedy to convene a committee of scientists to investigate the health consequences of smoking,
Surgeon General Luther Terry, who was trained in cardiac
medicine and had been assistant director of the National
Heart Institute, decided to quit smoking, although it took
him a couple of tries. On 11 January 1964, in a carefully or-
chestrated media event, he announced to much fanfare the
results of the study that his advisory committee had been
working on in secrecy for more than a year. The report represented a dramatic culmination of damaging studies
about cigarette smoking that scientists had been producing for nearly thirty years. It thereby ignited what had
been a simmering antismoking movement and led to immediate and intense political battles among industrial
leaders, scientists, and public officials over government's
role in regulating such a threat to public health, produced
by a powerful and profitable American industry. Looking
back, however, Terry has disparaged the "innocence" of
the antismoking movement during those years. Leaders,
including himself, naively assumed that publicizing scientific studies demonstrating smoking's harm to health
would handily convince the government to restrict the industry. Shrewd political tactics were not thought necessary; the scientific facts would suffice.[1]
   Unlike the movement to control alcohol advertising of
the 1950s, the initiative to regulate cigarette advertising was
spurred by the revelation of scientific findings that linked
the use of the product to illness and death, findings that

contained an element of surprise and unanticipated alarm and made for good press coverage. Yet the scientific indictment of cigarettes, while a necessary cause for the emergence of the postwar antismoking movement, was not the only impetus; other factors influenced the way the movement took shape in the 1950s and how it proceeded through the 1960s. These factors included the growth of scientific institutions and funding for their research along with Americans' reverence for science and medicine, a renewed embrace of social regulation, a heightened concern for "quality of life" issues in an affluent age, and the commitment by a select group of activist policymakers to the philosophy that government should take responsibility for the health of its citizens.

The tobacco industry proved a formidable opponent, and antismoking activists were much less successful in the 1960s than they had hoped to be. Although Congress and the Federal Communications Commission (FCC) did enact some policies to control cigarettes, particularly how cigarettes were marketed, the industry continued to thrive ten years after the release of the Surgeon General's Report. Nevertheless, the frustrations of the movement do not detract from the fact that it won many prominent converts and put several influential policy proposals on the table. Despite the more obvious success of Ralph Nader's auto-safety campaign in 1965, the cigarette labeling initiative of the same year is equally significant for marking the beginning of the recent consumer rights movement; it too illustrates important developments in American politics and culture.

Because antismoking hit the national policy stage in the early 1960s and engaged Congress and the Federal Trade Commission (FTC) in debate before the major environmental and consumer rights disputes of the 1960s and 1970s, the movement pioneered a new era of regulatory policymaking. By framing smoking as an impartial public health issue, the antismokers of this period—a select, technocratic group of scientists and policymakers—deliberately separated themselves from the moral approach used by the drys who fought alcohol and its marketing. The spirit underlying the control of a harmful and addictive substance shifted from a religious-moral basis to a secular-health basis. It is important to note, however, that morality still played a part in the movement to control cigarette marketing, so it is more accurate to describe its values as secular morality.

Although antismoking was a mainly top-down, technocratic movement before the 1970s, as early as the mid-1950s most Americans knew about scientific studies demonstrating cigarettes' harmfulness. Controversy over smoking in the 1950s focused on the way tobacco companies marketed their filter-tip cigarettes in the wake of health findings. Isolated policymakers, with the assistance of voluntary health organizations, pressed the issue, until the Kennedy administration established the Surgeon General's Committee on Smoking and Health. The committee, consisting of eminent scientists, physicians, and government officials, authoritatively pronounced that smoking caused cancer, thereby allowing antismoking advocates to gain entry into the national policy arena and propose cigarette marketing controls.

SCIENCE, HEALTH, AND CONSUMERISM

As the twentieth century progressed, so did the ascendance of science and medicine in American society. Faith in science pervaded culture and politics, and government officials increasingly came to rely on scientists' expertise as part of the policy process. As a British observer remarked in the 1970s, science had become "larger than life" in the United States. The medical profession in particular enjoyed a great deal of prestige during the first part of the century as its understanding of the germ theory and use of "magic bullet" medicine wiped out the threat of many deadly diseases such as cholera, tuberculosis, and polio. This approach to medicine served to depersonalize illness, going a long way toward removing premodern moral stigma from persons afflicted with infectious diseases. As more maladies could be treated and even cured, Americans did become much healthier by the 1950s, but, to the frustration of scientists and the public alike, "magic-bullet" medicine could not conquer all suffering. Chronic, multicausal diseases persisted and began to receive more emphasis and concern. This failure to remedy cancer, stroke, and heart disease was especially troubling because, in the increasingly affluent and secular postwar era, the "good life" had come to mean good health.[2]

As diseases in America shifted from infectious to chronic, medical scientists and national policymakers responded. Facilitating their responses were popular notions coming out of the New Deal era that American citizens should enjoy the right to good health and, furthermore, that the state should play a larger role in ensuring that right to health. Cancer was the first chronic disease to receive considerable attention from this partnership of scientists and government officials. As early as the 1930s, Americans fixated on cancer as a uniquely frightening, dangerous disease. Conquering cancer became an important national objective in the 1940s and 1950s, and Congress responded by creating the National Cancer Institute (NCI), one of the first national health institutes. Antismoking sentiment did not, however, take root in the NCI, for the scientists who controlled this agency disregarded preventive approaches and pushed on with their traditional laboratory science that focused on diagnosis and cure.[3]

While conventional science reigned in the federal cancer-fighting center, another type of medical science, epidemiology, was rising in favor as some scientists sought a new methodology in their attempts to understand the causes of chronic disease, especially cancer. Epidemiology focused on environmental and behavioral risks that led to disease and used demographic studies to make statistical causal inferences. Epidemiologists, who were more inclined to support preventive medicine, soon highlighted the relationship between cigarette smoking and cancer. The new emphasis on epidemiology was often at odds with the standard reliance on laboratory science.[4] This conflict was showcased in the debate over the health hazards of cigarettes in the 1960s when mainly laboratory scientists stood up for the tobacco industry to challenge the conclusions of epidemiologists who insisted that smoking caused cancer.

As they investigated the causes of chronic disease, many Americans, scientists and laypersons alike, paid increasing attention to lifestyle factors: diet, exercise, exposure to pollution, and smoking. This emphasis on lifestyle choices was in some respects a return to the pregerm theory era, when disease was more often attributed to moral failings. Once again the patient was blamed for poor personal choices. An emerging popular health movement yoked the lifestyle theory to an ideology of individual responsibility and championed antismoking as well as aerobic exercise and health foods. Along with continuing distress over the persistence of chronic disease, the ascendance of the health movement among white middle-class Americans and its advocacy of the lifestyle theory of disease in the 1970s and 1980s formed a supportive environment for antismoking sentiment.[5]

The rise of the consumer rights movement also contributed to the growth of the antismoking movement. Although a consumer movement had existed in America since the early twentieth century, the mid-1960s marked the beginning of the most recent and enduring movement of consumer rights activists and organizations. The movement, which flourished in the early 1970s, advocated a wide range of issues, from safety and health standards to increased political participation of American citizens. The interest in safety and health, exemplified by Ralph Nader's attack on the auto industry's negligent safety standards, as well as by several product labeling initiatives, increased Americans' awareness of hazards caused by legal products and especially sustained the policy campaigns against the tobacco industry.[6]

These political and cultural movements explain the persistence and growth of antismoking in the United States, but they do not account for its origins. Indeed, the postwar antismoking push started before the consumer rights movement attained influence in Washington and before the health movement really caught on in middle America. The impetus came from scientific studies in the 1940s and 1950s reporting the health hazards of smoking. A handful of federal policymakers started to pay attention to the issue in the late 1950s, and in 1964 members of Congress began to introduce major antismoking bills. Led by scientists, health organizations, and a few national officials, the 1960s initiative to curtail smoking and the advertising of cigarettes was not "grassroots" as the antialcohol movement had been. Although some religious groups, particularly Seventh Day Adventists, were agitating against smoking in these years, their sentiment was largely isolated and not articulated in a political arena.[7] The rise of antismoking as a national policy issue can best be explained by the conviction of certain elites, normally of a liberal or progressive bent, who believed that a nation's government should take responsibility for its people's health. Antismoking policymakers worked with health organizations, but they did not operate in a network of public interest groups as would become customary in health and consumer politics after the 1960s. Instead, the most effective antismokers were policy entrepreneurs, taking initiatives largely on their own and working to awaken public interest in particular pet causes.[8]

The antismoking initiative also found fertile ground on the national policy stage because Americans in the 1960s exhibited a renewed interest in social regulation, as opposed to economic regulation. Policymakers were less concerned with competitive practices of businesses than with negative externalities arising from industry, regardless of whether an industry was monopolistic. The trend toward social regulation came from the general affluence and optimism of the times. Americans developed high expectations not only for their economic well-being, but also for their physical and mental wellness. As more Americans than ever enjoyed a high standard of living, they lowered their "threshold for discomfort" and came to expect much more out of life than they had during harder times, paying increasing attention to more abstract and aesthetic "quality of life" issues. The new mass middle class embraced the idea of the "good life," which included not only two cars and a washing machine, but also such "amenities" as clean air and water. The persistence of chronic disease and the ever-present threat of premature death in their affluent and progressive society flouted their expectations and produced anxiety.[9] Compared to citizens of most other western nations, Americans seemed uniquely concerned about health and environmental issues.

The trend toward social regulation, then, did not occur because Americans were reacting to a sudden degeneration of living conditions. On the contrary, living conditions were, for most Americans, better than ever. Instead, it was Americans' values and perceptions that were changing. Increasing numbers of Americans became more committed to achieving social equality and environmental purity. Furthermore, some influential segments of the population developed a mistrust of traditional institutions, including industry, during this era.[10] In the context of Americans' heightened expectations of wellness and purity as well as their mounting misgivings about private industry, antismoking sentiment was an important element of the postwar trend toward environmentalism and social regulation as a whole.

ANTISMOKING BEFORE THE 1950S

Although many point to the publication of the Surgeon General's Committee Report on Smoking and Health in 1964 as the dawn of the recent antismoking movement, its origins lie in the early 1950s. Antismoking sentiment is as old as the European tobacco fetish, and the first American antismoking movement peaked in the early twentieth century as a sister crusade to the fight against alcohol. The early movement was led by Protestant-based organizations such as the Woman's Christian Temperance Union, the Young Men's Christian Association, and the Salvation Army, and prominent individuals, including Henry Ford and John Wannamaker. The preeminent leader of antismoking at the beginning of the century, though, was Lucy Page Gaston, a fanatical reformer who founded the Anti-Cigarette League of America in 1899 and believed smoking presented a moral and physical evil. Gaston preached that smoking caused the condition "cigarette face," stunted the development of boys, and inexorably led to more depraved crimes and misdeeds. Other members of the movement linked cigarette smoking to a whole host of maladies, including heart disease, emphysema, digestive problems, and nervous disorders. Lung cancer, however, was seldom mentioned since its incidence was very rare until later in the century. Although a handful of scientists and government officials lent their support, this early antismoking movement was primarily a grassroots campaign led by private citizens and religious organizations who were very often the same individuals and groups that supported the campaign for prohibition of alcohol. The moral impulses of the Progressives fostered the movement and persuaded many Americans that cigarettes were "a mark of deviancy."[11] It made considerable headway before the First World War: thirteen states prohibited the sale of cigarettes, and many more states, municipalities, and private businesses passed various restrictions on their sale and use.

The antismoking cause lost momentum during World War I, when cigarettes were popularized—and indeed patriotized—in rations packets to America's doughboys. The interwar years saw the glamorization of cigarettes through movies and advertising, and smoking increasingly became accepted among men and women of all classes who embraced the modern values of the progressing twentieth century. The Second World War further augmented the popularity of cigarette smoking, and, by the mid-1950s, 57 percent of men and 29 percent of women smoked. At the time that the surgeon general announced the results of his committee's study in 1964, 43 percent of the adult population smoked.[12] Of course, there remained a shrinking segment of middle America that, as with alcohol, viewed smoking as sinful.

The early antismoking movement also foundered because the scientific community largely withheld its support. Most doctors believed smoking to be innocuous and generally viewed antismoking activists as moral zealots.[13] The modern ethos of the interwar period stifled the antismokers and encouraged the smoking habit, and at the same time it stimulated scientific research and Americans' faith in scientific evidence—evidence that would soon prove smoking to be deadly. Ironically, then, medical science helped to quash the turn-of-the-century antismoking movement, but its findings became the driving force behind the modern antismoking movement.

As cigarette smoking was becoming widespread, and, as cases of lung cancer began to escalate, more scientists in Europe and the United States began to study the effects of smoking on the body. Their discoveries were not pleasant. In the 1930s German scientists established the link between the rise in cigarette smoking and the upsurge in cases of lung cancer, and American investigators used biostatistical methods to show that the life spans of smokers were shorter than those of nonsmokers. By the eve of World War II, scientists had published more than forty studies demonstrating the hazards of cigarette smoking. Because these reports were highly technical and confined to medical journals, though, the general public was unaware of the escalating medical evidence against cigarettes and continued to puff away without care.[14] This innocence would not last much longer.

THE MAKING OF A HEALTH CONTROVERSY

Cigarette smoking, along with the advertisement of cigarettes, became a subject for public discussion in the early 1950s when controversy revolved around filter-tip cigarettes, nicotine and tar content, and health claims made by manufacturers. Although the sentiment against cigarettes did not yet constitute a popular or a policy movement, fundamental arguments were being established that would underpin the anticigarette marketing campaign for the next several decades.

In the postwar years medical science brought even more evidence to bear against the increasingly popular habit. In 1950 three major studies that tightened the association between smoking and disease were published, and in 1953 Dr. Ernst L. Wynder and Dr. Evarts Graham of the Sloan-Kettering Institute of Cancer Research released a study showing that tar from tobacco caused cancer in mice. The most important U.S. study in this decade came from Dr. E. Cuyler Hammond and Dr. Daniel Horn of the American Cancer Society. For their massive epidemiological study, they recruited 22,000 volunteers to interview nearly 200,000 men in eleven states about their smoking habits and health conditions. At the conclusion of their study in 1954, Hammond and Horn announced that smokers were ten times more likely to die from lung cancer than nonsmokers, and heavy smokers were sixty-four times more likely to die of the disease than nonsmokers.[15]

It was not until 1952 that the American press picked up on the alarming findings that had accumulated over the previous fifteen years and began to disseminate them to the public. *Reader's Digest,* a magazine that did not accept cigarette advertising, chose to publish articles by antismoking activist Roy Norr that had originally appeared in the *Christian Herald,* whose editors had been leaders in the movement against alcohol advertising. *Reader's Digest*'s publication of the hard-hitting article "Cancer by the Carton" in December 1952 drew considerable attention, and it was soon picked up by other magazines and radio news programs. As one observer commented, "[T]he story was taken to the public by a wide variety of magazines, so that it could not be avoided by any literate smoker." *Reader's Digest* continued to feature critical articles about cigarettes through the decade. Television networks, in contrast, ignored the cigarette story in the 1950s because most of the major programs were sponsored by tobacco companies. A study of popular press coverage of the smoking and health issue reveals that the number of articles on this subject peaked in the mid-1950s and concludes that the majority of the American public had been informed that cigarettes were hazardous to health.[16]

This widespread dissemination of scientific studies about cigarettes triggered a brief health scare, and cigarette sales declined for the first time in twenty-one years. More doctors started advising their patients not to smoke. The scare was short-lived, and by 1956 cigarette sales had returned to their previous levels and set a new record for per capita consumption in 1960. The public knew of the dangers, but, after a short period of bombardment by effective cigarette marketing and clever industry public relations, it seems that most smokers chose to ignore the sharpening scientific evidence. Struggling to understand smokers' "psychological blackout" during the 1950s, one antismoking activist later theorized, "When new information clashes with long-standing beliefs, a mental reaction called 'cognitive dissonance' occurs." Although Americans were alerted to alarming evidence against cigarettes, they were not "incorporat[ing] this new information into their consciousness." Furthermore, as part of their rejection of sentimentalism in favor of professionalism, physicians as a group were skeptical of claims against smoking. Indeed, most physicians continued to smoke.[17]

Another factor restricting the spread of antismoking sentiment was the cautious stance taken by the American Cancer Society. The Society had been established in 1913 as a voluntary organization dedicated to research and education and was dependent on fund-raising. Many of its contributors, not to mention researchers and administrators, were smokers, so creating controversy about such a popular habit might hinder goodwill and free-flowing funds. As a further inhibition, federal law forbade voluntary organizations from political activity if they wanted to maintain a tax-exempt status. The American Cancer Society had to be coaxed into sponsoring the path-breaking Hammond and Horn study. In 1954 it was comfortable stating only that there was an "association" between lung cancer and smoking, and during the next few years the organization experienced an internal clash over how aggressively it should stand against smoking.[18]

THE INDUSTRY FIGHTS BACK: PUBLIC RELATIONS AND MARKETING STRATEGIES

Notwithstanding the incapacity of the fledgling antismoking movement to harness the scientific studies, the tobacco industry itself was largely responsible for the comeback in cigarette sales. Acutely aware of the recent studies that seriously implicated their products, tobacco companies huddled together in the early 1950s and emerged with a two-pronged defensive strategy designed to appease Americans' worries. First, in 1954 the Big Six tobacco firms formed an industry-wide research group, the Tobacco Industry Research Council (TIRC), whose stated purpose was to study the effects of smoking on the body. The Big Six—consisting of Philip Morris, R. J. Reynolds, Lorillard, American Tobacco, Liggett and Myers, and Brown and Williamson—claimed that they were very concerned about the recent reports about cigarettes and therefore wanted to take action themselves to confirm or deny the allegations that smoking was harmful. In reality, the TIRC was essentially a public relations, not a scientific research, effort. In fact the very first response of the tobacco companies to negative stories in the press—even before creating the research council—was to hire the public relations firm Hill & Knowlton. The industry even placed TIRC offices in the same building as the firm. In addition to designing protobacco advertisements and carefully crafting the industry's public statements, Hill & Knowlton worked behind the scenes to convince the media not to publish or broadcast negative reports. No real delineation existed between Hill & Knowlton and the TIRC; 50 percent of the TIRC's budget was marked for public relations purposes.[19]

The rhetorical war between antismoking activists and tobacco industry forces that Americans would grow accustomed to in the late twentieth century was already escalating in the 1950s, and the words were largely the same. Employing the counsel of their public relations firm, TIRC officials and scientists issued carefully worded statements to create doubt each time a damaging study was released.[20] These statements centered on one basic theme that tobacco executives would repeat again and again, like a mantra: "no conclusive scientific evidence" existed to implicate cigarettes because, in the words of TIRC lead scientist Clarence Little, "statistical association does not prove cause and effect." While mouthing these words, the industry dodged questions about tar and nicotine and tried its best to appear the innocent party, under attack by powerful and extremist forces. Before an audience of congressmen in 1957, Little, an acknowledged scientific expert in cigarette technology, including filters, offered this version of events when asked about the effectiveness of filter tips: "I wouldn't know about the filters, but the attack on tobacco was so well organized, so well propagandized, and so professional, that when it came first I think it stunned the industry wide awake." The industry, he continued, was dedicated to finding out "what the facts are, because if they [the problems] are true they have got to be corrected, if possible; and if they are not true, we have got to find out. We can't go along any more subject to violent attacks by people without taking steps to do the best we can to find out whether these attacks are well founded or not."[21] Little cleverly evaded the filter-tip question and instead constructed an image of an innocent, sincere, and victimized cigarette industry.

The industry's claims as to the purpose of TIRC were always disingenuous. Though the Council funded numerous research projects, rarely did the TIRC-sponsored projects actually study the relationship between smoking and human health, and the Council's board carefully screened out studies that might become damaging to the tobacco industry. The industry used the TIRC to establish close, co-optive relationships with major research centers and important scientists. In terms of its research function, then, the TIRC was a sham. The real intent of the TIRC was to offer Americans reassurances and make them believe that the tobacco industry cared and therefore could be trusted. The industry also created the research council so it could buy time to develop better strategies to deal with the damning scientific evidence they knew to be true. Quietly, most of the tobacco firms were engaged in their own health research and were replicating many of the damning studies in their own labs. Much evidence that has recently been revealed demonstrates that the companies knew very early on that cigarettes were addictive and deadly.[22]

The tobacco industry's second strategy to face down the health studies of the 1950s was to develop new types of cigarettes and market them as safer. Whereas the introduction of the filter-tip cigarette is the chief example of this strategy, the companies also portrayed king-size and mentholated varieties as less harmful to health. The development of filter tips was most embraced by the underdogs in the industry. For example, in 1952 the struggling firm Lorillard introduced the filter-tip brand Kent, advertised as "the greatest health protection in cigarette history." The debut of Kent, however, was less than successful, for it seems that the filter was too effective, rendering the cigarette almost flavorless. The trick to launching a successful filter-tip cigarette, the industry quickly learned, was to find a material that would filtrate some of the smoke but not reduce the taste. Industry laboratories busied themselves in the 1950s experimenting with different filter technologies. In the mid-1950s, the Kent filter was redesigned, and the brand became the second-most popular of the filter tips. Consumers were not informed, of course, that the cigarette tasted better because the filter was less effective.

At their inception in 1952, filter tips accounted for a mere 1.3 percent of the cigarette market; by the end of decade, their market share had surged to nearly 60 percent, overtaking regular cigarettes. Both the health scare and the tobacco manufacturers' exploitation of that scare caused the switch. While advertising expenditures for regular cigarettes declined in the mid-1950s, the Big Six spent lavish amounts advertising their filter and mentholated brands. Filter tips became the choice of smokers who were concerned enough about possible harm from smoking to switch to a "safer" cigarette but were not alarmed or committed enough to quit the habit.[23]

The marketing of filter-tip, king-sized, and mentholated cigarettes was, of course, a delicate business, for advertising them as "safer" meant that the companies were conceding that there was something dangerous about cigarettes. Upon the introduction of Kent, *Business Week* observed, "Lorillard is willing to push [its advertising claims] at the risk of damning, by inference, its nonfiltered cigarettes. Lorillard's willingness to go out on this limb shows how strong a groundswell is developing against the smoking habit."[24] Although this indirect acknowledgement troubled many cigarette executives, they charged ahead with marketing strategies that exploited the public's expanding anxieties about health, and a few firms were rewarded with soaring sales. Philip Morris advertised its filter-tip brand as "[t]he cigarette that takes the fear out of smoking," and its king-sized ads claimed that "coughs due to smoking disappear . . . parched throat clears up . . . that stale, 'smoked-out' feeling vanishes." Liggett and Myers boasted, "This is it. L&M filters are just what the doctor ordered." R. J. Reynolds depicted doctors smoking Camels. Kent's ad copy wondered, "Do you like a good smoke but not what smoking does to you?" After demonstrating that its cigarette left a lighter stain on fabric than did competing brands, one Kent advertisement even went so far as to point out to consumers that they were polluting themselves with tar: "Remember that, when you smoke, the same irritants that have caused the stains are drawn into your system." Even if the ads did not directly admit that smoking caused disease, they did concede that smoking could contaminate the body.[25]

Many cigarette ads in the early to mid-1950s thus hammered on the health theme to address consumers' apprehensions head-on. Because it was a potentially self-defeating tactic for the industry as a whole, some members refused to participate in the trend. But other companies could not resist the profit incentive and believed that "fear advertising" was a sure way to win more market share, regardless of the overall impact on the industry. Still, the companies' admissions were puzzling. *Business Week* wondered, "Why has the industry persisted in this 'negative' form of advertising, even when, as tobacco growers and others complain, it hurts the trade by making people conscious that cigarettes can be harmful?" The article offered an intriguing answer by pointing to motivational researchers who advised cigarette companies that "the majority of adult Americans have always been uneasy smokers, thanks to an inherited puritanical feeling about cigarettes and conviction from the state of their own bronchial tubes that cigarettes just aren't good for you." Therefore, what the "cigarette people" tried to do was "reassure the smoker that everything was all right—just as long as he smoked X brand, which, of course, is milder, easier on the throat, and so forth." Advertising guru Dr. Ernest Dichter notified cigarette companies that, in the current climate, "the advertiser who will help the smoker in his reexamination of smoking will have the edge. He must prove that he is on the side of the smoker." Dichter gave the tobacco industry the same advice he gave to the liquor industry: "[P]ush moderation for the sake of public relations."[26]

Ironically, then, for some cigarette companies, the health scare of the 1950s worked to their benefit. Cigarette advertisers stepped into the role of consoler and medical authority, "generously" helping Americans overcome their apprehensions about smoking. Cigarette advertising during the middle of the twentieth century provided a classic example of advertisers' ability to manipulate consumers' anxieties, promising that the product would deliver social success and physical wellness while threatening failure, discontent, and possibly ill health if the brand in question were not chosen.[27] But unlike other products that used this therapeutic tactic, the exaggerations and implications of cigarette advertising were grossly false and potentially deadly.

The health appeal was only one of the themes typically employed by skillful cigarette marketing in the 1950s. The promise of finding "taste," "flavor," "pleasure," "satisfaction," "refreshment," and "mildness" was ubiquitous in cigarette ads. The smoker would not only be protected from harm, but he or she would also discover relaxing pleasure from smoking X brand of cigarette. Lucky Strike's ads featured stylized paintings of women and personalized copy asking, "Why do I smoke? You know, yourself, you smoke for enjoyment. And you get enjoyment only from the *taste* of a cigarette. Luckies taste better—cleaner, fresher, smoother!" Philip Morris's Marlboro cigarettes, in contrast, appealed to masculinity and depicted men in the armed forces and men doing mechanical work on their cars until the brand turned to the iconic cowboy imagery in the 1960s. Brands such as Philip Morris's King Size and Old Gold and R. J. Reynolds's Camel used endorsements by celebrities, including Mickey Mantle, Tony Curtis, and Lucille Ball.

Some of the most famous and influential advertising campaigns of the postwar period promoted cigarettes. Prominent in print and on the radio, tobacco companies were also the biggest advertisers on television, sponsoring popular programs such as *Your Lucky Strike Theater*, *Arthur Godfrey and His Friends*, *Camel News Caravan*, *Candid Camera*, *The Flintstones*, and *I Love Lucy*. Most cigarette commercials featured addictive jingles, such as "Winston Tastes Good Like a Cigarette Should," and dancing cigarettes

"More Doctors Smoke Camels." Using the endorsement of a woman athlete, R. J. Reynolds's campaign for Camel cigarettes in the late 1940s sought to capitalize on Americans' postwar affluence as well as exploit their faith in medical authority and appease concerns about smoking's harm to health. *Life,* 21 July 1947.

For a Treat
instead
of a Treatment...
remember...

OLD GOLD

treats you right

Enjoy *today's* most pleasing cigarette with this assurance: No other leading cigarette is less irritating, or easier on the throat, or contains less nicotine than Old Gold. This conclusion was established on evidence by the U. S. Government.

Old Gold
CIGARETTES

Using imagery evoking adventure and sexual attraction, Old Gold's 1953 ad allayed consumers' fears and told them they deserved to indulge themselves in a "treat." Like many cigarette ads of this period, the copy reveals the company's perception that consumers were indeed worrying about cigarettes' harm to health and that the company needed to address these worries head on: "No other leading cigarette is less irritating or easier on the throat, or contains less nicotine than Old Gold. This conclusion was established on evidence by the U.S. Government." *Life*, 20 April 1953.

and cigarette packages with women's legs. The jingle in Chesterfield commercials, in contrast, was played over the imagery of cowboys smoking and rustling cows, while an unseen narrator declares the brand "the new choice of the men of America." Often, as in many television commercials of that era, the actor or announcer from the sponsored program either provided the narration for the commercial or simply performed the pitch on-screen without much interruption of the show in progress. Smoking also figured prominently in the programs themselves, using calculated product placements. As one ad executive explained, "[S]moking looks wonderful on television."[28]

Built on marketing and not on the utility of the product itself, the cigarette trade was the consummate consumer culture business.[29] Tobacco companies were in the forefront of another marketing trend. As the consumer culture increasingly focused on youth in the 1950s and 1960s, tobacco companies took the lead. In the search for new smokers, they sponsored television shows directed at children and developed extensive promotional campaigns on college campuses. By the mid-1960s, most ads featured romantically involved young men and women savoring an intimate moment by lighting each other's cigarettes. The prominent campaign for Salem Menthols accentuated these romantic tableaus with depictions of clean, fresh, and often adventurous outdoor scenes, dominated by lush greens and blues. By the middle of the 1960s, cigarette ads were notorious for their appeal to youth, making them easy targets for antismoking ire.[30]

EARLY CHALLENGES TO CIGARETTE MARKETING

Emerging antismoking activists recognized the power of cigarette advertising and sought to disarm the industry. In 1955 the FTC finally decided it should take action against the companies' bald health claims. As the agency responsible for ferreting out and eliminating false and misleading advertising, the FTC had a long history of involvement with the tobacco industry. Questionable health claims in cigarette advertising were not new in the 1950s; they had just become more exaggerated and plentiful in the era of filter tips. Beginning in the early 1940s, the FTC embarked on a half-hearted campaign to clean up cigarette advertising. To this end, it prosecuted, in individual cases, the five largest cigarette companies for instances of false and misleading advertising. The rulings proved meaningless because in some instances the cases lasted years and in the meantime the companies cleverly altered their advertising copy. As *Consumer Reports* observed, "No copywriter worth his Brooks Brothers suit would let an FTC order stop him from using health appeals if he felt they would be effective."[31]

In 1955 the FTC decided to try a new tactic to combat the increasingly egregious health claims in cigarette advertising. Instead of proceeding against individual cases of falsity, which had proven time-consuming and

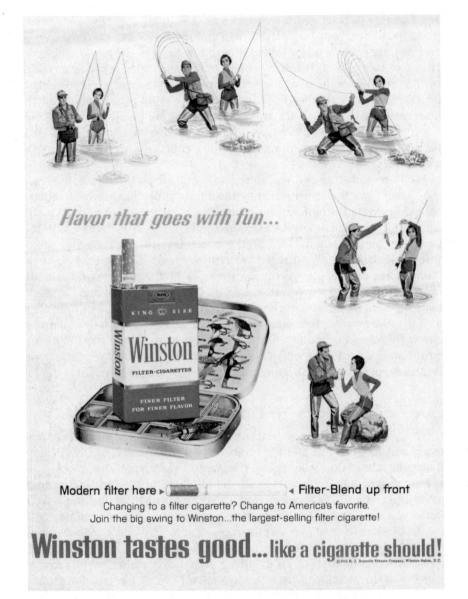

With a lighthearted, comical touch, Winston advertising in the mid-1960s emphasized "flavor" and "fun" for both men and women while consigning the nebulous information about its "Modern" filter to a minor place in the ad. Winston was one of many brands that excelled in using a catchy slogan, both in its print and broadcast marketing. *Life*, 5 June 1964.

ineffective, the Commission issued a seven-point guide to cigarette advertising. The tobacco companies were asked to refrain voluntarily from certain themes, such as testimonial by physicians, statements on the effects on parts of the body, and claims of reduction in tar and nicotine, in order to avoid formal prosecution. The companies generally complied, and their advertising began to focus more intently on promoting a brand's flavor, taste, and pleasure.[32]

As with the health scare, the FTC's action ended up working to the advantage of cigarette companies. Exposed to "fear advertising" for more than two years before the FTC moved in, consumers had been educated as to the function of a filter and the "safety" of filter-tip brands. Now, simply using the word "filter" in an advertisement, absent an explanation of its health virtues, was sufficient to attract smokers. The cigarette companies could push consumers' buttons without having to exploit potentially self-defeating health claims. Comparing the tobacco industry's strategy to Pavlov's conditioned-response experiment, antismoking journalist Roy Norr asserted, "The idea was, first, to run the series of ads that would make definite claims for the health protection through filtration, then, gradually, say nothing about health protection."[33] According to Norr, the new advertising restrictions played right into the cigarette companies' hands and actually enhanced their marketing effectiveness.

The FTC's limited actions with regard to cigarette advertising in the 1940s and 1950s have been reproved by government officials then and since. After criticizing the FTC for years of "stalling," in 1958 Representative John A. Blatnik of Minnesota, a lone antismoker, called the FTC's cigarette advertising guide "an apparently innocuous approach which turned out to have harmful effects." Blatnik complained that, because tobacco companies could no longer discuss the effectiveness of a filter or the levels of tar and nicotine in their advertising, consumers were led to believe that all filter-tip brands were equal—equally safe. Now, the only factor differentiating the brands in the consumer's mind was taste. Yet effectiveness of filters and levels of tar and nicotine *did* vary from brand to brand. Therefore, contrary to the FTC's edict of silence, Blatnik strongly believed cigarette advertising and product labeling should inform the consumer of these differences.[34]

The FTC's prohibition on advertising tar and nicotine did contain a loophole: references to the contents of a cigarette could be publicized if they were confirmed by independent scientific studies. In the second half of the 1950s, the tobacco industry received these studies when *Reader's Digest* and *Consumer Reports* tested the contents of each brand and published the results. The results, however, caused the industry considerable embarrassment because they revealed what cigarette manufacturers had been up to: loosening their filters to increase taste—and tar and nicotine—while at the same time leading consumers to believe that filter-tip cigarettes were

Playing up undisguised sex appeal, this close-up color photograph featuring a cool palette of blues to advertise this "fresh" menthol cigarette includes minimal copy and no hint of health concerns.

effective and safe. The tests showed that tar and nicotine levels were much higher than they had been in tests conducted on Kent and other brands in the early 1950s and that some filter tips, because they contained stronger tobacco, actually possessed higher levels than nonfiltered cigarettes. Most troubling to some observers was that these manipulations had been concealed from consumers.[35]

Outraged, Blatnik used his position as head of a House subcommittee to hold the first congressional hearing ever on the matter of cigarette advertising. The hearing, lasting six tedious days in the summer of 1957, featured highly technical testimony from scientists on both sides of the controversy and was notable for the complete absence of tobacco company executives. That the industry arrogantly refused to accept the subcommittee's invitation to testify clearly upset Blatnik, who wondered aloud, "I find it difficult to understand why this industry, which spends millions of dollars to advertise its products, should remain utterly silent in these proceedings in which it is the central figure."[36]

Significant testimony came from Roy Norr, who presented four policy proposals, all of which would be repeated, and some enacted, over the next twenty years. First, he demanded that Congress declare tobacco a drug and thereby place it under the regulatory powers of the Food and Drug Administration (FDA). Second, Norr proposed a labeling policy that would clearly state the government-verified tar and nicotine content on a package of cigarettes. Third, he asked Congress to outlaw testimonial cigarette advertising. Last, Norr argued that the FCC, with its mandate to protect the public interest on the airwaves, should determine that the advertisement of a controversial, not to mention deadly, product controverted the public interest and require that cigarette advertising be stricken from television and radio.[37] His ideas for regulating the product thus concentrated on regulating the way it was promoted, and this approach remained at the forefront of antismoking activists' policy efforts through the next decade.

Demonstrating that the early antismokers' primary concern was regulating cigarette advertising, Blatnik's 1958 subcommittee report reserved its sharpest reproach for the FTC. The Commission, the report maintained, had failed in its attempts to prevent deceptive cigarette advertising. The subcommittee blamed the Commission for allowing "the connection between filter-tip cigarettes and 'protection'" to become "deeply embedded in the public mind." The report demanded that the FTC scrutinize its structure, personnel, and procedures so that henceforth it would fulfill its "statutory duty" to prevent deceptive advertising. At the time, Blatnik's hearings and Norr's proposals were largely ignored, especially since cigarette companies did not directly participate. It was clear, though, that someone in power was paying attention. Not long after the release of the report, Blatnik's subcommittee was dissolved. Future hearings that had been scheduled on the cigarette matter were cancelled.[38]

In addition to Blatnik's futile efforts, another result of the release of tar and nicotine data by *Consumer Reports* and *Reader's Digest* was the materialization of the "tar derby" in the late 1950s. With the shroud of secrecy removed, tobacco companies competed to lower the tar and nicotine levels in their cigarettes and to boast of these decreases, which now could be confirmed by outside studies, in their advertising. Consequently, by the end of the decade tar and nicotine levels had fallen by almost 40 percent. The incentive was the same as during the period of "fear advertising": to play on anxieties and offer a safer cigarette, which consumers, educated by health reports, understood to be one with less nicotine and tar. The FTC, which could not seem to win, intervened to stop the tar derby and was rewarded with more criticism from antismokers. Throughout 1959 the Commission negotiated with the companies and in early 1960 announced that it had engineered a voluntary ban on references to tar and nicotine in cigarette advertising. Cigarette companies went back to emphasizing "taste" and "mildness," and, because they could no longer publicize their efforts to lower the nicotine and tar content, they stopped trying to build a safer cigarette.[39]

As the new decade approached, the filter-tip controversy receded, but not before Surgeon General Leroy Burney decided that a formal statement against cigarettes was in order. The American Cancer Society, the American Heart Association, the National Cancer Institute, and the National Heart Institute had participated in the Study Group on Smoking and Health in 1957, which reviewed studies on smoking and health and issued a call for more research. It also pressured the surgeon general to speak out against smoking. In response, Burney stated, "[T]here is an increasing and consistent body of evidence that excessive cigarette smoking is one of the causative factors in lung cancer." But he dampened the impact of these words by lending credence to the doubters: "[I]t is clear that smoking is not the only cause of lung cancer" and "the precise nature of the factors in heavy and prolonged cigarette smoking which cause lung cancer is not known." Two years later Burney was again persuaded to speak out against smoking in what *Newsweek* called "the most strongly worded warning against cigarette smoking yet made by a public official." This time Burney indicted cigarette smoking as "the principal cause" of lung cancer. He further made it clear to those Americans who were listening that filter tips could not eliminate the harmful contents of cigarettes.[40]

Burney's statements—along with the FTC's actions, Blatnik's congressional hearings, and even more damaging scientific studies—convinced the tobacco industry that a stronger trade association was needed to fend off attacks in an increasingly hostile climate. Deciding that disguising its public relations endeavors with a research front was ineffective against the growing threats, the industry created the Tobacco Institute in 1958 to carry out extensive public relations and lobbying efforts. The Tobacco In-

stitute was controlled by the chief executive officers of the member tobacco companies, which included all of the Big Six, and was funded by
those companies in amounts proportionate to each firm's share of the cigarette market. It quickly became one of the most powerful industry lobbying forces on Capitol Hill.

FORMING THE SURGEON GENERAL'S COMMITTEE

The industry did face a handful of enemies in Congress in the early
1960s. Mustering all her meager resources to fight the industry behemoth,
Senator Maurine Neuberger, a Democrat from Oregon, became the industry's chief congressional opponent. Her late husband, Senator Richard
Neuberger, had been committed to educating youth about the dangers of
both smoking and drinking. As the evidence against smoking accumulated
in the early 1960s, Maurine Neuberger adopted antismoking as her main
crusade and did her best to increase her fellow policymakers' awareness of
the matter. She even wrote a muckraking book, *Smoke Screen: Tobacco and
the Public Welfare* (1963). In her effort to spearhead the creation of an antismoking coalition, Neuberger corresponded with voluntary health and
medical organizations, wrote to the FTC, pestered the Kennedy administration, and tried to persuade like-minded senators to join her.[41]

Certain that the FTC had more power to regulate cigarette advertising
than it was using, in 1962 Neuberger wrote to FTC Commissioner Paul
Rand Dixon. "Any cigarette commercial or advertisement which fail[s]
to contain an adequate warning of the hazards of smoking," she argued,
"[i]s inherently deceptive." Echoing the drys' reason for banning all alcohol advertising, Neuberger urged the FTC to take action against the
whole class of cigarette advertising because it was all, by its very nature,
deceptive. Dixon replied that, in principle, the FTC did have "the power
to require affirmative warnings to avoid deception," but he was afraid
that, because the evidence against smoking had not been proven beyond a shadow of a doubt, any blanket FTC action against cigarette advertising would be strongly challenged and lead to a lengthy court battle. Neuberger was not pleased with his reply and consulted government
attorneys, who told her that Dixon was in error because "all that the
Commission is required to show is that its orders are based upon 'substantial evidence.'"[42]

Equally frustrated by the Public Health Service's lack of initiative on the
smoking issue, in 1962 Neuberger introduced a resolution in the Senate
calling for a massive education campaign on the health effects of smoking
and asking the president to establish a commission on tobacco and
health. Despite the support of six other senators, the resolution was
largely ignored by Congress and the administration. It did, however, cap-
ture the attention of the voluntary health organizations, which began to

rally around the idea of a presidential commission. By chance, a couple of months later, a reporter at a press conference asked President Kennedy what he intended to do about the cigarette controversy. Kennedy, who clearly had not been briefed on the issue, fumbled a weak reply. Quickly the White House called the Public Health Service and asked for advice. Motivated by the 1962 report of Britain's Royal College of Physicians that announced causal links between smoking and cancer, Kennedy's surgeon general, Luther Terry, was enthusiastic about indicting cigarettes. He agreed to form a committee to study the issue, the Surgeon General's Advisory Committee on Smoking and Health.[43]

The committee first met in November 1962. Its purpose was not to conduct its own research, but to compile and assess existing studies. To ensure its objectivity, only scientists who had not taken a public stand on the issue of smoking and health were selected for the panel. Moreover, the tobacco industry was given the authority to reject proposed members during the selection process. Although the committee was not uncovering new evidence about the health effects of cigarettes, its mission was crucial because it would provide government legitimation of the link between smoking and disease.[44] The purpose of the committee, therefore, was more political than it was strictly scientific. When the committee released its much-anticipated report more than a year later, in January 1964, it triggered the major policy events of the decade.

THE ANTISMOKING COALITION

As the Surgeon General's Committee prepared its report, antismoking activists and the cigarette industry were mobilizing their respecting forces. Consisting of voluntary health organizations, state and local public health officials, a few congressional members, the FTC, the Office of the Surgeon General, the Consumers Union, and some consumer-minded journalists, the antismoking coalition in the first half of the 1960s was loosely organized, operated under political restraints, and possessed unclear goals. It wanted to restrict cigarette smoking and, demonstrating its belief in the persuasive power of scientific evidence, seemed to settle on raising public awareness through warning labels and education campaigns as its main strategy. But questions about what the warning labels should say, where they should appear, and whether advertising should also be restricted were left unresolved. As both Blatnik and Neuberger had argued, the coalition thought that the FTC was best situated to mandate warning labels but, recognizing that the Commission had to answer to Congress, attempted to build antismoking sentiment there as well.

At first, the voluntary health organizations, led by the American Cancer Society, were at the forefront of the antismoking coalition. Despite its hesitancy in the 1950s, the American Cancer Society decided to take a hard-line stance against cigarettes in 1960. Convinced by the accumulating scientific evidence against smoking, it issued a strongly worded statement asserting that smoking unquestionably caused cancer. The Society proceeded to expand its antismoking educational campaign and fund more studies on smoking and disease.[45] As the largest and best-funded of the voluntary health organizations, and experienced in cooperating with both voluntary and governmental groups, the American Cancer Society was well-placed to lead the antismoking campaign. Yet like the other voluntaries, the Society's leadership restrained their political activism for fear of losing their tax-exempt status. Another weakness is that the health organizations were never as tightly coordinated as were the stakeholders in the tobacco coalition, nor did they possess the public relations skills or counsel of their opposition.[46]

Significantly, the American Medical Association (AMA) refused to join the informal coalition. More conservative than the other health organizations, the professional association was trying to avoid making powerful enemies as it devoted its resources to the battle against government-financed health insurance. To the dismay of many antismokers, the AMA even went so far as to accept tobacco industry money to conduct a long-term study of smoking.[47]

After the release of the Surgeon General's Report in 1964, the smoking controversy increasingly became a political matter that occupied the chambers of Congress and federal agencies and that called for more overt political tactics. As this shift to the formal policy realm occurred, the voluntary health organizations receded to the back rows of the antismoking coalition while members of Congress and activists in the bureaucracy ascended to the forefront.[48] Neuberger and Blatnik remained committed to the cause, and they were joined by Senator Frank Moss of Utah, who cosponsored antismoking bills and introduced his own. Although Moss was a Mormon, he always asserted that his religion had no connection to his crusade against smoking and the tobacco companies.[49] Like Neuberger, Moss was a policy entrepreneur in the Senate who identified a number of causes and acted upon them independent of public pressure. In 1963 Moss engaged in a letter-writing campaign to all cigarette manufacturers and television networks, imploring them to "take the glamour out of cigarette advertising," especially on television, which he believed was "particularly insidious because the ad comes right into the living room, and reaches all members of a family in a way that a newspaper or magazine ad would not."[50] Yet none of these figures was particularly influential. Before 1964, the power of antismoking in Congress was negligible. The coalition did win more congressional converts after the report's release, and it acquired an especially powerful adherent in the figure of Senator Warren Magnuson, chairman of the Senate Committee on Commerce. Even so, tobacco's influence in Congress, especially in the House, was always greater than antismoking pressure.

The tobacco industry's most powerful opponent in the federal government was not Congress but the formerly laggard FTC, which, under the leadership of Dixon, finally took a more proactive stance. Primed by Neuberger's argument that all cigarette advertising that failed to warn of harmful effects was inherently deceptive, Dixon was preparing to act against the entire tobacco industry. Realizing that the regulatory powers of the FTC always had been crippled by case-by-case prosecutions that companies invariably outmaneuvered, Dixon advocated a procedure by which the Commission could issue a ruling to apply to an industry as a whole. Accordingly, in 1962 the FTC announced a new rule-making power, called a trade regulation rule, and argued that the original legislation that had created the FTC allowed for such a procedure. In 1963, the Commission practiced using its new power against uncontroversial industries such as dry-cell batteries and sleeping bags.[51] But Dixon sensed that the Commission needed additional support from the federal government before unfurling its new rule-making power against the mighty tobacco interests, so he decided to wait for the release of the Surgeon General's Report before the Commission made its move.[52] When the FTC finally acted—by promulgating a trade-regulation rule that mandated warning labels on all cigarette packaging and advertising—it had a considerable effect. The subsequent policy developments of the 1960s were all in response to the initiatives of the FTC.

As for the role of the surgeon general in the coalition, before his committee's landmark report on smoking, he was a relatively weak figure. The report, however, captured public attention and caught the mood of the time regarding health and fear of contamination. Henceforth, the Office of the Surgeon General would enjoy new authority in the realm of federal policy, and reporters would turn to the surgeon general for information. Although the Office of the Surgeon General did not possess much influence in traditional policymaking circles, Terry and his successors were able to drum up considerable popular awareness and support for the antismoking cause by effectively employing the media.[53]

Rounding up the antismoking coalition was the fledgling consumer movement. The Consumers Union published an antismoking tract in 1963, but the organization did not yet enjoy much influence in national politics. More important was the influence of consumer-minded journalists. Although the media as a whole was resistant to airing the antismoking cause because of the money it derived from tobacco industry sources, several national journalists during the 1960s—namely, Elizabeth Brenner Drew, Drew Pearson, Jack Anderson, and Morton Mintz—were instrumental in reporting the antismoking point of view to the American public.[54]

Most activists in the antismoking coalition of the 1960s denied moral motivations and wished to be viewed as impartial defenders of public health who had no association with the temperance movement or the prohibitionist impulse. For instance, in its 1963 announcement of commitment to the antismoking cause, the Consumers Union assured readers that it had no interest in prohibition of cigarettes. Its leaders stated, "Our discussion will not consider any moral objections to smoking. . . . Smoking is now first and foremost a public health problem, and it is as such that we are concerned with it."[55] Although a secular concern for physical health and fair trade practices was in the forefront of the emerging antismoking attitude, the moral objection to cigarette smoking that was characteristic of antismoking sentiment in the first half of the century had not disappeared. For some Americans, no boundary existed between health and religious-moral concerns. For instance, in 1954 a biology instructor wrote *What's Wrong with Smoking* to summarize the current research on smoking and urge Americans, particularly Christian Americans, not to smoke because their bodies belonged to God and should be kept pure. Furthermore, he called cigarette advertising "propaganda" that "is a plot upon [a Christian's] spiritual character." Even Americans who were not devoutly religious carried with them the moral disapproval of cigarettes, as well as the notion established earlier in the century that smoking was a "bad habit." Such disapproval often became inseparable from purely scientific indictment.[56]

LIMITATIONS

The FTC was moving ahead with its plans to regulate cigarette marketing, but most agencies in the federal arena were as yet reluctant to speak out against cigarette smoking. Although the surgeon general actively pursued the matter, the department in which he was housed, the Department of Health, Education, and Welfare, did not share his enthusiasm. The department's secretary, Anthony Celebreeze, had implied that informing consumers of the health hazards of smoking was not the federal government's place. He reined in Surgeon General Terry and later advised Congress to reject cigarette labeling legislation. His resistance was never explained, but it certainly angered Senator Neuberger, who wrote of the heavy-smoking Celebreeze, "Who would rely on a narcotics addict to evaluate the hazards of narcotic addiction?"[57] While a few antismoking activists such as Roy Norr were arguing that the FCC and the FDA possessed the authority to take action against tobacco companies, both agencies avoided involvement. The FDA refused to include cigarettes as a substance for regulation under the 1960 Federal Hazardous Substance Labeling Act. The agency's strategy of playing it safe and protecting its standing in the business community greatly disappointed antismoking activists.[58]

Although the antismoking coalition included some state and local public health officials and organizations and enjoyed the support of groups such as the National Congress of Parents and Teachers, its strength was highly concentrated in Washington, D.C. Unlike the 1950s movement to ban alcohol advertising, the movement to require warning labels for cigarettes did not spring from church groups and thousands of evangelical women writing letters to their congressmen. Instead, it was initiated and guided by a core group of public servants and scientists who sought very little public input on the matter. Before the mid-1960s, the antismoking movement was not a widespread, popular movement but a classic example of a top-down, government-initiated reform. As sometimes occurs in U.S. politics, policies predated and even encouraged the emergence of a popular social movement and the establishment of public interest groups such as Action on Smoking and Health (ASH) and Group Against Smoking Pollution (GASP) in the late 1960s and 1970s.[59]

The antismoking coalition in the mid-1960s, isolated as it was from popular support and facing such a formidable opponent, had limited political power. Antismokers operated under the assumption that all they needed to do was inform the public of the hazards of cigarettes—simply provide the consumer with accurate information—and the consumers would make the rational choice to not smoke. The coalition underestimated both the power of cigarettes to addict their users and the power of the tobacco industry to combat health information. The biggest mistake, however, in the words of Luther Terry, was that "we overlooked our greatest ally in combating the cigarette industry: the large number of Americans who didn't smoke." The general population of nonsmokers was a vast resource that the coalition, situated in its government offices and hospital laboratories, certain that it would succeed based on the sheer weight of scientific evidence on its side, did not seriously think about tapping. Advocates of "consumers" and "health" always have a difficult time implementing protective measures against the opposition of special interest and industry groups, and this was all the more the case for the antismoking campaign of this period because it lacked the support of mobilized constituent interest.[60]

THE INDUSTRY COALITION

The tobacco industry, in contrast, possessed the two crucial sources of strength that the antismokers lacked: constituent support and enduring influence on Capitol Hill. Except for scientific evidence, the tobacco coalition had nearly everything else going for it—and it did a fairly good job of creating doubt about the evidence. The industry's strength, of course, was concentrated in the tobacco-growing states of the South, but retailers, wholesalers, and other business people involved in the tobacco trade across the country had an investment in tobacco's success as well. A favorite tactic of the coalition was to present statistics demonstrating how many Americans were dependent upon the tobacco trade for their livelihood. The industry skillfully mobilized these sources of political strength by projecting an image of the tobacco business as a big happy family comprising ordinary Americans who were fighting this battle together. As one observer notes, it was the tobacco farmers in particular who possessed "the kind of legitimacy that the tobacco companies want[ed] and desperately need[ed]." The industry knew Americans would tend to be unsympathetic toward wealthy and powerful tobacco manufacturers, but it understood that they would identify with an underdog—the tobacco farmer. This picture of an all-for-one, one-for-all tobacco industry was, according to one critic, "a myth perpetuated by the manufacturers to buy themselves goodwill with the public and with the farmers themselves." In reality, the manufacturers treated the farmers rather shabbily, but this strategy did manage to deflect some criticism away from the big corporations.[61]

The advertising and broadcast industries also had a significant stake in the continued prosperity of the tobacco industry and took their places as members of the coalition. By the mid-1960s, cigarette companies spent more than $250 million per year on advertising, and tobacco constituted television's largest advertiser. When antismoking activists honed in on advertising as a target for restrictive policies, advertisers and broadcasters further strengthened their ties with the tobacco industry and became one of cigarettes' loudest defenders in policy debates throughout the 1960s. Their involvement invigorated the coalition's strategy of using First Amendment arguments to oppose marketing controls.[62]

These sources of support formed the industry's "subgovernment"—a network of congressional members, agency officials, and industry groups that worked together across institutional boundaries to defend tobacco. The influence of the tobacco subgovernment in federal politics during the twentieth century is legendary.[63] Members of Congress from tobacco states enjoyed a disproportionate amount of power. The seats of power in both the House and the Senate chaired congressional committees, and nearly one-fourth of Senate committees and one-third of House committees were chaired by tobacco state congressmen in the early to mid-1960s. The tobacco industry's influence in Congress was further protected by skillful and connected lobbyists who maintained close and personal contacts with members of key congressional committees. Often, these political officials had formerly been involved in the tobacco trade, and the lobbyists had once been politicians. A classic example of subgovernment "incest" was Earle Clements, a former governor of Kentucky, former U.S. senator, and close friend of Lyndon Johnson, who was hired by the Tobacco Institute to act as the industry's chief lobbyist in the 1960s. As a former member of Congress, he benefited from floor privileges. Clements was probably the most powerful figure in the tobacco coalition and was responsible for the industry's success in several policy battles during that period. Later, Horace Kornegay, a former congressman from North Carolina, would serve as president of the Tobacco Institute. The industry was also fortunate to have Abe Fortas, a political intimate of President Johnson, on its side as part of the legal team of Philip Morris.[64]

Except for a few pockets of antismoking sentiment, the executive branch lent its support to the tobacco industry. The industry's strongest advocate in the federal bureaucracy was the Department of Agriculture, which for decades had propped up the industry with a generous system of price supports for the cultivation of tobacco. At the same time as the FTC and the Public Health Service were stressing the dangers of smoking and urging smokers to quit, the Department of Agriculture was distributing pamphlets and promotional films showcasing the virtues of smoking. The department's approach benefited from the tacit approval of President Johnson during the height of the smoking and health controversy. And tacit his stance was: the president, who had supported regulation on behalf of consumers on other matters, remained silent about the smoking issue even in his health message of February 1964, one month after the release of the surgeon general's bombshell report. During the battle over warning labels in 1965, the president and his office did not utter a word, even though the executive office's Bureau of the Budget could have intervened to coordinate policy as the Senate and House worked to compromise on legislation. Although he had quit smoking on doctor's advice, Johnson maintained close ties with industry figures, and he did not wish to further alienate southern states, which were critical in the civil rights struggle.[65]

Significantly, the tobacco manufacturers were also able to call upon the support of several scientists who stood up in hearing after hearing to question the evidence against cigarettes. Many of the scientists were paid for their testimony, but others genuinely doubted the causal link between smoking and lung cancer.[66] Having these scientists as members of the coalition was crucial because it allowed the industry to fight the antismokers on their own battlefield with credentialed soldiers. Indeed, the government hearings on cigarettes featured long days of scientists telling conflicting stories, and this lack of consensus was enough to create doubt in the minds of many members of Congress.

CONCLUSION

Great disparity existed between the two coalitions as they confronted the smoking controversy of the mid-1960s. The antismoking coalition suffered from several handicaps. First, its members simply could not command the level of political influence that their opponents could. They rarely were placed in powerful positions in the realms of traditional policymaking. The FTC had few friends in Congress, and even fewer in industry; the Public Health Service was impotent in cloakroom deal making;

and the health organizations did not pride themselves on crafty lobbying skills. To make matters worse, the coalition lacked cohesion, a distinct leader, and a clear objective. Antismokers sometimes contradicted each other during government hearings, and, because of their fear of being branded prohibitionists, few had the courage to state candidly that the policy objective was to decrease smoking.

In contrast, the tobacco coalition was united, organized, and unmistakably directed by the cigarette manufacturers under the auspices of the Tobacco Institute. Within the Tobacco Institute, Earle Clements and a team of lawyers coordinated all strategy, and coalition members enjoyed positions of influence on Capitol Hill.[67] As the policy battles of 1964 and 1965 approached, the tobacco coalition was certainly more politically powerful than its opponents, and—though it would not succeed in completely quashing regulatory legislation, which it realized was impossible—it would be able to diminish both the extent and the impact of such regulation.

Despite the antismoking movement's disappointment in the policy outcome, its effort in the 1960s is significant in the history of public health and marketing control movements. The politics of regulation had undergone a basic change in the 1960s. Moral reform voices had receded, and the alcohol industries were less threatened than at any time since the repeal of Prohibition. Yet new voices had arisen from scientific and health sources in another area: smoking. Antismoking in the 1960s marked a transition in twentieth-century policymaking from religious morality to a secular morality based on science.

5 THE WARNING LABEL DEBATE

In June 1965, with little publicity and no special ceremony, an unenthusiastic Lyndon B. Johnson signed into law the Cigarette Labeling and Advertising Act of 1965. The law required a warning label that stated, rather tepidly, "Caution: Cigarette Smoking May be Hazardous to Your Health" to be placed on all cigarette packages. It provided the opening salvo in the federal government's regulation of cigarette marketing and has served as the foundation on which the few subsequent pieces of congressional legislation on this matter have been built.

President Johnson's approval of the law followed substantial controversy during the legislative process. The public debates over the act highlighted differing orientations on significant questions about public life, private behavior, and governance in the second half of the twentieth century. The controversy exposed conflicting ideas about the proper role of the federal government in matters of public health when a lucrative and powerful private industry was involved. The disputes also centered on questions of how science should be used in public policy, and, perhaps most important, what lines could be drawn around commercial expression in a free enterprise system.

Throughout the debate, policymakers operated under the assumption that marketing was a powerful force in modern American society. Like the alcohol battle of the 1950s, the cigarette battle at the federal level was mainly fought on the limited ground of marketing, without escalating the conflict to consider curtailment of the sale or manufacture of the product itself. To most antismokers, marketing proved a legitimate arena for regulation because they assumed advertising techniques were so potent that restricting them, while countering with an antismoking marketing campaign of their own, would cause a decline in smoking. Controlling information disseminated to the public, the elite group of antismokers believed, was key, and their first goal was to mandate a warning label on cigarettes.

The point can also be made, however, that narrowing of the terms of debate to marketing occurred because marketing control served as safer ground for a contentious policy debate that involved personal habits of millions of Americans. Instead of attacking the habit directly, marketing regulation would strike at the industry's ability to promote it. The negative legacy of Prohibition was so strong that the possibility of banning or even restricting the production or sale (except to minors) of cigarettes was never even considered in a serious policy forum in these years. Instead, restricting the debate to the issue of marketing seemed to be a much more workable, much less risky place to stage a political fight. Both sides were content to keep the focus on advertising and product labeling. In terms of political strategy, they were being pragmatic: the industry forces had less to lose, and the antismoking camp had more to gain. This consensus on a limited arena for policy action was rarely discussed by the opposing forces or even commented upon by outside observers. Instead, it was tacitly accepted, with surprisingly little contemplation, that the cigarette policy battles of the 1960s would concentrate on questions of marketing.[1]

The stakeholders in the debate shared many of the same assumptions and dilemmas as did those who argued over alcohol advertising. Concerns over commercial free expression, personal liberty, protection of youth, and the efficacy of industry self-regulation all reappeared during the debate over the cigarette warning label. Yet the antismoking movement sharply differed from the temperance movement's crusade against alcohol advertising because of the authoritative scientific support for the antismokers' position. The antialcohol advertising movement did not have a single catalyst, let alone a scientific impetus, to incite widespread public concern. The cigarette policy discussion, on the other hand, was provoked in 1964 by the ringing Surgeon General Committee's Report. As the federal agency chiefly responsible for regulating commercial behavior, the Federal Trade Commission took a leadership role and tried to follow up on the Surgeon General Committee's recommendations with strict regulations. Congress quickly entered the fray, in part to impede the FTC, and thus the proper role of the federal government in protecting Americans from a proven health hazard became a matter of legislative debate.

RESPONSES TO THE REPORT: THE FTC AND CONGRESS

Armed with the conclusions of the Surgeon General's Report, a handful of government officials moved to act against the tobacco industry within a matter of weeks of its release. The conclusions themselves were not such a bombshell, but it was significant that the top health authority in the land had stated definitively that cigarettes were a hazard to health, and it became a hot story for the press. The lengthy report, written in highly technical and objective language, concluded that smokers died at a rate 70 percent higher than nonsmokers. The committee resolved, "Cigarette smoking is a health hazard of sufficient importance in the United States to warrant appropriate remedial action."[2]

The report had significant cultural and scientific repercussions. It was received with much credence by the press and, as far as public opinion polls indicate, by the American public as well. Even members of the media who had not been sympathetic to earlier reports of smoking's hazards fell in line and treated the findings as indisputable and authoritative. The ready acceptance of the report demonstrated Americans' widespread trust in the government and the scientific establishment before the 1970s, and the conclusions created a minor scare. Smoking did decline in the United States after its release—though it crept back up by the end of the year.[3] The report represented an important step for science because a government body whose members included esteemed scientists had affirmed epidemiological studies and thereby publicly authenticated epidemiology as a scientific discipline.[4]

Most important, though, was its political impact. The Surgeon General's Report raised the question of how science should be used when making public policy decisions. It was the report's decisive statement by an objective group of scientists that cigarettes could kill smokers that gave the Federal Trade Commission the confidence—and, according to the Commission, the authority—to take action. As far as the FTC was concerned, the report represented objective proof and therefore unquestionably could be relied upon in the public policy arena. The FTC's assumptions about the authority of the report and the objectivity of science in general, however, would be forcefully questioned by tobacco industry supporters as the battle wore on.

Yet the first major political conflict revolved not around the health and science disputes but rather the question of the FTC's jurisdictional authority to regulate cigarette marketing. Led by Commissioner Paul Rand Dixon and encouraged by Senator Maureen Neuberger, the FTC had been prepared to take action against the cigarette industry for at least a year before the report's release. Fully informed of its contents, the commissioners had been crafting a trade regulation rule that they waited to announce until a week after the report's release. Making use of its new rule-making power, the Commission proposed the restriction of cigarette advertising subject matter, including a ban on the disclosure of nicotine and tar content. The rule's most controversial component was the requirement of warning labels on both advertisements and cigarette packages. The Commission scheduled hearings on the rule for March of 1964 and declared it would become effective on 1 January 1965.[5]

Tobacco politics in the 1960s provides a premier example of the conflict between congressional and bureaucratic, or fourth branch, policymaking.[6] The FTC's rule on warning labels provoked an outcry from friends of the tobacco industry, who declared that the regulation was a matter for Congress, not a federal agency, to decide. At the FTC's hearings on its proposed rule, the industry's principal strategy was not to dispute the alleged health hazards but to present a legalistic challenge to the rulemaking authority of the FTC. The Commission responded that Congress had intended it to be a dynamic agency, actively seeking out and preventing deception in advertising—not just a "simple enforcement agency."[7] The tobacco industry immediately contacted its powerful allies in Congress in an effort to take the matter out of the aggressive FTC's hands and halt what it referred to as a power grab.

From an ideological perspective, many conservative policymakers, whether connected to the industry or not, were concerned about the power of the federal bureaucracy, and of the federal government in general, in American life. They regarded the FTC's action in this context, viewing it as an unwarranted intrusion into Americans' private lives and a violation of the rights of private enterprise. For example, during the 1964 cigarette hearings Representative Paul Schenck (R) of Ohio took the opportunity to vent his frustrations about bureaucratic power: "The people of the United States are more and more and more becoming regulated, becoming told what they can and cannot do and how they may or may not do it by rules and regulations of bureaus composed of members who have been appointed but never elected rather than by laws passed by the Congress, the Members of which are elected by the people of the United States." Representative Horace Kornegay (D) of North Carolina, soon to be head of the Tobacco Institute, argued that the FTC's cigarette ruling constituted a case of the "child" overpowering its "parent," and the child must be disciplined. Kornegay declared, "I believe it is imperative that this committee and the Congress take positive action to check the usurpation of authority by the Federal Trade Commission. The very heart of our Nation's economy—the free enterprise system—is at stake."[8] Because of such strenuous objections, substantial support existed in both the Senate and the House for suspending the FTC's rule on cigarette labeling.

In addition, in pragmatic terms, the tobacco lobby knew that it stood a better chance with a Congress that housed a disproportionate amount of powerful southern members than with the antagonistic FTC. The industry counted on the influence of tobacco congressmen, especially in the

House, to thwart the Commission's attack. Antismokers, in contrast, preferred to leave marketing policy in the hands of the FTC because they knew that the rule contained more teeth than anything that Congress would pass. Within weeks of the release of the Surgeon General's Report and the FTC's proposed rule, members of Congress responded to the cigarette controversy by introducing thirty-five pieces of legislation, many of them designed to impede the FTC.

It was a political fact of life that the House, which by its nature responds relatively quickly to special interests, was friendlier to the industry than was the Senate. Significantly, the chairmanship of the House Commerce Committee, to which these bills were referred, belonged to a tobacco industry sympathizer, Representative Oren Harris of Arkansas. The committee also counted as members Kornegay, James Broyhill of North Carolina, and Walter Rogers of Texas, all of whom were vocal opponents of the FTC and dedicated advocates of the tobacco industry. One antismoking activist observed, "The House Commerce Committee seemed totally in the grip of [chief tobacco lobbyist Earle] Clements and his allies."[9] It was with this committee of gentlemen that the cigarette makers knew they would find protection from the FTC.

The Senate's support for tobacco was less assured. Its Commerce Committee also included senators who spoke for the tobacco industry, but the committee was the seat of significant antismoking strength as well. Maurine Neuberger won a seat on the committee right before the policy fight. Even more important, the committee's chairman, the influential Warren Magnuson, sided with the industry's opponents in a much more decided way than he had during the alcohol marketing controversy. As a classic example of a cigar-chomping, scotch-drinking, rotund senator who liked to gamble, surround himself with Hollywood starlets, and operate in an "old boys' network," he seemed unlikely to champion consumer issues or take on the tobacco industry. Having nearly lost reelection in 1962, Magnuson decided he needed to augment his appeal by reconnecting to constituents and advocating the public interest. Some close advisors suggested consumer rights, and Magnuson took to the idea. Not long after, he hired a group of dedicated young and liberal staffers, including Yale law student Michael Pertschuk, who was a former member of Neuberger's congressional staff and an enthusiastic supporter of consumer rights and antismoking. Pertschuk remembers, "[M]y assignment: to help build a consumer record for Magnuson, identify opportunities, develop strategies, shepherd bills, and make certain that Magnuson received appropriate acknowledgement for his achievements." By the end of the decade, with the assistance of his bright new staff, Magnuson had authored eight pieces of consumer legislation, and the 1965 cigarette labeling act was one of the first of them.[10]

Another high-profile, if late-coming, supporter of the antismoking cause in the Senate was Robert F. Kennedy, who, like Magnuson, was made aware of the issue by an aide, in this case Peter Edelman, who was also committed to consumer issues. Neuberger had approached Edelman and asked him to persuade Kennedy to join her in antismoking activism in the Senate. With Edelman's assistance, Kennedy quickly educated himself about the smoking controversy and thrust himself into the forefront of the antismoking contingent with some hard-hitting and well-publicized speeches in the summer of 1965. From then until his death in 1968, antismoking was one of Kennedy's main causes.[11]

In stark contrast to the experience of congressional members who had fought for controls on alcohol advertising in the 1950s, the antismoking members of Congress operated in the absence of public pressure and received very little correspondence from interested constituents. The voluntary health organizations such as the American Cancer Society were reluctant to become involved in politics and did not mobilize their constituents in political support of antismoking measures. But the voluntaries were galvanized by the FTC's aggressive move against cigarette marketing and in the next few months created the Interagency Council on Smoking and Health in mid-1964. Joined by the Public Health Service and several congressional members, this mostly powerless ad hoc group attempted to counter the strength of the tightly knit tobacco industry.[12]

The industry, for the most part, was ready to negotiate. Observing the public response to the Surgeon General's Report and facing a harsh ruling by the FTC, at least a few tobacco executives began to see that a disclosure of health hazards was in all likelihood inevitable and they should try to work it to their advantage. Earle Clements, director of the Tobacco Institute, masterminded the tobacco industry's strategy throughout the policy debates of 1964 and 1965. Clements had long realized that some form of health warning was inescapable and that a warning label law passed by Congress, over whose members the industry wielded more control, could even be desirable.[13] First, a moderate piece of congressional legislation—a weakly worded message obscurely placed on packaging only—would fend off the rabid FTC. Second, a warning label would protect the industry from litigation. He calculated that, in an increasingly hostile political and public climate, acceding to some regulation would improve the industry's image. Like the distillers' admonitions to drink moderately and drive safely, a mild warning label might make the tobacco industry appear caring and responsible without meaningfully undermining their marketing messages and economic power. Clements worked hard to convince industry executives and tobacco congressmen of this political reality, but this capitulation to the inevitability of regulation occurred behind the scenes. Before congressional committees and the media, the industry continued to resist the idea of a warning label. Therefore, when the time came to make a deal, the industry would seem to be giving up much more than it actually was.

THE SELF-REGULATION STRATEGY

The tobacco industry, along with the broadcasting industry, also reacted to the Surgeon General's Report and the FTC's rule by engaging in more self-regulation. Hoping to prove to the nation's policymakers, as well as to the consuming public, that cigarette manufacturers were conscientious and did not require federal government oversight of their advertising as the FTC had proposed, the tobacco industry announced the formation of the Cigarette Advertising Code, Inc., in April 1964. This group of regulators, appointed by cigarette companies, would screen advertising to ensure that it met certain reasonable guidelines that had been spelled out in an agreed-upon code.[14]

The industry was mainly concerned not to offend sensibilities by overtly appealing to youth or by trumpeting health claims in their advertising. The code prohibited the use of athletes or celebrities who had "special appeal" to youth, nor could advertisements show a smoker who was participating in, or had just participated in, an athletic activity. It forbade the promotion of cigarettes at schools, on college campuses, or in comic books. The stipulation that attracted the most skepticism from critics declared that cigarette advertising should not appear "on television and radio programs, or in publications, directed primarily to persons under twenty-one years of age." Who could say what appealed to a person under twenty-one? The industry thought it could partially solve the problem of its appeal to youth by requiring that all actors and models were at least twenty-five years of age—in hopes everyone would assume young people could not be attracted by a twenty-six-year-old model. As for health claims, the code included many rules, but they were malleable and mostly left to the discretion of the person to be appointed code administrator. In practice, the code's health provision resulted in the elimination of "fancy, scientific names" and technical descriptions of filters from cigarette advertising.[15]

The cigarette manufacturers installed former New Jersey governor Robert Meyner as the administrator, lending the outfit an air of respectability. Meyner promised to examine all cigarette advertising carefully and vigorously prosecute through fines up to $100,000 the violators of the code. In fact, most of the tobacco companies, well aware of the hostile climate they confronted, had already made efforts to reform their advertisements. By mid-1964 most were unaffected by the code. A trenchant piece in the *Nation* titled "Too Little, Too Late—and Inept" pegged the code as "phony" and filled with meaningless guidelines. Antismoking activists noted that, although the code eliminated some of the more egregious abuses of cigarette advertising, it did not require an affirmative statement of warning and therefore was inadequate.[16]

Despite the criticism, the industry's political objective was largely achieved: the code persuaded many policymakers—if not in the FTC, then in Congress—that the industry could police itself and did not need federal government regulation to ensure fair advertising. A warning label on packaging would be enough to fulfill the government's responsibility for public health. The antismokers in the federal government, however, questioned whether industry self-regulation was sufficient to prevent objectionable marketing practices and, most imperative, cause a decline in smoking, so they continued to press for stricter advertising controls. Some policymakers took a middle ground: although they doubted that self-regulation would solve the problems at hand, they were willing to give the industry's advertising code some time to function before pushing for additional regulations.

The broadcasting and advertising industries also felt threatened by the FTC's ruling and leapt to the tobacco industry's defense. Broadcasters were highly dependent on cigarette advertising revenue—tobacco companies spent more than $100 million on television advertising alone and constituted the networks' largest advertiser. Like the cigarette companies, the broadcasters responded to the antismoking offensive with increased self-regulation. The National Association of Broadcasters developed new guidelines for cigarette advertising very similar to the tobacco industry's code.[17] Moreover, broadcasters were even more uneasy than their associates in the advertising and tobacco industries because, under the Federal Communications Commission Act, the national government bestowed licenses to broadcasters to use the airwaves, a public commodity, in "the public interest." The networks of course coveted cigarette advertising revenue, but they were wary of agitating the FCC.

Members of the advertising industry, however, did not practice under these licensing restraints and therefore were more apt to be defensive in the face of what they perceived as harassment. Feeling much beleaguered, the Advertising Federation of America issued a statement condemning "efforts by government and private organizations to make advertising the scapegoat in the controversy over lung cancer and cigarets [sic]." In May 1964 the *New Republic* reported that, according to interviews with twenty advertising men, advertisers who worked on cigarette accounts did not have "any pangs of conscience" about such work. One copywriter avowed that the Surgeon General's Report did not faze him, saying, "I'll take their [cigarette firms'] money. I write for the man who feeds me." Another advertising man pronounced the cigarette scare a mere "fad" and declared that "all this stuff about cigarettes and cancer will be forgotten this time next year."[18] Within a year, however, a cigarette labeling bill was emerging out of months of contentious debate in the House and Senate Commerce Committees, not to mention backroom dealing between tobacco lobbyists and congressional staffers, and, despite the industry's best efforts, the cigarette controversy was not forgotten.

STRATEGIES AND RHETORIC

The cigarette marketing controversy pertained to the enduring dilemma in American public policy over the balance between private rights and the public good. The 1964 and 1965 House and Senate Commerce Committee hearings on cigarettes, as well as the House and Senate floor debates on the cigarette labeling bills, considered critical issues regarding the rights of industry, the value of public health, the protection of youth, and the proper role of science in public policy. Policymakers confronted two related questions: is cigarette smoking harmful to health? and how should the federal government respond to the smoking-health problem?

Science and Health

On the question of harm to health, what was supposed to have been settled with the Surgeon General's Report clearly was not, as far as the tobacco coalition was concerned. The industry kept the controversy alive by presenting witness after witness, some of them paid to testify, to challenge the report's conclusions. For instance, Dr. Thomas H. Burford, chief of thoracic and cardiovascular surgery at a St. Louis hospital, avowed before the House Commerce Committee in 1964 that he neither thought cigarette smoking caused lung cancer nor believed that smoking was responsible for any shortening of life. "It's all statistical, and not causal, associations," he testified, not only contesting the Surgeon General's Committee, composed of some of the most respected figures in medicine, but also challenging the field of epidemiology. Several other doctors stood up after Burford that afternoon to reinforce his assertions. Comparable testimony, again presented by dozens of physicians in a row to achieve maximum effect, was delivered at the subsequent committee hearings.[19]

At the hearings, medical professionals who questioned the link between smoking and disease heavily outnumbered those who endorsed the causal connection. Probably assuming that the Surgeon General's Report spoke for itself and therefore no additional scientific witnesses were necessary, the only scientific witness presented by the antismoking camp for the first hearing was the surgeon general himself. Magnuson's aide Pertschuk observed that neither the surgeon general nor any of the heads of the voluntary health organizations was "prepared for the hostile, pseudoscientific cross-examination of the industry's friends in Congress. Under fire, the spokesmen for the voluntaries wilted or blustered; they proved less than compelling witnesses." In contrast, the industry's shrewd strategy of mobilizing a parade of scientific witnesses was largely successful in creating doubt in the minds of many congressional members about the health hazards of cigarettes.[20]

As a whole, the voluminous testimony of the scientists who spoke for the tobacco industry did not merely dispute the conclusions of the report, but challenged the validity of scientific methods and conclusions altogether. Policymakers were thus put in a difficult position: they had little experience with medical science, yet were being asked to make a decision based upon contested scientific evidence. They had to decide whether there could ever be enough scientific proof to warrant a public policy measure against cigarettes. Could they enact regulation if uncertainty existed? How much constituted enough proof for protective action—75 percent sure, 98 percent sure? The tobacco industry cannily demanded 100 percent certainty, and the surgeon general and like-minded scientists found themselves admitting that there was no such thing. During this debate, science undeniably had become political, and participating scientists had become "policy entrepreneurs." Could legislators treat this debate as they treated other political contests—as a brokering among equally interested and legitimate parties?[21]

Commercial Expression and Industry Power

Apart from science and policymaking, another crucial policy debate raised during the cigarette marketing controversy revolved around the principle of commercial free expression. The definitions and boundaries set by the tobacco industry and its opponents on commercial expression affected not only public policy, but also the wider consumer culture. The central question was whether an advertisement was inherently deceptive if it failed to disclose harmful effects. If so, what could the government do to correct the deception?

Opening the policy debate with their proposed rule, FTC commissioners claimed that cigarette advertising constituted misleading and deceptive advertising because it failed to admit the health hazards of smoking. It therefore constituted a special class of deception: deception through omission. The commissioners stated, "An advertiser's failure to disclose material facts in circumstances where the effect of nondisclosure is to deceive a substantial segment of the purchasing public is fully equivalent to deception accomplished through misleading statements or suggestions." To make matters worse, advertising for cigarettes—a product that could make one ill and die—showcased pleasure and carefree living. After conducting a comprehensive study of themes in cigarette advertising, the commissioners concluded, "Not only has the industry failed to disclose to the consuming public the dangers of cigarette smoking, its past and present advertising has camouflaged them. The cumulative effect of at least a decade of massive cigarette advertising has been to establish a barrier to adequate public knowledge and appreciation of the health hazards."[22] The FTC viewed cigarette advertising as a purposeful disinformation campaign that was aimed at seducing and deluding the public.

According to the FTC, the advertising of cigarettes should be held to a higher standard of truth than the advertising of most other consumer products because, as established by the Surgeon General's Report, deception in cigarette advertising was a life or death matter. The Commission was usually more attentive to regulating products that came into intimate contact with the body, particularly if they proved a danger to health even under normal conditions of use. The commissioners believed that these special characteristics applied to cigarettes as well. Furthermore, the commissioners argued, cigarettes were uniquely attractive to youth, a class of consumers that the FTC always had regarded as requiring special protection from misleading advertising. Last, they believed that cigarette advertising was so plentiful and effective, especially as it appeared on television, that it commanded great power over the consuming public. According to the commissioners, this overwhelming power should make the industry even more responsible and careful about how it wielded its influence.[23] The FTC, then, considered marketing to be a mighty force in the nation's economy and culture, a force that should be carefully monitored and controlled by the federal government.

When the debate moved to the congressional arena, more antismoking voices were heard, and they expanded on the case made by the FTC's leadership. The central argument of the antismoking camp was that the protection of public health took precedence over the protection of the rights of free enterprise. Claims of commercial free expression were invalidated when the product proved deadly. Antismokers strongly advocated a role for the federal government in cigarette regulation. To them, this was not a matter of First Amendment rights or of economics, but of public health and freedom from deception, and such a serious public health threat unquestionably warranted government action. Dr. Harold Diehl, a strong supporter of the warning label, testified that "a government which permits the sale and the advertising of a product which causes so much damage to health has a responsibility to continuously inform and impress upon the public the health hazards to which they are exposing themselves when they smoke cigarettes." Diehl tried to convince the Senate Commerce Committee of the importance of their impending decision by counseling, "Your committee apparently faces a basic issue as to whether in a democratic capitalistic society human health can be given precedence over financial gain for those who produce and sell a product which the highest health authority of our Government states is a serious hazard to health."[24]

Other antismoking members of Congress asked some tough questions about America's priorities when it came to big business and threats to health. Representative David King (D) of Utah argued that a responsible industry would have started to phase out the manufacture of cigarettes as soon as the evidence against smoking had emerged in the 1950s. Instead, according to King, the companies "elected to redouble their propaganda efforts to neutralize or even counteract the voice of reason. . . . At that point . . . the tobacco interests forfeited their claim on the sympathy of the Nation, as far as the economic argument is concerned." King wondered, "How long, may I ask, is the economic argument supposed to pass for valid? Are we to understand that the tobacco industry claims an everlasting investment in the corruption of America's health, and that in their judgment jobs will continue to weigh heavier than lives. . .?" Neuberger tried to connect the cigarette issue to larger populist issues championed by liberals in the 1960s, arguing that the industry's position was "that because the cigarette industry is big it should remain untouched by such pedestrian concerns as public welfare and safety. If ever there was an illustration of there being one law for the rich and one law for the poor, this is it."[25]

The stakeholder industries strongly disagreed with this picture and countered with their own dramatic tableau, portraying themselves as vulnerable victims of an attack on their commercial rights. Forcing them to place a warning label on their packages or advertisements violated their commercial free expression, which industry leaders interpreted as their right to advertise. They contended that, as long as the product was legal—and neither Congress nor the FTC had made any moves to prohibit cigarettes—the manufacturers should have relatively free rein in their marketing practices, at least as much as the manufacturers of any other legal consumer product. In his testimony before the House Commerce committee in 1964, R. J. Reynolds chairman Bowman Gray succinctly stated this sacred principle of the tobacco interests and perhaps all American consumer industries: "Advertising is basic to the successful distribution and sale of any consumer item on a national basis. The right to advertise is an essential commercial right and is virtually destroyed if one is required in every advertisement to caution against the use of the product." Through self-regulation, he argued, the industry itself could ensure the fairness of cigarette advertising without FTC or congressional intervention.[26] Framing the cigarette debate in terms of "freedom" versus "censorship" was a shrewd tactic. It appealed to policymakers who may have been opposed to smoking but were easily alarmed by threats to constitutional rights. It also appealed to congressional members who for financial or political reasons firmly supported the tobacco industry but wished to disguise that reality with lofty rhetoric.

Several congressional members claimed that cigarette marketing regulation, including a warning label, would serve as a dangerous precedent for government power over private commerce. Ross Bass (D) of Tennessee, one of the industry's most important supporters in the Senate, argued that, if a warning label were required in cigarette advertising, such advertising would necessarily have to cease. In effect, Bass claimed, the federal government was teetering close to prohibition and warned, "This outlawing of advertising of a commodity is in my opinion a very serious, a most serious proposition for the Congress to enter into. It is practically a new field." Senator Thruston Morton (R) of Kentucky declared an unwritten convention existed in the American marketplace that allowed businesses the freedom to say nearly anything they wanted in their advertising in order to sell their product. This convention, he asserted, protected cigarette advertising from government intervention.[27]

Senators Neuberger and Kennedy were skeptical of Morton's claim of an American custom of commercial free expression. They contended that numerous precedents existed in which the federal government had required statement of warning in advertising or had banned a product's advertising altogether, particularly in the case of over-the-counter medications. They further noted that it was not until the cigarette controversy that members of Congress challenged this policy. Neuberger remarked, "Congress did not feel constrained to leap to the defense of those [manufacturers of over-the-counter medications] in the name of the protection of the free enterprise system." She implied that Congress was bowing to the tobacco industry because of its economic clout and copious advertisements.[28]

Public Knowledge and a Warning Label

Antismokers fervently believed that industry self-regulation was inadequate, especially because the industry's Cigarette Advertising Code failed to require an affirmative statement of warning, either on packaging or advertising. Antismokers argued that federal government recognition of the health problem, represented by the requirement of a warning label, was of utmost importance in convincing Americans, especially young people who were considering taking up the habit, of the veracity of the health hazards of smoking.

To counter the warning label proposal, the industries used several different and often contradictory arguments. First, industry defenders contended that a label was unnecessary because, after the health scares of the 1950s and the wide publicity given to the Surgeon General's Report, the public was already well informed of the potential harm from cigarettes. Second, at the same time the manufacturers argued they were absolved from warning consumers about health hazards because the surgeon general had fulfilled that responsibility, they simultaneously denied the existence of those hazards, implying that a warning label would be false.[29]

Third, not only was a warning label unnecessary because Americans already knew the possible hazards of smoking, but the label would be ineffective, especially in its aim to deter youth from smoking, because consumers would ignore it and because youth were influenced by many factors other than marketing in their decision to start smoking. Indeed, the warning label might backfire, for putting a warning label—or as some members of Congress called it, a "skull and crossbones"—on cigarettes might actually encourage mischievous children to smoke.[30] Though not quite conceding the truth of the health hazard claims, industry representatives who made these points were in effect admitting that cigarette smoking did present a problem but were criticizing the warning label proposal as an ineffective solution. If followed to its logical conclusion, this line of argument meant that a warning label would be impotent and therefore would present no harm to the tobacco industry.

But industry representatives—sometimes the very same individuals who presented the "unnecessary and ineffective" argument—also used the opposite approach in their case against the warning label: the "doom and gloom" perspective. In their fourth approach, they contended that a warning label would be so powerful that it would spell the end of cigarette advertising and possibly the end of the tobacco business. What the warning label proponents were truly aiming at, the industry supporters claimed, was "backdoor prohibition." Bowman Gray testified that his company would "have to seriously consider discontinuance of advertising of its product under such circumstances. It does just negate the whole impact of the advertising." Gray agreed with Representative Kornegay that the warning label would "virtually eliminate competition as we know it in the industry." He liked to detail the extent of the tobacco economy in America, with emphasis on the "millions of persons" dependent on the industry for their livelihoods, and implied that legislation such as the warning label proposal could "seriously disrupt this important industry."[31]

In another approach, industry supporters repeatedly asked, If the health hazards are truly so terrible, why are regulators asking for only a minor warning label? If cigarettes were indeed so poisonous and deadly, why did they not press for an all-out ban? Senator Neuberger tried to justify the label legislation as "the most satisfactory middle ground," but many members of Congress criticized the warning label as a halfway measure and shrewdly proclaimed that government policy toward cigarettes should be all or nothing, knowing, of course, that "all" (prohibition) was completely unfeasible.[32]

In presenting these various lines of argument, the industry was trying to cover all the bases: a warning label would be bad policy because it was unnecessary, it was false, it would ruin the industry, or it would have no impact at all. Whichever way they argued it, industry representatives did agree that a warning label epitomized the federal government, particularly the Public Health Service and the Federal Trade Commission, playing "Big Brother" by imposing a partisan policy on Americans under the guise of public health and objective science. Representative Rogers even accused the Public Health Service of attempting to "brainwash the public." The tobacco industry astutely adopted the conservative ideology of the time and argued that a warning label on cigarette packaging and advertising was part of a larger pattern in the 1960s of government's increasing intrusion in Americans' personal lives. The industry tapped into the growing antigovernment sentiment of the 1960s, represented most by conservative Republicans and southern Democrats, the majority of whom supported the industry during the legislative fight and many of whom, ironically, had advocated the regulation of alcohol marketing and had close ties to the historic temperance movement. Adding further irony, industry supporters often compared cigarette regulation to America's failed experiment of Prohibition and portrayed their opponents as zealots on an absurd moral crusade to stamp out smoking, just like the drys of the early twentieth century.[33]

Antismokers responded to the industries' multifarious attack on the warning label policy by vigorously supporting government regulation when public health was so severely threatened and by presenting the labeling mandate as the most effective and least interventionist solution. Senator Magnuson stated that, even though surveys showed most Americans were aware of the Surgeon General's Report, "[t]oo many are still tempted to say, 'if cigarettes were really so harmful, the Government would certainly do something about it.'" The absence of such a government-mandated label, Magnuson and others believed, would lead consumers to assume that the federal government, like the tobacco industry, did not take the surgeon general seriously and considered cigarettes to be harmless. The FTC declared that, contrary to the industry's claims, the public's understanding of the health hazards could not be reliably measured. Commissioners reasoned that many people, seeing cigarettes for sale with no warning labels affixed to them and no other changes in their marketing, probably still thought the hazards were rumors or that the studies were in doubt. Besides, the FTC stated, "a deception, to be actionable, need not be universal." In other words, even if many Americans were well-informed, it only took the deception of one person to warrant regulatory action.[34]

But was a warning label the best policy solution? Some advocates acknowledged that the label would not solve the smoking problem, but insisted it was nonetheless an important first step, if only a symbolic one.[35] Federal government regulation of cigarette marketing, even if minor, was crucial to validate to the public the scientific conclusions about the health hazards. Other antismokers believed that a warning label would be more than a symbolic gesture and would actually curtail smoking in this country. Putting great faith in the rationality of consumers and the power of scientific risk findings, they assumed that, if consumers were provided with the best available information, they would make the right choice and not smoke. For instance, antismoking activist Senator Frank Moss stated he did not believe cigarettes could or should be prohibited, but "we can at least give the smokers and nonsmokers all the facts, and let them make up their own minds." Similarly, Neuberger advocated the label because she "believe[d] in the ability of the American people to make intelligent decisions when given all the facts."[36] Government, in their minds, would play the role of a neutral information-provider, not a partisan Big Brother, and would use its impartial power to counter the erroneous and manipulative impressions dispensed by the industry's advertising juggernaut and public relations machine. To them, the public's behavior could be determined by who controlled the information, and this control must be wrested from the industry.

The antismokers' most persuasive rationale for government intervention was the call to protect the nation's youth. While most members of Congress were not moved by the argument that a warning label was needed to protect adult smokers from themselves, they tended to sympathize with the case that children needed to be specially warned against a habit which everyone, on both sides, acknowledged should be taken up only by adults. Activists emphasized the vulnerability and susceptibility of youth both to the habit of smoking and to the glamour of cigarette advertising. The FTC argued that young people were largely uninformed of the health hazards of cigarettes because they rarely paid attention to the news and did not currently see any warning of these hazards on cigarette packages or ads. Commissioners believed that the impact of the Surgeon General Committee's Report was already fading, and when in a few years the next crop of adolescents was deciding whether to start smoking, they more than likely would be unaware of the report's conclusions.[37] For these reasons, the federal government urgently needed to follow through with regulatory action, and the optimal regulation, most antismokers agreed, was a warning label on advertisements. A package label would do little good because the smoker had already made the decision to purchase cigarettes and smoke. A warning in advertising, however, would be much more effective in reaching nonsmokers, especially youth, who had not yet made up their minds.[38]

Discrimination and the Comparison with Alcohol

Further contending that government intervention in cigarette marketing would be unfair and unprecedented, industry supporters argued that, in comparison to other hazardous consumer products, the government was discriminating against cigarettes. Senator Bass asked the surgeon general, "Is it fair for us just to single out this industry and say we are going to do everything we can to knock you out of business, and let all the rest of them go?"[39] When comparing cigarettes to other harmful products, the product that was typically brought up, especially by southern members of Congress, was alcohol, which they avowed presented as bad, if not worse, of a health problem as cigarettes. Tobacco congressmen accused the Public Health Service and the FTC of ignoring the problems created by alcohol and thereby unfairly attacking cigarettes. Several constituents wrote angry letters to antismoking members of Congress, demanding to know why they were paying more attention to cigarettes than to alcohol. For instance, Mrs. R. E. Mattice wrote to Magnuson: "You must indeed be a very busy man to bother with such nonsense as this. Why not suggest labelling the liquor bottles and make the producers of old 'demon rum' label the health hazards? Liquor does more harm—a thousand times more harm—than cigarettes."[40]

Antismokers, however, discounted tobacco's association with alcohol as well as the notion of unfair discrimination against cigarettes. The FTC emphasized that alcohol could be consumed safely in moderation, but any consumption of cigarette smoke could prove hazardous, and cigarettes were more addictive to more people than was alcohol. Furthermore, the FTC contended, the alcohol industries were already well regulated by a system of controls that "has no parallel in the cigarette industry." As evidence, the commissioners cited the "comprehensive and detailed" regulations imposed by the Department of Treasury upon the alcohol industries and further claimed that those industries conformed "to stringent industry-wide codes which long predate any efforts by the cigarette industry at systematic self-regulation." Led by the FTC, the antismoking camp thought that the tobacco industry's attempt to derail the cigarette warning label initiative by pointing out that alcoholic beverages did not have warning labels was unreasonable.[41]

The Slippery Slope

A strong component of the industry's discrimination argument was the alarmist "slippery slope" theme. According to this proposition, once warning labels and advertising controls were imposed on cigarettes, every other potentially harmful product in America's consumer market, from fatty foods to automobiles, could expect the same. Senator Morton began his testimony in the 1965 Senate hearing by cautioning, "I hope we don't panic here. . . . [T]he first thing you know, we are not going to be able to eat anything, smoke anything, for that matter, or drink anything." And Representative Kornegay wondered aloud, "Once this ball starts rolling, where will it stop? What industry, what product in this country would be safe from regulation in the area that we are talking about . . .?"[42] Many congressional committee members, perhaps because they were steeped in a cold war, domino-theory mindset, appeared to be persuaded by the slippery slope line of reasoning. Again, the fear was that allowing regulation in the case of cigarettes would open the floodgates to intrusive and excessive government intervention in Americans' private lives.

MACHINATIONS AND OUTCOME

When the hearings concluded and the House and Senate committees began deliberations, everyone understood that some kind of warning label legislation was inevitable. The bill that would eventually become the Cigarette Labeling and Advertising Act of 1965 was largely drafted by Senator

Magnuson's aide Michael Pertschuk. Young, inexperienced, and lacking the support of a public interest movement, Pertschuk caved under the immense pressure of the tobacco industry lobbyists, particularly the sharp and powerful Earle Clements.[43] As a result, his bill required a warning label to be placed on cigarette packaging only, and it preempted any other federal, state, and local action regarding the marketing of cigarettes. The FTC had stated that, unless Congress specifically prevented it from acting, it would press forward with its rule that required warning messages in advertising. The key purpose of the preemption clause, therefore, was to prevent the FTC from enforcing its rule, ensuring the industry's wish that only product packaging would display a warning. Also, because many states had warning label legislation in the works, the industry pressed for the preemption to bar any other governmental body from enacting a stronger warning message. Consequently, Magnuson's preemption clause weakened the bill and antagonized many antismokers. In fact, the bill was so geared toward the industry's interests that it was nearly identical to the bill under consideration in the House, authored by tobacco industry supporter Walter Rogers.

But Magnuson's bill was not the only warning label measure placed before the Senate committee. Neuberger, a more entrenched and impassioned antismoker than Magnuson, had proposed a bill that required a warning label on cigarette packages, mandated the disclosure of nicotine and tar levels on packages, and included a vague proposal to eliminate cigarette advertising that appealed to children. Most important, Neuberger's version supported the FTC in its intention to regulate cigarette advertising. The dispute between Neuberger's and Magnuson's bills centered on FTC authority. Unlike in the House, where a decision in favor of the tobacco industry was assumed, the Senate committee confronted a difficult decision between two bills representing differing positions on federal agency power and tobacco industry clout. Senators deliberated over the merits of the preemption clause and over how long such a moratorium on federal agency action should last. In an eleven-to-two vote, the committee favored Magnuson's bill, but antismokers did amend it to limit the preemption period to three years.[44]

The major difference between the House and Senate bills was that the House committee had suspended FTC action indefinitely. Both committees publicly justified the preemption by pointing to the industry's efforts at self-regulation. The House committee seemed assured that the industry's Cigarette Advertising Code had indeed improved the "character of cigarette advertising," and no further regulation was necessary, but the Senate decided it would give the industry three years to see whether the industry's code, along with smoking education campaigns and the warning label on packages, would ameliorate the problems caused by cigarette smoking.[45]

Most antismoking activists, however, deplored any government policy on smoking that left untouched cigarette advertising. Several members of Congress, including Frank Moss and Robert Kennedy, vigorously opposed the preemption clause, even with a three-year limit, and pledged to filibuster the bill when it came up on the floor. In the House, Representative John Moss of California accused the Commerce Committee of legislating "to the whims of a special interest." "The endorsement of this legislation," he argued, "puts the Federal Government in the position of saying that cigarette smoking constitutes a serious health hazard, but that traditional guardians of public health . . . cannot act to protect their citizens if they believe a warning statement in cigarette advertising would do so." Others argued that the preemption was unprecedented in federal law and amounted to special treatment for the tobacco industry. The FTC, the Department of Health, Education, and Welfare, and the National Interagency Council on Smoking and Health (which encompassed thirteen voluntary health organizations) all opposed the preemption clause. The controversy also attracted the attention of the liberal organization Americans for Democratic Action, which added its voice to the protests against the weak cigarette labeling bills.[46]

In conference committee, members of the Senate and House Commerce Committees hammered out a compromise. Under pressure from tobacco lobbyists, they agreed to the watered-down warning: "Caution: Cigarette Smoking May Be Hazardous to Your Health" instead of Neuberger's proposal, which stated smoking "is dangerous to your health." To smooth over the most glaring discrepancy, the House acceded to the Senate's three-year limit on the preemption of regulation by other government bodies. In exchange, the Senate loosened its rules for the placement and size of the warning label on packages and granted the industry's wish to extend the preemption expiration from 1 January to 1 July 1969, to push the issue into the next session of Congress and allow the tobacco interests more time to maneuver. Another provision of the bill, proposed by the Senate members of the conference committee, required annual reports from the FTC and the Department of Health, Education, and Welfare on the current state of cigarette advertising and health research and allowed the agencies to make policy recommendations.[47]

Antismokers in Congress made last-ditch attempts to strengthen or kill the emasculated labeling bill that emerged from conference committee. In the House, a few members tried unsuccessfully to pass amendments to strengthen it, but none of their protests or amendments really mattered. It was clear to everyone that the antismoking contingent in the House lacked clout. The tobacco lobby already had their votes lined up, and, to no one's surprise, the cigarette labeling bill easily passed the House, 286 to 103.[48]

In the Senate, Kennedy and Neuberger, with the assistance of Americans for Democratic Action, lobbied their fellow senators to join them in supporting an amendment to reduce the preemption period to one year. Although it failed, a respectable showing of twenty-nine senators supported the reduction. When the bill came up for the final vote in the Senate, five antismoking senators—four Democrats and one Mormon Republican—opposed it. But by this time, their cause had lost adherents. This small yet dedicated group was discouraged to learn that other pillars of the antismoking camp, such as the National Interagency Council on Smoking and Health, had decided to support what they considered a mockery of a bill in the expectation that something was better than nothing. In fact, Neuberger even voted for it, reasoning, "this is the first time in the history of the United States that our Government will have gone on record as showing that it is believed there is some relation between smoking and disease. I believe that an educational process is going on."[49] Still, she joined Kennedy and six other members of Congress in sending a letter to President Johnson, urging him not to support the bill. Johnson remained silent and signed the bill.[50]

AFTERMATH AND ASSESSMENT

After the final vote, Magnuson, the named author of the bill, took credit for "a forthright and historic step toward the responsible protection of the health of this Nation's citizens." Tobacco congressmen chimed in with similar disingenuous statements and patted themselves on the back because they knew that the legislation really represented a victory for the tobacco industry.[51] Journalist Elizabeth Brenner Drew saw these pronouncements for what they were. In her insightful *Atlantic Monthly* article "The Quiet Victory of the Cigarette Lobby: How It Found the Best Filter Yet—Congress," she wrote, "[T]he tobacco industry's success at winning from Congress what it wanted while still providing the lawmakers with an opportunity to appear to be all in favor of health was a brilliant stroke."[52]

That the Cigarette Labeling Act served the industry's interests was no secret. The wording of the label was weak, and it appeared only on packaging. Federal agencies as well as states and municipalities were forbidden from requiring other labels, and advertising was left unregulated. The legislation certainly was less stringent than what the FTC rule would have required. Drew could not have made it clearer in her exposé when she declared, "[T]he bill is not, as its sponsors suggested, an example of congressional initiative to protect public health; it is an unabashed act to protect private industry from government regulation." FTC Commissioner Philip Elman deemed the act "one of the dirtiest pieces of legislation ever." The *New York Times* agreed, calling the labeling bill a "shocking piece of special interest legislation" and arguing that the minor concession of a label on packages was a "maneuver to distract attention from this surrender to tobacco interests."[53]

When Michael Pertschuk told his friend Stanley Cohen, Washington reporter for *Advertising Age,* about the legislation, Cohen replied that the bill, especially its preemption clause, was "shocking, shocking." After listening to his friend's reaction, Pertschuk then realized that he had been "overwhelmed, and even seduced, by the glittering phalanxes of a corporate lobby" and had given the tobacco industry nearly everything it had wanted. In a later interview, Pertschuk reflected, "I got caught up in the game plan and did something for which I was not at all proud. . . . I knew that I was really participating in an effort which was in effect cutting off the potential for regulating cigarette advertising." At the time he believed "that the tobacco industry was so powerful and had so many allies in the Senate and in the House, that it would be futile to stand in the way of this legislative juggernaut. So I thought I might as well go along with it and gain the credit for Magnuson as the author of the Bill putting the warning on the package."[54] Magnuson, too, had adopted this attitude of inevitability and firmly believed that the Cigarette Labeling Act was the best legislation that could have passed. He explained to a constituent, "[T]he choice was between excluding advertising and no bill at all. The overwhelming majority of the public health experts agree with me that the bill we passed is much better than no bill at all. You may be assured that I will continue to work for proper safeguards in cigarette advertising." Maurine Neuberger and the National Interagency Council on Smoking and Health also resigned themselves to this reality while promising future action.[55]

In some sense, though, the labeling act can be viewed as an antismoking victory. The antismoking movement in these years should not be dismissed because of the industry's ability to emasculate its proposals. Its existence and efforts, not yet supported by a wider public interest movement, were significant. Although the warning label legislation accomplished less than what reformers had hoped for and much less than what effective regulation of a deadly substance would demand, it did mark official federal government recognition of the problems caused by smoking. It put smoking on the national agenda as a valid issue for Congress and federal agencies to control, and it provoked national-level debate on the federal government's authority to regulate private enterprise and protect public health. Furthermore, it is important to remember that the industry did have to make some concessions. Although it won many strategic victories during the policy battle, many industry members would have preferred no legislation at all.

The cigarette labeling legislation that passed, though weakened by the preemption clause and the refusal to touch advertising, did provide the means for subsequent and stronger actions to control the marketing of cigarettes because it required annual reports from the FTC and the Public Health Service. Provided with this opening, the agencies would not let the issue die. Although prevented from taking any formal action for the remainder of the 1960s, they heightened their antismoking activism and, in the reports they presented to Congress, continually appealed for more stringent measures.[56] Kennedy, Moss, and other members of Congress also continued their activism. By 1969, when the preemption clause's term was about to end, another round of vigorous policy debate over cigarette marketing control seized the federal government.

CONCLUSION

Much of the journalistic and scholarly analysis of this episode in cigarette policymaking concentrates solely on the fascinating political machinations behind the labeling act and explores the questions of which side won and why. Appreciating the raw politics and financial interests that underlay, and in many cases determined, the direction of government policy toward cigarettes is important in understanding marketing control. But the ideological factors that influenced policy debates and outcomes should not be discounted. The ideological arguments presented by both sides were part of an ongoing political-cultural debate that pitted public health against commercial free expression and posed questions about science and objectivity. The central dilemmas raised by the cigarette controversy asked what Americans would accept in their consumer culture and how highly Americans valued public health when it conflicted with the interests of private enterprise.

Not only did the tobacco industry achieve victory in the political fray because of its money, connections, and other resources, but it also prevailed in the ideological contest. In addition to its many other advantages, the industry's charges of discrimination, zealotry, and government intrusion, along with its articulation of the principle of commercial free expression, resonated widely among the nation's policymakers. The antismokers' arguments did not match the potency of the industry's ideological arsenal; the abstract ideology of "public health" could not muster enough rhetorical power to serve as a rallying cry in Americans' struggle to control a profitable industry that made and sold a substance that many consumers desired and that caused the biggest threat to the nation's public health. As America's postwar prowess was peaking, Americans and their policymakers were not ready to confront and challenge the troubling aspects of their pervasive consumer culture, perhaps best represented by the dilemmas surrounding the control of the tobacco industry, arguably the nation's largest and most influential advertiser. In the mid-1960s conflict between commercial free expression and public health, the values of consumerism prevailed.

THE NEXT PUSH

Restricting Advertising

Federal government activity on the cigarette marketing front exploded between 1966 and 1970. Convinced that the warning label law was inadequate, and informed by new scientific studies offering added proof of the deadly consequences of smoking, most antismoking activists believed they needed to take further action to curb smoking, moving from the labeling approach to more interventionist proposals for restricting advertising. Against the backdrop of a burgeoning consumer rights movement and the public's increasing suspicion of business in general, sentiment against both the smoking habit and the big tobacco companies intensified and spread through more sections of the federal government. As part of a growing propensity in American society to question authority and challenge established institutions, the political fortunes of the antismoking campaign, framed as a movement to protect innocent people from an industry that threatened their lives, unquestionably advanced during the second half of the 1960s.

Conflict over commercial free expression dominated the political discussions, but the debates over policy shifted from a focus on labels and health information to a concern over broadcast advertising and exposure to youth. The key questions were whether broadcast advertising, as opposed to other forms of marketing, provided a unique danger to children; and if and how the government could restrict cigarette advertising on television and radio, over constitutional objections. During these years the industry continued to develop its personal liberty arguments. Realizing that their challenge to scientific reports of health hazards was losing effectiveness, industry leaders tried to shift the terms of debate to a question of rights. Although the cigarette makers and their supporters certainly were exploiting, and in some sense manufacturing, the personal liberty and free speech issue, it constituted an important ideological sticking point for many policymakers. Cigarette marketing restrictions once more invoked dilemmas basic to American democratic and consumer society.

Policy efforts during these years featured a mixture of congressional and federal agency action, and combined informal pressure tactics with legislative and administrative mandates. While a handful of committed congressmen were striving to persuade the tobacco companies to refrain voluntarily from certain advertising practices, the Federal Communications Commission issued a decision requiring "equal time" for antismoking messages on broadcast media. At the end of the decade, when efforts to convince the industry to regulate itself more vigorously had failed and the labeling act's preemption clause had expired, Congress passed a new law to ban cigarette advertising from television and radio and strengthen the warning label.

Although activity on these matters was lively and fairly well publicized, the antismoking movement continued to be highly centralized among national policymakers and state level public health officials. This small group of activists may have sensed growing public support for initiatives against the tobacco companies, but they still did not receive, nor did they attempt to organize, genuine grassroots political support for their efforts. (One citizen action group, Action on Smoking and Health, operated on Capitol Hill in the late 1960s, but its organizational development was weak and its popular reach limited.)[1] Until the 1970s, when the focus began to shift to local restrictions on smoking in public places, antismoking policy largely remained a top-down, federal government initiative.

SEARCHING FOR SOLUTIONS BEYOND
THE WARNING LABEL

In the second half of the 1960s, many policymakers, including some prominent antismokers, still had faith in the efficacy of industry self-regulation. They clung to a tradition of corporatism holding that, with public guidance, private parties could pursue and protect the public trust. Influenced by this tradition, some expected Congress's requirement of a warning label to prod the industry into voluntarily exhibiting further responsibility in its marketing, especially because, in its report accompanying the legislation, the Senate had warned that themes in cigarette advertising must not counteract the message in the warning label.[2] Right after passage of the labeling act, dissatisfied members of Congress, particularly Senator

Warren Magnuson—with perhaps a naïve understanding of the industry's politics and his own influence over them—tried to instigate more industry responsibility along these lines.

After the reality set in that the legislation had played right into the industry's hands, and after encountering public criticism for his role in that debacle, Magnuson felt ashamed, and resolved to do penance. Determined to show the public and his colleagues he was not in the industry's pocket and would not let the issue fade with his emasculated labeling bill, he pledged to stay on the cigarette makers' backs and force them to clean up their advertising. Meanwhile, he exposed the contradictions in the federal government's policies toward smoking by questioning the U.S. Department of Agriculture's subsidization of tobacco growers, saving his harshest criticism for the department's funding of the film "Worlds of Pleasure," which extolled smoking.[3]

Magnuson embarked on a crusade of sorts to exhort the tobacco companies to curb their advertising and especially to stop marketing their products to children. In private correspondence, he revealed his aim to engineer for cigarettes something like the distilled spirits situation in which the manufacturers voluntarily removed their advertising from broadcast media. Magnuson clearly viewed alcohol and tobacco policy in a similar light and had credited himself with keeping spirits' advertising off television by periodically threatening the distillers with regulatory action.[4] In letters to Cigarette Advertising Code administrator Robert Meyner, Magnuson pressured the industry to cease its sponsorship of television programs that attracted young viewers. Just two months after passage of his labeling act, Magnuson expressed his ire, in both letters to the industry and a speech to the Senate, that a Kent cigarette commercial had immediately preceded a performance by the Beatles on the *Ed Sullivan Show* and that the television program *Gilligan's Island* was sponsored by the American Tobacco Company. He claimed that such advertising practices effectively negated the warning labels and thus defied the Senate report that stated such negation of the label would not be tolerated. In his correspondence with Meyner, Magnuson questioned whether the industry was truly able to police itself responsibly and wondered "whether, indeed, additional legislation is necessary concerning restraints upon cigarette advertising." As a further threat, he reminded the tobacco interests that cigarette advertising recently had been banned from television in Great Britain.[5]

Instead of being put to rest by the warning label law, the dilemma grew, accompanied by delicate policy questions: how could government protect youth from the marketing of a legal consumer product? In what ways could media's audiences be limited without trampling on First Amendment rights? Apart from an outright ban on television advertising, a solution to the problem of exposure to youth proved elusive. Nearly every television show, along with many popular radio programs and magazines, attracted at least some percentage of youthful viewers, and the most popular programs, such as the *Ed Sullivan Show* and major sporting events, drew large audiences of both children and adults. Meyner agreed with Magnuson that an important part of his job as code administrator was to eliminate cigarette advertising's appeal to youth, but he found himself, in the words of one observer, "faced with the ghastly problem of somehow separating [appeals directed primarily to youth] from appeals made to young and old alike, which under the code are completely permissible." The code's requirement that the actors be at least twenty-five years of age did not mollify Magnuson and like-minded officials. Meyner did finally devise a formula that prohibited the broadcast of cigarette advertising on a program attracting at least 45 percent of viewers who were younger than twenty-one. (He chose the standard of 45 percent because the latest census had found that 41 percent of the population was under the age of twenty-one.) The new guideline meant that more cigarette sponsors shifted to programs broadcast later in the evening.[6] Magnuson dropped the matter for the time being, but he and Robert Kennedy would take it up again in 1967 with added persistence.

Although it had its knuckles rapped by the preemption clause in the labeling law, the Federal Trade Commission refused to crouch in the corner. The FTC joined Magnuson's offensive against objectionable cigarette advertising in November 1965, when it wrote to all cigarette companies, tobacco industry associations, and the National Association of Broadcasters Broadcasters, warning that it would "proceed against advertising which tends to negate or obscure the health warning on the package." Furthermore, in a challenge to industry self-regulation, the FTC told the companies it considered their advertising code "to be inadequately designed to achieve Congress's objective that the public should in no way be misled or dulled into a false sense of security." But Meyner was steadfast in his defense of the industry's system of self-regulation, declaring that the code was "completely compatible with the Cigarette Labeling Act." Meyner also told the commissioners their concerns were outdated, for many of the themes identified as objectionable in the FTC's report were now prohibited under the code.[7]

Although it had not radically changed the face of cigarette advertising, the industry's effort at self-regulation did result in some modifications in the mid-1960s. Advertisers found they had to be more careful and clever to comply with the code, yet they did not have to abandon some of the most effective themes in cigarette advertising. One adman explained, "You can't win a swimming meet, then pull yourself out of the pool and reach for a cigarette, the way we used to do it. . . . So we're limited to the less athletic sports. We go sailing, we go trout fishing. We can have boy-girl fun in the water, but if we want to show surfing, the smokers are on the beach waiting." He explained another new tactic: "[T]he guy who has been swimming or water skiing, he'll change his clothes or put on a shirt, to indicate a time lapse—then he's allowed to smoke." A further change in advertising, the adman continued, was that "nobody is allowed to inhale deeply any longer. Nor is he permitted to do a big take, or reach with a huge smile. . . . It isn't supposed to look like they're taking dope. We need a very short, fast draft, and then a very fast exhale. . . . It's not the greatest thing that ever happened to him. It's just good." He concluded by observing, "You see, the cigarette companies are in a strange spot these days—they're trying to say the stuff's great and not say it, at the same time." These alterations did not prove a major obstacle for the cigarette companies, and, most important, they did not dampen sales. A tobacco executive reflected, "That's the reason no one is really worried about the code. They can't stop us from showing good-looking people doing good-looking things."[8] And it was this precise tactic—portraying cigarette smoking as attractive—that was the industry's most persuasive selling point. Ironically, as cigarette advertising came under increasing attack, its sell became softer, which not only assuaged, or at least stymied, its critics and prolonged its tenure on television, but also turned out to be a more effective way to sell cigarettes. Self-regulation was not such a bad deal after all, and the cigarette makers probably understood this all along.[9]

While tobacco industry members blithely faced criticism of their advertising campaigns through 1967, broadcasters felt more nervous. As members of an industry licensed to broadcast in the "public interest," they saw themselves as more vulnerable to charges of corrupting youth. After the New York office of the NAB's code authority prepared a study declaring "the cumulative impact of cigaret [sic] commercials on the air is to make smoking seem universally acceptable, attractive and desirable," the association tightened its cigarette advertising guidelines. In terms of portraying athletic activity, the NAB's guidelines were now more stringent than the tobacco industry's.[10]

Three major cigarette manufacturers chafed against the new NAB rules and complained about having to submit their advertising to both the Cigarette Advertising Code and the NAB for approval. An internal NAB memo reported that "over-all cooperation by cigaret [sic] manufacturers has become more token than real." As early as 1967, some NAB officials were predicting the imminent end of broadcast cigarette advertising, and the NAB general counsel advised broadcasters to begin looking for sources of revenue to replace it.[11] As the pressure heightened, the two industries, which in the past had joined forces to fight the antismokers, found themselves increasingly at odds. By 1969, when a ban on broadcast cigarette advertising was impending, the broadcasters and the tobacco executives would try to sell each other out.

THE TAR AND NICOTINE DISPUTE

Industry self-regulation requires significant cooperation among industry members, and it was only a matter of time before the tobacco companies let competition undermine their solidarity under the Code. Intraindustry disputes were abetted by actions of certain antismoking government officials, and the biggest cause of dissension was the question of whether cigarette marketing should disclose tar and nicotine levels. Since 1960, the FTC had forbidden such disclosures in an effort to halt the fraudulent claims that had provoked the 1950s tar derby. The FTC triggered the new debate when, persuaded by leading antismokers, particularly Daniel Horn, director of the newly established National Clearinghouse on Smoking and Health, it did an about-face in early 1966 and suspended its earlier rule. Subsequently, the Commission set up a laboratory to test the contents of cigarettes, allowing it to authenticate the companies' tar and nicotine claims.[12]

Despite the green light from the FTC, the industry's code continued to forbid mention of nicotine and tar in advertising. The atmosphere had changed significantly since the 1950s, when tobacco companies had exploited the health theme by discussing "smoker's cough" or the power of their filters to block harmful tar from entering the lungs. The industry understood, first, that misleading statements pertaining to nicotine and tar had landed them in trouble in the past, and, second, it was in the interest of at least most brands not to draw attention to health matters. The most important reason why cigarette manufacturers did not want to disclose their contents, however, was their understanding that packing their cigarettes with undisclosed high amounts of these substances was what attracted and hooked their customers. Meyner's stated rationale for continuing the prohibition was that because no connection had been proven between smoking and illness, tar and nicotine information was meaningless. In other words, disclosing the contents would imply that some cigarettes were safer than others, and thus at least some cigarettes were hazardous—an implication most members of the industry wished to avoid.[13]

But one company, Lorillard, was gratified by the FTC's decision because it wanted to tout the low nicotine and tar levels in its Kent brand. In a threat to the industry's unity, Lorillard officially broke from the code in late 1966 and pressed on with its marketing campaign for Kent, emphasizing the hot-button theme of health. As an additional menace, Lorillard executives developed amicable relationships with Magnuson and his aide Michael Pertschuk, both of whom supported the tobacco company in its tar and nicotine position. The industry's solidarity further deteriorated when American Tobacco abandoned the code in 1967. Although the industry finally revised its code in 1968 to allow nicotine and tar information in cigarette advertising, only a few brands took advantage of the sanction.[14]

REGULATING BROADCAST CIGARETTE ADVERTISING

The climate continued to worsen for the cigarette companies as the policy discussion increasingly focused on a broadcast advertising ban, revisiting the controversy over the limits of commercial free expression. Dissatisfied with the earlier focus on a product label, antismokers chose as their next arena the regulation of radio and television because they believed that, compared to print media, broadcast media were passively received and could much more effectively permeate the consumer's senses. They assumed that radio and especially television were more difficult to tune out and avoid, and therefore advertising messages in broadcast media were more controlling and dangerous, especially to youth. Robert Kennedy contended that, among all media, television was "particularly formative of youth attitudes."[15]

Furthermore, antismokers considered broadcast media to be unique because the airwaves served the public interest and therefore were regulated by the Federal Communications Commission. No other media had its own federal government regulatory commission. Senator Ralph Yarborough (D-TX), in an antismoking speech before the Senate in 1968, characterized the broadcast airwaves as a "national resource, like rivers and mountains" that belonged to all Americans. Yarborough distinguished radio and television from print media by contending that "a newspaper or magazine is privately owned and can pursue its own advertising policy, but the communication spectrum above the earth cannot be anyone's private property." Kennedy and others noted that broadcasters had already admitted their difference from other media when they voluntarily banned the advertisement of hard liquor and firearms; they naturally should extend this policy to cigarettes as well.[16] Convinced that they possessed the legal authority to regulate broadcast advertising, the antismokers' next policy objective became the curtailment and ultimately the ban of cigarette advertising from the air.

In 1967 a movement began in earnest either to persuade broadcasters and cigarette manufacturers to remove cigarette advertising from radio and television voluntarily or to mandate this removal through congressional legislation. Three principal developments contributed to the push for a broadcast ban. First, the FTC and the Public Health Service released their highly critical reports on cigarette marketing and the health consequences of smoking, respectively, as required by the 1965 labeling law. To the dismay of industry supporters, it became clear that neither of these federal government agencies had been muzzled by the law's preemption clause. Second, Senator Kennedy began an aggressive campaign to persuade the tobacco and broadcasting industries to cease marketing cigarettes to youth. Finally, the FCC ruled that, under its Fairness Doctrine, broadcasters must allow a significant amount of time for antismoking messages.

The FTC and Public Health Service Persist

The FTC's strongly worded 1967 report to Congress included a thorough review of the themes used in cigarette advertising and concluded that, when compared with cigarette advertising before the labeling law, "there has been no significant change in the basic appeals made. Advertising continues to depict smoking as an enjoyable activity while ignoring completely the health hazards." Similar to the temperance activists in the 1950s who complained that alcohol ads never showed skid rows, violence, or disease, the FTC criticized cigarette ads for failing to depict "an habituated cigarette smoker with a hacking cough . . . [or] the tension felt by a chain smoker when he runs out of cigarettes." To the FTC, both the industry's efforts at self-regulation and the warning label on packages failed to overcome the power of advertising to create the impression of smoking "as a harmless and enjoyable social activity that is not habit forming and involves no hazards to health." The Commission recommended stronger wording for the warning label as well as its inclusion in cigarette advertising.[17]

Commissioner Philip Elman, however, believed that these recommendations did not go far enough and in a separate statement advocated banning cigarette advertising from broadcast media. Elman, like many antismokers, believed "the airwaves constitute[d] a public resource" and that broadcast cigarette advertising proved more insidious than advertising in other media. He argued a warning message in advertising would be meaningless because "we can be sure that all cigarette commercials will be skillfully written to blot out the effect of the warning." To his mind, cigarette advertising could be effectively curbed only by prohibiting it altogether from television and radio and including a stronger and more conspicuous warning label in other forms of cigarette marketing.[18]

By the next year, the Commission had adopted Elman's position, and its 1968 report to Congress recommended the complete ban of cigarette advertising from television and radio. Significantly, in support of the proposed broadcast ban one commissioner contrasted cigarette policy with alcohol policy, arguing that they ought to be congruous: "[T]he hazard to health presented by cigarette smoking is at least as great as that associated with liquor consumption, and the exposure of this hazard to teenagers is far greater. Yet the states have instituted rigorous controls on advertising of liquor, and no hard liquor advertisements appear on TV. I believe that the evidence at hand fully supports the institution of a similar ban on cigarette advertising." Dissenting from his colleagues, chairman Paul Rand Dixon opposed a broadcast ban as too drastic. In a separate statement he argued that, if a warning label appeared in broadcast advertising, "the public interest would be sufficiently protected" and no ban would be necessary.[19] These opposing viewpoints on the advisability of a ban created a dilemma in the antismoking movement that would prompt controversy through 1969 and after.

The Public Health Service's reports to Congress reviewed more than two thousand studies relating to smoking and health published since the Surgeon General's Report of 1964. The 1967 and 1968 reports concluded that recent research more strongly linked smoking with illness, providing additional validation to the conclusions made in 1964. In August 1968, while stopping short of a call for its ban, the surgeon general recommended drastic changes in cigarette advertising and the implementation of more potent antismoking campaigns. Bolstered by the aggressive and somewhat surprising recommendations of the FTC and the Public Health Service, the American Cancer Society and the World Conference on Smoking and Health took a significant step for the movement by publicly advocating the termination of all cigarette advertising.[20]

Under siege, the tobacco industry geared up its public relations machine to retaliate against both agencies. The Tobacco Institute blasted the Public Health Service report as "a mixture of unsupported recommendations and a few carefully chosen citations" and charged that it ignored copious research to the contrary. Robert Meyner took on the FTC, pointing out falsities and questionable statistical methods in its report. As for the FTC's rationale that a cigarette ad was inherently deceptive if it failed to disclose potential harm, Meyner responded, "The Code has not descended to the illogical position that the absence of any claim in these areas is automatically a claim that cigarette smoking is safe."[21] But to most commissioners and many other antismokers, this position was precisely logical and was the principal reason why broadcast cigarette advertising, if not all cigarette advertising, had to be stopped.

RFK On the Scene

Although he had been largely absent from the antismoking crusade since the passage of the labeling act, Kennedy rejoined the movement with vigor in 1967, adding heat to the flames surrounding the tobacco industry. Like Magnuson, he pegged his hopes on industry self-regulation and believed the best solution would arise when the companies voluntarily restricted their marketing. Kennedy asked all of the tobacco companies to make a greater effort to regulate themselves and especially to curb their appeal to young people. Perhaps, he wrote to the companies, "your own action in the coming month would make . . . legislation, as well as an experimental ban [on broadcast advertising] unnecessary." But Kennedy did not wait for the companies' responses. During the next month he introduced three antismoking bills in an effort to pressure the industry into voluntary action. His first bill required a warning label in all cigarette advertising and gave the FTC the power to regulate the form and position of the warning in the advertisements. The second bill empowered the FCC to restrict cigarette advertising's appeal to youth in broadcast media, for instance by prohibiting the broadcast of cigarette ads before 9 p.m. (a proposal drawn up by the National Congress of Parents and Teachers). And in an effort to persuade, or coerce, the companies to manufacture safer cigarettes, Kennedy's most innovative bill proposed the imposition of higher taxes on those cigarettes that contained more tar and nicotine.[22]

Other members of Congress remained committed to the regulation of cigarette marketing during these years. Nevertheless, although four years had passed since the release of the Surgeon General's Report, a genuine grassroots antismoking movement still had not emerged to support and pressure them. Forty-two House members joined together under the leadership of Representative John Moss (D-CA) to sponsor bills similar to those proposed by Kennedy, but they did not even receive a hearing.[23] Antismoking politicians understood that these policy proposals were only symbolic. Considering the absence of active public support, none of the legislation stood a chance for passage before 1969, the year that the 1965 labeling law would expire. Pertschuk, still working for Magnuson and the Senate Commerce Committee, told *Consumer Reports* that most of the mail received by senators in support of antismoking measures came from "doctors or religious fundamentalists." In his view, "It will take much more broad-gauged public pressure to get a law through."[24]

Kennedy continued his activism by inviting industry executives to a "summit meeting," during which advertising issues and his legislative proposals would be discussed. At the meeting, which occurred in October of 1967 in Washington, D.C., and included about thirty people, Kennedy assuaged the industry men by reiterating his preference for industry self-regulation and his opposition to prohibition, yet he did not hold back when he pushed the executives to find ways to diminish cigarettes' appeal to youth. For instance, he suggested that the companies withdraw their ads from television and radio during early evening, "prime time" hours. Kennedy was particularly bothered by tobacco sponsorship of televised professional football games because he was certain many young boys watched them. Kennedy asked the executives to use a lower standard than 45 percent for determining a youth audience and recommended going even further by establishing a ceiling on the absolute number of young people who viewed programs sponsored by tobacco companies. He reasoned that, even if a football game drew less than 45 percent of its viewing audience from youth, the audience was still so large that millions of youth were being exposed to cigarette commercials. He also tried to persuade the companies to refrain from depicting smoking as so attractive and enticing and to follow the lead of liquor advertisers by encouraging moderate consumption in their marketing campaigns. Nothing much came of this meeting, for relations deteriorated when Kennedy discovered that, although one company had acceded to his earlier request to cease sponsorship of professional sporting events on television, another cigarette manufacturer had taken over the sponsorship contract right when the summit meeting began. Kennedy considered this a show of "bad faith" and stopped the discussions.[25]

Kennedy not only reached out to the tobacco companies, but also involved the sports establishment and the broadcast industry in his discussions about cigarette marketing. He wrote to all professional team owners, head coaches, league commissioners, and National Collegiate Athletic Association officials, asking them to do what they could to curb cigarette advertising during sporting events. He also wrote to the heads of the broadcast networks, trying to persuade them of their responsibility to guard the public health, even in the absence of a government mandate. Simply, he asked the networks to accept fewer cigarette advertisements. He also repeated some of the suggestions he had made to the tobacco executives, including late night broadcast of cigarette ads and changing the standards for determination of a youth audience. Broadcasters, though, were resistant to his proposals and complained they were being unfairly singled out by antismoking activists. Julian Goodman, president of NBC, responded to Kennedy, "Since young people are included in the audiences for magazines, newspapers, billboards, and most radio and television programs, the sense of your suggestion is tantamount to a proposal that all cigarette advertising be barred."[26] Goodman's statement spoke to the difficulty in restricting children's access to mass media, but government officials such as Kennedy were determined to find a policy solution.

The FCC Mandates Fairness

Debates over the rights and responsibilities of the broadcast media grew more heated as a result of the FCC's ground-breaking 1967 decision applying the Fairness Doctrine to cigarette advertising. For at least ten years antismoking activists had been arguing that, as the guardian of the public's airwaves, the FCC should regulate cigarette advertising on television and radio. After passage of the cigarette labeling act, the FCC warmed to this idea, especially because its chairman, Rosel Hyde, was a Utah Mormon, and its powerful general counsel, Henry Geller, was a committed antismoker.[27] Signaling the Commission's increasingly antismoking bent, in 1966 an FCC official delivered a speech very critical of broadcasters—at the National Association of Broadcasters' annual meeting, no less—and lambasted them for their irresponsibility on the issue of cigarette advertising. He claimed, "From the cigarette advertising presently being carried on radio and television stations, no one would ever know that a major public controversy is in progress as to the harmful effects of cigarette smoking on the American public." In the FCC's opinion, "the sign on broadcasting's door for cigarette advertisers reads 'Business as usual.'" The FCC official characterized the smoking issue as a "major test of self-regulation for the broadcast industry," and told his audience that the industry had "not only failed to pass this test of self-regulation—it hasn't even taken it."[28]

Not long afterward, the Commission received a letter from a young lawyer named John F. Banzhaf III, arguing that the Fairness Doctrine should be applied to cigarette advertising. The Fairness Doctrine was a tradition in American broadcasting that had been codified several times since the 1920s, both by the federal government and by broadcasters themselves. It held that broadcasters should provide equal time to air opposing views on controversial issues of importance to the public, and the FCC considered it to be the bedrock principle of responsible broadcasting. One commissioner asserted that the Fairness Doctrine "ensures that the most powerful medium of mass communication in our society does not stifle competition in the market place of ideas." But over the forty-some years of its existence, the doctrine had never specifically been applied to advertising. Instead, it pertained mainly to political issues, personal attacks, and other controversies on which a broadcast station might be prone to editorialize.[29]

Antismoking advocates were not the first to think of using the Fairness Doctrine to restrict advertising. In 1948, drys urged the FCC to apply the doctrine to alcohol advertising, but the Commission demonstrated the federal government's reluctance to deal with alcoholic beverages by dodging the issue and refusing to make a determination. But in 1967, when the issue was cigarettes, the FCC seized the use of the doctrine. As one commissioner who was dubious about the ruling on cigarettes observed, it was not that any administrative principle had changed since 1948, it was simply that the commissioners were, as a group, opposed to cigarette smoking.[30]

In reaction to Banzhaf's complaint and also to Senator Magnuson's urgings to employ the doctrine, in June 1967 the FCC declared the applicability of the Fairness Doctrine to cigarette advertising. It required television and radio stations to provide a reasonable amount of time—the ruling stopped short of requiring equal time, and the ratio ended up being about one to three—to antismoking messages, as a way to counter prodigious cigarette advertising. According to the ruling, cigarette smoking unquestionably constituted a controversial issue of public importance. Cigarettes were a unique case, the FCC argued, because their normal use endangered the lives of millions of Americans; they clearly proved a unique threat to public health. The Public Health Service, Congress, and the Federal Trade Commission had all stated as such, the FCC emphasized. It was simply a matter of decency for broadcasters, who accepted millions of dollars of cigarette advertising revenue, to also provide some information about the hazards of this product.[31]

The FCC's ruling, which came as a surprise to most everyone, especially the broadcasting and tobacco industries, caused an uproar and sparked a lively debate over the constitutional role of government in the media and commerce. Several congressmen, most from tobacco states but some from other parts of the country, addressed Congress on several occasions to draw attention to the iniquities of the FCC ruling. Undoubtedly, it was a landmark decision and a departure from past policy. One member of Congress declared that the ruling contained the "potential of dramatically altering the content of public broadcasting." North Carolina's Walter Jones was harsher in his depiction of the ruling's impact, calling it "staggering in its invasion of congressional authority and its usurpation of power over the news and programming content of our radio and television stations." A congressman from California, who was also an advertising executive, was similarly distressed by the potential damage, both politically and constitutionally, of the FCC's decision. He viewed it as "a gross power grab by a Federal agency trying to control the content of programming of our Nation's broadcasting media. . . . We must not allow regulatory bureaucrats to dictate what broadcasters—or any other of our free media must tell audiences. And they must not be allowed to dictate the terms under which legal products may be advertised. Such Big Brotherism is not the way of free democracy."[32] While these opponents' condemnation echoed the criticism of the FTC's ruling in 1964, the FCC's ruling was even more troubling because it involved government intervention into the media and therefore touched even more directly on cherished First Amendment rights.

FCC Commissioner Lee Loevinger, though ultimately concurring with the Fairness Doctrine ruling, was deeply troubled by its implications. He insisted the doctrine was meant to apply to "news," "commentary," and "discussion of public issues," categories that excluded advertising. The NAB agreed with Loevinger's assessment and released a statement that asserted "product advertising in and of itself does not involve the discussion of a public issue." NBC declared that cigarette ads did not explicitly discuss whether smoking is or is not a health hazard and therefore should not be viewed as controversial. Commissioner Nicholas Johnson, by contrast, defended the doctrine's application to advertising by declaring that, because advertisements were "an important and substantial part of the information put before the public by television and radio broadcasting," they should not be exempt from fairness considerations. Because cigarette advertising took a controversial position that was "of the public moment," Johnson asserted, the FCC was justified in requiring the "other side" to be aired.[33]

Commissioner Loevinger had other reasons for disputing the FCC's ruling. In a statement that speaks to the question of values and policymaking, Loevinger argued that, at base, the FCC's decision was based on "sentiment" rather than on "legal authority." In the last few years he had become thoroughly convinced that smoking was extremely hazardous and agreed wholeheartedly that the cigarette industry should be restricted. In a moralistic statement, Loevinger called the marketing of cigarettes to young people "something very close to wickedness," but he recognized that his antismoking convictions were based on sentiment and doubted that the Commission had the legal jurisdiction to require antismoking messages in broadcast media. Loevinger asked his fellow commissioners to question what the term "public interest" really meant and to distinguish their sentiments from their legal reasoning. "The 'public interest,'" he wrote, "is a judgment encompassing whatever the person making the judgment deems to be socially desirable." We must be careful, he counseled, because "the Commission has not been given a roving mandate by Congress to do whatever it may regard as socially desirable (i.e. 'in the public interest')." Although Loevinger did not go as far as those members of Congress who accused the FCC of "Big Brotherism," he did point out a valid concern about the power of federal agencies to dictate their values to the nation, especially the FCC in its influence over the media.[34]

Opponents were also disturbed by the "slippery slope" capacity of the FCC's ruling. Could not the FCC proceed to require "equal time" for every advertised product that attracted adversaries? Would we next see antiautomobile messages and antimargarine public service announcements? Representative Jones exclaimed, "[M]y head reels as I consider the possibilities of the evils that may be committed under the enormous stretching of the innocuous sounding 'fairness doctrine.'" Another member of Congress was convinced that antialcohol messages would be the next topic under consideration by the FCC.[35] Just as those who argued that once warning labels were mandated for cigarettes, every other objectionable product would have a warning label slapped on it, opponents of the FCC ruling believed that the federal government had set yet another dangerous precedent in the realm of marketing and media.

Another objection to the FCC ruling stemmed from the design of the 1965 labeling law. A group of congressmen, as well as Commissioner Loevinger, maintained that the FCC's action violated the preemption clause that had forbidden federal agency regulation of cigarettes, but the FCC believed it was not subverting but indeed upholding the intention of the 1965 Act by implementing the "smoking education campaigns" that were also called for in the legislation.[36]

Commissioner Johnson replied to critiques of the ruling by reiterating that the cigarette was a very unique product in that it constituted a dire threat to human health through its normal use. Every other hypothetical case for Fairness Doctrine applicability, he asserted, was "more questionable" than the case of cigarettes. True, he conceded, "this decision *could* be extended to other situations." But as in all legal procedures, the Commission would carefully consider each case to decide whether it met the test of being a "controversial issue of public importance." He doubted whether any other advertised product would reach the level of controversy and significance of cigarettes. Trying to put the ruling in perspective, Johnson reminded the opponents that the FCC had not gone so far as to mandate a broadcast ban on cigarette advertising, and he predicted that the requirement of time for antismoking messages would not negatively affect the tobacco or broad-casting industries. According to Johnson, when he considered other routes that the federal government could take to restrict cigarette marketing, the rul-ing was only "a mild form of regulation." Most broadcasters, though, consid-ered the FCC's action harsh and appealed the ruling.[37]

In the appeal, the federal appeals court upheld the FCC, disappointing champions of commercial free speech. The decision, however, exposed the antismoking movement's dilemma over the status of cigarette advertising in terms of constitutional law and government regulation. Could advertising be viewed as public expression, subject to regulation just as any other form of speech would be? Or was advertising in a separate category, protected by a unique principle of commercial free speech and therefore exempt from FCC oversight? The FCC had portrayed cigarette advertising, and advertising in general, as contributing to the marketplace of ideas and public issues, but such a characterization of advertising would leave it open to First Amend-ment protection. The court, though it ultimately supported the Fairness Doc-trine ruling, used a different argument, minimizing advertising's role in American public life and concluding it did not enjoy the same First Amend-ment protections as did other types of expression. Presiding Judge David Bazelon wrote, "[T]he speech which might conceivably be chilled by [the Fairness Doctrine] ruling barely qualifies as Constitutionally protected speech. . . . As a rule it does not affect the political process, does not con-tribute to the exchange of ideas, does not provide information of matters of public importance, and is not, except perhaps for admen, a form of individ-ual self expression. It is rather a form of merchandising, subject to limitation for public purposes like any other business practices." In making that argu-ment and carefully defining the cigarette case as unique the appeals court minimized the constitutional issues at stake in order to preclude review by the Supreme Court. Still, because it determined that the FCC could in a sense regulate commercial advertising, the decision set an important precedent for marketing policy and for the consumer movement more generally.[38]

As a result of the Fairness Doctrine ruling, Americans in the late 1960s saw and heard numerous, imaginative, and by most accounts effective an-tismoking spots on television and radio. In addition, these years saw the first notable decline in the number of smokers since the brief scare follow-ing the publication of the Surgeon General's Report in 1964. Many ob-servers believed the fierce antismoking campaign being waged in the broadcast media had caused the decline in smoking as well as measurable increases in antismoking attitudes as documented by public opinion sur-veys. The situation had never looked better for antismoking advocates, and they were determined to take advantage of the moment and push for a complete ban on broadcast cigarette advertising. Many of the activists, however, failed to realize that a broadcast advertising ban would arrest the counteradvertising currently required by the FCC.[39]

Tobacco industry members acutely understood that their political influence and public image were suffering. Trying to recapture the offensive, the industry planted pro-tobacco articles in *True* magazine and the *National Enquirer,* causing something of a scandal when the true authorship was revealed.[40] In addition, the business magazine *Barron's* published a hard-hitting piece in October 1967 entitled "Dangerous Lengths: The Federal Crusade Against Smoking Has Gone Too Far." After detailing the recent efforts of the "tyrannical" antismoking movement, including the actions of "the demagogue" Robert Kennedy, the article declared, "What began a few years ago as a seemingly well-intentioned, if disturbing, effort to brainwash the citizenry into kicking the habit thus has spiraled into a crusade as menacing and ugly as Prohibition."[41] The tobacco industry eagerly ordered numerous reprints of the *Barron's* article and distributed them to policymakers and other potential friends across the nation.

Tobacco executives tried other tactics to strengthen their hand as they prepared for the legislative battle in 1969. The Tobacco Institute released a pamphlet entitled "The Cigarette Controversy: Eight Questions and Answers" as part of the industry's ongoing effort to cast doubt on the solid scientific evidence against cigarette smoking. In addition, Horace Kornegay, who had been congressman from North Carolina, took a new job as a star lobbyist for the Tobacco Institute. Now, both Kornegay and Earle Clements, as former members of Congress, had floor privileges. Despite these moves, the industry's strategy could not overcome the antismoking forces as readily as it had four years earlier.

THE POLITICS OF 1969: MANEUVERING A BROADCAST BAN

Everyone with a stake in the cigarette policy arena was focused on the summer of 1969, when the labeling law's preemption clause was set to expire. Once more, the nation's policymakers faced tough questions about commercial speech, bureaucratic versus legislative power, and the authority of scientific evidence. Although many of the questions were the same as in the earlier debate, power relations had altered since 1965.

Antismoking Advantages, Strategies, and Dilemmas

As before, congressional committees held extensive hearings on the cigarette controversy—House Commerce Committee Chairman Harley Staggers pronounced them the longest congressional hearings in his memory—and much of the testimony repeated that heard in 1964 and 1965.[42] There was, however, a palpable difference. By 1969, the antismoking movement's influence in Washington, D.C., had grown significantly, and its leaders were more savvy and politically sophisticated. Pertschuk and Magnuson were determined not to repeat the mistakes they had made during the 1965 legislative process. Although the movement suffered from the loss of Robert Kennedy, who was assassinated in 1968, Senator Frank Moss of Utah emerged as an effective spokesman for the cause. Federal agencies were more united, persuasive, and aggressive than they had been five years earlier, and antismoking organizations such as the American Cancer Society had become, in the words of one commentator, "far more vocal and visible." Add to that the growing numbers of committed members of Congress, and the antismoking coalition in the federal government proved formidable in 1969.[43]

In addition, as journalist Elizabeth Drew and others observed, antismoking sentiment seemed to be catching on among the American public. One important factor in the rise of the antismokers' fortunes was that the consumer movement and Ralph Nader had become more politically fashionable in the late 1960s. As Drew noted, "[A] number of politicians have learned that defending the consumer is good politics." The tobacco industry was also hurt by the fact that many of Clements's political contacts were no longer in positions of power after 1968. And most damaging, the tobacco industry no longer enjoyed the staunch support of the broadcasting and advertising industries. Drew commented, "Despite the cigarette industry's warning that what is at stake is the freedom to advertise in general, the advertising industry is keeping its distance." The broadcasting industry had special reasons for withdrawing from the tobacco coalition.[44]

The antismokers' political strategy was to let the preemption clause, which had restricted federal agencies' ability to regulate cigarettes, expire by thwarting the tobacco coalition's efforts to extend the 1965 labeling act. Once freed from the clause, the FTC would finally be able to implement its 1964 rule that required warning messages in cigarette advertisements, and the FCC could continue to push for further regulations of broadcast cigarette advertising. Both agencies were certain to be aggressive. Just before the 1969 showdown, the FCC stated its intention to ban cigarette advertising from broadcast media. The surprise announcement ignited another contentious debate about the limits of federal agency power, especially as it involved restrictions on media, an area many policymakers believed dangerously impinged on fundamental American freedoms. Again, the specter of Big Brother was raised.[45]

Presented with the proposals of the FTC and the FCC, antismokers confronted a dilemma: should broadcast cigarette advertisements be allowed to continue if they featured a warning message, or would it be better to ban broadcast cigarette ads altogether? What would be the best policy to protect public health? While most members of the antismoking coalition, including most FTC commissioners, supported a broadcast ban, important figures such as Surgeon General William Stewart and the FTC's Paul Rand

Dixon did not. Stewart and Dixon opposed a ban because they firmly believed that instead of seizing information from the American public, a democratic consumer society would be better served by the conferral of even more information. More information to the consumer, they believed, would come from allowing cigarette ads that included an effective warning and from the continuation of antismoking messages as required by the Fairness Doctrine. Allowing both sides of the smoking controversy to present their ideas, this camp of antismokers argued, would provide true democratic free expression.[46] In contrast, most antismokers believed broadcast cigarette advertising was so powerfully insidious that a warning message could never counterbalance it. They painted their objective as protecting the nation's youth from the hazards of smoking, not preserving the industry's right to advertise or defending some abstract concept of freedom, and the most effective measure to prevent children's exposure to cigarettes was the termination of broadcast advertising. To them, a free market of ideas did not apply in this situation where the consequences were deadly and the cigarette marketers held so much influence.

Another ramification to be considered was the effect on warning labels: if a broadcast ban were enacted, the FTC's proposal to require warning labels in advertising would apply only to print media. Antismokers had always considered print advertising less damaging and tended to discount the impact of a warning message in a print ad. If broadcast cigarette advertising were to cease, however, a warning label in print would become more critical. Antismokers, especially Senator Moss, feared and fully expected that, in the event of a broadcast ban, the industry would divert its advertising money to extensive, and thus more powerful, print campaigns. Therefore, ensuring the right of the FTC to implement warnings in advertising remained a top priority of the antismoking movement.[47]

The Broadcasters Face Reality

Although serious about ordering a broadcast advertising ban, the FCC was willing to negotiate with the broadcast industry. In the enduring belief that industry self-regulation was preferable to government decree and because of concerns about violating the First Amendment, the Commission—as Magnuson, Kennedy, and Moss had been doing for years—gave the broadcasters the opportunity to reject cigarette advertising themselves. Trying to appease the FCC, broadcasters spent much of the year exploring ways to restrict cigarette advertising. For example, the broadcasters entertained proposals for time restrictions and prohibiting actual smoking in TV ads. The National Association of Broadcasters also considered, but did not adopt, a proposal to minimize the depiction of cigarette smoking in programming as well.[48] But the broadcasters did not, at least at first, welcome the idea of an advertising ban and losing the nearly $250 million dollars spent by tobacco companies on broadcast advertising and sponsorships. Not willing to jettison this immense source of revenue until all other avenues had been tried, broadcasters held onto the hope that, if the broadcasting and tobacco industries could maintain a united front, the House, at least, would come through with legislation that would continue to preempt FCC and FTC action.[49]

But by the spring of 1969, when the strength of the antismoking movement was increasingly evident, many participants and observers predicted that broadcast cigarette advertising soon would be terminated, whether the broadcasters cooperated or not. Tellingly, in a May 1969 article, Elizabeth Drew quoted a tobacco industry attorney asserting that "it is inevitable that TV advertising is going to end one way or another." The attorney criticized the industry he worked for, arguing that it "should have been working out an orderly withdrawal with the congressional staffs and agencies. Warren Magnuson and Bob Kennedy offered them the chance. Instead, the sentiment is to fight this down to the wire and it could end up in a mess, with the industry the likely loser. Right now they're getting hammered by the antismoking ads, which are better than their own, and by the antismoking people who are increasingly effective." As evidence that the broadcast industry had begun to confront the hard reality, *Newsweek* reported that "major networks were toying with sample operating budgets that exclude cigarette advertising revenues." A broadcast ban seemed all the more realistic and threatening because cigarette advertising already had been banned from broadcast in Denmark, France, Italy, Norway, Sweden, Switzerland, Czechoslovakia, and England.[50] Finally, without consulting the tobacco industry, the broadcasters announced a three-and-a-half-year phase-out plan for cigarette advertising.[51]

The broadcasters' proposal was unprecedented in American commerce. Hard liquor manufacturers had never broadcast on radio or television in the first place, so neither they nor the broadcasters had confronted the problem of how to withdraw a whole class of advertising from those media. The voluntary termination of a veritable institution in mid-twentieth-century American consumer society—broadcast cigarette advertising— would not only be a significant reformation of American advertising but also a delicate political maneuver. Ideally, the broadcast and tobacco industries together would agree to a plan to end broadcast advertising, but such unity proved elusive by the late 1960s. With so much money at stake, inter- and intraindustry mistrust flared. The tobacco industry was alarmed by the broadcasters' phase-out proposal. Although they realized that the termination of broadcast advertising might actually benefit them financially and politically, tobacco executives did not want to be outmaneuvered.

THE TOBACCO INDUSTRY'S FINAL MANEUVERS

The tobacco interests did not have much to worry about in the House of Representatives. Antismokers, though vocal, could claim only forty votes there. During the House hearing, the two sides fought the tired battle over whether smoking really constituted a hazard to health. In its deliberations, during which the tobacco lobbyists were granted privileged seats in the Presidential Gallery, the House did not even consider a broadcast advertising ban. Much to the industry's delight, the bill that emerged from the House extended the preemption on federal agency action for six more years and merely strengthened the wording of the warning label on packaging.[52]

By contrast, the industry had much to fear from the Senate. Supported by a number of other senators, Magnuson and Pertschuk had decided they were not going to engage in the kind of negotiating and compromising with the tobacco lobby that they had done in 1965. Pertschuk set the tone for the Senate committee hearing when he opened with a twenty-minute screening of cigarette commercials, showcasing them in all their glamorous and fun-loving glory. According to *Consumer Reports,* when the industry realized that it faced "almost certain defeat in the Senate," it "naturally began to talk compromise." Already angry at the broadcasters because of their phase-out plan, the tobacco industry took advantage of the unfavorable situation in the Senate by pulling the rug out from under the networks. During the Senate hearing, the cigarette representatives made the surprise announcement that they would pull out of broadcast media by 30 September 1970—almost three years earlier than the broadcasters' plan. To add to the broadcasters' consternation, the tobacco companies offered to go off the air even earlier than 30 September the date when advertising contracts expired, if the networks would release them from their contracts.[53]

The industry's new strategy dramatically shifted the playing field. One member of the Senate committee observed, "Suddenly the tobacco companies were putting themselves in a heroic role." Joseph Cullman, head of Philip Morris and chairman of the Tobacco Institute, declared that the companies' offer to withdraw voluntarily from broadcast media indicated "a new atmosphere of understanding of our responsibility."[54] But the industry was not motivated by a newfound concern for public health. Company executives saw political and financial advantage in terminating broadcast advertising. Demand for cigarettes was largely stable and inelastic, and the brands had little to differentiate them, so cigarette advertising was, in the words of Pertschuk—who understood exactly what the industry was doing—"a costly contest in prime time." Curtailing advertising was most beneficial to the firms with the largest market shares because a ban would make it almost impossible for new brands to be launched. In other words, a ban would stabilize competition and restrict new entrants. Furthermore, being on the air meant that effective antismoking messages were also on the air. It was therefore not difficult to grasp the industry's political strategy in volunteering for a broadcast ban. *Business Week* recognized it: "By surrendering gracefully, the tobacco industry hopes to salvage something. Washington observers think it will get some rewards for sparing Congress the task of legislating a major industry off the public airwaves." Although some senators were disinclined to offer the industry any relief, many were gratified by the industry's offer and did, as *Business Week* predicted, make concessions.[55]

Now it was the broadcasters' turn to be furious, and they raised legitimate constitutional objections to a broadcast ban. Broadcasters had intended to end cigarette advertising on their own terms, preserving as much revenue as possible, but the tobacco executives had just double-crossed them. An irate Vincent Wasilewski, head of the NAB, charged that, in violation of the Fifth Amendment, the government was discriminating against broadcasters in favor of print media. If there was something wrong with cigarettes, he demanded, cigarette advertising should be banned in all media. Even better, the product itself should be banned, not the advertising. In a move that incensed Senator Moss, the networks announced that they would not release the cigarette companies from their advertising contracts. Moss replied to Wasilewski in astonishment, "You ask us to reject the offer of the cigarette companies to withdraw from broadcast advertising—a goal sought by virtually every major public health group in this country—on the grounds that Congressional sanction of such withdrawal would violate the 'principle of equality between competing advertising media.'" Revealing the antismoking movement's belief in the power of TV as well as the sequence of its political strategy, he continued, "Do you really believe that magazine and newspaper advertising are the equal of television advertising in their impact on the American family? . . . Of course I would like to see the end of cigarette advertising in all media. . . . But I do not intend to let congress sacrifice the hard won victory over cigarette advertising on television and radio on the phony altar of 'equality.'"[56] In response to the broadcasters' charges, the FCC insisted that in ordering a ban on broadcast cigarette advertising, it was not trying to discriminate against broadcast media, but that its jurisdiction only applied to broadcasting. The Commission further indicated it would support Congress if it chose to mandate an advertising ban in all media.[57]

In the final twist to the story of the broadcast ban, neither the broadcast nor the tobacco industry was permitted to end broadcast cigarette advertising voluntarily. Despite federal policymakers' preference for industry self-regulation, Congress decided to decree the ban. Over the lone objections of Moss, who continued to be dedicated to industry self-regulation, the Public Health Cigarette Smoking Act of 1969 banned cigarette advertising from radio and television beginning 2 January 1971. (As a concession to the industry, the ban was set for 2 January to allow cigarette companies to advertise during the college football games on New Year's Day.) Once policymakers determined that the cigarette companies would need an antitrust exemption in order to execute a coordinated withdrawal from broadcast media, they balked. The new legislation also strengthened the existing warning label on cigarette packages. Industry interests wanted the new warning label to state that "excessive" smoking was dangerous, but the health forces prevailed and the warning label was changed to "Warning: The Surgeon General has determined that cigarette smoking is dangerous to your health." Last, acceding to industry supporters, the legislation continued to preempt FTC action until 1 July 1971, a provision that displeased most antismokers. President Nixon signed the controversial law on 1 April 1970.[58]

TAKING THE BAN TO COURT

After passage of the act, the broadcasters aired their constitutional objections to the new legislation before a federal court. In the landmark case *Capital Broadcasting Company v. Mitchell* in 1971, the federal court concurred with past decisions holding that "product advertising is less vigorously protected than other forms of speech" and upheld the broadcast ban, thus setting an important precedent in commercial expression law. In addition, by accepting the assumption that broadcast advertising was more damaging to children than print advertising, the court rejected the broadcasters' argument that the ban was discriminatory and thus violated their Fifth Amendment rights. Nevertheless, a persuasive dissent by Justice J. Skelly Wright laid out several unanswered questions pertaining to marketing regulation policy and the nature of advertising. Wright's chief concern was that the courts and policymakers contradicted each other in their definitions of advertising as public speech, a contradiction already evident during the Fairness Doctrine appeals court proceedings.[59] Wright also used his dissent to scorn the 1969 law, charging that the tobacco industry had once again outmaneuvered the antismoking movement. Many policymakers and scholars then and now agreed with him. Dashing antismokers' hopes and validating the industry's strategy, cigarette sales had not plummeted in the absence of broadcast advertising. In fact, after cigarette advertising was removed from television and radio, most of the accompanying antismoking commercials also vanished, and cigarette consumption almost immediately turned upward. The tobacco industry continued to thrive during the 1970s.[60]

Expanding on Paul Rand Dixon's and Surgeon General Stewart's position, Wright expressed his belief that true free expression would benefit the antismoking cause. He argued that the best circumstances had existed when cigarette advertising was still on the air and the Fairness Doctrine had required counteradvertising. In his view, the ill-advised broadcast ban "cut off debate on the value of cigarettes just when [the FCC ruling] had made such a debate a real possibility. The theory of free speech is grounded on the belief that people will make the right choice if presented with all points of view on a controversial issue." Wright further believed the tobacco interests had taken advantage of the new phase in antismoking policymaking: "Indeed, it was presumably the very success of the [Fairness] doctrine in allowing people to make an informed choice that frightened the cigarette industry into calling on Congress to silence the debate." Deciding that the broadcast ban violated the industries' First Amendment rights, Wright thought the government had overstepped its boundaries. The government, he argued, was permitted to advocate a certain position in a public controversy, but once it took steps to "monopolize the debate or to suppress the expression of opposing points of view on the electronic media by making such expression a criminal offense," it had gone too far. Wright declared the state "cannot impose silence merely because it fears that people will be convinced by what they hear and thereby harm themselves."[61] Despite Wright's passionate objection, the majority of the court disagreed.

Wright and a small group of antismoking activists, including the surgeon general, wanted to escape the antismoking movement's central contradiction: in the past it had used a "freedom of information" rationale to support the requirement of a warning label, but now it advocated the suppression of information in its quest for smoking control. The majority of the movement, though, was not troubled by the contradiction because they saw no problem with suppressing information they considered wrong and harmful to impressionable children. In fact, they considered such a suppression to be a duty—perhaps a moral duty—in the protection of public health.

CONCLUSION

Like Justice Wright, many viewed, and continue to view, the 1969 law just as they view the first labeling law: as a tobacco industry victory cleverly engineered to look like an antismoking success. The antismokers, many charge, made a grave mistake when they chose to trade the Fairness Doctrine ruling for a complete ban on broadcast cigarette advertising. Yet, just as with the first law, it can be argued that the broadcast ban was not a complete coup for the tobacco industry. The ban signaled to the public that the cigarette was not legitimate enough to be allowed on TV, the most popular and pervasive communication medium. As such, the policy contributed to the growing antismoking sentiment among at least certain groups of Americans.[62]

Passage of the 1969 law ended congressional involvement in the regulation of cigarette marketing for the next decade. Except for Senator Moss's persistent efforts to convince tobacco companies not to transfer, and publishers not to accept, massive advertising money into print media, Congress largely left the cigarette marketing issue alone until the early 1980s, when antismoking Representative Henry Waxman (D-CA) revived the fight, resulting in a 1984 law that mandated rotating warning labels.[63] Even without congressional leadership, there continued to be new developments in cigarette marketing policy during the early 1970s because of the ongoing interplay between the tobacco industry and its federal regulator, the FTC. By the end of 1970 all except one cigarette company finally agreed to disclose tar and nicotine levels on their cigarette packages. Freed from preemption, when the FTC moved forward on its intention to require warning messages in print advertising, the tobacco industry, except for two companies, voluntarily included the warning. The FTC backed off at this point but eventually did enforce its advertising rule in January 1972, finally achieving the antismoking movement's marketing control objectives from 1964. The FTC followed up by ordering an investigation of the cigarette industry in 1976, but it was stalled by the courts until 1979. The decade also saw the antismoking activism of President Jimmy Carter's Secretary of Health, Education, and Welfare, Joseph Califano, Jr. In those years, the movement entered its next phase by turning its attention to eliminating smoking from public places, starting with public carriers and public buildings, and exhibiting more concern for the rights of nonsmokers.[64]

In a momentous step for consumer rights campaigns in general, the five years since the release of the Surgeon General's Report saw the majority of the antismoking movement escalate its policy aims while altering its rationales. Cigarette marketing control began under the assumption that simply adding authoritative information to the marketing mix would solve the smoking problem; by the end of the decade most antismokers had abandoned this proposition, now convinced that notification of risk must be accompanied by censorship of the misleading messages conveyed by the industry's marketing. In other words, marketing control had come to mean the right information should supplant the wrong information because consumers could not be trusted to choose good health over desire. The tobacco industry nevertheless successfully dodged the implications of the new regulation philosophy when it could.

The 1960s experience with cigarette marketing control reaffirmed the American tradition that commercial expression was not completely free— or possibly not free at all, depending on the nature of the product. At the same time, the controversies surrounding the labeling law, the application of the Fairness Doctrine, and the broadcast ban exposed significant challenges to that tradition, challenges that would be taken up again when new temperance activists tried to restrict alcohol marketing. The cigarette marketing policy debates demonstrated that Americans, or at least their national policymakers, were deeply divided over issues basic to American consumerism and democracy.

PART III

*The New Temperance Movement
and Alcohol Marketing Restrictions,
1970s and 1980s*

THE POLITICAL, LEGAL, AND SCIENTIFIC CONTEXT OF REGULATION

After the 1950s movement to ban alcohol advertising faded, concern about alcohol marketing virtually disappeared from national politics during the ensuing decade and a half. But by the mid-1970s a new temperance movement, labeled "neo-prohibition" by its critics, was placing alcohol advertising back on the federal government's radar.[1] Similar to past temperance movements, it sought to reduce overall alcohol consumption in society, focused on preventing the most vulnerable groups from drinking, and viewed the commercial promotion of alcoholic beverages as injurious and unscrupulous. Like its predecessors, it chose setting limits on consumer desires as a main site for political battle, but leaders of this largely secular and public health–oriented movement adopted more modest goals than had the prohibitionists at the beginning of the century and the drys at midcentury. Instead of advocating the prohibition of all alcohol advertising from all media, they proposed a range of marketing reforms, including mandating warning labels on packaging and advertising, banning advertising from radio and television, and requiring counteradvertising.

For this new effort, however, progress was slow. Although expressions of concern about alcohol advertising surfaced during the years of the Carter administration, they did not gain sufficient attention to become part of the national political agenda until the mid-1980s. Significantly, these were the years when an antiregulatory temper was soaring in Congress as well as in key regulatory commissions, a development that severely hindered the movement's success.

The emergence of alcohol marketing control initiatives in these years was part of larger political and social phenomena. The consumer rights, personal health, and public health movements, all of which emphasized individuals' "right to know" to maximize their well-being, abetted the campaigns for alcohol marketing controls. Widespread anxieties about youth, mass media, and consumerism were evident in the agendas of many public interest organizations as well as in the FTC. Furthermore, the alcohol studies field experienced a major shift from the alcoholism perspective, which had opposed controls on alcohol sales and marketing, to a public health perspective, which advocated restrictionist policies toward alcohol. Rising rates of alcohol consumption in the 1970s contributed to the general salience of alcohol issues in American society, and both government officials and the popular media devoted considerable attention to the problems of youth consumption, drunk driving, and Fetal Alcohol Syndrome.

Using the antismoking movement as a model for tactics and rhetoric, the late-twentieth-century temperance movement consciously separated itself from its earlier incarnations by cloaking itself in the language of science and public health, eschewing the overtly moral tones of its forebears. One observer remarked, "[W]hile prohibitionists sought to save the drinker's soul, today's campaigners want mainly to ensure his neighbors' safety."[2] But, unlike the movement to control cigarette marketing, the new effort to restrict alcohol advertising sought mass support almost from the beginning, and it enjoyed backing from a considerable number of public interest organizations. It combined the centralized, technocratic leadership characteristic of the antismoking movement with a mass-based approach associated with the earlier temperance movement. Also important, it shared with both preceding movements the tendency to moralize public health concerns and focus on the threat to innocent youth.

Alcohol control advocates, however, were even more susceptible than antismoking activists to being pegged as moral zealots, partly because the substance in question was alcohol, which most Americans consumed in moderation and had stronger cultural connections to the ridicule evoked by reminders of Prohibition, and partly because of the way new temperance leaders used science. Although they adopted the scientific model, the activists relied more on social scientific evidence than on medical or biological science and necessarily had to discuss the social effects of drinking. This situation led new temperance reformers to explicitly examine the impact of media and advertising on behavior, a relationship that the antismoking leaders had not systematically explored, and for the most part these studies did not provide the kind of hard evidence that skeptical and resistant policymakers demanded.

The new climate of concern about alcohol problems along with the pioneering work of the antismoking and consumer rights movements seemed to augur well for the alcohol marketing control initiatives, but other powerful factors in American politics dampened their prospects. Shifts in the federal government's position on regulating the media and advertising along with new developments in the Supreme Court's view of commercial speech shaped the political environment in which the new temperance movement operated. As antiregulatory attitudes came to predominate in Washington, D.C., and as advertising was afforded more protection under the First Amendment, the chances for effective regulation of alcohol marketing grew slim.

THE EMERGENCE OF NEW TEMPERANCE

The movement rose during this period for several reasons. Americans were reacting to the rise in consumption of alcoholic beverages in the 1960s and 1970s when per capita consumption reached its highest level since before Prohibition. This increased consumption meant more alcohol problems in society: more tragic drunk driving incidents, more cases of cirrhosis and other health-related alcohol problems, and more—or at least more prominent—teenage and college-age drinking. These visible problems produced an inclination to use more coercive strategies aimed at reducing the host of negative consequences associated with widespread alcohol use. Furthermore, Americans seemed more willing to meddle in others' drinking habits. *Business Week* suspected that enough time had passed for the "post-Prohibition distaste" for intervening in others' personal behavior to have faded. Many observers noted a transformation in Americans' drinking patterns during the 1980s, and it became a popular topic in the media. In one of several *New York Times* features on the new temperance movement during the decade, science writer Jane Brody observed, "The onetime status symbol of being able to hold one's liquor is yielding to a new social pressure to drink lightly, if at all." The rate of increase in per capita consumption of alcohol began to flatten by the late 1970s and decline during the 1980s.[3]

The Contribution of Health Movements

Affecting this new trend toward low to moderate alcohol consumption, at least among adults, was the heightened interest in health and fitness in the 1970s and 1980s. No longer did a martini lunch seem compatible with a productive and fit workday. In the quest for wellness, upwardly mobile Americans would rather reach for a bottle of spring water than a beer and rather spend their after-work hours exercising at a gym than enjoying a cocktail hour. Fostered by several factors, including a reaction against the drug excesses of the 1960s, the mounting focus on self in the "Me Decade," and continuing developments in medicine pointing to preventive approaches, two health movements arose and intertwined during this period: a public health movement and a personal health movement. Both stressed prevention, focused on prudent behavioral choices, such as drinking, smoking, and exercise, and were sometimes at odds with the traditional medical field.[4] The movements diverged, however, in their constituencies and ideologies.

The public health movement consisted of professionals who thought about health in terms of the community—pursuit of the "common good"—more than the individual. In their pursuit of ethical practice, public health professionals tried to avoid "blaming the victim" by focusing on "exposure to risk within populations" rather than on "agent-causality." Dan Beauchamp, a leader in the field, argued that responsibility lay not with individuals but with government because the protection of public health was "best seen as a collective function," whereas "voluntary mechanisms" would not succeed.[5] The personal health movement, in contrast, was a popular trend emphasizing individual responsibility for health and lifestyle modification. Its constituency was mostly upper and middle class, and its focus on self meant there was little broader public concern, especially not for the health and opportunities of less privileged groups of Americans. These factors lent the movement an undeniable moral dimension, for it dealt with intimate personal behavior and seemed to imply that one's illness was one's own fault for not living "right." The personal health movement's individualistic tone, furthermore, meant that government regulation was not central to its aims, a tendency that meshed nicely with the deregulatory climate and "new individualism" of the era.[6]

Both health movements fostered the new temperance orientation toward alcoholic beverages, but the new temperance leaders, most of them professionals, wished to align themselves with what they viewed as the more ethical and authoritative public health perspective. An alignment with medical professionals lent the new temperance movement more credibility, and in turn, the public health movement supported the new temperance quest for government controls.

Antisubstance Abuse Campaigns

The health movements' disapproving view of alcohol consumption extended to tobacco and other drugs, substances to which alcohol was increasingly linked in these years, and the temperance viewpoint often became subsumed in the period's prevalent substance-abuse prevention campaigns, which also muddied the distinction between scientific objectivity and values. Constantly reminded by pressure groups and professionals that alcohol is a drug, more policymakers took note of the inconsistencies between the policies and attention directed toward narcotics and the neglect and leniency toward alcoholic beverages. In 1971 the *New York*

Times published an editorial on alcohol policy that began, "This country's worst drug problem—in terms of numbers of individuals seriously affected, annual economic loss and similar indices—is neither heroin nor marijuana nor any other of the drugs newly come to fashion. Rather it is that terrible old and reliable destroyer of lives: alcohol." The Carter administration's drug policy addressed alcohol and tobacco, and Nancy Reagan's "Just Say No" campaign also included alcohol, though the focus remained on narcotics and she drew criticism from some new temperance advocates. The Anti-Drug Abuse Act of 1986 encompassed both illegal drugs and alcohol, and in the mid-1980s, the White House Office of Substance Abuse Prevention began using the phrase "alcohol and other drugs" in its literature.[7] Portraying alcohol advertising as "drug-pushing" was a common rhetorical strategy used by groups pressing for alcohol advertising restrictions so they could link their campaign to the moral opprobrium usually reserved for narcotics.[8]

Much more so than the fight against illegal drugs, though, new temperance activists looked to the antismoking movement as a model, both in methods and goals. Temperance historian David Musto observed in 1986 that antialcohol reformers were trying to achieve the same transformation in popular attitudes toward drinking as had been achieved for smoking. Building upon the antismoking movement, however, required ignoring the significant differences between alcohol and tobacco. Musto wrote, "In the concern for health, alcohol becomes a substance, just like tobacco becomes a substance." The *New York Times* argued that the two products should be conceptualized and treated in the same way, stating that Americans and their policymakers needed to "view excessive alcohol consumption with at least as much public distaste as it does excessive cigarette smoking."[9]

Activism against cigarettes continued to escalate in the 1980s, most prominently by local and state voluntary organizations and government officials that secured clean air laws in public places and workplaces. The new political mobilization of nonsmokers and the achievement of no-smoking spaces were boosted by a 1986 Surgeon General's Report declaring that environmental tobacco smoke constituted a major health hazard to nonsmokers. Surgeon General Everett Koop proved a charismatic leader for the cause, pressing for a "Smoke Free Society by 2000." National advocacy groups such as Doctors Ought to Care, Action on Smoking and Health, Group Against Smoking Pollution, and Michael Pertschuk's Advocacy Institute lent action and energy to the campaign at local and national levels, though the groups were poorly coordinated. The Coalition on Smoking or Health, founded in 1981, showed the national health organizations becoming more organized and aggressive, and its director, attorney Matthew Myers, worked with Representative Henry Waxman to pass the 1984 law requiring rotating warning labels. A few personal liability lawsuits in the works against tobacco companies appeared promising, though this had not yet become a dominant strategy. By the end of the decade, most participants in the movement agreed that a total ban on cigarette marketing was the goal.[10]

Nevertheless, the antismokers confronted considerable obstacles. The 1984 law incorporated significant concessions to industry interests, including exemption from liability. The movement's controversial fight against government price supports for tobacco was going nowhere, and the industry's public relations machine continued to churn out denials of scientific evidence. Little had changed in the industry's marketing tactics, and in 1988 a fresh appeal was made to young people when R. J. Reynolds introduced the character Joe Camel in campaigns for its Camel brand. Antismokers still had no support from the White House or the Food and Drug Administration, and the FTC had retreated from its earlier commitment. Waxman's new bill to restrict cigarette advertising was easily shot down in 1990. Still, attitudes toward smoking had experienced a major transformation since 1964, and polls at the end of the 1980s showed high levels of intolerance for smokers.[11]

The new temperance movement learned from the antismokers to focus on health problems and use the language of science as it made the case for marketing restrictions. In 1984, sociologist Robin Room observed that the public health literature devoted much more attention to cigarette smoking than to alcohol problems and speculated it was because society emphasized the health effects of smoking but the social and moral effects of drinking.[12] In a conscious endeavor to separate themselves from the drys, new temperance activists tried to avoid moral overtones by sticking to a script that covered birth defects, cirrhosis, brain damage, and cancer, as well as traumatic injuries and deaths caused by car crashes and other drinking-related accidents. Activists constantly distanced themselves from the historic prohibition movement, and they displayed no cognizance of the 1950s movement to ban alcohol advertising. Instead, they saw their heritage in the antismoking movement of the 1960s. One leader told Congress, "We have caught on because of the tobacco stuff."[13] New temperance activists wanted to borrow the legitimacy that came from the health evidence against cigarettes. For the same reason, they associated themselves with the antisubstance abuse and health movements of the period, and they largely succeeded in gaining recognition from public health professionals.

The Public Health Perspective

The transformation to a new temperance orientation was also occurring in the academic setting among professionals in the alcohol studies field. In the late 1960s, the field started to shift from a focus on the disease of alcoholism to an emphasis on alcohol problems, more broadly defined. Often called the "public health perspective," the new model was part of the larger public health movement and advocated restrictionist policies toward alcohol to prevent alcohol problems among the general American population. Its adherents rejected the dichotomy between alcoholism as deviant and social drinking as normal, arguing, on the one hand, that so-called social drinking often became problematic and, on the other, that all alcoholics were not diseased for life.

The shift, however, was not complete; some professionals clung to the tenets of the alcoholism paradigm that had predominated in the 1950s and 1960s and continued to focus on the individual alcoholic, emphasize treatment, narrowly define alcohol abuse, and oppose restriction on the availability, use, and marketing of alcoholic beverages. The alcoholism movement continued to ascend at the federal government level, most evident when Congress created the National Institute on Alcohol Abuse and Alcoholism (NIAAA) in 1970, an agency which in its first years concentrated on funding treatment programs and research on alcoholism and accepted the norm of moderate, or social, drinking. Morris Chafetz, director of the NIAAA in the early 1970s, firmly believed that alcohol problems afflicted only a small minority of Americans who were alcoholics and that everyone else could and should drink—though responsibly. He therefore opposed policies that restricted access to alcoholic beverages. Congress's Uniform Alcoholism and Intoxication Act of 1971, which decriminalized public drunkenness, also attested to the continued influence of the alcoholism movement among policymakers. The 1970s also saw no increase in the national excise tax on alcohol, and, adjusted for inflation, alcohol taxes actually shrunk.[14]

But by the mid-1980s, the public health perspective had won enough converts in the field to transform both discourse and government action on alcohol problems. The new direction was worldwide and was particularly influenced by the studies of European and Canadian social scientists and statisticians that connected the increased incidence of drinking-related problems in a society to high levels of total consumption of alcoholic beverages in that society. In the United States, public health activists recommended that the government place warning labels on alcoholic beverage products; double the national excise tax and then index it to the inflation rate; standardize the widely varying state regulations regarding hours of sale, age limits, taxation, and so on; restrict alcohol advertising and engage in "counteradvertising" campaigns; and pass stronger laws to punish drunk drivers.[15]

In *Beyond Alcoholism: Alcohol and Public Health Policy* (1980), Dan Beauchamp applied the principles of the public health profession to alcohol policy and recommended that the government's goal should be minimal use of alcohol in society. Directly challenging the alcoholism movement, he argued, "the image of social drinking as the frequent but nonproblematic use of alcohol is well suited to the industry's purposes. . . . In formulating its policy, the government must not be misled into defining social drinking as the ideal or principal goal of public policy." And on the subject of marketing regulation, Beauchamp advocated advertising restrictions and counteradvertising campaigns because he believed, significantly, that the policy toward alcohol marketing should be brought "into conformity" with policy for cigarette marketing.[16]

Corresponding to broader trends in U.S. culture and politics, including the health, antisubstance abuse, and consumer movements, the public health perspective grew increasingly influential. The most important groups to embrace the new perspective were the NIAAA, which started to sponsor public health studies and established a research center devoted to prevention, and the National Council on Alcoholism, which had been the leading popularizer of the now-discarded alcoholism perspective. The National Academy of Science and the American Public Health Association also adopted the new orientation, and by the late 1980s the Department of Health and Human Services had become a new temperance advocate. While noting the remaining opposition to the movement, in 1984 Robin Room was calling the shift a "substantial revolution."[17] Although it is difficult to discern a precise relationship between scholarly movements and popular attitudes, the growing tendency among professionals and academics to define alcohol problems broadly and advocate coercive strategies likely fed the popular trend. The academic movement certainly influenced public policy—though not nearly as much as the restrictionists wished.

CONSUMER RIGHTS REGULATION

The rise and decline of the consumer rights movement also determined the trajectory of the new temperance movement. Propelled by Ralph Nader and his followers and influenced by an overall disenchantment with private industry, consumer rights proved to be a politically attractive issue, especially for Democratic legislators. Yet this phenomenon was broad-based and mushroomed outside of the usual arenas of partisan politics. Sometimes termed "the new regulation" to set it apart from earlier industry-specific regulatory initiatives, the consumerist thrust during the late 1960s emanated not from the executive branch but from the simmering citizens' movement, a small yet energetic force of public interest lobbyists and journalists and their congressional allies.[18]

Its momentum took the movement through the mid-1970s, when one of its major concerns was the inadequate regulation of misleading advertising. Advocates argued that the consumer possessed the right to know maximal information about consumer products, and it was the manufacturers' responsibility to provide this information, good and bad. New temperance advocates, like antismoking activists, saw themselves as part of the consumer movement and used the "maximum information" rationale to press for warning messages on alcoholic beverage packaging and advertising, as well as counteradvertising campaigns.[19]

The FTC's Activism

The history of the FTC in the 1970s and 1980s, dramatically shaped by the changes in presidential administrations, illustrates the consumer movement's inconstant influence in national politics. The opening volley in a struggle that would result in a fairly proconsumerist Nixon administration occurred when the so-called Nader report on the FTC was released in 1969. The report flayed the agency for neglecting consumer issues, singling out its loose and ineffective regulation of advertising for special criticism, and called on the FTC to abandon its case-by-case procedure and adopt an industry-wide prosecutorial approach to better protect the "perpetually aggrieved consumerate." As the authors surveyed the FTC's "crimes of neglect" over the previous decade, they managed to point to one area in which the Commission had gone the distance and performed as it should: cigarette marketing in the 1960s. The report noted, "The singularly unusual case of the FTC's action on deceptive cigarette advertising is indicative of what the FTC would be capable of if properly directed and motivated." Otherwise, they claimed, the FTC was appallingly inept.[20] The Commission's leadership in cigarette marketing regulation, then, was an exception, and it remained to be seen whether it would apply the same commitment and resources to alcohol marketing control.

Richard Nixon responded to criticism of the FTC's consumer record by appointing reformist commissioners, and the agency spent the early 1970s seeking solutions to ethical problems inherent in modern advertising. The Senate Commerce Committee, which had become the stomping ground of several proconsumer senators, took advantage of the outrage provoked by the Nader report and eventually passed legislation that strengthened the FTC's rule-making power. In a time when the word "consumer" had become synonymous with "the people," a grassroots movement, allied with key members of Congress, had prodded a sluggish federal agency into action against "the interests" on behalf of "the people." To some observers, the period 1970 to 1973 constituted the pinnacle of the consumer rights movement.[21]

Signaling its new activism, in late 1971 the FTC held a series of hearings that inquired into not only the theories and methods of the advertising business, but also the impact of advertising on consumers. The bulk of the hearings examined the question of how advertising, especially advertising shown on television, affected young children. The impact of television, particularly televised violence, on children had become a matter of public importance during the late 1960s and early 1970s. The public interest organization Action for Children's Television, founded by a group of Boston area mothers in 1968, put pressure on the government by petitioning federal government agencies to restrict and improve advertising directed at children. Children's advocates and advertising restrictionists considered television most dangerous because children were likely to spend more than three hours a day watching it, and statistics showed that more than 90 percent of children watched television every week, including nearly all the programs that adults viewed. Adding to the saliency of this issue, the Surgeon General's Scientific Advisory Committee on Television and Social Behavior initiated an inquiry and issued a report on the matter, and a congressional committee held hearings on the problem in 1972.[22]

The report released at the conclusion of the FTC's hearings found that advertising was neither particularly manipulative nor as omnipotent as many of its critics regularly pronounced, yet the Commission did pursue regulatory policies aimed at making advertising more accountable and truthful. One proposal, heavily influenced by the Naderites, was a program of ad substantiation in which advertisers would be required to offer proof for every advertising claim. Although the complete program, which would have been a bureaucratic nightmare, never came to fruition, the Commission did grow more aggressive in demanding proof for questionable claims from individual advertisers. As a result, the burden of proof increasingly shifted from the FTC, which previously had been expected to document why an advertisement was misleading, to the advertiser, who now had to prove why the advertisement was truthful. While consumer advocates viewed this transfer of power as salutary, a possible unintended consequence of the FTC's new hard-nosed approach was a shift by advertisers to more "ethereal realms" in an attempt to dodge the regulators' search for "verifiable claims."[23]

The FTC's advertising control initiatives along with the widespread concern over television's impact on youth set the stage for a movement to restrict the advertisement of beer and wine and deemphasize alcoholic beverages in television programs. Although the FTC's hearings on advertising did not specifically mention the advertisement of cigarettes and alcohol, Leo Bogart's influential analysis of television, *The Age of Television: A Study of Viewing Habits and the Impact of Television on American Life* (1972), singled out the advertising of those two products as especially troublesome because of their negative impact on children. Some critics looked at not only brand advertisements, but also general programming, criticizing television shows for depicting a much higher incidence of alcohol consumption than in real life and for showing drinking as a way to solve problems or provide relief.[24]

COUNTERADVERTISING AND THE FCC

Even more controversial was the FTC's support of counteradvertising and its pressure on fellow regulatory agency, the FCC, to mandate it. The practice of counteradvertising had been tried—successfully, in the view of many reformers—in the case of cigarette advertising during the late 1960s. Despite the FCC's emphatic and specific denials that its Fairness Doctrine could be applied to other classes of advertising, public interest groups nevertheless tried to use the cigarette precedent to require counteradvertising for products and issues such as snowmobiles, military recruitment, gasoline —and alcoholic beverages. The tobacco lobby's predictions of a "slippery slope" had, in this instance, come true. To the consternation of many industry groups, the FTC backed the growing effort to extend the Fairness Doctrine and proposed that the FCC require broadcast networks to offer free time to groups wishing to dispute controversial advertising claims. Policymakers therefore found themselves in the early 1970s revisiting the question of whether the Fairness Doctrine should be applied to commercial advertising.[25]

In this debate, the counteradvertising proposal quickly encountered strong opposition, both ideological and bureaucratic. Former FCC Commissioner Lee Loevinger, who had penned the dissent from the Fairness Doctrine ruling on cigarette advertising, continued to object to the doctrine's expansion. Now an attorney in private practice speaking before an American Marketing Association conference in 1973 entitled "Advertising and the Public Interest," Loevinger argued that "those who demand free broadcasting time to answer ads are, at best, zealots, and, at worst, publicity seekers or crackpots." He called counteradvertising "the antithesis of free speech" because it was in fact "government mandated and controlled speech," and viewed it as part of the FTC's effort, on behalf of its "militant" consumer group constituency, to jettison the rule of objective law in favor of biased standards based upon its skewed concept of the consumer's interest.[26]

In addition to vocal conservatives such as Loevinger, the FCC itself rejected the premise of counteradvertising and enjoyed tacit support from the White House. In 1974, after receiving petitions from several public interest groups requesting that the Fairness Doctrine be applied to whichever product or service was in question, the FCC decided that these disputes had gone too far. The Commission issued a statement reiterating that it had applied the doctrine to cigarettes as a unique case, and it refused to extend the doctrine to any other commercial advertising.[27] This reluctance on the part of the FCC presaged a broader leaning toward antiregulatory philosophy in the government and did not bode well for the emerging alcohol marketing control movement.

The Precipitous Decline of Consumer Regulation

Not only was the FCC backtracking, but the FTC also retreated from its regulatory activism. Buoyed in a unique historical moment in the early 1970s when a coalition of journalists, activists, and policymakers came together to promote consumerist values, the FTC by the mid-1970s found the air leaking from behind its sails. Proconsumer President Carter appointed activists to the FTC, and to chair the Commission, he chose former Magnuson aide, Senate Commerce Committee staffer, and Ralph Nader ally Michael Pertschuk. Furthermore, on the specific question of alcohol marketing regulation, the Carter White House supported warning labels. But the consumerists were no match for the antiregulatory thrust that increasingly dominated the political environment in the late 1970s.[28]

The concern about media's impact on children persisted under the chairmanship of Pertschuk. In defiance of the growing conservatism around him, Pertschuk's chief cause while at the helm of the FTC was the "kidvid" crusade—the movement to regulate or even ban television advertising directed at children. The corporate world and its accumulating friends in the federal government had little patience for these consumer rights initiatives. They especially were resistant to proposals that aimed to curtail what businesses often claimed as the most cherished right of free enterprise: the right to advertise, and particularly the right to advertise on television. By 1979, a powerful anti-FTC backlash had struck Washington.[29]

Corporations in all areas of private enterprise were scrambling during the 1970s to change their corporate image to cope with and hopefully co-opt the influential consumer rights movement. In response to increasing hostility from consumer rights activists and the FTC, the broadcast and advertising industries fortified their trade organizations and stepped up their public relations efforts in the early 1970s, forming the National Advertising Division (NAD) and broadcasting a "Radio Free America" public relations campaign urging Americans, "Let's keep broadcasting free in America."[30] Businesses in general became better organized and more involved in Washington politics, especially by taking advantage of political action committees, and strengthened their ties with Congress. The crucial support provided to the FTC by consumer advocates in the Senate as well as by grassroots activists had withered by this time through death, retirement, and political defeat. In its place stood a new orientation that prioritized deregulation and was influenced by free-enterprise economists. Accordingly, members of Congress were treated to a litany of grumblings about the FTC, usually in wildly overblown rhetoric about anti-Americanism and the threat of overregulation. Many congressional members supported proposals to gut, and even to thoroughly dissolve, the FTC.[31]

As these proposals went forward, President Carter came to the FTC's defense, and the resulting legislation was not as harmful as consumer advocates had feared. Nevertheless, as would prove significant in hampering the antialcohol advertising campaign, the Federal Trade Commission Improvements Act of 1980, which Pertschuk has called a "triumph of business," removed the Commission's ability to use the principle of "unfairness" to regulate commercial advertising. Congress directed the FTC to prosecute only advertising that met the narrower criteria of "deception." Looking back on the impact of the new legislation, Pertschuk wrote: "rule making at the FTC had received so severe a political pummeling that once fearless commissioners began to fear to tread." The "kidvid" proceeding, along with several other initiatives, closed. An agency that for years had been criticized for being too sluggish was now denounced and even disciplined for being too activist.[32]

The "political pummeling" that occurred during the last year of the Carter presidency helps explain why the FTC acted much more cautiously as it approached the alcohol advertising issue than it had toward cigarette advertising in the 1960s and early 1970s. The antiregulatory trend only intensified as the "Reagan Revolution" brought new, conservative officials to the federal government. Many Reagan appointees were in fact deregulators who advocated turning matters over to the free market. New FTC chair James Miller III's philosophy of regulation was nearly the polar opposite of that of his predecessor, Pertschuk. Influenced by the "law and economics" school of thought that was increasingly promoted at universities across the country and spearheaded by scholars at the University of Chicago, Miller argued that regulatory action should be based on cost-benefit analysis, not humanitarian values or fuzzy ideas about the "public interest." To him, the public interest meant the preservation of free markets. The FTC's staff size decreased during the 1980s, and, not surprisingly, the agency cut way back on its prosecutions of corporations, especially big corporations, for antitrust and other anticonsumerist transgressions.[33] Under Miller, the Commission had no interest in pursuing alcohol marketing control, and he ordered that investigations against Somerset Importers, maker of Johnnie Walker scotch whiskey, and Anheuser-Busch be terminated and that a citizens' petition advocating regulation of alcohol advertising be declined.[34]

Similarly, new FCC chair Mark Fowler's concept of the broadcaster's duty to the public interest varied sharply from former commissioners' philosophies. Since he rejected the notion of broadcasters as "trustees of culture," the Fairness Doctrine and public interest broadcasting did not find support from him or the Reagan administration in general. In 1985, the FCC strengthened its dismissal of the Fairness Doctrine as a regulatory tool by asserting that it had "a chilling effect on the marketplace of ideas," and in 1987 the FCC repealed the doctrine altogether. This hands-off attitude toward broadcast regulation was reinforced when, because of an antitrust inquiry, the National Association of Broadcasters suspended its self-regulatory code in 1982.[35]

As the conservative project to reduce the size of government went forward, at least in terms of social regulation, the new temperance movement exposed inconsistencies in the New Right's ideology. The New Right struggled with the contradiction between freedom and moral restraint as it confronted America's consumer culture. Its attitude toward media and advertising regulation proved rather paradoxical: on the one hand, conservatives viewed "big media" as a threat to the nation's morals and particularly to the values of children; on the other hand, they seemed to view government intervention as equally threatening and debasing.

Many Reagan supporters opposed alcohol consumption for moral reasons and made antisubstance abuse a key part of its social agenda, yet they remained even more opposed to government interference in private enterprise, signaling an important shift from the era when moral conservatives opposed to alcohol championed intrusive government regulation. Consequently, except for a few religious-based and voluntary campaigns, the conservatives' challenge to the media was limited during the 1980s.[36] In stark contrast to the experience of the 1950s, the new movement for alcohol marketing controls did not become a favored political cause of religious conservatives.

THE SUPREME COURT REEVALUATES
COMMERCIAL SPEECH

The free-market scholars who influenced Miller and others in the Reagan administration had been questioning the regulation of commercial advertising since at least the mid-1970s. Increasing litigation, as well as this antiregulatory theorizing, meant that much more attention was directed to commercial free speech questions than during previous decades. Influential University of Chicago economist Ronald Coase, for instance, argued that commercial actions and ideas could not be differentiated from political actions and ideas, and thus the two realms, economic and political, should be treated the same under the law, and advertising should enjoy First Amendment protection. Arguing that subjecting an advertisement to competition in the marketplace would determine its falsity or truth "through acceptance or rejection," he opposed the FTC's regulation of advertising. The Commission's intervention in this function of the free market, he declared, was "completely alien to the doctrine of free speech."[37]

Opponents of advertising regulation had been encouraged in recent years by several court decisions that expanded First Amendment protection of commercial advertising. The customary distinction between political speech and commercial speech that went back centuries in English common law survived the arrival of the First Amendment because American lawmakers generally believed that commercial speech could not be characterized as "free and open" discourse. This common law principle was codified in 1942 in the Supreme Court case of *Valentine v. Chrestensen* that upheld New York City's right to ban handbill advertisements. Although Justice William O. Douglas, one of those in the majority on *Valentine*, later declared that the decision had been "casual, almost offhand," and "has not survived reflection," it has served as the precedent for all subsequent assertions that commercial speech does not enjoy First Amendment protection on par with other types of speech.[38]

Beginning with the 1964 case of *New York Times v. Sullivan,* the Court began to reevaluate the implications of *Valentine* and make distinctions between kinds of advertising that were protected and kinds that were not. In a series of cases in the 1970s, the Court extended constitutional protection to advertisements not because it was bowing to corporate interests, but because it was protecting consumers from anticompetitive business practices. In these cases, the products or services in question differed from the ordinary advertisement of consumer products such as appliances or soda. The *New York Times* case involved an editorial advertisement on the civil rights movement; *Bigelow v. Virginia* (1975) dealt with the advertisement of abortion services; *Virginia State Board of Pharmacy v. Virginia Citizens Consumer Council* (1976) involved the advertisement of prescription drug prices by pharmacists; and *Bates v. State Bar of Arizona* (1977) upheld the advertisement of attorneys' services. All of these advertisements, the Court stated, were different from the type of advertisement at issue in *Chrestensen* because they "did more than simply propose a commercial transaction. [They] contained factual material of clear 'public interest.'" Furthermore, the Court pronounced that all advertising fulfills a public purpose because "commercial speech serves to inform the public of the availability, nature, and prices of products and services, and thus performs an indispensable role in the allocation of resources in a free enterprise system."[39] The Court's reasoning was close to what Coase was arguing at about the same time—that commercial speech was vital and should not be interpreted by the judiciary as an inferior form of speech.

Although the Court's new direction on the question of commercial speech was generally interpreted as proconsumerist, new temperance reformers, who also believed they were acting in the consumer's interest, viewed the litigative trend in the opposite light. They understood that the extension of protection to any class of commercial advertising, even if it were to help women find legal abortion services, would impair the government's ability to regulate alcohol advertising. Justice William Rehnquist resisted the "wavering" lines that the Court was trying to draw between advertisements that deserved First Amendment protection and those that did not and remained wedded to the principle laid down in *Valentine* that "a purely commercial proposal is entitled to little constitutional protection," no matter the factual content of the ad. Rehnquist viewed the Court's widening protection for commercial advertising as "far-reaching" and "troublesome" because it would open the door for protection of advertisement of "liquor, cigarettes and other products the use of which it has previously been thought desirable to discourage."[40] His concern was justified, for by the late 1970s it seemed that *Valentine* had been nearly overturned, delighting most advertisers—especially advertisers of beer and wine, who were preparing for a legislative fight—and making them hopeful for a future of expansive marketing practices.

But in the 1986 case of *Posadas de Puerto Rico Assoc., dba Condado Holiday Inn v. Tourism Company of Puerto Rico,* the Court seemed to backtrack on this litigative trend by deciding that, although gambling was legal in Puerto Rico, the government was authorized to restrict the advertisement of gambling casinos. *Posadas* caused beer and wine advertisers special concern because it approved the restriction of another kind of "sin" advertising, which indicated that the Court was less likely to extend constitutional protection to commercial speech when it involved the promotion of "bad habits." Most troubling to alcoholic beverage producers was the Court's argument that because the Puerto Rican government could have gone further by entirely prohibiting the practice of gambling, "it is permissible for the government to take the less intrusive step of allowing the conduct, but reducing the demand through restrictions on advertising." The decision thus seemed to open the door for precisely what advocates of alcohol marketing control intended: to continue to allow the manufacture and sale of alcoholic beverages but reduce the demand for them through advertising controls.[41]

Although *Posadas* appeared to be a boon for their cause, new temperance advocates had reason to be cautious. The decision had been closely contested, five to four, and in his dissent, Justice William Brennan argued that in its recent decisions the Court had undeniably established that commercial speech was protected by the First Amendment, a "fact" that the majority in *Posadas* had "totally ignore[d]." He contended that the Court had relied too much on the opinions of the Puerto Rican government as to the effect of gambling advertising and did not hear actual proof that such advertising would indeed cause harm.[42] Proof would become a troublesome question. Although the new temperance movement mustered several law professors to testify before Congress that restrictions on alcohol advertising would be found constitutional, it was difficult for the movement to offer convincing proof that alcohol advertising caused harm. Many suspected that the reasoning that had resulted in the *Posadas* decision would not be replicated in the case of controls on alcoholic beverage advertising.

Two U.S. district court decisions on the subject of alcohol advertising also left the advertising restrictionists wondering about success on the federal level. In Oklahoma and Mississippi, courts in the 1980s upheld intrastate bans on alcohol advertising, but the U.S. Supreme Court declined to rule on the First Amendment implications of the cases, side-stepping a definitive position on the constitutionality of alcohol advertising restrictions. Instead, activists on both sides of the alcohol control issue were left to speculate about how the Supreme Court would rule on proposed restrictions, based on the mixed and tentative decisions on commercial speech over the last ten years.[43]

SCIENTIFIC EVIDENCE AND ADVERTISING

The problem of scientific evidence constituted a major obstacle to the new alcohol control movement. The alcohol advertising controversy of the 1950s scarcely had concerned itself with scientific proof for the harmful effects of advertising, for that battle had been fought on mainly moral and anecdotal grounds. The antismoking movement of the 1960s, though it based almost its entire case on scientific evidence, was mostly concerned with physiological effects of the substance and did not really explore the psychological impact of advertising. It did not have to—once policymakers were convinced by the evidence that smoking caused illness and death, they moved rather quickly to institute marketing controls without first requiring proof that the controls would work.

By the time of the new temperance movement, the expectation of a scientific rationale for regulatory policymaking was taken for granted, yet this time it would not be enough for marketing control advocates to prove that the product could be harmful to certain groups of consumers. That, it seemed, was assumed; no Surgeon General's Report revealing the effects of alcohol was necessary, as it was for cigarettes. Instead, policymakers, egged on by the movement's opponents, demanded that the restrictionists scientifically demonstrate that the *marketing* of alcohol was harmful to consumers. This inquiry entailed a different kind of science, one conducted by sociologists, psychologists, and media specialists, not medical doctors or epidemiologists, and one that operated on a different and looser evidential standard than "hard" or medical science. Researchers conducted abundant studies on the impact of alcohol advertising, but they often contradicted one another, and none could provide the level of certainty that satisfied the more conservative FTC or Congress.[44]

Because policy debates largely hinged on the demand for scientific proof of marketing's effects, they spoke to broader questions about the relationship between science and policymaking. Public health expert Lawrence Wallack observed, "It may well be that the traditional tools of science simply cannot provide the clarity in this area necessary to resolve major issues: the ensuing debate on [alcohol] advertising must also be a debate on the role of science in determining social policy."[45] The dilemma affected other policy areas that shared the new temperance movement's concern with media impact, especially policy discussions about television's influence on youth. For instance, the demand for "evidence" also handicapped the opponents of televised violence, an issue that concerned Surgeon General William Stewart. During these debates, researchers tried on several occasions to explain to resistant members of Congress that the measurement of media impact was not the kind of cut-and-dry science that they were accustomed to gathering before making policy. During the

Senate's 1972 hearing on television and social behavior, Surgeon General Stewart attempted to explain the weaknesses of social scientific data and urged that action was called for nonetheless: "The data on social phenomena such as television and violence . . . will never be clear enough for all social scientists to agree on the formulation of a succinct statement of causality. But there comes a time when the data are sufficient to justify action. The time has come." Others similarly argued that scientific proof of causation did not apply to media and advertising impact because there simply were too many confounding variables.[46]

Like marketing control advocates before them, proponents of restrictions on alcohol advertising believed that advertising was a powerful and menacing force in contemporary American society. Most reformers assumed that advertisers enjoyed the ability to manipulate consumers, and in the case of alcohol and youth, such manipulation was insidious and must be stopped. Leaders of the movement to ban broadcast beer and wine ads in the 1980s wrote, "Advertising . . . is a sophisticated art, making use of decades of accumulated knowledge and experience, playing on the consumer's most private insecurities, fears, and desires. Advertising not only affects our purchasing decisions; it also affects our vision of society, our attitudes toward other people, and our philosophical beliefs." Children, they argued, were more vulnerable than adults to advertising's manipulative effects because youth were "open to a variety of images as they seek social acceptance and clarification of their own identity. Adults are more set in their ways."[47] The flashpoint of youth and advertising remained as important an element in advertising control movements as it had been in the 1950s.

Social scientific explanations of media impact research were based on a similar set of assumptions about how advertising functioned in society. As sociologist Rose Goldsen explained, "Conventional wisdom insists on establishing a measurable connection between exposure to the ads and [behavior] as 'proof' that they do anything at all. But we miss the culture-shaping power of commercials if we think that's how they do their main work." As for alcohol advertising, she argued, how they "did their work" was by saturating the environment with glamorized depictions of alcohol and alcohol-related lifestyles. They made the alcohol culture seem "familiar" and "admirable" to children, who, in their aspirations to adulthood, internalized these depictions over time. Lloyd Johnston, a social psychologist from the University of Michigan's Institute for Social Research, told his congressional audience, "It seems to me there is some evidence that advertising does affect consumption, and certainly there is evidence in other product areas, like cigarettes. But it seems to me—and this may sound funny coming from a scientist—that we ought not suspend common sense while we wait for a scientific answer." In fact, he continued, there may never be an answer because, "[i]n a society in which advertising totally permeates the society, you cannot set aside an experimental group of youngsters and let them grow up without beer advertising."[48]

Despite the urgings of these credentialed experts, most policymakers continued to demand a higher standard of evidence before they would enact the kinds of marketing controls that the restrictionists demanded. After holding a hearing on proposed beer and wine advertising restrictions, the chairperson of a Senate subcommittee reported it "could not find evidence to conclude advertising influences nondrinkers to begin drinking or to increase consumption. . . . Our subcommittee record contains no facts which would justify legislation to censor advertising of beer and wine products." If Congress, composed of politicians and laypersons, could not understand the inconstant nature of social science and would not act to control alcohol marketing, perhaps the federal bureaucracy would respond. But the FTC—which had acted eagerly against cigarette advertising without stopping to obtain evidence of its potential effects on consumers— also refused to move against alcohol advertising. As a rationale for its inaction, the Commission cited the lack of evidence showing that alcohol ads "expressly urge individuals to become problem drinkers." The Commission admitted that it would not act unless it learned of "extensive, and perhaps *unobtainable* evidence" of the effects of alcohol advertising.[49]

Policymakers were skittish, especially in the antiregulatory atmosphere of the 1970s and the 1980s, about creating regulatory policy that intervened in personal behavior and in the media. Whether the issue was alcohol advertising, advertising directed at children, or violence on television, most members of Congress, the FCC, and the FTC thought they would get burned by this political hot potato unless they could demonstrate that the regulation was based on indisputable science, especially when the issues in question were so intimately related, first, to First Amendment and personal liberty concerns, and second, to economically powerful interests.[50] The demand for incontrovertible evidence on a matter for which such evidence was unattainable provided a way for policymakers to rationalize their refusal to regulate alcohol advertising without appearing to support egregious alcohol ads.

Industry members encouraged this strategy by pointing out contradictions in social scientific studies and reminding legislators that, "[l]acking such scientific proof, it would seem to be an ill-considered legislative move to mandate either a ban or counteradvertising." Public interest groups, on the other hand, bemoaned this mindset and urged policymakers to let their common sense guide them and to think of all the young people who were put at risk while researchers quibbled over data percentages. Michael Jacobson, one of the leaders of the 1980s movement to ban broadcast alcohol advertising, responded to the industries' demand for scientific evidence by insisting that the industries should be asked to prove "that the $750 million worth of radio and television advertising does *NOT* increase alcohol consumption and alcohol problems." This, he asserted, should be the scientific test applied by policymakers when considering marketing control measures.[51]

Although it seemed that they were often defeated by the demand for scientific proof of media impact, new temperance activists did try to use science to their advantage by representing alcohol restriction as a public health matter. Alcohol caused the deaths through disease, accidents, and crimes of nearly 100,000 Americans each year. After invoking copious statistics and descriptions of medical problems, they could profess, much more convincingly than had the drys of the 1950s, that they were not prohibitionists and were not motivated by a moral agenda.[52] The public health approach was dominant when new temperance activists pushed for a health warning label, which they did eventually win. And when they presented the scientific evidence for Fetal Alcohol Syndrome, they were even more successful at placing their marketing restriction initiatives in a public health and scientific arena. Discussions of alcohol advertising's impact on youth, however, usually led activists to mix scientific evidence with ethical judgments.

BUILDING THE NEW TEMPERANCE COALITION

In addition to drawing support from the academic, professional, and government organizations that had switched to the public health perspective on alcohol control, by the 1980s the new temperance movement enjoyed the leadership and support of numerous public interest groups. These groups included the Center for Science in the Public Interest (CSPI), a nonprofit consumer-advocacy organization; Remove Intoxicated Drivers; the National Parent-Teacher Association; and Action for Children's Television. Like the antismoking movement, the new temperance movement originated from technocratic sources of leadership, but, lacking the scientific footing of a recent bombshell "discovery" and the credibility of an eye-opening Surgeon General's Report, activists needed to demonstrate overwhelming popular support for restrictionist policies to compel the federal government to act. Although there was some scientifically based urgency that pressured policymakers, particularly the identification of Fetal Alcohol Syndrome, it was not enough to drive the policy movement, so new temperance activists also relied on the mass-based tactics of other social movements.

Like the old temperance movement, the new movement put together an impressive national coalition to press for its policy goals. Under the leadership of CSPI, more than twenty groups formed Project SMART (Stop Marketing Alcohol on Radio and Television); by the height of the antialcohol ad campaign in 1985, Project SMART claimed hundreds of member organizations. Aiming to demonstrate to policymakers the popular support for its cause, and thus the grassroots advocacy of this social issue, one of Project SMART's main strategies was to collect one million signatures on a petition against broadcast alcohol advertising.[53]

But the groups and leaders who played the most important roles in the new temperance campaigns were quite different from the church-dominated old temperance coalition. Demonstrating the movement's association with the broader consumer rights movement, CSPI was founded in 1971 by scientists influenced by Ralph Nader. By the late 1970s, only one of the founders, Michael Jacobson, remained, and the organization focused on his area of specialty, nutrition and food additives. In 1982 CSPI extended its interest to alcoholic beverages' effect on physical and social well-being and created the Alcohol Policies Project, headed by George Hacker, to advocate a public health approach to alcohol policy. Jacobson and Hacker, who saw themselves principally as consumer rights advocates, were the chief nongovernmental leaders of the alcohol restriction movement and the spokesmen for Project SMART.[54]

Only a handful of organizations with ties to the old temperance movement joined the new coalition, and very few religious leaders appeared at the several congressional committee hearings held on alcohol marketing during the 1970s and 1980s. The only religious denomination to join Project SMART was the United Methodist Church. Significantly, it was a denomination that had fallen away from its firm commitment to traditionally dry positions as its leadership moved in a more mainline, arguably liberal, direction.[55] Its participation signaled the less strident and less religiously conservative tenor of temperance politics. The American Council on Alcohol Programs (the new name of the National Temperance League) and the Woman's Christian Temperance Union also signed on to Project SMART, but neither group played a leadership role in the coalition or appeared at the congressional hearings during this period.[56] The Southern Baptist Convention retained its stated commitment to abstinence, and, although it did not formally join Project SMART, a representative of the Convention's Christian Life Commission regularly sent statements to Congress in support of policies to restrict alcohol marketing. The Mormon Church also stated its support for the initiatives. Otherwise, despite the surge of religious right activism during this era, no other church groups politically supported the predominantly secular new temperance campaigns.[57]

One important nonparticipant in Project SMART and its campaign to restrict advertising was Mothers Against Drunk Driving (MADD). Founded in 1981 by a woman whose daughter had been killed in a drunk-driving accident, MADD struck a chord with Americans and spread quickly, reaching 350 local chapters by 1984. MADD, which became influential in shaping government policies toward alcohol, focused on the individual drunk driver and not on the product itself. Its resulting message—go ahead and drink, but just don't drive—was perfectly acceptable to the alcoholic beverage industry, which used the same approach in its public service announcements. Although it is difficult to tell whether MADD's single-issue and conservative approach was what attracted alcohol industry funding or whether its alliance with the alcohol industry was what prevented the group from extending its advocacy to other alcohol policy issues, the important point is that it accepted industry money and did not, until later in the 1980s, join the more aggressive movement to restrict the marketing of alcoholic beverages.[58]

As evidenced by the popularity of MADD and similar anti–drunk driving groups, the issue of drunk driving peaked in salience during the 1980s. Alcohol misuse appeared on the national agenda during the decade in other forms as well, including the perception of rising youth drinking and concern about Fetal Alcohol Syndrome. The alarm over alcohol consumption by teenagers dovetailed with concerns about drunk driving to foster a movement to raise the drinking age to twenty-one in every state across the nation, an objective realized in 1984.[59] The identification of Fetal Alcohol Syndrome began to be reported in the popular press in the early 1970s but encountered resistance when some scientists and government officials questioned whether light drinking was harmful to a fetus and challenged the surgeon general's recommendation that pregnant women practice total abstinence.[60] This dispute represented another prime example of nonscientific policymakers struggling to make sense of scientific debates. Despite the challenges, the vast majority of the medical profession advised pregnant women not to drink because no safe level of alcohol consumption was known, and public health advocates publicized Fetal Alcohol Syndrome as the most prevalent preventable birth defect. Although drunk driving and youth drinking were important symbolic issues on which to base the advertising restriction movement, Fetal Alcohol Syndrome particularly moved policymakers because, like the smoking-cancer scare, it involved a recent "discovery" of which many Americans might not be aware, it was based on medical science, and it involved harm to innocent children.

THE ALCOHOL INDUSTRY'S FORTUNES AND MISFORTUNES

The new temperance movement was also reacting to, and at the same time causing, changes in the alcohol industry's marketing techniques and product development during this period. The alcohol consumption curve turned downward in these years as a result of several factors, including demographic changes, health concerns, new temperance attitudes, and, in the early 1980s, a poor economy. Alcoholic beverage companies tried several new strategies to defy the consumption trend and appeal to new markets. Just as the tobacco companies reacted to health scares by pushing low-tar and filter brands, brewers pushed light, low, and nonalcoholic beers to take advantage of more temperate and health-conscious attitudes.

"Would good friends really play this hard for a beer?" Beer advertisements in the 1980s often featured young, athletic men and women having fun in the sun. This Michelob Light ad shows the newer emphasis on light beers and appeals to both conviviality and competition. *Sports Illustrated*, 23 May 1983.

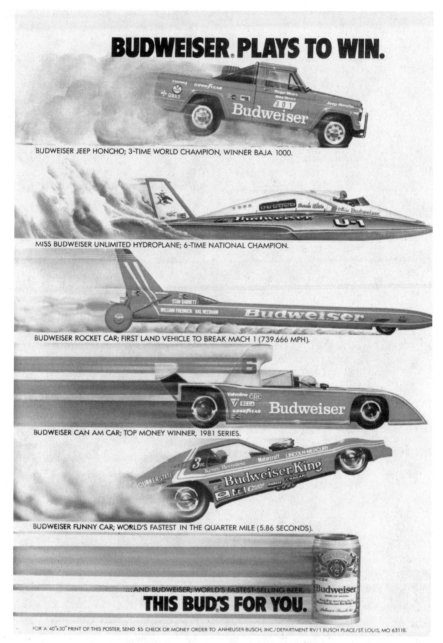

BUDWEISER. PLAYS TO WIN.

BUDWEISER JEEP HONCHO; 3-TIME WORLD CHAMPION, WINNER BAJA 1000.

MISS BUDWEISER UNLIMITED HYDROPLANE; 6-TIME NATIONAL CHAMPION.

BUDWEISER ROCKET CAR; FIRST LAND VEHICLE TO BREAK MACH 1 (739.666 MPH).

BUDWEISER CAN AM CAR; TOP MONEY WINNER, 1981 SERIES.

BUDWEISER FUNNY CAR; WORLD'S FASTEST IN THE QUARTER MILE (5.86 SECONDS).

...AND BUDWEISER; WORLD'S FASTEST-SELLING BEER.
THIS BUD'S FOR YOU.

FOR A 40"x30" PRINT OF THIS POSTER, SEND $5 CHECK OR MONEY ORDER TO ANHEUSER-BUSCH, INC./DEPARTMENT RV/1 BUSCH PLACE/ST. LOUIS, MO 63118.

Alcoholic beverage companies excelled in sponsoring sporting events in the 1980s, as demonstrated by this Budweiser ad touting its sponsorship of various racing sports and associating its product with speed and success. The copy at the bottom encourages readers to purchase a poster of the advertisement, illustrating the extension of the company's merchandising efforts. *Sports Illustrated,* 2 May 1983.

If you think the shapely stir their Seagram's 7 with Diet Coke® just to save calories... think again. They stir for the great taste, too! Prove it to yourself. Enjoy it in moderation, today. The shapely stir. Guaranteed to turn heads.

Counting calories? Stir with Seven & Diet Coke®

Seagram's

"Guaranteed to Turn Heads." Seagram's appealed to health-conscious and body-image concerns, particularly for women, while using sexuality and skin to promote its beverage. Marketing to the changing tastes of the 1980s, instead of depicting its whiskey straight or on the rocks, which was characteristic of the male-centered spirits advertising before the 1960s, Seagram's urges consumers to mix the liquor with a diet soft drink. *Sports Illustrated,* 18 July 1983.

And just as tobacco companies sought to reach new consumer segments by marketing to and designing special brands for women, African Americans, and youth, alcohol manufacturers also vigorously pursued these markets. Because bitter beer and dark spirits were traditionally conceived as men's beverages and unappealing to women and children, the alcohol industry promoted wine, vodka, and sweet drinks such as wine coolers and prepared cocktails. Indeed, one of the great marketing success stories of the 1980s was the wine cooler. The beer, wine, and spirits industries now positioned themselves as competitors in the wider beverage market that included soft drinks, juice, and bottled water.[61]

The companies targeted minorities more than ever before by placing specific billboards in urban neighborhoods and pushing products such as malt liquor with high alcoholic content. Brewers also stepped up their marketing efforts to youth. One of the most famous and successful beer advertising campaigns to appeal to children during the 1980s was Anheuser-Busch's campaign for Bud Light that featured Spuds MacKenzie, a cute party dog. The marketing of beer to college students had become especially aggressive in the 1980s, with sexual "spring break" ads and the promotion of contests that encouraged binge drinking. Also during this period alcohol firms heightened their visibility by sponsoring rock concerts and major sporting events, both of which reached large numbers of young people.[62]

Moreover, always present was the drive by a handful of distilled spirits companies and advertising agencies to increase their marketing effectiveness by airing their ads on radio and television. The mid-1960s saw Rum Superior of Puerto Rico commercials on a New York City TV station, in 1970 a group of television stations based in Philadelphia solicited spirits ads, in 1980 *Advertising Age* reported that at some advertising agencies "there has been plenty of shop talk about placing liquor ads on cable," and in 1984 Ted Turner considered soliciting hard liquor ads for his cable television channels. But all of these attempts were quashed by the trade associations of the spirits and broadcast industries and by threats from government officials; broadcast advertising of spirits remained taboo.[63]

Despite the industries' attempts to expand their marketing efforts and reach new consumers, the consumption curve continued to slump in the mid-1980s. *Impact,* a publication that covered the alcoholic beverage industry, reported that from 1980 to 1987, beer consumption fell 7 percent, wine dropped 14 percent, and distilled spirits, beset by temperate attitudes and changing tastes, decreased by 23 percent. One advertising executive blamed "tougher laws, public advertising campaigns, and peer pressure" for the decline in alcohol sales.[64] Although the companies certainly lamented the impact on their bottom line, they were able to use their economic misfortune to political advantage against the advertising restrictionists. Proudly displaying charts that showed advertising expenditures increasing while consumption was decreasing, they trumpeted that here was proof that advertising did not cause consumption, let alone abuse, of alcoholic beverages. By the mid-1980s, not only could industry representatives claim that their opponents had no evidence of advertising's link to consumption, but they could provide hard-to-ignore evidence to the contrary.[65]

Apart from this strategy, which normally tongue-tied the restrictionists, the industry used several other tactics to defeat new temperance policy proposals. Perhaps most important, the industry was a major contributor to politicians across the country. Alcohol researchers James Mosher and David Jernigan stated in the 1980s that the industry "is considered one of the most formidable lobbies in the country" and has built up its clout to "protect itself from legislative intrusion into its marketing domain." The public health lobby, they claimed, could not compete. The beer, wine, and spirits industries were also successful at forging links with other industries, such as the broadcasting, advertising, entertainment, and restaurant industries, as well as with public interest groups such as Mothers Against Drunk Driving and Students Against Drunk Driving as a way to augment their lobbying power and undercut criticism. Savvy political players like the tobacco companies, members of the industry also staved off criticism by donating millions of dollars to organizations and causes associated with minorities and with the arts.[66] A primary way that the industries sought to improve their public image was through public service campaigns, usually concentrated on drunk driving. Furthermore, just as in the 1950s, the industries fended off regulation by touting their self-regulatory efforts as evidenced by their trade associations' advertising codes.

CONCLUSION

The industries' political clout was thus strong, almost insurmountable, as the new temperance movement launched its campaign to regulate alcohol marketing. Taking cues from the antismokers, temperance advocates had adapted to a more secular public arena, especially surrounding health and drug issues, and they were nourished by developments in the public health and alcohol studies fields as well as by political and cultural trends such as the consumer rights movement, the rising influence of public interest groups in American politics, and Americans' increasing attention to lifestyle factors affecting personal health. As had marketing restrictionists before them, they were tapping longstanding cultural tensions in America, showing that many, regardless of political party affiliation, maintained discomfort with what seemed an increasingly out-of-control consumer culture. Yet other legal and political trends impaired the movement's success. The Supreme Court was allowing commercial advertising more constitutional protection, and, even more significant, antiregulatory attitudes had become dominant in key areas of the federal government. Although it attracted support and attention by training its focus on the problem of alcohol and innocents (drivers, youth, and the unborn), the new temperance movement also foundered on the difficult territory of scientifically proving advertising and media impact on behavior.

Furthermore, although alcohol consumption had decreased in American society during this period, drinking did not experience the massive shift in disapproval that smoking did. Most Americans continued to drink alcohol in moderation and considered their consumption harmless, hardly worthy of government oversight. Many Americans, therefore, possessed an intrinsic resistance to government regulation of what they considered a personal and private behavior and were susceptible to politicians and industry members who painted the new temperance activists as paternalistic neoprohibitionists. The debates over alcohol marketing controls in the 1970s through the early 1990s would find the new temperance movement trying several political and rhetorical strategies in its attempt to counter the popular, political, and legal strands of resistance.

POLICY CONTESTS

Warning Labels and Advertising Controls

Hoping to draw attention and concern to what he believed were deplorable marketing practices by the alcohol industries, in 1987 Senator Strom Thurmond, surrounded by beer advertising posters, made a high-profile speech on the Senate floor lambasting Anheuser-Busch for its Spuds MacKenzie marketing campaign and accusing the whole industry of pushing drink to youngsters. Demonstrating that alcohol politics make strange bedfellows, Thurmond, a conservative Republican from South Carolina, had teamed up with Representative John Conyers, the African American Democrat from Detroit, to push a warning label bill through Congress, twenty years after Thurmond had first introduced it. Despite glaring differences in their political ideologies and agendas, Conyers and Thurmond became friendly over their shared alarm about alcohol abuse and their common belief that alcohol marketing was, at least in part, to blame. Garnering support from both sides of the aisle, including politicians such as Al Gore (D-TN) and Orrin Hatch (R-UT), and from numerous public advocacy and health groups, the warning label measure finally passed in 1988.[1]

The new temperance initiative to control alcoholic beverage marketing lasted nearly two decades. Yet, despite its willingness to put several different policy proposals on the table, it attained few of its goals. The campaign for government control of alcohol marketing began in the 1970s but did not become a true public interest movement until the early 1980s, when many groups in American society became interested in alcohol controls and a genuine new temperance sensibility blossomed. During this period the movement passed through several phases and confronted many of the same dilemmas faced by previous marketing control movements, particularly with regard to free speech, mass media, the protection of youth, and the politicization of scientific evidence. The marketing policy proposals fell into two main categories. The first involved only a government-mandated warning label on the container, whereas the second dealt with regulations that affected advertising, ranging from restrictions on advertising content, mandated counteradvertising, a warning message in advertisements, to an outright broadcast advertising ban.

When alcohol restrictionists stuck with the less-ambitious product label proposal, they chiefly used a scientific–public health approach and generally succeeded in acquiring the antismoking movement's credibility in federal policy circles. But when the movement tried to pass legislation to alter advertising—a more intrusive strategy for restraining consumer desires—restrictionists often strayed from the health approach and employed more psychological and moral arguments. At these points, the new temperance movement more closely resembled the old. The moral approach, along with policymakers' growing reluctance to regulate commercial speech, strenuous opposition from the affected industries, and resistance from privacy-loving Americans who bristled at any intimation of prohibition, all combined to defeat the alcohol advertising control proposals.

PHASE ONE: THE 1970S CAMPAIGN FOR LABELS

During the 1970s, the effort to regulate alcohol marketing was not yet a popular movement. Instead, it largely came, as had the advocacy of tobacco marketing control in the 1960s, from a handful of government officials and growing numbers of academics and medical professionals. None of the initiatives found success, yet the events and controversies in these years were important for mobilizing support for an advertising restriction movement from a public health perspective and for bolstering the connection to the antismoking and substance abuse campaigns.

Early Efforts in Congress

Taking advantage of the commotion surrounding cigarette marketing in the late 1960s, some antialcohol members of Congress seized the moment to highlight what they saw as a double standard applied to alcohol in relation to cigarettes and thereby entered the orbit of the emerging new temperance cause. Most valuable in the Senate was Thurmond, the teetotaler who, like many southern drys, opposed tobacco controls but liked the idea of warning labels when applied to alcoholic beverages. He first introduced his bill to require warnings on distilled spirits in 1967, two years after Congress passed the cigarette warning label law, and several other senators from tobacco states pledged their support to alcohol labels. Thurmond, though, was not proposing such a measure merely as a means to combat tobacco regulation; he was deeply committed to alcohol marketing controls as a way to stop alcohol abuse and would propose the warning label, soon extended to all alcoholic beverages, during every Congress until its passage in 1988.

Although his conservative and Southern Baptist roots signified a connection to the old temperance movement, Thurmond proved a crucial congressional leader of the new temperance perspective on alcohol control. Many years before the clinical identification of Fetal Alcohol Syndrome and massive attention to drunk driving had heightened Americans' interest in the public health threat of alcohol, Thurmond's public addresses stressed the health problems caused by alcohol abuse. Not only did he borrow the warning label idea from the antismokers, whom he resolutely opposed, but he also adopted their scientific approach. Presaging the public health perspective that would come to dominate the alcohol studies field, in 1967 Thurmond stated that alcoholism used to be viewed as a moral issue but "is increasingly being viewed as the serious health problem that it is" and discussed the physical ailments associated with its consumption. Further situating his proposal as a scientific and not a moral policy, he averred that the warning label was "not a prohibition measure" but simply "an objective guideline upon which [the consumer] can base his own judgment or spur him on to further inquiries." When he next introduced his bill in 1969, the ostensibly stodgy conservative described the warning label as "essentially a consumer protection measure" that was in accord with the escalating consumer rights movement because its purpose was simply "to make the public aware of the dangers" of alcohol misuse.[2] Although his proposal was notably unsuccessful for two decades, Thurmond did understand how an alcohol marketing control proposal should be positioned in the contemporary political environment.

This period also found a group of congressional members proposing bills to prohibit beer and wine broadcast advertising during certain hours of the day and bills to prohibit the tax deductibility of alcohol advertising, which they believed constituted a government subsidy of drug pushing. Many of these politicians hailed from California and represented populations of Seventh Day Adventists and Mormons, but other sponsors were from the Midwest and the South, and their party affiliations and political ideologies varied. They operated in the absence of a national grassroots or professional movement.[3]

Wayne Morse, the Democrat from Oregon famous for opposing America's involvement in Vietnam, was the Senate's sponsor of a 1967 bill to prohibit broadcast advertising of alcohol between 3 p.m. and 10 p.m. Morse introduced his bill in the same session that Robert Kennedy proposed legislation to do the same for cigarettes, demonstrating that it was not just traditional protobacco, antialcohol southerners who proposed—or threatened—coordinating the federal government's policies toward alcohol and cigarettes. During a speech delivered in support of both Morse's and Kennedy's bills, Senator Ralph Yarborough (D-TX) stressed the danger of exposing children to advertisements for products that harmed health. Emphasizing the similarities of alcohol and tobacco from a public policy standpoint, Yarborough noted, "Just as Senator Morse has detected and pointed out to us the anomaly of alcoholic beverage advertising directed at those under 21 years of age, the very able and perceptive Senator from New York has brought to light the impropriety of cigarette advertising directed toward the same audience." Echoing these proposals, the Consumers Union later called for a ban on both cigarette and alcohol advertising.[4] None of the alcohol legislation proposed during these years made progress, but it is instructive to see how protests against alcohol and cigarette marketing intertwined.

The alcohol marketing issue was next taken up by Senator William Hathaway, a Democrat from Maine who had grown concerned about alcohol marketing a few years previously and now chaired the Subcommittee on Alcoholism and Narcotics. Congressional reforms in the early 1970s had devolved most activity to a proliferation of subcommittees, and Hathaway, like many members of Congress, used his authority to hold hearings as a way to publicize his pet concerns without actually trying to pass legislation. In 1976, he held a hearing to investigate "the effects of advertising and other media on alcohol abuse," and although it did not register on the national radar, the proceedings revealed the basic issues of debate that would endure through the early 1990s and beyond. Trying to expose negligence and urge action, Hathaway made a point to interrogate federal agencies and the broadcast networks about their positions on and jurisdiction over alcohol advertising. Like Senators Edwin Johnson and Warren Magnuson before him, Hathaway hoped that the industries and the federal regulators could address the problems caused by irresponsible advertising and programming without resorting to congressional intervention.[5]

The BATF Resists Labeling

Also in the mid-1970s, a proposal to require a list of ingredients on alcohol labels caused a commotion that pitted the consumer rights movement against the alcohol industries and flustered government regulators. Alcoholic beverages had always enjoyed exemption from food labeling regulations, but now consumer advocates, in particular the Center for Science in the Public Interest, wanted to remedy what they saw as an unfair and possibly dangerous situation.[6] The push for ingredient labeling represented more of a concern about food safety and protecting persons with allergies than about excessive alcohol consumption, but the controversy demonstrates the intransigence of both the Bureau of Alcohol, Tobacco, and Firearms (BATF) and the alcohol industries to any marketing regulations. Established in its current form in 1972, the BATF resembled its predecessors in the Treasury Department by fostering the industries' economic development and stability without much concern for public health or temperance matters. As such, the agency was generally viewed as an ally of the alcohol industries it regulated.

The Food and Drug Administration, which was in the midst of requiring stronger standards for nutrition labeling on foods, also tried to acquire the authority to mandate ingredient labels on alcoholic beverages, but with the support of federal courts, the BATF maintained its jurisdiction over all alcoholic beverage labeling and marketing matters. The FDA nevertheless continued to apply heavy pressure to both the BATF and the White House in favor of ingredient labels, and as a result the BATF promised to study the issue.[7] In 1980 the Bureau finally announced that, beginning in 1983, it would require ingredient labels on alcohol containers. In 1981, however, it retracted the order, explaining that it was following the directive of a Reagan administration order calling for deregulation in federal agencies. In accordance with the typical cost-benefit analysis that dominated policymaking during the Reagan era, the BATF stated that "the ingredient labeling regulations would result in increased costs to consumers and burdens on industry which are not commensurate with the benefits which might flow from the additional label information." According to the *New York Times*, the Reagan administration "killed" the ingredient label proposal.[8]

The ingredient label debate, along with the jurisdictional wrangling between the BATF and the FDA, influenced the simultaneous battle to require a health warning label on alcoholic beverages. Thurmond's bill was receiving more attention by this time and in 1978 had garnered a hearing by Hathaway's subcommittee, largely because of the heightened interest in Fetal Alcohol Syndrome, an issue that reinforced the positioning of alcohol control as protecting innocents, in this case protecting fetuses from their mothers' behaviors.[9] By 1977, the FDA was concerned enough about Fetal Alcohol Syndrome to ask the BATF to also order a health warning label on alcohol products. Still smarting from being enjoined from ingredient labeling matters, FDA Commissioner Donald Kennedy wrote, "Quite frankly, if the FDA retained jurisdiction over the labeling of alcoholic beverages, it would waste no time in commencing proceedings to require labeling warnings." The special assistant to the president for health issues, Peter Bourne, also wrote to the Bureau, urging it to listen to the FDA on this issue.[10]

Despite these entreaties, in 1979 the BATF announced that, after study, it had found that health warnings were not necessary and instead advocated a voluntary educational effort. In the meantime, the Bureau had received more than three thousand letters from opponents of the label, most of them generated by an industry-engineered correspondence campaign. The Bureau revealed its antiregulatory bias when a spokesman stated that "people are tired of being told what to do by the Government." The alcohol industries, of course, were delighted with the BATF's dismissal of a warning label. Industry members then formed the Beverage Alcohol Information Council to implement the requested public awareness campaign on Fetal Alcohol Syndrome, a campaign that did not include broadcast spots and that many public health advocates have considered inadequate, though the BATF declared itself satisfied with the industry's efforts.[11]

The BATF's decision, however, was not the final word on the warning label as the 1970s came to a close. The Senate, the White House, and the Department of Health, Education, and Welfare continued to push for the label, with Fetal Alcohol Syndrome as the prime motivating factor, and in 1979 the Senate passed a bill that required a tame health warning label. The House, however, did not show interest in the label, and the measure died. Although the Senate once again held hearings on a warning label and Fetal Alcohol Syndrome in 1982, 1979 was the closest that the warning label bill came to passage until nearly ten years later.[12]

Debating Government Intervention

Political debate over the warning label during these years revolved around many of the same issues raised to support and oppose the cigarette warning label. Some opponents hoped to prevail by arguing the label would financially harm the many businesses involved in the manufacture and sale of alcohol, but more common was the "slippery slope" strategy that also had been a favorite tactic of the tobacco industry. Slapping a warning label on alcohol, a substance that has been known since ancient times to impair human functioning, would lead to the labeling of every product that was potentially hazardous. Americans, they argued, were overwarned. Furthermore, such a mandate would represent overzealous government intervention into free enterprise and private behavior. Senator Gordon Humphrey (R-NH) encouraged his colleagues to halt the federal government's paternalistic tendencies by opposing the label. He lamented: "Americans today are besieged by a barrage of Government warnings to do this, not to do that, and so on. The Federal Government, always with good intentions, manages to delve into every aspect of Americans' lives. The result? Suspicion and distrust. The health warning label is just another example of good intentions gone astray."[13]

But label advocates, especially Senators Thurmond, Hatch, and Donald Riegle (D-MI) and the FDA's Kennedy, contended that a warning message was vital to inform the public about harm to a fetus, impairment of driving, and other alcohol-related health hazards. While the government was mandating warning labels on products such as cigarettes and saccharin, it seemed to Thurmond and others that leaving one off of alcohol—a product that resulted in the deaths of tens of thousands of Americans every year—would be a glaring oversight and signify that the U.S. government was evading its responsibility to protect its citizens' health. The government, Donald Kennedy asserted, had an obligation to inform consumers, especially special populations at risk (such as pregnant women), of potential hazards. Trying to make the proposal more palatable to conservative legislators, he emphasized that the label was not intended to tell consumers how to behave but was simply meant to provide them with better information with which to make the decision whether or not to drink.[14]

Orrin Hatch reconciled his conservatism with the labeling proposal by arguing that it "require[d] minimum Government intrusion into industry." Hatch agreed that labeling was the best means to increasing awareness and saving lives, which explained why "we have a long tradition of Government mandated warning labels." To those who warned of the government becoming Big Brother if such a label were required, Hatch defended the label as "an appropriate mode of Government action." He explained, "A warning label educates without requiring a particular behavior, leaving the individual free to govern his own conduct, while better informed about the consequences." The label would leave the decision to drink up to the individual, and, Hatch asserted, "Congress trusts Americans to make the right decision when they are provided with accurate information." The label, he continued, was crucial because it would demonstrate, even if only symbolically, the federal government's acknowledgement of the serious health hazards caused by alcohol consumption and its obligation to make consumers aware of those hazards.[15]

Opponents discounted these predictions, claiming that warning labels, in particular the cigarette label, had not been shown to be effective and did not reduce consumption of the product. In rebuttal, Kennedy contended, "[E]ven if only a small number of people change their behavior, it seems to me that those people have a right to know what their Government had legitimately concluded about scientific evidence of a risk. Even if only one percent of them opt for that change, it seems to me that the Government's obligation is nonetheless clear." Thurmond used a similar rationale, arguing that, if the warning label prevented just "one potential alcoholic from taking his first drink" or just one intoxicated person from deciding to drive, "it is worthwhile and constructive legislation." Labeling was the right policy even if massive behavioral change could not be measured.[16]

As had advocates of a warning label on cigarette packages, those who pressed for a warning on alcohol containers fought the implication that they were morally motivated. Opponents often implied that the labeling movement was only building upon antialcohol attitudes encouraged by temperance advocates of yesteryear and using the public health argument as a shield. For instance, one opponent of the label stated, "[W]e should ask ourselves . . . whether we are in danger of labeling a particular substance not because it is more dangerous to more people but because we feel more willing to give it a bad name." In response to these kinds of charges, Commissioner Kennedy assured his congressional hearing audience that "our attitudes toward both ingredient and warning labels are motivated strictly by a philosophy that citizens have a right to make informed health choices for themselves—and not by any ethic that seeks to deny access to alcohol on moral grounds." Other restrictionists, such as Thurmond and Riegle, continued to stress the "firm medical and factual basis" of the warning label proposal.[17]

The debate over alcohol warning labels did, however, diverge from the cigarette fight because, except for some heated controversy over Fetal Alcohol Syndrome, which never reached the level of the tobacco industry's challenge to health hazards, the alcohol and media industries did not deny that alcohol consumption caused problems. The industries did, however, dispute the restrictionists' position on the extent of alcohol problems in American society and whether marketing played a role in causing them. Some new temperance activists asserted that every drinker was susceptible to hazards and that every pregnant woman who consumed any alcohol put her baby at risk; therefore, a warning message should reach every potential consumer by being featured on the container. Opponents of the label, on the other hand, believed that alcohol problems afflicted only a small percentage of the population; therefore, a warning label was a misguided approach. Mark Keller, a leader in the alcohol studies field, argued that the warning would actually be harmful because it would in effect "cry wolf" by threatening everyone. "Alcoholic beverages," Keller asserted, "are not harmful to probably 90% or more of drinkers," and these "normal" drinkers would quickly learn that the warning was "not true." This perception of falsity would lead "those who are subject to harm"—the genuine problem drinkers—to disregard the messages on the label.[18]

Keller believed, as did many other opponents, that the label was a panacea, an easy answer to a complex problem that should be addressed by broader educational efforts. Morris Chafetz, former director of the National Institute on Alcohol Abuse and Alcoholism (NIAAA), called the label an "oversimplified, inadequate response to the problem." DISCUS, the distillers' trade association, also employed the argument that warning labels were "inappropriate because they delay comprehensive solutions to alcohol-related problems." (Presumably, these "comprehensive solutions" would not affect the distillers' marketing practices.) Label advocates agreed with these opponents that educational campaigns were needed to raise awareness, but they denied the implication that a warning label was meant to abdicate the government's responsibility to support other antialcohol efforts. For instance, Senator Hatch acknowledged that the label was not a cure-all and would be most effective only in conjunction with other educational programs.[19]

Despite the restrictionists' strong arguments for a warning label and the support they enjoyed from the Carter White House, the opposition prevailed in 1980. The alcohol industries, along with related industries that profited from the sale of alcohol, unleashed their lobbying power to defeat the proposal. They were joined by figures in the alcohol field such as Chafetz and Keller who clung to the perspective that controls on alcohol created undeserved stigma and would backfire, and by the agency given responsibility to regulate the industries, the BATF. But by the mid-1980s, the alcohol field and the national political arena was seized by a new temperance perspective that championed marketing controls as effective policy with which to address widespread alcohol problems.

PHASE TWO: BUILDING SUPPORT FOR
A BROADCAST BAN

In the early 1980s, at the same time conservatives were dominating the nation's top posts, alcohol-related issues exploded on the political scene. The congressional agenda became crowded with proposals to address birth defects, drunk driving, and drinking age. Moreover, television news and talk shows were devoting programs to alcohol problems and the attendant policy questions. Accompanying these issues was a public interest campaign pushing for alcohol marketing controls, particularly for a ban on broadcast advertising. This new temperance initiative differed from the recent attempt to adopt a warning label in not only its more ambitious goal but also its increased attention to social and psychological problems caused by alcohol consumption. Although the physical health hazards of alcohol were still emphasized, the new campaign concentrated on alcohol advertising's corruption of heavy drinkers, women, and especially youth through psychological appeals. Furthermore, consumer and public health groups—not federal policymakers—took the lead in this phase of the marketing control movement.

The Center for Science in the Public Interest (CSPI) set the tone for the initiative to ban alcohol advertising from radio and television by publishing *The Booze Merchants: The Inebriating of America*, a tough exposé of the alcohol industries and a vigorous argument for restriction of their marketing practices. In the same year, 1983, *Advertising Age* featured an extensive story about the mounting campaign for alcohol advertising restrictions, demonstrating the spreading influence of the new temperance movement in many sectors across the nation, including state governments, public interest organizations, the national media, and the federal government.

Advertising Age stated that the attack on alcohol advertising was "fueled by an apparently grass-roots movement" and noted how it emanated from the widespread attention lately paid to drunk driving. One alcohol company executive reacted, "[I]t's a very real threat—certainly one that the industry should be taking seriously. It's a growing phenomenon."[20]

To cap off 1983 as a key year for the emergence of the advertising restriction movement, CSPI organized a coalition of twenty-nine groups to press for federal government action. Their first move was petitioning the Federal Trade Commission to take a number of actions: ban alcohol advertisements aimed at youth, require counteradvertisements for remaining alcohol ads, require warning labels in print alcohol ads, and ban other "youth-oriented" marketing tactics. For several reasons, including FTC chairman James Miller's antiregulatory outlook and the Commission's customary practice of deferring to the BATF on alcohol marketing matters, the CSPI's coalition did not expect that the FTC would act favorably on the petition. Even so, the coalition's strategists decided to start with the federal agency that twenty years prior had led the initiative for similar curbs on cigarette marketing before moving on to Congress with its demands.[21]

Escalating the movement, CSPI next formed Project SMART, and its principal demands—the ban of broadcast beer and wine advertising *or* government-mandated counteradvertising—became the policy proposals deliberated by Congress. In addition to launching its massive petition drive to demonstrate "a groundswell of grass-roots support" for these restrictions, the coalition held press conferences and started building relationships with key policymakers.[22]

Even before Congress announced its intention to respond to this invigorated movement, the alcohol and broadcast industries grew unnerved by Project SMART's burst of activism. In 1984 the three television networks came together, in what *Advertising Age* called "an unusual cooperative effort," to produce a video that showcased their recent programming efforts to fight alcohol abuse. Later that year, a nervous Stroh Brewing Company met with the three networks' top executives to judge their commitment to battling the new temperance movement. In hopes of preventing federal government action, the industries' trade associations scrambled to reinforce their self-regulatory codes. The distillers announced a "New Initiatives in Moderation" public relations campaign, and the United States Brewers Association for the first time mentioned drunk driving and special concerns for younger audiences in its advertising code.[23]

Even the BATF took a dim view of the legislative threat and warned brewers that they should regulate themselves more vigorously if they wanted to avoid a ban. At a meeting of the National Association of Beer Wholesalers, a BATF official counseled the brewers, "This industry has done a very good job speaking out against alcohol abuse, but wet t-shirt contests and chug-a-lug contests on college campuses will undo a lot of that good work. Unless the industry takes a good look at these and other tactics, there is a very real possibility that the authority for reform will be put in the hands of Congress and that beer and wine advertising will be banned." The association's chairman then rallied his members for a fight by using scare tactics: "[I]f pressure groups succeed in getting beer and wine ads off the airwaves, outright sales bans will be their next goal. . . . Don't kid yourselves . . . these neo-Prohibitionist groups have no other goal than to put us out of business."[24] The brewers listened carefully and voted to commit half a million dollars to political action committees to defeat the restrictionist movement.

The fear was real. In 1985, though it is seldom remembered as such, a proposed ban on broadcast beer and wine advertising became a top item on the national agenda. At the beginning of the year, *Advertising Age* proclaimed, "Beer and wine advertising on television looks to be *the* issue of 1985" and called it a "major political football." Furthermore, the magazine prophesied, "[W]e see 1969 [ban on broadcast cigarette advertising] all over again." It quoted a "well-placed government source" as stating that "this will be one of the biggest issues of the congressional year, right behind the budget." *Advertising Age* also reported that "the alcohol advertising issue has become the top priority at the NAB [National Association of Broadcasters], AAF [American Advertising Federation], USBA and virtually all other interested groups." At a national conference of television broadcasters, members of the House Telecommunications Subcommittee warned the broadcasters that, "[i]f [the ban legislation] gets to the floor, you're dead." The president of the American Broadcasting Company well understood the threat and vowed that the networks, which stood to lose more than $700 million in advertising revenues, would strenuously contest the restrictionists. He also warned his fellow executives not to "repeat the passive approach" that they had taken in the sixties when Congress banned broadcast cigarette advertising.[25]

Both houses of Congress rushed to schedule hearings on "*the* issue of 1985." The Senate's hearings came in February, and the House heard testimony in May. Despite the ad ban campaign's increasing momentum, which many observers predicted would steamroll through Congress, the alcohol industries found encouragement from other sectors of the federal government. Under pressure from Congress's accelerated timetable, the FTC finally rejected the CSPI's petition, which it had been sitting on for nearly a year and a half, arguing—in stark opposition to its stance on cigarette regulation in the 1960s—that such a decision should be made by elected members of Congress, not federal bureaucrats.[26] The industries were also no doubt pleased that a White House official, Virginia Knauer, a special advisor to President Reagan and head of the U.S. Office of Consumers Affairs, made a statement opposing an alcohol advertising ban. Furthermore, FCC commissioners questioned Project SMART's proposals,

and one commissioner went so far as to call the proposed ban "discriminatory" and "unconstitutional" and told broadcasters they "ought to be
outraged."[27] The new temperance movement should have heeded these
signals of dissent coming from powerful players in the federal arena.

ARGUMENTS AND RHETORIC OVER
ADVERTISING CONTROLS

The controversy over alcohol advertising controls revealed significant
divisions in Americans' positions on the federal government's role in restricting private industry and promoting public health in the late twentieth century. Senator Paula Hawkins (R-FL), chair of the subcommittee that
held hearings on the broadcast ban, declared that "some of the prime
moving forces of 20th century American society" were "lined up on either
side" of the alcohol advertising issue.[28] The debates extended into the
early 1990s and ranged widely, examining the unique characteristics of alcohol advertising, the relationship between cigarettes and alcoholic beverages, the broader power of advertising to affect behavior, legal questions
of commercial speech, and the adequacy of self-regulation.

Morality and Science

Although the restrictionists paid heed to public health concerns, most
of their critique of alcohol advertising was based upon social-cultural—
which in many instances was indistinguishable from moral—grounds. Indeed, many of their arguments were identical to those made by advocates
of an alcohol advertising ban in the 1950s, even though new temperance
activists were largely unaware of that earlier movement. For example, the
authors of *The Booze Merchants* concluded their castigation of the alcoholic
beverage industries not with a statement of how curbs on alcohol advertising would improve physical health, but rather how they would lead to a
healthier mental outlook. They wrote, "*The overall goal of this attack should
be to change the very way people think about alcohol and drinking.* Drinking
can have a place in many of our lives and in our society, but it should
never be seen as a way of demonstrating manhood or femininity, of promoting one's chances of success in various endeavors, or of solving personal problems." In another instance, a professor of law equated the
advertisement of alcohol with other "immoral" behaviors when he
stated, "[I]t would be exceedingly odd if government could protect
children from the broadcast of indecent language, but not from the
thousands of commercials encouraging them to believe that the consumption of alcohol is an integral part of the good and merry life."[29]
Many new temperance advocates increasingly painted the presence of

alcohol in American society as a threat to family and to proper social relations, much as had the older temperance movement.

Despite their attention to social and psychological concerns, ad ban supporters were careful to present themselves as a secular public interest movement and to avoid an association with religious morality. Nevertheless, industry representatives challenged the restrictionists' claims of scientific support, branding the activists "zealots" and "social engineers." New temperance leaders desperately wanted to cloak themselves in the shroud of scientific credibility similar to that donned by the antismoking movement, but they fell short of presenting the verifiable evidence that many policymakers demanded. Project SMART constantly confronted its opponents' accusation that its proposals were based on "ideology and speculation," not hard science.[30]

Alcohol and Cigarettes

Participants in the debate over alcohol advertising invoked abundant and deliberate comparisons between alcoholic beverages and tobacco products. The House Subcommittee on Telecommunications, Consumer Protection, and Finance invited John Banzhaf, the lawyer who had played a leading role in promoting cigarette marketing regulation, to testify on the proposals to control alcohol advertising. Banzhaf saw many parallels between alcohol and tobacco and believed these similarities distinguished them from other consumer products. First, "both of these products contain very powerful drugs." Second, both are "strongly addictive, at least to a certain number of people." Third, he asserted, "both are unbelievably deadly." When it was his turn to testify, however, CSPI's Michael Jacobson reminded his audience that, because of its acute and immediate mind-altering effects, alcohol was deadly in a way different from cigarettes, and this could actually make it more dangerous. "It takes cigarettes decades to kill people," he declared, "whereas alcohol could kill the drinker or innocent people in a matter of a minutes." As an additional contrast to cigarettes, Jacobson pointed to the social problems caused by alcohol, stating, "[A]lcohol, much more so than cigarette smoking (the other major potentially deadly habit promoted by advertising) ruins millions of families and careers and undermines the educational experience of our young."[31]

Opponents of advertising controls also made a distinction between alcohol and cigarettes, but with a different twist. Trying to disassociate the alcohol controversy from the cigarette scare, which by this time was accepted as legitimate, they argued that because the properties of the two substances were so dissimilar, the policies applied to them should be differentiated as well. Whereas Jacobson attempted to depict alcohol as more damaging than cigarettes, his opponents argued precisely the opposite. They emphasized again and again that, whereas even moderate use of cigarettes was harmful, moderate consumption of alcohol was safe and enjoyable. New temperance advocates could not deny this reality, and it was probably the most damaging argument used against their policy movement.[32]

Advertising and Behavior

Advocates of an advertising ban began their critique with a firm assumption that advertising influenced behavior. Advertising caused people to consume products, and consumption produced commercial growth, which, asserted the leaders of Project SMART, was not undesirable per se. The advertising of alcohol, they held, was different and, except for cigarette advertising, uniquely dangerous because when it caused consumption of the product it also created ascendant social and public health problems. At one hearing, a doctor representing the American Academy of Family Physicians declared, "[A]lcohol advertising contributes to a climate characterized by dangerously benign attitudes toward alcohol. Alcohol advertising helps to perpetuate myths that alcohol is innocuous and that signs of alcohol abuse can be ignored."[33] Alcohol advertising, activists insisted, was meant as camouflage and subterfuge; not only did it hide the problems of alcohol misuse, but it helped cause them. It failed to tell the whole truth about the consequences of alcohol consumption and therefore was false and misleading.

In contention, members of the advertising, broadcasting, and alcohol industries vigorously denied that alcohol ads had any impact on alcohol abuse. The industries presented many studies that failed to demonstrate a link between advertising and consumption, poking holes in research that made that connection. They then presented even more studies concluding that alcohol abuse and youth drinking were caused by factors such as peers, families, socioeconomic environment, and physiological characteristics. Indicting the media, the industries asserted, was the easy answer to a complex problem. One industry spokesperson stated, "To blame advertising for the tragic effects of alcohol abuse is to controvert the best available social science." It was crucial for the industries to challenge the media impact argument because, if they could establish that advertising did not create alcohol problems, it would follow that restricting alcohol advertising would not solve them.[34]

New temperance advocates, however, adeptly turned the industries' nonimpact argument against them, pointing out a glaring inconsistency in their argument. The industries prided themselves on their public service announcements promoting moderate drinking, and they vaunted these self-regulatory efforts at every opportunity. One disgusted restrictionist declared, "We are to believe knowing 'when to say when' can influence young people, but 'the night belongs to Michelob' doesn't. We are led to believe 'Spuds MacKenzie' can lead people to drink responsibly, but not to drink." She threw down the gauntlet: "[I]f advertising has no effect on attitudes or consumption, then everyone should stop wasting time and money on antidrug or antidrinking and driving or any kind of prevention or moderation messages."[35] Either advertising influenced attitudes and behavior, restrictionists challenged, or they did not—the industries could not have it both ways, no matter what the social scientific studies said.

The Appeal to Youth and Other Markets

New temperance adherents believed alcohol advertising turned particularly insidious when it was purposefully aimed at vulnerable groups, namely, heavy users, young people, and women, and Project SMART presented abundant examples of alcohol ads targeted at these three markets. Reformers insisted that alcohol advertising was dangerous for heavy users because, though advertising may not cause alcoholism, it served as a constant reminder of the availability and desirability of alcoholic beverages and provided the alcoholic with "a rationale for drinking." They also considered it inappropriate to advertise alcoholic beverages, especially newer products such as light beer and fruit-flavored alcoholic drinks, specifically to women in an effort to expand the market for alcohol.[36]

Most shocking to the advocates of an advertising ban, though, was the marketing of alcohol to youth. They charged that alcohol advertisers cleverly used messages of "social success, wealth, athletic prowess, [and] sex" to associate their products with an attractive lifestyle and lure youngsters, who were defenseless and searching for a social identity, into getting hooked on alcohol. New temperance advocates argued that children were besieged by "confusing and contradictory" messages about alcohol, especially when they encountered the allure of alcohol advertising at the same time that government and schools deployed "just say no" campaigns.[37] In addition, many of these ads featured risk-taking activities such as hanggliding and kayaking, which again proved especially tempting to irrational young people. The most appalling examples of alcohol marketing practices were to be found on college campuses and in college newspapers. All in all, this advertising, which they lambasted for relying on emotional appeals and ignoring facts and caution, created false and damaging impressions for vulnerable children about growing up and fitting in within American society. Leaders of Project SMART stated, "Given the susceptibility of youth to advertising, alcohol advertising on television significantly contributes to the general attitude that drinking is a healthy activity and the norm for our society."[38] The statement implied that drinking was not, or should not be, normal, and thus was deviant and wrong.

The industries, of course, contended that their advertising was not aimed at youth. Alcohol ads, they maintained, used tactics similar to the ads for most other products, such as attractive settings, pretty, youthful people, and fun activities. An Anheuser-Busch executive vigorously denied that his company had intentionally designed Spuds MacKenzie to appeal to youth and employed the facile argument that children were not allowed to drink, so "what is in it for us to aim at kids, anyway?" Another opponent of restrictions declared, "It would be a mistake to think that the use of these splendid images is a sign that the advertising targets young people. It turns out that all of us, not just those in the 14–25 age bracket, like to see ads with gorgeous people having fun." If children were attracted to the ads as well, advertisers claimed, that certainly was not what they had intended.[39] Instead, the purpose of their advertising was to build brand loyalty, not attract new consumers. Opponents of marketing controls assured policymakers that alcohol manufacturers were not trying to expand their market and certainly were not plotting to attract underage customers. As had marketing restrictionists before them, new temperance activists disputed this claim by presenting abundant examples of advertisements clearly aimed at young people. Over and over they called the industries' brand argument nonsense.[40]

The industries were more convincing when they showed that, as alcohol advertising expenditures had risen over the last several years, consumption rates and the incidence of alcohol problems had actually declined. After displaying statistics and graphs, industry representatives insisted this was the ultimate proof that their advertising could not be connected with alcohol abuse. The evidence was difficult to refute, but restrictionists replied that many other factors in American society, including lower drinking ages and tougher drunk driving laws, had caused the drop in drinking and alcohol-related crimes and illnesses. Regardless of declining consumption, they maintained that alcohol advertising was still promoting a drug that caused harm to health and social relations and therefore needed to be regulated.[41]

Industry Self-Regulation

To contest such negative portrayals of their advertising, the industries employed many of the same arguments exploited by alcohol and cigarette companies throughout the previous thirty years in repeated attempts to stave off marketing controls. Industry executives nearly exhausted the self-regulation tactic by constantly touting their achievements at curtailing advertising and programming on television and radio. The networks avowed they were applying their standards on alcohol commercials more stringently and had become more sensitive to how alcohol was portrayed to youthful audiences. The NAB claimed that television programs had toned down the depiction of drinking and touted several shows, such as *Hill Street Blues*, *Cheers*, and *The Facts of Life*, that had recently featured stories about alcoholics. At the congressional hearings, the brewing, distilling, and wine industries exhibited their respective advertising codes and discussed in depth their educational campaigns on drunk driving and moderate drinking.[42]

Yet restrictionists insisted the industry's efforts were far from adequate. "Frankly," declared a leader of CSPI, "we think their oft-stated concerns about drinking and driving and their recent barrage of brochures, media kits, and so-called educational materials are a sham." CSPI's Jacobson argued that the industries' public service announcements and campaigns had been recently undertaken only as a response to public pressure and predicted that as soon as threats of legislation faded, the industries' concern would disappear.[43] Representative John Seiberling (D-OH), sponsor of the House bill to ban alcohol advertising in 1985, stated the industry's public service announcements constituted only about 3 percent of the total alcohol advertising appearing on radio and television. Others pointed out that the announcements were rarely broadcast in prime time. Moreover, the industries' messages focused on excessive consumption of alcohol or the act of drunk driving, implying that moderate use of alcohol was harmless as long as one did not drive. Testifying in support of advertising regulation, a physician representing the American Medical Association argued, "Present messages about knowing your limit do not provide an understanding of the health effects of alcoholic beverages, and furthermore, they are often lost in the barrage of advertising that repeatedly links drinking with good times." New temperance adherents believed that all consumption of alcohol was potentially problematic and that all consumers needed to be better educated about the risks.[44] The industry's voluntary efforts could not be relied upon, making more coercive measures by the federal government necessary to protect the public.

Commercial Free Expression

Participants in the multiple alcohol advertising hearings also confronted the questions that had been churning in some legal and policy circles since the early 1970s: First Amendment protection of commercial advertising. The proposed ban on broadcast alcohol advertising promised to be a perfect test case for an ultimate decision on the constitutionality of regulating commercial speech. The industries repeatedly declared to policymakers, already apprehensive about the proposals before them, that marketing regulations were unquestionably unconstitutional. Back in the 1950s the industries also had employed the theme that it was their "constitutional right to advertise," but now they could point to an impressive list of Supreme Court decisions to buttress their contention that alcohol advertising was protected by the First Amendment. Since the Court's 1980 ruling in *Central Hudson v. New York,* restrictions on commercial speech had to pass a test requiring that the restriction represent a substantial government interest and that it constitute an appropriate measure with which to address that interest. Opponents of regulation were convinced that an alcohol ad ban would not pass the *Central Hudson* test because the Court would find the ban more restrictive than necessary to address governmental concern about alcohol abuse.[45]

Control advocates responded that a ban on broadcast alcohol advertising would nevertheless prove constitutional, basing their argument on the traditional view that commercial speech had always deserved less protection than other forms of speech. They could also point to a key case to support their position, *Capital Broadcasting Co. v. Mitchell* (1971), in which the Court had found the prohibition on broadcast cigarette advertising constitutional. The industries countered that the *Capital Broadcasting* case predated the new decisions and, if brought before the Court now, the cigarette broadcast ban would not pass the *Central Hudson* test.[46] CSPI's George Hacker called the industry's claims of First Amendment rights "a diversion; at best a distortion of all legal history concerning commercial speech, and at worst a sly mockery of important free speech guarantees that were never intended to protect advertising of potentially lethal and addictive products in dangerous ways." Similarly, a civil liberties lawyer siding with the ban movement told Congress alcohol advertising was less deserving of constitutional protection than other types of advertising because it involved a product that caused deaths and injuries to thousands of innocent people. He reminded his congressional audience that, although the Supreme Court lately had been affording protection to certain types of advertising, it had "never applied its commercial speech approach to a case in which physical safety of others was a serious concern." He believed that in the case of alcohol advertising the Court would use a "special standard that would permit government regulation even more readily than the *Central Hudson* approach would permit." In addition, he declared, the Court always had been more inclined to regulate content in broadcast media than in other forms of media and expression.[47]

Counteradvertising

As part of the commercial free speech dispute, the alcohol advertising controversy also addressed the question of the federal government's authority to require counteradvertising. Because Project SMART proposed either a broadcast advertising ban or equal time for counteradvertising, policymakers needed to consider the current state of the Federal Communication Commission's Fairness Doctrine. Believing that they could learn another lesson from the antismoking movement, many restrictionists expected that the counteradvertising proposal would in fact be more effective than an outright broadcast ban in influencing public attitudes toward alcohol consumption. It was widely believed that the anti-smoking messages required by the FCC from 1966 to 1970 had successfully dampened per capita smoking, only to see smoking rise when the messages ceased with the broadcast ban. Some industry members agreed with this assessment of the cigarette precedent and were as fearful of an equal time mandate as they were of a ban. For instance, one advertising executive declared, "[T]hey are trying to suggest that counteradvertising is a compromise, and it's not." And the USBA president called the counteradvertising proposal "a ban in sheep's clothing." Though it never caused a major rift in the movement, some new temperance activists favored counteradvertising over a ban because they thought keeping health messages constantly in the public eye was preferable to terminating all information, positive and negative, about alcoholic beverages.[48]

The industries offered a powerful and ultimately convincing case that government-ordered counteradvertising was ill advised. Reminding Congress of the FCC's 1974 decision that the Fairness Doctrine no longer applied to product advertisements, the NAB argued any legislation mandating counteradvertising would repudiate federal government policy. Passing Project SMART's proposal, the industries declared, would unleash the slippery slope that the FCC had spent the previous decade trying to shore up. Such a policy, especially one that went so far as to require one-to-one equal time—for even the FCC's cigarette ruling had mandated a ratio of only one public service announcement to every four cigarette commercials —was extreme and misguided, they asserted.[49]

Supporters of the counteradvertising proposal replied that alcohol advertising should be exempt from the government's current position on the Fairness Doctrine. According to Representative Seiberling, alcohol ads "promote a special kind of product which present unique problems thus requiring separate and unique treatment." And because the advertising of wine and especially beer was so extreme in its abundance and its themes, this "imbalance justifies the requirement of equal time."[50] Congress, however, was not persuaded.

Despite the flurry of activism and apparent strength of Project SMART, its proposals died quickly and quietly after the 1985 congressional hearings. By the middle of the year, the campaign for an advertising ban or counteradvertising had ended. Neither congressional subcommittee that held hearings evinced enthusiasm about reporting legislation, and Seiberling could not even find a cosponsor for his bill based on SMART's proposals. *Advertising Age* speculated that the industries had won over members of Congress with their promises of further self-regulation and continuing industry-funded public service announcements. Although this was probably true, the defining factor in the ad ban movement's swift defeat was more likely the powerful and moneyed lobbying juggernaut of the alcohol, advertising, and broadcast industries combined with the prevailing antiregulation climate in Washington.[51]

PHASE THREE: REVIVAL OF THE WARNING LABEL

Not to be defeated, the new temperance movement took advantage of the reauthorization of the NIAAA in 1986 by amending the bill to require warning labels. A first sign that the label was back on the agenda came in mid-1986 when the American Medical Association joined the active restrictionists in recommending warning labels on alcoholic beverages as part of a "five-point program" to address the unhealthy consequences of alcohol consumption. Also, only one year after it was thought that the alcohol marketing issue was old news, the *New York Times* featured the dispute over warning labels in its "60 Second Debate" column. Thurmond, who had not been active in the more extreme broadcast ban movement of the previous three years, reestablished his leadership by presenting the familiar arguments in favor of the label, including the oft-noted parallel to the cigarette warning label. Perhaps to distinguish it from the failed advertising control proposals, he emphasized that a label requirement was not an intrusive policy because it merely provided information.[52]

Thurmond's adversary in this "60 Second Debate" was F. A. Meister, the president of DISCUS who used three main arguments to oppose labels. First, he claimed that everyone, including teenagers and pregnant women, already knew the dangers of "excessive drinking." Second, and in contradiction to his argument that everyone already knew all there was to know, he used the panacea argument: that labels would provide a "false sense of security that we . . . have done our duty to educate everyone on alcoholism . . . while in reality we have accomplished little or nothing." Last, he knew of no new health hazards discovered by recent research that would warrant such a label. In fact, he stated, recent research had uncovered health *benefits* from moderate consumption of alcoholic beverages.[53]

The warning label amendment failed in 1986, but during the next two years, developments on the labeling front accelerated on both local and national levels. State legislation to require warning labels on alcohol containers was moving ahead in Massachusetts and California, two classic bellwether states, and several states had instituted extensive public awareness campaigns for Fetal Alcohol Syndrome. The *New York Times* again spotlighted the warning label debate in its op-ed section, this time pitting Patricia Taylor of CSPI against James Sanders of the Beer Institute, and Thurmond attracted publicity with his Spuds MacKenzie speech.[54]

John Conyers added his voice and considerable influence among liberals and racial minorities to the movement, raising awareness of the adverse effects of alcohol abuse on African American communities. Studies showed that blacks suffered from alcohol-related health problems to a greater extent than whites, leading Conyers to claim that "these health statistics are creating two Americas." His involvement reflected a recent direction in the new temperance movement toward examining the influence of alcohol and its marketing on ethnic and racial minorities. The CSPI published *Marketing Booze to Blacks* in 1987 and *Marketing Disease to Hispanics: The Selling of Alcohol, Tobacco, and Junk Foods* in 1989 to highlight this concern, which had not previously been prominent in the restrictionists' arsenal of arguments.[55] Opponents contended that the attempt to restrict advertising to women and minorities smacked of paternalism for it assumed that these groups were "not capable of making the same choices about products as others can."[56]

Thurmond's warning label bill once again made its way to the Senate floor in the spring of 1988. Similar to legislation recently passed for cigarettes, this version, cosponsored in the Senate by Howard Metzenbaum (D-OH), Tom Harkin (D-IA), and Dan Evans (R-WA), and supported by Orrin Hatch and Ted Kennedy, required four rotating labels to be depicted on the packaging of all alcoholic beverages. These labels featured the familiar themes about impairment of driving ability and causation of birth defects but added to them: "Warning: Alcohol is a drug and may be addictive" and "Warning: This product contains alcohol and is particularly hazardous in combination with some drugs." More than ninety organizations pledged their support to the initiative, including most of the former members of the defunct Project SMART along with MADD, the AMA, the American Academy of Pediatrics, and the National Rainbow Coalition. Thurmond heralded a recent Gallup poll showing that nearly 80 percent of Americans supported health warning labels on alcohol.[57]

During the hearing chaired by Al Gore, the new temperance movement returned to the more circumscribed public health approach. Proponents argued that Americans were largely uninformed about health hazards caused by alcoholic beverages and presented a panel of medical experts to explain these hazards and support the label. Gore and others believed that the birth defects component of the label had, "by far, the strongest case behind it" and could not understand how the necessity for such a warning could be denied. Several advocates stressed that warning labels were a policy tool that had proven effective in educating the public about risks and appeared widely on products such as artificial sweeteners and aspirin without much controversy. An exasperated Conyers declared, "[A]ll we are asking for are warning labels, not a war against alcoholism or shutting them down or taxing them to death. All we are saying is let's put some counter-information on the table. If we can put information labels on bubble bath and stepladders and aspirin, give me a break—we're talking about a drug here." Later in the hearings, a physician echoed Conyers's frustration at the double-standard applied to alcohol when she stated, "If we can label diet soda, it is certainly time we recognized the health hazards of alcohol, not merely to thousands, but to millions of Americans." Gore concluded by arguing, "You know, this is 1988. Come on. It is time."[58]

Gore was right: after twenty-one years, the label's time finally had come. The industries that had fought labeling so successfully for decades now lessened their resistance, in part because of mounting new temperance campaigns on the state and local levels and in part because of the industries' increasing realization that labels would offer them protection from liability suits.[59] But the industry won major concessions, producing legislation that was watered-down from earlier versions. First, the law preempted state and local labeling requirements, and second, instead of four or five rotating messages, it required all distilled spirits, beer, and wine containers to carry one message: "Government warning: (1) According to the Surgeon General, women should not drink alcoholic beverages during pregnancy because of the risk of birth defects. (2) Consumption of alcoholic beverages impairs the ability to drive a car or operate machinery and may cause health problems." Furthermore, the law, which was to take effect in November 1989, allowed the BATF to set requirements for typeface, size, and placement of the label. Within a year, the new temperance activists were expressing dissatisfaction with the BATF's specifications, which they argued had resulted in "virtually microscopic warning labels." Gore claimed that "heavy pressure from the industry appears to be playing a major part in undermining the new warning program" and accused the BATF of "game playing." Gore, Thurmond, Conyers, and others pushed for the BATF and the industries to make the labels as "conspicuous and effective as possible" and hinted, in a veiled threat, that unless they saw more commitment to the warning label on packaging, they would push for warnings in alcohol advertisements as well.[60]

PHASE FOUR: THE FAILED INITIATIVE TO REQUIRE A WARNING MESSAGE IN ADVERTISING

In the meantime, Surgeon General Everett Koop had turned his attention to the dangers presented by alcohol marketing, a move that caused genuine alarm among industry members. At Dr. Koop's high-profile Drunk Driving Workshop in late 1988, he featured a panel on advertising and marketing comprised mainly of advocates of government regulations. Aware that the new temperance movement wanted to put advertising restrictions back on the political agenda, industry leaders were afraid that, if Koop's workshop advocated marketing controls, Congress would be inclined to act. Within two months, many advertising and broadcasting groups had filed statements of opposition with the Surgeon General concerning the panel. The NAB, for instance, argued in its statement that drunk driving was a problem associated with the illness of alcoholics and the recklessness of young people and could not be addressed with advertising restrictions.[61]

When Koop left office in June 1989, he issued ten recommendations from the Drunk Driving Workshop, only two of which dealt with marketing. The recommendations were much tamer than the industries had expected, asking only for a vague restriction on marketing practices that appealed to youth and for more voluntary counteradvertising. One relieved advertising executive stated, "The surgeon general rejected by implication the vast majority of proposals from his workshop's advertising panel" such as a broadcast ban, warning messages in advertising, and mandatory counteradvertisements. But once out of office, Koop became much more aggressive against alcohol advertising and called for an all-out ban on broadcast beer and wine advertising.[62]

Although Congress remained unenthusiastic about enacting further controls on alcohol marketing, the new temperance movement made one last drive for regulation by backing a bill to require warning messages in all alcohol advertising. Just as the industries had feared, Conyers asserted that requiring a warning in advertising was "the next logical step" after mandating a label on packaging. Another new temperance activist, Christine Lubinski, of the National Council on Alcoholism, claimed that the new proposal had "unbelievable grass-roots support, but politically, it is one of the most difficult battles to wage." She attributed congressional reluctance to members' fear of losing media coverage as retribution. The alcohol interests, congressional members well understood, pumped an estimated two billion dollars a year into broadcast, print, and other media industries.[63]

The bill, called the Sensible Advertising and Family Education (SAFE) Act of 1990, was sponsored by Senator Gore, Senator John Glenn (D-OH), and Representative Joe Kennedy (D) of Massachusetts, but it failed to come to a vote. Kennedy and Strom Thurmond, another odd political pairing, reintroduced the SAFE Act in 1991 and again in 1993.[64] Also during the early 1990s, Surgeon General Antonia Novello made raising consciousness about teen drinking a major part of her program and skewered alcohol advertising for its part in encouraging youth consumption.[65] Another factor that encouraged passage of the advertising warning message, this one dealt by chance misfortune, was the death of Thurmond's twenty-two-year-old daughter at the hands of a drunk driver during the spring of 1993. The tragedy prompted Senate leaders to finally call for a committee vote on the SAFE bill.[66]

In the end, the advertising warning proposal, which never enjoyed much congressional support and was fought by powerful industry interests, failed. Its failure effectively marked the end of the new temperance movement's drive for congressional action to curtail alcohol marketing.[67] George Hacker argues that the elderly Strom Thurmond was tired of fighting the industries, particularly the broadcast industry. Hacker also emphasizes that in 1994 the Democrats, who were always the biggest supporters of the movement, lost the House of Representatives. Because the new temperance movement's allies were desperately trying to protect their own threatened programs, it was more difficult to convince them to support new antialcohol proposals. After nearly fifteen years of pushing for marketing regulations, the movement could count one policy achievement, the requirement of an obscure and, in many people's view, ineffective warning label on the packaging of alcoholic beverages. How much of a victory it was, along with the overall success of the alcohol marketing restriction movement, remains in doubt.

CONCLUSION

Alternating between a scientific-health and a social-moral approach, the new temperance movement exposed America's unresolved dilemmas concerning the role of science and social science in policymaking, the power of advertising in a consumer society, and government's ability to protect vulnerable groups (namely children, women, minorities, and alcoholics) from legal commercial practices. Although the new temperance movement's efforts to curtail alcohol marketing displayed many similarities to the antialcohol advertising movement of the 1950s, its approach proved much more secular and succeeded in attracting a surprising number of self-identified liberal, nonreligious public interest groups and professionals to its cause. It also was supported by nearly all the important medical organizations. The ascendance of the antismoking movement—based on science yet maintaining ethical values attendant to demands for corporate responsibility—in the intervening years was a crucial factor in this shift. This secularity did not mean that the recent movement was any less "moral." As anthropologist Solomon Katz has theorized, a new secular morality arose in the 1970s and 1980s around cultural phenomena such as the antismoking and antialcohol movements chronicled here.[68] Fused with a public health rationale and a consumer rights sensibility, and enjoying support from secular, authoritative figures such as the surgeon general, the new temperance movement's arguments for reining in abuses of consumer culture were persuasive to a wider range of Americans and their policymakers than was the Christian movement in the 1950s. But it could not overcome Americans' increasing reservations in the last quarter of the twentieth century about government paternalism, invasion of privacy, and encroachments on freedom, concerns that the powerful alcohol, media, and advertising industries effectively exploited.

CONCLUSION

The Elusive Quest for Restraints

Near the end of December 2001, the National Broadcasting Company announced a departure in its advertising policy: the network would effectively break the taboo against spirits advertising on TV by airing hard liquor advertisements on programs shown after 9 p.m.[1] Condemnation of NBC's move was swift and, significantly, articulated by diverse critics as moral authorities joined political and scientific leaders in voicing strong objections. Linking alcohol consumption to other traditional vices, conservative newspaper columnist Cal Thomas wondered, "What else would NBC advertise if it felt it needed the money? Perhaps prostitution, since that apparently is what NBC is engaged in as it sells airtime to the liquor industry. . . . NBC might as well let gamblers advertise." For Thomas, opening the gates to hard liquor ads was one more case of television teaching young people to "shoot up schools, have sex outside of marriage," and challenge authority in general.[2]

Although one might be inclined to discount Thomas's perspective as the overreaction of a moral conservative, the American Medical Association echoed his outrage, calling NBC's decision "shockingly irresponsible" and "greedy." The chairman of the AMA accused the network of "putting its desire for profit far above the health of our nation—especially young people, who develop many of their ideas and expectations about alcohol from watching TV." Former Secretary of the Department of Health, Education, and Welfare Joseph Califano also strongly condemned NBC, detailing how the network's putative safeguards of children's welfare were full of holes. Asserting that "self-regulation cannot withstand the pressure to produce profits. Federal regulation or legislation is needed," he revived the call for a government ban on alcohol advertising.[3]

At the beginning of the twenty-first century, scientific and moral voices continued to converge to construct a secular morality that denounced the commercial promotion of potentially hazardous substances. Thomas ended his piece by reflecting, "We're always debating where to draw lines, or whether to draw them at all." The basis of the decades-old controversy over both cigarette and alcohol marketing, which can be applied to Americans' wavering discomfort with advertising in general, has revolved around whether a democratic society can draw lines around its consumer culture. If so, who should draw those lines and on what basis? Should government take a larger role in marketing regulation? Should marketing be regulated on the basis of scientific evidence or moral concerns? Americans seeking more control over consumerism have confronted other serious questions. Could a business's marketing operation be separated from its manufacturing and retail capacities as a target for regulation? Could (and should) the youth consumer market be separated from the adult market so that restrictions applied only to young people, leaving adults free to access controversial advertising and harmful products? And last, was any of this regulation constitutional?

At base, controversies over alcohol and cigarette promotion embody how Americans and their policymakers in the second half of the twentieth century confronted and accommodated questionable business practices in a free society, struggles that were also reflected in the environmental and consumer rights movements of this period. Although they share an association with the old temperance movement, the alcohol and cigarette marketing control movements of the postwar era illustrated what some scholars have identified as the postmaterial critique of uncontrolled consumerism.[4] They reflected an affluent society's accentuated concern with not only risk and wellness, but also the complicity of the increasingly pervasive media, the chief messenger of the mass consumer society that, ironically, helped engender these concerns in the first place.

The marketing control debates tapped into tensions between the strong traditions of restraint, virtue, and health and the equally powerful ideals of individualism, liberty, and economic gain. Americans have felt ambivalent— and vaguely guilty—about their rampant consumerism, especially as it involves and attracts children, who are framed as the most innocent and vulnerable victims of marketers' manipulations. They have been troubled by the contradiction between their incessant appetite for consumer goods and their traditional desire for limits and restraint, which progressively translated into a new religion of good health. This conflict between value systems was laid bare when the subjects of dispute were alcohol and cigarettes because these products, along with their promotion, involved

unique ethical problems. The campaigns against the marketing of cigarettes and alcoholic beverages not only encompassed the general disapproval of glamorous and therapeutic advertising, but also resulted from
specific objections to the promotion of substances posing risk to health,
livelihood, and, according to some, respectability. In the end, these efforts, while significant for revealing the enduring discomfort many Americans harbored toward unregulated consumerism, have been mostly inef-
fectual, and the lines between acceptable and unacceptable marketing
practices remain unclear and shifting.

GOVERNMENT REGULATION AND FREE ENTERPRISE

A critical question in postwar American commerce has been to what extent government and industry should be responsible for safeguarding the
consuming public from risk. Evincing a conviction that crossed party
lines, activists in all three marketing control movements believed that
government had an undeniable obligation to protect and inform its citizens. This commitment to positive government, descended from the Progressive Era and solidified during the New Deal, reached its peak in the
1960s and 1970s, when many groups and interests championed an activist
federal government, especially in matters of social regulation. In the words
of one advocate of alcohol marketing control, government had an urgent
duty to remedy the "badly tilted" decision-making field, and many restrictionists, such as Robert Kennedy on the issue of cigarettes and his son Joe
Kennedy with regard to alcoholic beverages, formulated this duty in terms of
protecting public health instead of establishing moral principles.[5] Even as
many Americans in the 1970s and beyond came to distrust government intervention in private behavior, and their policymakers became increasingly
reluctant to enact further regulation, marketing restrictionists pressed on
with their firm belief that the federal government should be able to define
how alcohol and cigarettes were depicted in the marketplace.

On the issue of corporate responsibility, many Americans had come to
consent with the consumer rights perspective, encapsulated in the argument of Joe Tye, a leading antismoking advocate who in 1984 declared, "It
is reasonable to expect that when significant evidence suggests that a
product is dangerous, those engaged in selling it should adhere to a standard of conservatism, whether they believe the evidence or not. They
should not depart from this standard until the safety of the product has
been determined." Furthermore, Tye asserted that industry's duty to inform
consumers of possible hazards "arises as soon as there is credible evidence
that the risk is real, not when the last shred of doubt in the manufacturer's
mind is resolved."[6] Yet, although most people have agreed that if something
were wrong or even potentially wrong with a product its manufacturer would
have a duty to inform its consumers, many Americans and their lawmakers

have had difficulty with the idea of the state forcing a reluctant business to make such disclosures and change their marketing practices.

The First Amendment dilemma that hampered marketing control movements over the last fifty years remained unresolved as America entered the twenty-first century, and it constitutes one of the most significant commercial questions in recent American jurisprudence. Neither liberals nor conservatives have developed a unified position on commercial free speech, as contingents in both camps seek to retain some control over consumer culture, but the courts have indicated growing tolerance for unfettered marketing practices. Ten years after it appeared to advocate less protection for commercial speech in the *Posadas de Puerto Rico v. Tourism Company of Puerto Rico* case, the U.S. Supreme Court took a new direction and ruled in 1996 that a Rhode Island ban on alcoholic beverage price advertising was unconstitutional. In deciding the Rhode Island case, several justices concluded that "a state legislature does not have the broad discretion to suppress truthful, nonmisleading information for paternalistic purposes." The Court continued to demonstrate strong support for commercial speech in a 1999 case that struck down a ban on casino advertising in New Orleans. Observers noted the repercussions for cigarette and alcohol marketing controls, with one commentator writing, "[I]f anyone wanted to bring the Marlboro Man back to the airwaves, the *Greater New Orleans* decision could provide all the ammunition necessary." Finally, after years of avoidance, in 2001 the Court ruled on the most salient question of commercial speech in recent history, the constitutionality of cigarette advertising bans. In *Lorillard Tobacco Co. v. Reilly,* the Court unanimously found that a Massachusetts law prohibiting the advertising of tobacco products within a thousand feet of playgrounds, parks, and schools violated the First Amendment. Justice Sandra Day O'Connor noted, "As the State protects children from tobacco advertisements, tobacco manufacturers and retailers and their adult consumers still have a protected interest in communication." Furthermore, Justice Clarence Thomas asserted that no difference existed between commercial and noncommercial speech in the eyes of the law. *Lorillard* constituted a decided blow to marketing regulation initiatives.[7]

Nevertheless, restrictionists continued to insist that commercial speech did not warrant constitutional protection, especially when that speech promoted harmful behaviors. Lawrence Gostin and Allan M. Brandt maintained that a ban on cigarette advertising would actually advance freedom because consumers would be free to make decisions without the interference of misleading and overwhelming marketing messages.[8] The antismoking movement, whose momentum soared in the 1990s, was unwilling to acquiesce to the Court's decisions. Increasingly, its activists turned to liability suits as a strategy to curtail and punish the tobacco industry and pressed the Food and Drug Administration to regulate tobacco as a drug. The cigarette makers eventually won the bout with the FDA when the Supreme Court ruled in the industry's favor, but, threatened by endless lawsuits, in 1998 the industry negotiated a $243 billion settlement with the state attorneys general, a settlement that also required major limitations on cigarette marketing practices, such as bans on outdoor advertising, brand name merchandise, and the use of cartoons. Despite the new restrictions, four years after the settlement tobacco companies were spending 125 percent more on marketing, and the major public health organizations persist in pressing the federal government to mandate stricter regulations.[9]

THE PROBLEM OF SCIENCE AND VALUES
IN POLICYMAKING

The three marketing control movements also illustrate the escalating role of science in policymaking and in American society in general. As the twentieth century advanced, decision making became more dependent on scientific evidence, and in public life religious authority was increasingly displaced by scientific expertise and bureaucratic powers. An important backdrop for the recent antismoking and antidrinking movements has been the postwar development of the scientific establishment along with the growth in funding available for health science research. Improved scientific techniques meant that researchers were able to detect products' health risks that previously had gone unnoticed. Scientists and social scientists had become the country's modern-day priests in the policymaking arena on a whole host of issues, from atomic energy to school desegregation, and most Americans—but clearly not all—were more apt to trust scientific authorities, such as a U.S. surgeon general, than they were religious leaders, such as a bishop of the Methodist Church, to influence public policy decisions.[10] The religious drys' futile campaign against alcohol advertising during the 1950s was in part a reaction against this shift to a more secular political culture. As contrasted with the 1950s movement in which the federal bureaucracy kept its distance, the leadership role taken by several federal agencies in the subsequent cigarette and new temperance antiadvertising campaigns was one mark of the secularization of tobacco and alcohol control movements. These issues had been better adapted to fit the secular public style and thus gained growing mainstream acceptability.

But the increasing reliance on science did not turn policymaking into a cut-and-dry process or reduce the ideological component. The controversies over alcohol and cigarette consumption provide striking case studies of nonexperts struggling to make sense of contradictions in scientific evidence and still formulate policy. As with many other policy issues in the postwar period, such as pesticides and nuclear energy, government officials involved in cigarette and alcohol marketing debates had to assess risk on the basis of disputed evidence. They were asked to make immediate decisions on questions that, like most scientific problems, needed more research and on which answers of absolute certainty might never be reached.[11]

The scientific debates that ensued during the cigarette and second round of alcohol marketing hearings caused considerable confusion among many policymakers as to the nature of scientific research and what constituted evidence and facts. Many believed, or wanted to believe, that science was objective and static, but the policy discussions about alcohol and tobacco revealed the inescapably political and dynamic nature of science. As policymakers found themselves overwhelmed with conflicting scientific evidence, they confronted the question of how much was sufficient for the government to enact regulation, especially when that policy would encroach upon free enterprise and free expression. Could restrictive policies be undertaken when scientific uncertainty existed? Usually with encouragement from the affected industries and their allies, policy discussions sometimes became caught up on questions about the nature of science, diverting decision makers from debate about the policies themselves.[12]

SECULAR MORALITY AND THE FOCUS ON YOUTH

Related to the relationship between science and policymaking was the tension between science and values. Many concerned citizens and policymakers hoped that on the questions surrounding alcohol and tobacco science would lead the way out of the inexorable struggle between value systems emphasizing community and order and those prizing individualism and freedom. But rarely can science be divorced from its social-cultural context, and subjectivity is especially manifest in scientific assessment of risk and definitions of good health, realms which easily become moralized and, relatedly, politicized. These political controversies often saw ostensibly neutral scientists develop into political actors. Because scientific indictment of a substance easily slid into moral disapprobation, discussions of the effects and propriety of alcohol and cigarette marketing muddled any clear distinctions between values and science, between morality and health.[13] All three of the movements studied here incorporated to some degree moral motivations. Comparing the arguments used by the drys of the 1950s with those articulated by subsequent marketing restrictionists demonstrates this continuity. Still, we can discern a clear shift from the religious morality of the 1950s movement to the secular morality of the later movements against cigarette and alcohol marketing that relied on secular experts and frequently disavowed moral impulses. Many of the policy discussions revolved around similar themes confronted in earlier debates but were informed by new evidence about addictions.

The issue on which scientists and other secular figures were most likely to abandon their supposed objectivity was the problem of children drinking and smoking. The fear of corrupting innocent youth played a key role in each of the marketing control movements, and restrictionists in all three periods accused the manufacturing, media, and advertising industries of deliberately appealing to, and thereby exploiting, youth in their cigarette and alcohol advertisements. For instance, one medical doctor who testified on behalf of the National Tuberculosis Association at congressional hearings on cigarette labeling in 1965 departed from the medical discussion to indict cigarette advertisers for their role in the rising incidence of youth smoking. The scientist voiced the beliefs of many antismokers when he charged that children were "subjected to extremely clever allures carefully developed by the advertisers."[14] The charge of manipulation of innocents was an important theme of the morality play that emerged from the scientific findings of hazards to health.

Restrictionists were most troubled by television and the extent to which it influenced children's attitudes and behaviors. Television's use of sight, motion, and sound as well as its pervasive and universal presence in American living rooms have made it a supreme shaper of values in postwar society. Historically, most Americans, particularly of the middle class, had conceived of the family home as a shelter protecting the child from the corruption of the consumer marketplace. With the advent of commercialized radio and especially television, it became more difficult—and some would argue, impossible—to maintain the boundary between the home and the marketplace. Television, and advertising on television, appeared most threatening of all because children had such easy and frequent access to it.[15] The antimarketing movements before the 1970s used mainly intuitive and personal evidence as they made these claims of media and advertising impact on young people's values and behaviors. The new temperance movement, however, was able to draw upon a plethora of new social scientific studies, and much of the policy debate during the last period revolved around the reliability of media impact research.

The movements' shared focus on the threat to children can be understood as an expression of the reformers' own struggles with the seductions of consumer culture. In other words, framing cigarette and alcohol marketing control as a youth problem resulted less from a specific concern for children than from a manifestation of wider adult anxieties about declining cultural standards. Moral conservatives and liberal consumer rights advocates coincided in the belief that children's innocence was in part a function of their isolation from commercialized desires. The appeal of advertising to children, especially when the advertising promoted products that society believed children should not consume, seemed to showcase the worst tendencies of consumer culture—the baldest form of manipulation that in subtler ways affected us all. Control proponents from various ideological positions used their advocacy of advertising and media standards for children as a way of establishing their standards of restraint and propriety for all of society. They wanted to draw a boundary somewhere so as not to yield to a complete encroachment of consumer culture on authentic values and experiences. The attack on cigarette and alcohol advertising's appeal to children thus represented a distillation of a broader critique of the values promoted by unrestrained consumerism in American society as a whole.[16]

The anxiety concerning youth continued into the next century. NBC's proposal for advertising hard liquor was designed to avoid, or at least have the appearance of avoiding, youth audiences by allowing the ads to be broadcast only at night. In 2003 the distilled spirits industry association DISCUS attempted to assuage restrictionists' demands for constraint by establishing a 30 percent threshold: member companies pledged not to market their products in outlets where more than 30 percent of the audience was expected to be underage. Dissatisfied restrictionists, though, next pressed for a 15 percent threshold.[17] Since the 1940s, participants in the debates over alcohol and cigarette advertising have proposed varying broadcast schedules and placement formulas in an effort to dodge youthful audiences. None of the plans proved feasible, and all, including the most recent ones, attracted criticism because of the realities of late-night television viewing by abundant numbers of American children as well as the technical matter of time zone differences. Furthermore, youth in the late twentieth century consumed much of the same media as adults, including televised sporting events and adult-oriented situation comedies, making the isolation of the youth market from the adult market unworkable.[18] Despite the sustained and popular pursuit of strategies to restrain consumerism, the attempts have been largely futile.

COMPARING OUTCOMES

The unimpressive achievements of the two movements against alcohol marketing as contrasted with the relatively more successful campaign against cigarette marketing reveals how the technical and historical differences between the substances entered politics. Admittedly, cigarettes continued to be one of the most heavily advertised products in the last twenty years of the twentieth century—even without the employment of broadcast advertising. In addition to the traditional print ads, tobacco companies were major outdoor advertisers and used other types of promotional spending, such as sponsorship of sporting events and rock concerts, to maintain strong recognition with its target audiences: youth, minorities, and blue-collar workers. One of the tobacco companies' chief strategies for dealing with the decline in its public image was to diversify by purchasing nontobacco companies. Another strategy has been targeting overseas markets, particularly in Asia and the third world, for massive cigarette sales to make up for the decline in the U.S. market. Through these successful strategies, as well as the fact that at the end of century a substantial minority of Americans continued to smoke, the tobacco industry continues to thrive in the twenty-first century.[19]

Nevertheless, when compared with the alcoholic beverage industries, the tobacco business, and particularly cigarette advertising, faces a considerable threat, and legal challenges to the industry continue to advance. Most significant, cigarette marketing has seemed more troubling than alcohol marketing because cigarettes prove much more deadly under normal conditions of use. Because of this widespread and popular perception of tobacco's proven hazards, and, in spite of constitutional and political barriers, antismokers have been relatively successful at persuading government to regulate the promotion of cigarettes.[20] The history as well as the future direction of alcohol control, in contrast, is much more inconsistent and ambiguous. Advocacy groups and some government officials continue to agitate against the alcoholic beverage industries, yet rules for retailing and distribution across the nation are liberalizing, and many cable television channels now prominently feature hard liquor commercials, a trajectory that could not be imagined for cigarette distribution and promotion in the current climate.[21]

Although many of the impediments that antialcohol activists have faced were the same as those encountered by antismokers, particularly constitutional objections and the economic power of the industries, alcohol restrictionists have encountered even greater obstacles. Alcohol restrictionists often noted that policymakers were more comfortable regulating, or merely discussing, cigarette smoking and illegal drug use than they were talking about or combating alcohol problems. A spokesperson for the Tobacco Product Liability Project, which monitors lawsuits against both cigarette and alcohol manufacturers (again demonstrating the perception of linkage between the two products) observed in 1989 that "the alcoholic beverage industry has escaped many of the restrictions and requirements imposed on the tobacco industry in the last two decades."[22] Americans' and their policymakers' skittishness when presented with proposals to regulate alcohol marketing, as opposed to cigarette marketing, has derived from alcohol's closer historical association with moral imposition and intolerance. George Hacker, who remains a leading advocate of alcohol marketing controls, argues that alcohol policy is much more nebulous and difficult than cigarette policy and believes that the new temperance movement has been "much more hamstrung by the legacy of Prohibition" than has the antismoking movement.[23]

Resistance to alcohol controls can also be attributed to the reality that many potential supporters of regulation were themselves moderate consumers of alcohol. A majority of adult Americans drink alcoholic beverages in some amount, estimated at 65 percent of the population in 1999, and consider their consumption pleasurable and harmless. This consumption phenomenon has diminished the felt need for restrictions on the promotion of alcohol, and only when the discussion is framed as protecting children and fetuses have Americans grown disposed to its regulation. Support for antismoking controls, on the other hand, has profited not only from the widespread disapproval of youth smoking, but also from the substantial decrease in the smoking rate among adults across this period, from more than 40 percent of Americans in 1965 to around 25 percent in the mid-1990s.[24] The social acceptability of smoking has experienced a much more substantial decline than the acceptability of drinking. Also shaping the public's perception of the acceptability of drinking and smoking, the mainstream media regularly runs stories about studies that show the benefits of alcohol consumption while virtually no reports of the positive effects of smoking are ever publicized.[25] Therefore, although alcohol and tobacco have been linked together as "bad," the moral and thus political valence of each has differed.

Although the advocates of an alcohol advertising ban in the 1950s were on the whole very different from the supporters of cigarette and alcohol marketing control afterward, they all agreed that the federal government should vigorously regulate the promotion of risky consumer goods, especially when those goods were promoted through powerful media to consumers they viewed as vulnerable and uninformed. Each group of reformers to some degree posed a critique of America's expanding consumer culture and its most conspicuous expression, modern marketing. By the 1970s, these calls for restraint attracted both avowed conservatives and, more likely, self-identified liberals to the causes. Like the broader consumer rights movement, the advocates of alcohol and cigarette marketing regulation wanted to make consumerist practices safe and accountable; at the same time, they often sought to impose their moral or ethical standards for acceptable and unacceptable behaviors, not only on industry, but also on consumers.

The antismoking movement has been particularly influential as a model for campaigns seeking marketing regulation of suspect products by using scientific evidence mixed with social attitudes. The approach was applied, not as effectively, in the case of alcohol marketing control and has been extended to issues such as the marketing of fatty and junk foods and marketing to children in general.[26] As such, the marketing regulation movements studied here, although much less successful than their adherents wished, influenced each other and created momentum for agitation against the unrestricted promotion of products and ideas deemed harmful to the physical and social body in American consumer society. Their quest for limits, in the face of powerful countervailing business trends and cultural values, endures.

NOTES

INTRODUCTION—HEALTH, MORALITY, AND FREE SPEECH

1. U.S. Senate, Committee on Interstate and Foreign Commerce, *Liquor Advertising Over Radio and Television,* 82nd Cong., 2nd sess., 1952, 22.

2. Quoted in "AMA Prescribes Strong Medicine," *Advertising Age,* 21 July 1986, S17; Mark Edward Lender and James Kirby Martin, *Drinking in America: A History,* rev. ed. (New York: Free Press, 1987), 199–201.

3. Thurmond quoted in "Senator Raps Spuds MacKenzie Promotion," *Marketing News,* 4 December 1987, 24.

4. Gary Cross, *The Cute and the Cool: Wondrous Innocence and Modern American Children's Culture* (New York: Oxford University Press, 2004), and *An All-Consuming Century: Why Commercialism Won in Modern America* (New York: Columbia University Press, 2000), 249, 109; Ellen Seiter, *Sold Separately: Children and Parents in Consumer Culture* (New Brunswick, N.J.: Rutgers University Press, 1993); James Gilbert, *A Cycle of Outrage: America's Reaction to the Juvenile Delinquent in the 1950s* (New York: Oxford University Press, 1986).

5. Lizabeth Cohen, *A Consumers' Republic: The Politics of Mass Consumption in Postwar America* (New York: Alfred Knopf, 2003), 8–12; Jean-Christophe Agnew, "Coming Up for Air: Consumer Culture in Historical Perspective," in John Brewer and Roy Porter, eds., *Consumption and the World of Goods* (London: Routledge, 1993), 19–39.

6. John C. Burnham, *Bad Habits: Drinking, Smoking, Taking Drugs, Gambling, Sexual Misbehavior, and Swearing in American History* (New York: New York University Press, 1993), 100. Roland Marchand, *Advertising the American Dream: Making Way for Modernity, 1920–1940* (Berkeley: University of California Press, 1985), argues that advertising promoted urban and modern values.

7. Peter N. Stearns, *Battleground of Desire: The Struggle for Self-Control in Modern America* (New York: New York University Press, 1999).

8. Michael Schudson, "Delectable Materialism: Second Thoughts on Consumer Culture," in David A. Crocker and Toby Linden, eds., *Ethics of Consumption: The Good Life, Justice, and Global Stewardship* (Lanham, Md.: Rowman & Littlefield, 1998), 253–60; Daniel Horowitz, *The Morality of Spending: Attitudes Toward the Consumer Society in America, 1875–1940* (Baltimore: Johns Hopkins University Press, 1985).

9. Solomon Katz, "Secular Morality," and Howard Leichter, "Lifestyle Correctness and the New Secular Morality," both in Allan M. Brandt and Paul Rozin, eds., *Morality and Health* (New York: Routledge, 1997).

10. Cross, *An All-Consuming Century.*

11. Christian Smith, "Introduction: Rethinking the Secularization of American Public Life," in Christian Smith, ed., *The Secular Revolution: Power, Interests, and Conflict in the Secularization of American Public Life* (Berkeley: University of California Press, 2003), 1–79.

12. John Greenaway, *Drink and British Politics Since 1830: A Study in Policy Making* (Houndmills, Hampshire: Palgrave Macmillan, 2003), 1–6.

13. Cross, *The Cute and the Cool*, 164.

14. "Tobacco, Alcohol, and Ads: Charting an Independent Path," *Advertising Age*, 30 January 1989, 16; Richard McGowan and J. F. Mahon, "Collaborating with the Enemy: Tobacco, Alcohol, and the Public Good," *Business in the Contemporary World* 7 (1995): 69–92; Meredith Minkler, Lawrence Wallack, and Patricia Madden, "Alcohol and Cigarette Advertising in Ms. Magazine," *Journal of Public Health Policy* 8 (Summer 1987): 164–79; Warren Breed and James DeFoe, "Drinking and Smoking on Television, 1950–1982," *Journal of Health Policy*, June 1984.

15. Burnham, *Bad Habits*, 5–6, 86. Cassandra Tate, *Cigarette Wars: The Triumph of 'the Little White Slaver'* (Oxford: Oxford University Press, 1999).

16. "Liquor Propping up Some Cigaret Ads," *Advertising Age*, 26 July 1984: 46–47; Matthew P. McAllister, *The Commercialization of American Culture: New Advertising, Control and Democracy* (Thousand Oaks, Calif.: Sage, 1996), 179–80, 197–200; David Buchanan, *Beer and Fast Cars: How Brewers Target Blue-Collar Youth Through Motor Sport Sponsorships* (Washington, D.C.: AAA Foundation for Traffic Safety, 1990).

17. T. J. Jackson Lears, "From Salvation to Self-Realization: Advertising and the Therapeutic Roots of the Consumer Culture, 1880–1930," in Fox and Lears, eds., *Culture of Consumption;* D. Altman, "How an Unhealthy Product Is Sold: Cigarette Advertising in Magazines, 1960–1985," *Journal of Communications,* 1987, 37:95–106; Michael Jacobson, R. Atkins, and George Hacker, *The Booze Merchants: The Inebriating of America* (Washington, D.C.: Center for Science in the Public Interest, 1983).

18. Senator Howard Baker at U.S. Congress, Senate, Consumer Subcommittee of the Committee on Commerce, *Cigarette Advertising and Labeling*, 91st Cong., 1st sess., 22 July 1969, 169.

19. Allan M. Brandt, "The Cigarette, Risk and American Culture," *Daedalus* 1990, 119(4):156; Mark E. Rushefsky, *Making Cancer Policy* (Albany: State University of New York Press, 1986), 6; Charles Rosenberg, "Banishing Risk," in *Morality and Health*, 49; Joseph Gusfield, "The Social Symbolism of Smoking and Health," in Robert L. Rabin and Stephen D. Sugarman, eds., *Smoking Policy: Law, Politics, and Culture* (New York: Oxford University Press, 1993), 50–77.

20. Howard Leichter, *Free to Be Foolish: Politics and Health Promotion in the United States and Great Britain* (Princeton, N.J.: Princeton University Press, 1991), 26; "The FTC as National Nanny," *Washington Post*, 1 March 1978, A22.

1—TEMPERANCE AND MASS SOCIETY

1. C. P. Trussell, "Testimony Asks Senate Committee to Act on Langer Bill," *New York Times*, 13 January 1950, 12:4; John W. Ball, "55 Witnesses Appear to Ask Interstate Ban on Liquor Ads," *Washington Post*, 13 January 1950, 1:6; "Old King Alcohol," *Time*, 23 January 1950, 11–12; "Junius Jr. at the Press Table," *The Voice*, March 1950, 12.

2. Gaines Foster, *Moral Reconstruction: Christian Lobbyists and the Federal Legislation of Morality, 1865–1920* (Chapel Hill: University of North Carolina Press, 2002).

3. Methodist Church, *Journal of the 1952 General Conference*, 1846–47, *Journal of the 1956 General Conference*, 1922, and *Journal of the 1960 General Conference*, 1725.

4. Alice G. Knotts, *Fellowship of Love: Methodist Women Changing American Racial Attitudes, 1920–1968* (Nashville: Abingdon Press, 1996).

5. "World Temperance Sunday," *The Voice,* September 1939, 19; "Methodists Plan Great Temperance Advance," *American Issue,* April 1947, 2; Bishop Wilbur Hammaker, "Have You Started?" *The Voice,* January 1949, 4–5, "The Second Commitment Day," *The Voice,* May 1949, 4, and "The Methodist Board of Temperance: Its Origins and Development," *The Voice,* November 1953, 7, 11. "Methodists Mobilize Against Liquor Traffic," *American Issue,* November 1953, 3. Circulation figures in *N. W. Ayer & Son's Directory: Newspapers and Periodicals 1930–1969* (Philadelphia: N. W. Ayer & Son, 1969).

6. Ruth Bordin, *Woman and Temperance: The Quest for Power and Liberty, 1873–1900* (New Brunswick, N.J.: Rutgers University Press, 1990), 96; Alison Parker, *Purifying America: Women, Cultural Reform, and Pro-Censorship Activism, 1873–1933* (Urbana: University of Illinois Press, 1997), 9, 27–32. Circulation figures in *N. W. Ayer & Son's Directory.*

7. Joseph Gusfield, *Symbolic Crusade: Status Politics and the American Temperance Movement* (Urbana: University of Illinois Press, 1963), 3; John C. Burnham, *Bad Habits: Drinking, Smoking, Taking Drugs, Gambling, Sexual Misbehavior, and Swearing in American History* (New York: New York University Press, 1993), 1–22.

8. Frederick Lewis Allen, *Only Yesterday: An Informal History of the Nineteen-Twenties* (New York: Harper & Brothers, 1931), 195–206; Edward Larson, *Summer for the Gods: The Scopes Trial and America's Continuing Debate Over Science and Religion* (New York: Basic Books, 1997).

9. Gusfield, *Symbolic Crusade,* 4.

10. Burnham, *Bad Habits,* 39–44.

11. Kenneth Rose, *American Women and the Repeal of Prohibition* (New York: New York University Press, 1996), 101–102, 66; George Marsden, *Religion and American Culture* (San Diego: Harcourt Brace Jovanovich, 1990), 204–5.

12. David Riesman, *The Lonely Crowd: A Study of the Changing American Character* (New Haven, Conn.: Yale University Press, 1950); William H. Whyte, *The Organization Man* (New York: Simon and Schuster, 1956); Lori Rotskoff, *Love on the Rocks: Men, Women, and Alcohol in Post–World War II America* (Chapel Hill: University of North Carolina Press, 2002), 198.

13. Joseph Gusfield, "Social Structure and Moral Reform: A Study of the Woman's Christian Temperance Union," *American Journal of Sociology* 61 (November 1955): 221–32.

14. Jon Stone, *On the Boundaries of American Evangelicalism: The Postwar Evangelical Coalition* (New York: St. Martin's Press, 1997), 14.

15. Roy L. Smith, "The Sacred Responsibility of Example," *American Issue,* December 1948, 8; Robert Wuthnow, *The Restructuring of American Religion: Society and Faith Since World War II* (Princeton, N.J.: Princeton University Press, 1988), 42; James Gilbert, *A Cycle of Outrage: America's Reaction to the Juvenile Delinquent in the 1950s* (New York: Oxford University Press, 1986.)

16. Parker, 138, 140, 225.

17. Richard F. Hamm, *Shaping the Eighteenth Amendment: Temperance Reform, Legal Culture, and the Polity, 1880–1920* (Chapel Hill: University of North Carolina Press, 1995), 12–14, 34–35; Foster, 80–81; Lori Ginzberg, *Women and the Work of Benevolence: Morality, Politics, and Class in the Nineteenth-Century United States* (New Haven, Conn.: Yale University Press, 1990), 98, 110; Jed Dannenbaum, *Drink and Disorder: Temperance Reform in Cincinnati from the Washingtonian Revival to the WCTU* (Urbana: University of Illinois Press, 1984), 10, 85; Jack S. Blocker, Jr., *American Temperance Movements: Cycles of Reform* (Boston: Twayne, 1989); Alan Hunt, *Governing Morals: A Social History of Moral Regulation* (Cambridge: Cambridge University Press, 1999), 10.

18. "Drys a Power in Washington," *American Issue,* January 1960, 6; Gusfield, *Symbolic Crusade,* 163.

19. Ginzberg, 77–82; Hamm, 203–204, 209; Rose, 101. Foster, 247–54.

20. Elizabeth Smart to Senator Wallace White, 28 January 1947, and Smart to White, 30 January 1947, both in National Archives and Records Administration (hereafter NARA) Record Group (hereafter RG) 46, Commerce Committee, 80th Cong., S. 265, Box 9; Annalee Stewart to Senator Edwin Johnson, 10 March 1950, NARA, RG 46, Commerce Committee, 81st Cong., S. 1847, Box 23; Wilbur Hammaker to Johnson, 12 April 1950, NARA RG 46, Commerce Committee, 82nd Cong., S. 2444, Box 1; Clinton Howard to Johnson, 24 May 1950, NARA, RG 46, Commerce Committee, 81st Cong., S. 1847, Box 23.

21. Hamm, 236–39; Foster, 207–208; Parker.

22. Ronald Roizen, "The American Discovery of Alcoholism, 1933–1939" (Ph.D. diss., University of California, Berkeley, 1991), 39, 180–207.

23. Distilled Spirits Institute, Inc., *Annual Report* (Washington, D.C., 1946), 12; Idem., *Annual Statistical Review* (Washington, D.C., 1951), 40–41; Idem, *Annual Statistical Review of the Distilled Spirits Industry* (Washington, D.C., 1960), 47. As for beer, 9.43 percent of Americans lived in areas dry for beer in 1947, and this figure remained mostly constant for the next decade. *Brewers' Almanac* (Washington, D.C.: United States Brewers Association, 1949), 108; *Brewers' Almanac* (Washington, D.C.: United States Brewers Association, 1960), 100–107.

24. Jay L. Rubin, "The Wet War: American Liquor Control, 1941–1945," in Jack S. Blocker, Jr., ed., *Alcohol, Reform, and Society: The Liquor Issue in Social Context* (Westport, Conn: Greenwood Press, 1979), 235–58; Rotskoff, 46–51.

25. *Advertising Age,* 16 April 1956, 88.

26. See C. P. Trussell, "Liquor Ad Fight Widens in Scope," *New York Times,* 27 April 1958, 84:3; "Bills Restricting Liquor Advertising are Before 8 State Legislatures, AFA Reports," *Advertising Age,* 30 March 1953, 44; Edward B. Dunford, "States Can Stop Sale of Advertised Liquors: New and Sweeping Powers Bestowed by 21st Amendment," *American Issue,* February 1947, 3–4.

27. Lawrence Samuel, *Brought to You By: Postwar Television Advertising and the American Dream* (Austin: University of Texas, 2001), 87.

28. Walter O. Cromwell, "Who Pays the Bill? Modern Advertising Contributes to Immensity of Liquor Problem," *American Issue,* June 1947, 5.

29. George Gallup, *The Gallup Poll: Public Opinion 1935–1971* (New York: Random House, 1972), 43, 203, 251, 322, 356, 549, 596, 771, 877, 925, 1296–97, 1477, 1666, 1991; Harold Y. Vanderpool, "The Wesleyan-Methodist Tradition," in Ronald Numbers and Darrel Amundsen, eds., *Caring and Curing: Health and Medicine in the Western Religious Traditions* (New York: Macmillan, 1986), 344; Roizen, "The American Discovery," 40.

30. Clarence Hall and Rev. Dutton Peterson, U.S. Senate, Committee on Interstate and Foreign Commerce, *Liquor Advertising,* 81st Cong., 2nd sess., 1950, 47, 94; Paul Bosley, U.S. House of Representatives, Committee on Interstate and Foreign Commerce, *Advertising of Alcoholic Beverages,* 84th Cong., 2nd sess., 1956, 66.

31. Colvin quoted in "Liquor Advertising Hit," *New York Times,* 14 December 1947, 60:5; Hammaker found in "At Langer Bill Hearing Congress Powerless to Pass Anti-Ad Bill, Industry Asserts," *Modern Brewery Age,* January 1950, 88; "High Tide in Washington," *The Voice,* December 1953, 4; "House Resumes Hearings on Liquor Advertising," *Christian Century,* 26 May 1954, 629; Duke K. McCall, "New Year's Message," *American Issue,* January 1953, 1.

32. Burnham, 23–25; Gusfield, 4; Rotskoff, 36–37.

33. Joseph Dubin, "As We See It: Swallowing the Dry Line," *Modern Brewery Age,* August 1952, 21; "Heublein Ads Push 'Duet Drinking' but Wives Aren't Shown," *Advertising Age,* 24 February 1958, 193; "Brewery, Broadcaster Spokesmen Hit Back at Attacks on Radio, Television Programs," *Modern Brewery Age,* October 1952, 34, 80–85; Robert G. LaForge, "Misplaced Priorities: A History of Federal Alcohol Regulation and Public Health Policy" (Ph.D. diss., Johns Hopkins University, 1987), 286; Rotskoff, 41.

34. Rotskoff, 41, 194, 198–99

35. Roizen, "The American Discovery of Alcoholism"; Jay L. Rubin, "Shifting Perspectives on the Alcoholism Treatment Movement 1940–1955," *Journal of Studies on Alcohol* 40 (1979): 376–86; Blocker, 145–46; E. M. Jellinek, *The Disease Concept of Alcoholism* (New Haven, Conn.: Hillhouse Press, 1960); Rotskoff, 65.

36. Ernest Kurtz, *Not-God: A History of Alcoholics Anonymous* (Center City, Minn.: Hazelden, 1979); David A. Ward, "Conceptions of the Nature and Treatment of Alcoholism," in Thomas Watts, ed., *Social Thought on Alcoholism* (Malabar, Fla.: Robert E. Krieger, 1986), 9–24; Blocker, 139–51; Rotskoff, 65.

37. Burnham, 82–83; Henry Bretzfield, *Liquor Marketing and Liquor Advertising: A Guide for Executives and Their Staffs in Management, Sales and Advertising* (New York: Abelard-Schuman, 1955), 25; Roizen, "The American Discovery," 284; LaForge, 286–90; General Frank R. Schwengel, president Joseph E. Seagram and Sons, "External Problems of the Industry," at The Seagram Family Association First Convention, 1951, 127–28, in Hagley Museum and Library, Seagram Collection, Acc. 2173, Series III, Box 3; "Conference Draft—Hill and Knowlton Study, LBI," 11, n.d., Box 97, Folder 1, John W. Hill Papers, Wisconsin Historical Society.

38. Howard Haggard, "Editorial: The Proposed Massachusetts Label and Its Place in Education Against Inebriety," *Quarterly Journal of Studies on Alcoholism* 6 (June 1945): 1–3.

39. Blocker, 151–53.

40. Blocker, 149; Rubin, 380.

41. Mark Edward Lender and James Kirby Martin, *Drinking in America: A History*, rev. ed. (New York: Free Press, 1987), 188; "Alcoholic Neutralism," *American Issue*, November 1955, 2; George Eads, "Militant Ladies of WCTU Renew Attack on 'Arrogant, Corrupt Liquor Forces,'" *Modern Brewery Age*, November 1952, 56, 86–89; Hugo Hecht, "Alcoholism is a Preventable Disease," *American Issue*, June 1952, 4–5; Edward Rees, *Congressional Record*, 9 August 1954, 13846; Rubin, "Shifting Perspectives," 380; Roizen, "The American Discovery, " 89–90.

42. William L. White, *Slaying the Dragon: The History of Addiction Treatment and Recovery in America* (Bloomington, Ill.: Chestnut Health Systems, 1998), 178–80; Roizen, "The American Discovery," 239, 249–50; Penny Booth Page, "E. M. Jellinek and the Evolution of Alcohol Studies: A Critical Essay," *Addiction* 92 (December 1997): 1619.

43. Ronald Roizen, "How Does the Nation's 'Alcohol Problem' Change From Era to Era? Stalking the Social Logic of Problem-Definition Transformations Since Repeal." Presented at Historical Perspectives on Alcohol and Drug Use in American Society, 1800–1997, College of Physicians of Philadelphia, 9–11 May 1997; Rotskoff, 65, 67, 85–86; White, 180; Page, 1623.

44. Robert Tournier, "The Medicalization of Alcoholism: Discontinuities in Ideologies of Deviance," in Watts, ed., *Social Thought on Alcoholism*, 39–51; Blocker, 150.

45. John W. Ball, "Drys Ask Senators to Banish Whisky's 'Men of Distinction," *Washington Post*, 13 May 1947, 3:3; "Old King Alcohol," *Time*, 23 January 1950, 11–12.

46. "Does 'Beer Belong' to Radio-TV or Radio-TV Belong to Beer?" *Christian Century*, 25 May 1955, 612; "Network President Says—'We're a Willing Servant of the Beer Industry,'" *American Issue*, September 1954, 4–5.

47. "Circulation," *The Voice*, January 1938, 3; "Curb on Ad Space for Liquor Scored," *New York Times*, 11 April 1951, 50:1; Bretzfield, 176; "Saturday Evening Post Will Publish Liquor Advertising in Policy Change," *New York Times*, 28 August 1958, 25:5.

48. "Advertising and Marketing News," *New York Times*, 19 July 1954, 28:4; "Washington Star Drops 1914 Stand; To Accept Liquor Ads," *Advertising Age*, 29 October 1956, 2; "Newspapers Lifting Alcohol Beverage Ad Ban," *Modern Brewery Age*, September 1957, 26; "Saturday Evening Post," *New York Times*; Carl Spielvogel, "Advertising: Post Joins Liquor Media List," *New York Times*, 31 August 1958, 6:1; "Post Finds

Liquor Ads Are Now 'Compatible,'" *Advertising Age,* 1 September 1958, 1, 58; "Drys Urge Post to Reconsider Its New Liquor Policy," *Advertising Age,* 8 September 1958, 2; "Nuyens Believes Liquor Ads on Air Makes Sense," *Advertising Age,* 17 November 1958, 58.

49. James Patterson, *Grand Expectations: The United States, 1945–1974* (New York: Oxford University Press, 1996), 343–55; Samuel, *Brought to You By,* x, xii, 3.

50. Jackson Lears, *Fables of Abundance: A Cultural History of Advertising in America* (New York: Basic Books, 1994), 252–53; Patterson, 343–45; Gilbert, 7; Samuel, 22.

51. Gilbert, 6, 18, 212–14; Frederic Wertham, *Seduction of the Innocent* (New York: Rinehart and Company, 1953).

52. Lears, *Fables of Abundance,* 254–56; Roland Marchand, *Advertising The American Dream: Making Way for Modernity, 1920–1940* (Berkeley: University of California Press, 1986); Vance Packard, *The Hidden Persuaders* (New York: D. McKay, 1957).

53. Raymond A. Bauer and Stephen A. Greyser, *Advertising in America: The Consumer View* (Boston: Division of Research, Graduate School of Business Administration, Harvard University, 1968), 133–35, 140–41, 210–26; Samuel, xix, 9, 26–28, 50.

54. "National Distillers to Run 8-Page Ad in May Coronet," *Advertising Age,* 12 April 1954, 30; "Distillers' Use of Newspaper Space Reported Greater," *Advertising Age,* 9 January 1950, 16; "Brewers Spending $1.50 Per Barrel on Ads, Compared With $1.40 in '53," *Advertising Age,* 14 June 1954, 18; "Schenley Drive for Canadian Whisky is the Heaviest Ever," *Advertising Age,* 4 October 1954, 64; William Freeman, "News of the Advertising and Marketing Fields," *New York Times,* 10 February 1957, 10:5.

55. "News of Advertising and Marketing," *New York Times,* 6 August 1956, 26:4; John Crichton, "The Liquor Business: How It Has Grown in 20 Years Since Repeal," *Advertising Age,* 30 November 1953, 2, 44–57; "Radio-TV Unit Backs Ads," *New York Times,* 1 January 1955, 10:8; "Whisky in 3 of Top 10," *American Issue,* October 1954, 5; "Saturday Evening Post Will Publish Liquor Advertising in Policy Change," *New York Times,* 28 August 1958, 25:5.

56. "Ad Copy Should Speak of Home Life, Cheer, Say Dichter," *Advertising Age,* 27 January 1958, 3; Ernest Dichter, *Strategy of Desire* (Garden City, N.Y.: Doubleday, 1960).

57. Samuel, 41, 59–62; Lears, *Fables of Abundance,* 251; Colston E. Warne, "The Case Against Advertising," *Consumer Reports,* April 1949, 150, 185; "Margaret Mead Exposes Admen—They Hate Humans," *Advertising Age,* 22 August 1955, 2; James McCarthy quoted in "Admen Told to Spank Delinquent Brothers," *Editor and Publisher,* 14 June 1952, 76; Stanley Cohen, "Trust-Busters Turning to Advertising," *Advertising Age,* 1 February 1954, 127.

58. Gilbert, 3, 76, 212; Lears, *Fables of Abundance,* 252–54.

59. Leo Bogart, *The Age of Television: A Study of the Viewing Habits and the Impact of Television on American Life* (New York: Frederick Ungar, 1956), 98–101, 184; Lynn Spigel, *Make Room for TV: Television and the Family Ideal in Postwar America* (Chicago: University of Chicago Press, 1992), 50–51; Samuel, 72–73; Gary Cross, *An All-Consuming Century: Why Commercialism Won in Modern America* (New York: Columbia University Press, 2000), 107, 109, 126–28.

60. U.S. House, *Investigation of Radio and Television Programs,* 82d Cong., 2nd sess., 952. Fred Lardner, "What's Brewing in Washington," *Modern Brewery Age,* May 1952, 26–27, 87–88; "As We See It: A Repeat Performance," *Modern Brewery Age,* June 1952, 17; "Initial Hearing in Radio-TV Probe Turns into Field Day for Top Drys," *Modern Brewery Age,* June 1952, 20, 81–82; "Radio, TV Spokesmen Assail Dry Pressure to Censor Airwaves," *Modern Brewery Age,* July 1952, 18; "Radio, TV Defended at a Hearing Here," *New York Times,* 24 September 1952, 38:2; "Viewer Complaints Against TV Commercials Aired at House Committee Hearing in New York," *Advertising Age,* 29 September 1952, 44.

61. U.S. Senate, Subcommittee to Investigate Juvenile Delinquency of the Committee on the Judiciary, Hearings on S. Res. 62, 84th Cong., 1955, 69–76; "Donovan Hits Dry Propaganda Linking Juvenile Delinquency to Drinking," *Licensed Beverage Industries Newsletter,* July–August 1954, 1.

62. Rotskoff, 228, 232.

2—THE INDUSTRIES' REGULATORY RESPONSE

1. John Crichton, "The Liquor Business" *Advertising Age,* 30 November 1953, 2, 44–57; Attorney Daniel Bernheim quoted in Robert Alden, "Advertising: Legal Twists Top Liquor Woes," *New York Times,* 14 June 1960, 58:2.

2. "Beer's Future Looks Good, But More Advertising Needed, Wholesalers Told," *Advertising Age,* 9 November 1953, 48; "Liquor Retailers Told to Modernize, Use More Advertising," *Advertising Age,* 27 September 1954, 24.

3. Pamela E. Pennock and K. Austin Kerr, "In the Shadow of Prohibition: Domestic American Alcohol Policy since 1933," *Business History* 47(July 2005): 387.

4. LaForge, 186, 196–97, 202, 217.

5. Ibid., 229–31.

6. Ibid., 226–27.

7. Ibid., 202, 218–19, 236–43.

8. "U.S. Gives Mild Slap to Brewers for Copy Claims," *Advertising Age,* 12 April 1954, 2; Joseph Dubin, "As We See It: Let's Kill 'Fattening' Fallacy," *Modern Brewery Age,* April 1954, 21; "Liquor Industry Cautioned on Ads," *New York Times,* 8 May 1957, 75:1; "What's Brewing in Washington," *Modern Brewery Age,* November 1959, 17; "Advertising for Addiction," *American Issue,* 9 November 1959, 2.

9. Stanley Cohen, "Treasury, Not Client, Has Last Word on Alcohol's Ad Problems," *Advertising Age,* 14 December 1953, 2, 32–35.

10. Robert G. LaForge, "Misplaced Priorities: A History of Federal Alcohol Regulation and Public Health Policy" (Ph.D. diss., Johns Hopkins University, 1987), 152–53; Mark Edward Lender and James Kirby Martin, *Drinking in America: A History* (New York: Free Press, 1987), 170.

11. Henry Bretzfield, *Liquor Marketing and Liquor Advertising: A Guide for Executives and their Staffs in Management, Sales and Advertising* (New York: Abelard-Schuman, 1955), 172–74; C. P. Trussell, "Liquor Ad Fight Widens in Scope," *New York Times,* 27 April 1958, 84:3; Crichton, "The Liquor Business," 46.

12. "Liquor Industry Presses for Cut in 'Killing Tax,'" *Advertising Age,* 12 January 1953, 54; Crichton, "The Liquor Business," 2, 44–57; Charles Downes, "Sales Frustration Leads to Shifts of 29 Beer, Wine, Liquor Accounts," *Advertising Age,* 31 October 1955, 3; Seagram's Inter-Company Business Symposium, 1951, 121, in Seagram Collection, Hagley Museum and Library, Acc. 2173, Series III, Box 282.

13. Jack S. Blocker, Jr., *American Temperance Movements: Cycles of Reform* (Boston: Twayne, 1989), 137.

14. "Schenley May Use Radio, Television," *New York Times,* 29 July 1949, 25:2; Joseph Dubin, "As We See It: Swallowing the Dry Line," *Modern Brewery Age,* August 1954, 21; Joseph Dubin, "As We See It: Time for Counter-Pressure," *Modern Brewery Age,* March 1956, 21; "Anti-Liquor Ad Bill Likely to Pass in House," *Advertising Age,* 9 April 1956, 22; George Eads, "Drys Spearhead New Prohibition War," *Modern Brewery Age,* December 1956, 53.

15. "New Tactics Seen in Drys' Campaign," *New York Times,* 17 January 1950, 24:2; Seagram's Inter-Company Business Symposium, 124–25.

16. "The Drys Today Wear a Deceiving New Look," *Modern Brewery Age,* April 1958, 100–101.

17. Richard McGowan, *Government Regulation of the Alcohol Industry: The Search For Revenue and the Common Good* (Westport, Conn.: Quorum Books, 1997), 48–49; Blocker, 136–37.

18. "Budweiser's New Slim Can is Aimed At Woman Buyer," *Advertising Age,* 12 December 1955, 37; Lippincott and Margulies Industrial Designs, Inc., "Whose Brand of Beer Is That?" in Hagley Museum and Library, Acc. 2206, Box 1; "Brewers Foundation Puts 'New Look' Into Color Magazine Ads," *Advertising Age,* 7 May 1956, 3; "Liquor Industry Distills New Ad Plans As It Starts to Shed Long-Standing Taboos," *Printers' Ink,* 7 November 1958, 9–10; Lennen & Newell Research Department, "Importance of Women in the Use of Alcoholic Beverages," June 1962, in Seagram Collection, Acc. 2126, Box 782.

19. "Club Pours Water on Plan to Push Liquor to Women," *Advertising Age,* 26 January 1959, 42.

20. Bretzfield, 175; LaForge, 275–82.

21. Crichton, "The Liquor Business."

22. "Liquor Industry Presses for Cut," 54; Doyle, Dane, & Bernbach, *Four Roses Fact Book,* 1962, 7–8, in Seagram Collection, Acc. 2126, Box 762.

23. McGowan, 53; United States Brewers Foundation, *Brewers Almanac* (New York: USBF, 1958), 86. Distilled Spirits Institute, "The Local Option Fallacy," n.d. in Seagram Collection, Acc. 2173, Series III, Box 48.

24. Lord Calvert ads in Seagram Collection, Acc. 2173, Box 89; Seagram's Inter-Company Business Symposium, 98–99; Lender and Martin, 173.

25. My analysis of alcoholic beverage advertising is based on ads in *Life* magazine from the years 1947, 1950, 1952, 1957, and 1960, and ads in the Seagram Collection, Hagley Museum & Library, Acc. 2173 and Acc. 2126.

26. "Advertising: Marketing Men Go to Fore," *New York Times,* 21 November 1958, 48:2; "Distillers Should Be Wary," *Advertising Age,* 3 November 1958, 12.

27. "Comments" on Hill & Knowlton Recommendations, Box 97, Folder 1, John W. Hill Papers, Wisconsin Historical Society (hereafter Hill papers); "Progress Report of Women's Division Liaison to WAABI," 26 October 1951; Manual for Women's Association of Allied Beverage Industries; R. E. Joyce, Vice President National Distillers Products Corporation to Kerryn King of Hill & Knowlton, 7 December 1951, all in Box 99, Folder 6, Hill Papers.

28. "Heublein Ads Push 'Duet Drinking' but Wives Aren't Shown," *Advertising Age,* 24 February 1958, 193; "Liquor Trade Bans Appeal to Women," *New York Times,* 2 January 1952, 83:4; "Liquor Industry Distills New Ad Plans As It Starts to Shed Long-Standing Taboos," *Printers' Ink,* 7 November 1958, 9–10; "Advertising: Women Invading Liquor Field," *New York Times,* 12 August 1958, 48:3; see Seagram's Golden Gin ads, Seagram Collection, Acc. 2173, Box 107.

29. "Report and Recommendations to LBI," 26 October 1951, Box 97 Folder 1; Box 95, Folder 6, Hill Papers.

30. Emphasis in the original, *Life,* 30 January 1950.

31. Emphasis in the original, *Life,* 20 March 1950.

32. Distilled Spirits Institute, "Repeal Facts," 1940s-1950s, in Seagram Collection, Acc. 2173, Box 283.

33. Seagram Collection, Acc. 2173, Boxes 11, 85, 108, 110, 180, and 199.

34. Bretzfield, 18.

35. "Liquor Men Decry Radio Advertising," *New York Times,* 10 August 1949, 33.

36. Blocker, 7.

37. "Beer Seeks Friends," *Business Week,* 6 August 1938, 32.

38. National Association of Broadcasters and *Modern Brewery Age,* "Do's and Don't's For Beer Advertising," in "Here's How (brewers use radio advertising)," National Archives, Record Group 46, 80th Cong., S. 265, Box 10, n.d.

39. Ibid.

40. USBF quote from "Brewers Foundation Puts 'New Look,'" *Advertising Age;* "Schaefer Brewing Discovers Women," *Advertising Age,* 2 February 1953, 3; James Seid-

check, "Brewers Appeal to Feminine Market with Low Calorie Themes," *Advertising Age,* 29 March 1954, 71; "Get Beer Into Mom's Grocery List, Selzer Urges," *Advertising Age,* 13 May 1957, 67.

41. I examined the "Beer Belongs" campaign in *Life* magazine.

42. Lawrence Samuel, *Brought To You By: Postwar Television Advertising and the American Dream* (Austin: University of Texas Press, 2001), 72, 112–13.

43. *Classic Commercials: The Early Years* (St. Laurent, Quebec: Madacy Entertainment Group, 2002).

44. Crichton, "The Liquor Business."

45. Wine Advisory Board advertisements, Seagram Collection, Acc. 2173, Box 291.

46. Joseph Dubin, "A Counter-Attack," *Modern Brewery Age,* January 1950, 13; Joe Kroyzend, "Just Thinkin' Out Loud," *Modern Brewery Age,* January 1950, 28.

47. Fred Lardner, "What's Brewing in Washington," *Modern Brewery Age,* April 1950: 4, 40.

48. "McBee Diary" 23 June 1950, Box 96, Folder 3, Hill Papers.

49. Wachtel at Seagram's Inter-Company Business Symposium, 121.

50. "Schenley May Use Radio, Television," *New York Times,* 28 July 1949, 25:2; "And Now, Liquor?" *Newsweek,* 1 August 1949, 37.

51. "Airing of Liquor Ads Sparks NAB Conflict," *Advertising Age,* 20 October 1958, 2; "Crack in the Dike on Liquor Ads," *Broadcasting,* 20 October 1958, 31–33; "Hard Liquor on the Air: Part II," *Broadcasting,* 27 October 1958, 35–36; "Nuyens Seeks Radio Outlets As WCRB Withdraws," *Advertising Age,* 12 January 1959, 1.

52. "Let's Break Out the Bottle," *Broadcasting,* 28 October 1957, 130; "The Cork Doesn't Fit," *Broadcasting,* 18 November 1957, 142; "Liquor Ads," *Broadcasting,* 3 November 1958, 5.

53. Fellows quoted in "Airing of Liquor Ads," *Advertising Age.* Also see "Distillers Should be Wary," 12; Carl Spielvogel, "Advertising: Plugs for Cigarettes," *New York Times,* 24 November 1958, 49:2; "Nuyens Seeks Radio Outlets," *Advertising Age.*

54. "Beer, Wine Ads on TV Scored in House Report," *New York Times,* 18 August 1954, 26:1; "NARTB Moves to Cut Out Drinking on TV Commercials," *Advertising Age,* 11 October 1954, 36; Joseph Dubin, "As We See It: An Important Step Forward," *Modern Brewery Age,* May 1955, 21; Robert Alden, "Advertising: Liquor Taboo on TV Widened," *New York Times,* 10 October 1960, 50:3.

55. "Drys Lose Out in Plea to Ban Beer Programs," *Modern Brewery Age,* January 1953, 38.

3–LEGISLATIVE BATTLES

1. George W. Eads, "Reconciled Drys Plan Aggressive Prohibition Moves," *Modern Brewery Age,* March 1950, 104; Norman Marshall, National Commander of the Salvation Army, at U.S. Senate, Committee on Interstate and Foreign Commerce, *Alcoholic Beverage Advertising,* 85th Cong., 2nd sess., 1958, 72 (hereafter Senate hearing, 1958.)

2. Aaron Haberman, "From Moral Majority to Righteous Minority: School Prayer and the Transformation of the Christian Right," paper delivered at the American Historical Association meeting, January 2005. Edward O'Brien of DSI, at U.S. Senate, Committee on Interstate and Foreign Commerce, *Liquor Advertising,* 80th Cong., 2nd sess., 1948, 129, 135 (hereafter Senate hearing, 1948); E. J. Soucy of New Hampshire Wholesale Beverage Association, Joseph Brady of International Union of United Brewery, Flour, Cereal, Soft Drink, and Distillery Workers of America, William Gretz of William Gretz Brewing Company, at U.S. Senate, Committee on Interstate and Foreign Commerce, *Liquor Advertising,* 81st Cong., 2nd sess., 1950, 113, 189, 215 (hereafter Senate hearing, 1950).

3. Eads, "Reconciled Drys"; "Celler, Klein Hit Anti-Beer Ad Bill," *Broadcasting,* 24 May 1954, 134. The petitions, one of the largest collections in the post-WWII congressional records, receive special mention in the *Guide to the Records of the United States Senate at the National Archives 1789–1989* (U.S. Senate Bicentennial Publication, 1989), 75.

4. "Old King Alcohol," *Time,* 23 January 1950, 11–12; "At Langer Bill Hearing Congress Powerless to Pass Anti-Ad Bill, Industry Asserts," *Modern Brewery Age,* January 1950, 17–18; "House Listens to Pleas of Drys for Ban on Liquor Ads," *Advertising Age,* 24 May 1954, 1, 8; "The Ladies Wait for the Door to Open," *Broadcasting,* 31 May 1954, 80; "Churchmen Press for Liquor Curbs," *New York Times,* 23 April 1958, 37:1.

5. "Senators Cool to Dry Quest for Liquor Ad Ban," *Advertising Age,* 28 April 1958, 3; "Testimony of Bryson Bill Ends," *Broadcasting,* 31 May 1954, 80.

6. Fred Lardner, "What's Brewing in Washington," *Modern Brewery Age,* June 1954, 36, 120; "Democratic Congress May Ease Ad Worries," *Advertising Age,* 8 November 1954, 1, 84; Lardner, "What's Brewing in Washington," *Modern Brewery Age,* December 1954, 34; Joseph Dubin, "As We See It: No Room for Complacency," *Modern Brewery Age,* May 1956, 13.

7. Homer Socolofsky, *Arthur Capper: Publisher, Politician, and Philanthropist* (Lawrence: University of Kansas Press, 1979), 20, 96, 100, 175; "Ex-Senator Capper Dies of Pneumonia," *New York Times,* 20 December 1951, 31:1; "Arthur Capper of Kansas Dies; Senator 30 Years," *St. Louis Dispatch,* 20 December 1951, 18:1; Eric Burns, *The Spirits of America: A Social History of Alcohol* (Philadelphia: Temple University Press, 2004), 274.

8. "The Senate's Most Expendable," *Time,* 20 March 1950, 18. "Senator Langer, 73, G.OP. Rebel, Dead," *New York Times,* 9 November 1959, 1:7; Glenn H. Smith, *Langer of North Dakota: A Study in Isolationism, 1940–1959* (New York: Garland, 1979).

9. "Ed Johnson's Record Unique," *Denver Post,* 31 May 1970, 36:1; Fred Lardner, "What's Brewing in Washington," *Modern Brewery Age,* April 1950, 4; "Sen Johnson Wants Publishers Out of Radio, TV Business," *Advertising Age,* 3 May 1954, 149.

10. Johnson to Senator Charles Tobey, 22 November 1949; Johnson to John W. Snyder, Treasury, 26 July 1949; Lynch, Treasury, to Johnson, 14 September 1949; and Johnson to Lowell Mason, FTC, 23 May 1950, all in NARA, RG 46, Commerce committee, 81st Cong., S. 1847, Box 23; Jason Mead, FTC, to Johnson, 14 August 1951, NARA, RG 46, Commerce committee, 82nd Cong., S. 2444.

11. Teller to Johnson, 22 January 1952 and 6 February 1952, NARA, RG 46, Commerce committee, 82nd Cong., S. 2444.

12. Johnson to Mildred Hoffman, 24 April 1952, NARA, RG 46, Commerce committee, 82nd Cong., S. 2444; Clinton Howard to Johnson, 24 May 1950, NARA, RG 46, Commerce committee, 81st Cong., S. 1847, Box 23.

13. *Congressional Record,* 77th Cong., 2nd sess., 8508; *Congressional Record,* 1947, 6676–78; "J.R. Bryson Dead, Congressman, 60," *New York Times,* 11 March 1953, 33:6; Fred Lardner, "What's Brewing in Washington," *Modern Brewery Age,* March 1955, 31–32; Stanley Cohen, "This Week In Washington," *Advertising Age,* 25 April 1955, 74.

14. Kerryn King of Hill & Knowlton to Adm. F. E. M. Whiting, President, Licensed Beverage Industries, 2 January 1951, Box 95, Folder 6, John J. Hill Papers, Wisconsin Historical Society.

15. Joseph Dubin, "As We See It: No Room for Complacency," *Modern Brewery Age,* May 1956, 13.

16. "Reanimated Drys Are Making Gains," *New York Times,* 1 June 1947, 7:3; "Groups Map Fight on Liquor Ad Law," *New York Times,* 30 August 1949, 35:2.

17. Joseph Dubin, "As We See It: Time for Counter-Pressure," *Modern Brewery Age,* March 1956, 21; "Anti-Liquor Ad Bill Likely to Pass in House," *Advertising Age,* 9 April 1956, 22; Arthur Garel, "What's Brewing in Washington," *Modern Brewery Age,* April 1956, 29; Garel, "What's Brewing in Washington,'" *Modern Brewery Age,* July

1956, 24; "This Week in Washington," *Advertising Age,* 20 August 1956, 48; Garel, "What's Brewing in Washington,'" *Modern Brewery Age,* August 1956, 26.

18. *Congressional Record,* 1954, 13851–52; U.S. House of Representatives, Committee on Interstate and Foreign Commerce, *Advertising of Alcoholic Beverages,* 83rd Cong., 2nd sess., 1954, 10 (hereafter House hearing, 1954); "Liquor Men Warned of 'Hush-Hush' Trend," *New York Times,* 9 January 1947, 26:7; "TV Liquor Ad Ban Is 'Pusillanimous': Celler," *Advertising Age,* 21 July 1958, 2, 77.

19. Senate hearing, 1948, 10, 17.

20. *Congressional Record,* 1949, 11732; *Congressional Record,* 1954, 9511.

21. Shelby Scates, *Warren Magnuson and the Shaping of Twentieth-Century America* (Seattle: University of Washington Press, 1997), 107, 170, 189, 218; Timothy J. McMannon, "Warren G. Magnuson and Consumer Protection" (Ph.D. diss., University of Washington, 1994); U.S. Senate, Committee on Interstate and Foreign Commerce, *Liquor Advertising,* 84th Cong., 2nd sess., 1956, 148 (hereafter Senate hearing, 1956); Senate hearing, 1958, 61, 78, 140–41; "Senate Questions Radio Commercials," *Broadcasting,* 13 February 1956, 84; Magnuson to Luis Munoz-Marin, 1 August 1957, NARA RG 46, Commerce committee 85th Cong., S. 582, Box 227, Folder 2; "Senators Threaten New Legislation as Publisher Buys Radio for Liquor," *Advertising Age,* 28 August 1961, 3, 194; "Senate Unit to Probe Broadcast Liquor Ads," *Advertising Age,* 30 March 1964, 1, 89; "No Letup Likely in Liquor Ad Ban, NAB Tells Senate," *Advertising Age,* 20 June 1966, 3, 136.

22. "Churchmen Press for Liquor Curbs," *New York Times,* 23 April 1958, 37:1; Mrs. Hazel Hartman to Magnuson, 25 August 1958, NARA, RG 46, Commerce committee, 85th Cong., S. 582, Box 227, Folder 1; Magnuson to Mrs. Denver Golladay, 25 October 1956, and Magnuson to Mrs. Roy Cummings, 15 October 1956, NARA, RG 46, Commerce committee, 84th Cong., S. 923, Box 248, Folder 1.

23. U.S. Senate, Committee on Interstate and Foreign Commerce, *Liquor Advertising,* 80th Cong., 1st sess., 1947, 71–72 (hereafter Senate hearing, 1947); "Advertising News and Notes," *New York Times,* 13 June 1947, 34:5.

24. Reed and Johnson to Senator Wallace White, 28 July 1947, "Report of Subcommittee," NARA, RG 46, Commerce committee, 80th Cong., S. 265, Box 9.

25. Senate hearing, 1948, 21–24

26. Ibid.

27. Ibid., 30–41.

28. Ibid., 7.

29. "Schenley May Use Radio, Television," *New York Times,* 29 July 1949, 25:2; "FCC Says It Can't Forbid Liquor Ads," *New York Times,* 16 August 1949, 31:2. Johnson to Paul Walker, Acting Chair, FCC, 26 July 1949, NARA, RG 46, Commerce committee, 81st Cong., S. 1847, Box 23.

30. Johnson to unknown, 31 January 1952, NARA, RG 46, Commerce committee, 82nd Cong., S. 2444; Paul Walker, Acting Chairman, FCC, to Johnson, 11 August 1949, NARA, RG 46, Commerce committee, 81st Cong., S. 1847, Box 23.

31. U.S. Senate, Committee on Interstate and Foreign Commerce, *Liquor Advertising Over Radio and Television,* 82nd Cong., 2nd sess., 1952, 18, 24, 26, 105, 117–23, 127–31 (hereafter Senate hearing, 1952); Teller to Johnson, 22 January 1952; "Washington: Radio-TV Liquor Advertising Ban Dies in Committee," *Editor and Publisher,* 29 March 1952, 8.

32. U.S. House of Representatives, Committee on Interstate and Foreign Commerce, "Advertising of Alcoholic Beverages," Report No. 2670, 83rd Cong.

33. Joseph Dubin, "As We See It: Swallowing the Dry Line," *Modern Brewery Age,* August 1954, 21; "Fight Ban on Beer, Wine Commercials, NARTB Head Urges," *Advertising Age,* 12 September 1954, 1; Val Adams, "Alarming Precedent," *New York Times,* 12 September 1954, 13:1; *Congressional Record,* 1954, 13851–52.

34. Joseph Dubin, "As We See It: The Broadcasters Report," *Modern Brewery Age,* January 1955, 11. "NARTB Moves to Cut Out Drinking on TV Commercials," *Advertising Age,* 11 October 1954, 36; Fred Lardner, "What's Brewing in Washington," *Modern Brewery Age,* February 1955, 30, 109–10.

35. National Woman's Christian Temperance Union, *Annual Report,* 77th Annual Convention, 1951, 152–53; Colvin, Senate hearing, 1947, 48; Clarence Hall, William Plymant, Senate hearing, 1950, 49–50, 78; Clayton Wallace, Temperance League of America, Senate hearing, 1948, 58, and Senate hearing, 1958, 63.

36. Edward Dunford, attorney for the National Temperance League, Senate hearing, 1956, 107–38; Representative James Davis at U.S. House of Representatives, Committee on Interstate and Foreign Commerce, *Advertising of Alcoholic Beverages,* 84th Cong., 2nd sess., 1956, 16–17 (hereafter House hearing, 1956).

37. Wallace, Senate hearing, 1952, 168; Hall, Senate hearing, 1950, 49.

38. Colvin, Senate hearing, 1950, 57; Hammaker, Senate hearing, 1947, 8.; Endrews, Senate hearing, 1948, 48.

39. FTC report, Senate hearing, 1950, 10.

40. C. Aubrey Hearn of Southern Baptist Convention, and Hall, Senate hearing, 1950, 63, 49, emphasis added.

41. B. B. McGimsey of Texas Brewers' Institute, Joseph Brady, James Short of Florida State Council of Brewery Workers, Jenkins, Riley, Senate hearing, 1950, 177, 185, 202, 259, 263.

42. House hearing, 1954, 27, 17.

43. Braucher, O'Neill, Senate hearing, 1950, 255, 218; Dr. James Greene, Pittsburgh Chamber of Commerce, Senate hearing, 1948, 42; Soucy, R. E. Joyce of DSI, Frank Fernbach of Congress of Industrial Organizations, Senate hearing, 1950, 114, 123, 126, 364; Celler, House hearing, 1954, 10.

44. Soucy, Flanigan, Senate hearing, 1950, 113, 124; Greene, Senate hearing, 1948, 42; Joyce, E. V. Lahey of USBF, John Dwight Sullivan of Advertising Federation of America, and Short, Senate hearing, 1950, 126, 159, 183, 202.

45. Lahey, Sullivan, Brady ,Ronald Hidde of Wisconsin State Council of Brewery and Soft Drink Workers, John Marshall of Ohio Brewers Association, and Riley, Senate hearing, 1950, 160, 183–86, 196, 212, 263; Hester, House hearing, 1954, 150; Greene, Senate hearing, 1948, 42–43.

46. Hall, Rev. Dutton Peterson, Methodist, Senate hearing, 1950, 47, 94; Paul Bosley, National Conference of Methodist Youth, House hearing, 1956, 66.

47. Joyce, Hester, and Sullivan, Senate hearing, 1950, 127, 166, 183; Greene, Senate hearing, 1947, 42–43.

48. Celler, Brady, House hearing, 1954, 10, 104; Hester, Senate hearing, 1950, 166.

49. "Hearing Set on Liquor Ads," *New York Times,* 18 May 1954, 60:2.

50. House hearing, 1954, 32, 63; Halvorson, U.S. Senate, Subcommittee of the Committee on Interstate and Foreign Commerce, *Liquor Advertising,* 83rd Cong., 2nd sess., 1954, 86; W. R. White, President of Baylor University, House hearing, 1956, 41.

51. Teller to Johnson, 22 January 1952; "Washington," *Editor and Publisher.*

52. Soucy, Sullivan, Jenkins, Isaac Diggest, Association of National Advertisers, Senate hearing, 1950, 114, 184, 259, 326; O'Brien, Anthony Ferro of New York Brewery Workers, Senate hearing, 1948, 135, 155.

53. Brady, Senate hearing, 1950, 185; Thomas Owens, New England State Council of Brewery Workers, House hearing, 1954, 122. Hester, Senate hearing, 1952, 117; and Ferro, Senate hearing, 1948, 155.

54. Hammaker, Senate hearing, 1947, 8, and Senate hearing, 1952, 22. Senator Glen Taylor, Senate hearing, 1947, 22; Wallace, Henry Johnson, Senate hearing, 1948, 57, 75; Samuel McCrea Cavert of Federal Council of the Churches of Christ in America, Rev. Peterson, Senate hearing, 1950, 23, 94.

55. Ivy, Senate hearing, 1950, 354 and House hearing, 1956, 132–40; Roger Storms, *Partisan Prophets: A History of the Prohibition Party, 1854–1972* (Denver: National Prohibition Foundation, 1972).

56. Turner, Senate hearing, 1948, 56; Hooton, W. A. Scharffenberg of American Temperance Society, Senate hearing, 1952, 62, 70; Colvin, Senate hearing, 1947, 48; Reverend Dr. Norman Vincent Peale, Senate hearing, 1958, 21.

57. Emerson, Senate hearing, 1950, 42; Wallace, Senate hearing, 1948, 57; Coor, Senate hearing, 1952, 55.

58. Hobbs, Senate hearing, 1950, 67; Hooton, Senate hearing, 1952, 60.

59. Sherwood, Louise Jones, Senate hearing, 1950, 53, 350.

60. I. S. Ernst of United Brethren Church, Senate hearing, 1950, 44; Peale, Senate hearing, 1952, 31; Representative Davis, House hearing, 1954, 24; Strom Thurmond quoted in "Senators Cool," *Advertising Age*, 48.

61. Dr. Norman Lovein, Georgia Temperance League, Senate hearing, 1950, 107; Taylor, Senator hearing, 1947, 22.

62. Dr. J. Warren Hastings of National Christian Church, Senate hearing, 1950, 110; Sherwood, Senate hearing, 1950, 54; Hammaker, House hearing, 1954, 19; Ashton, Coor, Senate hearing, 1952, 25, 54.

63. Cross, Wallace, Senate hearing, 1950, 68, 341. Halvorson, Senate hearing, 1952, 20; Peale, Senate hearing, 1958, 21.

64. O'Brien, Senate hearing, 1948, 131; Brady, Mrs. Franklin Sartwell of Woman's Association of Allied Beverage Industries, and Childs, Senate hearing, 1950, 185, 310, 313; Hester, Senate hearing, 1952, 117; Brady, House hearing, 1954, 107.

65. Cavert, R. H. Martin, editor of the *Christian Statesman* and president of the National Reform Association, Senate hearing, 1950, 23, 371; Halvorson, Martin, Senate hearing, 1952, 19, 38; Strom Thurmond, Senate hearing, 1956, 47.

66. O'Brien, Senate hearing, 1948, 135; Soucy, Joyce, Ellis Slater of Frankfort Distilleries, and Brady, Senate hearing, 1950, 113, 126, 135, 185; Hester, Senate hearing, 1958, 230.

67. Wallace, Senate hearing, 1952, 169, 172; Hall, Peterson, Senate hearing, 1950, 47, 94; Elizabeth Smart, WCTU, House hearing, 1954, 48.

4—EMERGENCE OF THE POSTWAR ANTISMOKING MOVEMENT

1. Luther Terry, Foreword to Elizabeth Whelan, *A Smoking Gun: How the Tobacco Industry Gets Away With Murder* (Philadelphia: George F. Stickley, 1984), ix–x; Richard Kluger, *Ashes to Ashes: America's Hundred-Year Cigarette War, the Public Health, and the Unabashed Triumph of Philip Morris* (New York: Alfred A. Knopf, 1996), 259–60; Stephen Klaidman, "How Well the Media Report Health Risk," in Edward J. Burger, Jr., ed. *Risk* (Ann Arbor: University of Michigan Press, 1990), 128–29.

2. James T. Patterson, *The Dread Disease: Cancer and Modern American Culture* (Cambridge, Mass.: Harvard University Press, 1987), 51, 142, quote on 181; Allan Brandt, "Behavior, Disease, and Health in the Twentieth-Century United States: The Moral Valance of Individual Risk," in Allan M. Brandt and Paul Rozin, eds., *Morality and Health,* (New York: Routledge, 1997), 53–77; Joseph R. Gusfield, "The Social Symbolism of Smoking and Health," in Robert L. Rabin and Stephen D. Sugarman, eds., *Smoking Policy: Law, Politics, and Culture* (New York: Oxford University Press, 1993), 54; Allan Brandt, *No Magic Bullet: A Social History of Venereal Disease in the United States since 1880* (New York: Oxford University Press, 1985).

3. Patterson, 97, 135–36, 140, 167, 190, 200.

4. Brandt, "Behavior," 60–62; Mark Rushefsky, *Making Cancer Policy* (Albany: State University of New York Press, 1986), 28.

5. Participants in the new orientation include Donald Ardell, *High Level Wellness: An Alternative to Doctors, Drugs, and Disease* (Emmaus, Pa.: Rodale Press, 1977); Leon Kass, "Regarding the End of Medicine and the Pursuit of Health," *Public Health* 40 (1975):11–12; John H. Knowles, "The Responsibility of the Individual," *Daedalus* 106 (Winter 1977): 57–80. Observers and critics include Charles Rosenberg, "Banishing Risk," in *Morality and Health,* 44–49; Brandt, "Behavior," 63–70; Michael S. Goldstein, *The Health Movement: Promoting Fitness in America* (New York: Twayne, 1992), 129–43; Sylvia Noble Tesh, *Hidden Arguments: Political Ideology and Disease Prevention Policy* (New Brunswick, N.J.: Rutgers University Press, 1990), 45–48.

6. Elizabeth Brenner Drew, "The Politics of Auto Safety," *Atlantic Monthly,* October 1966, 95–102; Ardith Maney and Loree Bykerk, *Consumer Politics: Protecting Public Interests on Capitol Hill* (Westport, Conn.: Greenwood Press, 1994); Michael Pertschuk, *Revolt Against Regulation: The Rise and Pause of the Consumer Movement* (Berkeley: University of California Press, 1982), 12, 17, 20.

7. Kenneth Dole, "News of the Churches: Is It Wrong to Smoke?" *Washington Post,* 30 January 1954, 9:1; "5-Day Plan Helps Smokers to Quit," *New York Times,* 18 April 1963, 37:1.

8. James Q. Wilson, "The Politics of Regulation," in James Q. Wilson, ed., *The Politics of Regulation* (New York: Basic Books, 1980), 370; Robert A. Kagan and David Vogel, "The Politics of Smoking Regulation: Canada, France, the United States," in Rabin and Sugarman, eds., *Smoking Policy,* 24; Pertschuk, 10, 20.

9. Michael D. Reagan, *Regulation: The Politics of Policy* (Boston: Little, Brown, 1987), 88, 90; Raymond Tatlovich and Bryon W. Daynes, eds., *Social Regulatory Policy: Moral Controversies in American Politics* (Boulder, Colo.: Westview Press, 1988), 2–3; Patterson, 138–39; Samuel Hays, "Three Decades of Environmental Politics: The Historical Context," in Michael J. Lacey, ed., *Government and Environmental Politics: Essays on Historical Developments Since World War Two* (Washington, D.C.: Woodrow Wilson Center Press, 1989, 1991), 25.

10. Kagan and Vogel, 41; Leonard Silk and David Vogel, *Ethics and Profits: The Crisis of Confidence in American Business* (New York: Simon and Schuster, 1976); Mary Douglas and Aaron Wildavsky, *Risk and Culture: An Essay on the Selection of Technical and Environmental Dangers* (Berkeley: University of California Press, 1982), 10.

11. Cassandra Tate, *Cigarette Wars: The Triumph of 'the Little White Slaver'* (Oxford: Oxford University Press, 1999), 57.

12. Kluger, 113–14; Larry C. White, *Merchants of Death: The American Tobacco Industry* (New York: Beech Tree Books, 1988), 27. Statistics on smoking from Office on Smoking and Health of the Centers for Disease Control and Prevention, "Smoking Prevalence among U.S. Adults, May 2005," <http://www.cdc.gov/tobacco/research_data/adults_prev/prevali.htm>.

13. Tate, 39–64; Ronald J. Troyer and Gerald E. Markle, *Cigarettes: The Battle Over Smoking* (New Brunswick, N.J.: Rutgers University Press, 1983), 51; Kluger, 66; John C. Burnham, "American Physicians and Tobacco Use: Two Surgeons General, 1929 and 1964," *Bulletin History of Medicine* 63 (1989): 1–31.

14. Tate, 120, 139–40; Kluger, 106–11; Troyer and Markle, 51.

15. Kluger, 132–36, 145–48; E. L. Wynder and E. A. Graham, "Tobacco Smoking as a Possible Etiologic Factor in Bronchogenic Carcinoma," *Journal of the American Medical Association* 143 (1950): 329–36; E. Cuyler Hammond and Daniel Horn, "The Relationship between Human Smoking Habits and Death Rates: A Follow-Up Study of 187,766 Men," *Journal of the American Medical Association* 154 (1954): 1316–28. Another significant early study was Richard Doll and Bradford Hill, "Smoking and Carcinoma of the Lung. Preliminary Report," *British Medical Journal* 2 (1950): 739.

16. Roy Norr, "Cancer by the Carton," *Reader's Digest,* December 1952, 7–8; Robert Sobel, *They Satisfy: The Cigarette in American Life* (Garden City, N.Y.: Anchor Books, 1978), 168; Troyer and Markle, 56–57, 71. Thomas Whiteside, *Selling Death: Cigarette Advertising and Public Health* (New York: Liveright, 1971), 45; Patterson, 211; W. Kip Viscusi, *Smoke-Filled Rooms: A Postmortem on the Tobacco Deal* (Chicago: University of Chicago Press, 2002), 139–41.

17. Sobel, 169–70; "Cigarette Scare: What'll the Trade Do?" *Business Week,* 5 December 1953, 58–68; Whelan, 2; Burnham, "American Physicians," 12–14, 24; Kluger, 184.

18. Kluger, 107, 146–47, 506.

19. Philip J. Hilts, *Smokescreen: The Truth behind the Tobacco Industry Cover-Up* (Reading, Mass.: Addison-Wesley, 1996), 14–15.

20. David Courtwright, "'Carry on Smoking': Public Relations and Advertising Strategies of American and British Tobacco Companies since 1950," *Business History* 47 (July 2005): 421–32.

21. For an example of a Hill & Knowlton press release, see "Gaps Still Exist in Knowledge of Lung Cancer and Heart Disease, Says Little," 19 April 1963, in Senator Frank E. Moss Papers, University of Utah, MS 146, Box 93, Folder 13. A. Lee Fritschler, *Smoking and Politics: Policymaking and the Federal Bureaucracy* (New York: Appleton-Century-Crofts, 1969), 18; Kluger, 168–69, 210; U.S. House of Representatives, Subcommittee of the Committee on Government Operations, *False and Misleading Advertising (Filter-Tip Cigarettes),* 85th Cong., 1st sess, 1957, 55 (hereafter cited as House hearing, 1957).

22. Hilts, 11, 15; Kluger, 149, 164–65, 184, 205–206; Robert H. Miles, *Coffin Nails and Corporate Strategies* (Englewood Cliffs, N.J.: Prentice-Hall, 1982), 64–65.

23. "Filter Cigarette Linked to Increase in Smoking," *New York Times,* 29 September 1958, 29:7; Federal Trade Commission, *Trade Regulation Rule for the Prevention of Unfair or Deceptive Advertising and Labeling of Cigarettes in Relation to the Health Hazards of Smoking* (Washington, D.C., 22 June 1964), 35–37, 75.

24. *Business Week,* 22 March 1952, 27; Terrence H. Witkowski, "Promise Them Anything: A Cultural History of Cigarette Advertising Health Claims," *Current Issues and Research in Advertising* 13 (1991): 393–409.

25. Cigarette advertisements from *Life* magazine in the 1950s and 1960s.

26. "Cigarette Scare," *Business Week,* 58–68. John E. Calfee, "The Ghost of Cigarette Advertising Past," *Regulation* 10 (November/December 1986), 40.

27. Roland Marchand, *Advertising the American Dream: Making Way for Modernity, 1920–1940* (Berkeley: University of California Press, 1985), xxi, 335–63; T. J. Jackson Lears, "From Salvation to Self-Realization: Advertising and the Therapeutic Roots of the Consumer Culture, 1880–1930," in Richard Wightman Fox and T. J. Jackson Lears, eds., *The Culture of Consumption: Critical Essays in American History 1880–1980* (New York: Pantheon Books, 1983), 19.

28. *Classic Commercials: The Early Years* (St. Laurent, Quebec: Madacy Entertainment Group, 2002); Lawrence Samuel, *Brought To You By: Postwar Television Advertising and the American Dream* (Austin: University of Texas Press, 2001), 19, 73, 100–101, 174.

29. Federal Trade Commission, *Trade Regulation Rule,* 52–57; "Cigarette Scare," *Business Week,* 58–68; Allan M. Brandt, "The Cigarette, Risk, and American Culture," *Daedalus* 119 (1990), 157; Ruth Brecher and Edward Brecher et al., *The Consumers Union Report on Smoking and the Public Interest* (Mount Vernon, N.Y.: Consumers Union, 1963), 143.

30. "Cigarettes: The Industry, Its Advertising, and How Harmful Are They?" *Consumer Reports,* February 1953, 63; "Catch Em On the Campus," *Nation,* 5 November 1960, 339.

31. "Cigarettes: The Industry," *Consumer Reports,* 63; "FTC Rules against Lucky Strikes," *Consumer Reports,* August 1951, 353.

32. "FTC Trying to Get Voluntary Compliance," *Business Week,* 25 September 1954, 124, 129; "Cigarette Trade Yawns at FTC Ad Rules," *Business Week,* 1 October 1955, 56.

33. Norr, House hearing, 1957, 271.

34. Blatnik, "Making Cigarette Ads Tell the Truth," *Harper's,* August 1958, 45–49; Calfee, 35–45.

35. Lois Mattox Miller and James Monahan, "The Facts Behind Filter-Tip Cigarettes," *Reader's Digest,* July 1957, 33–39; and "Cigarettes: The Industry," *Consumer Reports.*

36. Blatnik, House hearing, 1957, 204.

37. Norr, ibid., 272–73.

38. U.S. House of Representatives, The Legal and Monetary Subcommittee of the Committee on Government Operations, *False and Misleading Advertising (Filter-Tip Cigarettes),* 85th Cong., 2nd Sess., H. Rept. 1372, 20 February 1958, 25; Susan Wagner, *Cigarette Country: Tobacco in American History and Politics* (New York: Praeger, 1971), 88–90; Maurine Neuberger, *Smoke Screen: Tobacco and the Public Welfare* (Englewood Cliffs, N.J.: Prentice-Hall, 1963), 54. The historical record is unclear as to why Blatnik's subcommittee was dissolved.

39. Richard L. Madden, "Cigaret Strife: Firms Open New Round of Filter Innovations, Step up Ads, Promotion" *Wall Street Journal,* 24 January 1958, 1:1; Calfee, 42; Wagner, 93.

40. "Cigarette Controversy Smokes Up Here and Abroad," *Newsweek,* 22 July 1957, 58–59; "Dr. Burney's Alarm," *Newsweek,* 7 December 1959, 66; Leonard M. Schuman, "The Origins of the Report of the Advisory Committee on Smoking and Health to the Surgeon General," *Journal of Public Health Policy,* March 1981, 22; Federal Trade Commission, *Trade Regulation Rule,* 10–11.

41. "Sen. Neuberger Asks U.S. Subsidy to Counteract Liquor, Cigaret Ads," *Advertising Age,* 26 May 1958, 12; Neuberger, *Smoke Screen;* also see Neuberger to Senator Frank Moss, 11 January 1964, Moss Papers, Box 93, Folder 4.

42. Neuberger, 57–59.

43. Senate Joint Resolution 174, 23 March 1962, in National Archives, Record Group 46, 89th Cong., S. 559, Box 12. Neuberger, 60–61; Fritschler, 37–39.

44. Daniel S. Greenberg, "The Burning Question: Tobacco and Politics," *The Reporter,* 30 January 1964, 34–35; Schuman, 23–25; Brandt, "The Cigarette, Risk," 163–65.

45. Kluger, 168–69, 203–4, 222.

46. Courtwright, 426.

47. Federal Trade Commission, *Trade Regulation Rule,* 12; Kluger, 200, 203, 222, 286; "More Research is Urged on Smoking-Health," *Tobacco News,* March 1964, 1; *Congressional Record,* 1964, 8157.

48. Troyer and Markle, 76.

49. Memo, n.d., Moss Papers, Box 93, Folder 13; Moss to Anna Baker, 12 March 1969, Moss Papers, Box 93, Folder 16; Moss to John Thorson, 3 September 1969, Moss Papers, Box 93, Folder 22.

50. Moss to cigarette companies and broadcasters, 17 April 1963; Correspondence with tobacco companies and broadcast networks are found in Moss Papers, Box 93, Folders 1, 18, 20, 21, 23, and Box 339, Folder 13.

51. Stanley Cohen, "Cigaret Rule Seen Typifying New 'Help Business' Spirit of FTC," *Advertising Age,* 23 March 1964, 74; Fritschler, 74.

52. Fritschler, 75.

53. Brandt, "Cigarette, Risk," 166.

54. Brecher et al.; Pertschuk, 33.

55. Brecher et al., 175.

56. Neal Buffaloe, *What's Wrong With Smoking* (Grand Rapids, Mich.: Zondervan, 1954), 26–27; Goldstein, 116–17; Gusfield, 62.

57. Neuberger, 17; Fritschler, 31.

58. Neuberger, 128–29; Kluger, 222.

59. Randall B. Ripley and Grace A. Franklin, *Congress, the Bureaucracy, and Public Policy* (Pacific Grove, Calif.: Brooks/Cole, 1991), 3.

60. Terry, "Foreword," in Whelan, x; Robert L. Rabin and Stephen D. Sugarman, "Introduction," in Rabin and Sugarman, eds., *Smoking Policy*, 5; Fritschler, 35, 120.

61. White, 48; Melvyn D. Read, *The Politics of Tobacco: Policy Networks and the Cigarette Industry* (Brookfield, Vt.: Avebury, 1996), 30.

62. Elizabeth Brenner Drew, "The Quiet Victory of the Cigarette Lobby: How It Found the Best Filter Yet—Congress," *Atlantic Monthly*, September 1965, 76–80.

63. Read, 25, 36; Douglass Cater, *Power in Washington: A Critical Look at Today's Struggle to Govern in the Nation's Capital* (New York: Random House, 1964), 17–25; Fritschler, 3.

64. Ripley and Franklin, 6–8; Hilts, 182–84; Wagner, 137, 155; Kluger, 270.

65. Fritschler, 29, 116; Whelan, 102; Wagner, 137, 149; Peter Taylor, *Smoke Ring: The Politics of Tobacco* (London: Bodley Head, 1984), 171.

66. Burnham, "American Physicians," 24–29.

67. Wagner, 150, Fritschler, 124–25; Gideon Doron, *The Smoking Paradox: Public Regulation in the Cigarette Industry* (Cambridge, Mass.: Abt Books, 1979), 49.

5—THE WARNING LABEL DEBATE

1. Robert Sobel, *They Satisfy: The Cigarette in American Life* (Garden City, N.Y.: Anchor Books, 1978), 191; Thomas Whiteside, *Selling Death: Cigarette Advertising and Public Health* (New York: Liveright, 1971), 44.

2. U.S. Public Health Service, *Smoking and Health: Report of the Advisory Committee to the Surgeon General of the Public Health Service,* (Washington, D.C.: Government Printing Office, 1964); "Being Nonchalant About Smoking," *Time*, 24 January 1964; Leonard M. Schuman, "The Origins of the Report of the Advisory Committee on Smoking and Health to the Surgeon General," *Journal of Health Policy* (March 1981), 26; Michael Housman, "Smoking and Health: The 1964 U.S. Surgeon General's Report as a Turning Point in the Anti-Smoking Movement," *Harvard Health Policy Review* 2 (Spring 2001); Richard Kluger, *Ashes to Ashes: America's Hundred-Year Cigarette War, the Public Health, and the Unabashed Triumph of Philip Morris* (New York: Alfred A. Knopf, 1996), 260.

3. Joseph R. Gusfield, "The Social Symbolism of Smoking and Health," in Robert L. Rabin and Stephen D. Sugarman, eds., *Smoking Policy: Law, Politics, and Culture* (New York: Oxford University Press, 1993), 54; "Smoking—One Year Later," *Time*, 22 January 1965, 58.

4. Allan Brandt, "The Cigarette, Risk, and American Culture," *Daedalus* 119 (1990), 165.

5. FTC, *Federal Register*, 1964, 8325–26.

6. A. Lee Fritschler, *Smoking and Politics: Policymaking and the Federal Bureaucracy* (New York: Appleton-Century-Crofts, 1969); U.S. House of Representatives, Committee on Interstate and Foreign Commerce, *Cigarette Labeling and Advertising*, 88th Cong., 2nd sess., 1964, 60–75, 80–110 (hereafter House hearing, 1964); U.S House of Representatives, Committee on Interstate and Foreign Commerce, *Cigarette Labeling and Advertising—1965*, 89th Cong., 1st sess., 1965, 32–34 (hereafter House hearing, 1965); U.S. Senate, Committee on Commerce, *Cigarette Labeling and Advertising*, 89th Cong., 1st sess., 1965, 245–53, 392–401 (hereafter Senate hearing, 1965).

7. FTC, *Trade Regulation Rule for the Prevention of Unfair or Deceptive Advertising and Labeling of Cigarettes in Relation to the Health Hazards of Smoking* (Washington, D.C.: Government Printing Office, 22 June 1964), 79.

8. Schenk and Kornegay, House hearing, 1964, 93, 135.

9. Michael Pertschuk, *Giant Killers* (New York: Norton, 1987), 36–37.

10. Pertschuk, 25; Magnuson and Jean Carper, *The Dark Side of the Marketplace: The Plight of the American Consumer* (Englewood Cliffs, N.J.: Prentice-Hall, 1968); Magnuson, "Consumerism and the Emerging Goals of a New Society," in Ralph M. Gaedeke and Warren W. Etcheson, eds., *Consumerism: Viewpoints from Business, Government, and the Public Interest* (San Francisco: Canfield Press, 1972); and Magnuson and Elliot A. Segal, *How Much for Health?* (Washington, D.C.: R. B. Luce, 1974).

11. Memos from Edelman to Kennedy, Robert F. Kennedy Senate Papers, John F. Kennedy Presidential Library (hereafter RFK Senate Papers), Legislative Subject File 1965–1968, Box 14, Folder 6/65–9/65.

12. Kluger, 285.

13. Fritschler, 117; Kluger, 278–79.

14. Hill and Knowlton press release, "Cigarette Manufacturers Announce Advertising Code," 27 April 1964, National Archives and Records Administration (hereafter NARA), Record Group 46 (hereafter RG), Senate Committee on Commerce, Box 15, Folder: Tobacco Industry; "Cigarette Firms Establish Strict Advertising Code," *Tobacco News,* September 1964, 4.

15. Cigarette Advertising Code printed in *Advertising Age,* 4 May 1964, 178; Robert Meyner to Paul Rand Dixon, 11 April 1967, Senator Frank E. Moss Papers, MS 146, Special Collections, Marriott Library, University of Utah, Box 213, Folder 1.

16. "Our Ads Already Conform to Code, Cigaret Men Say," *Advertising Age,* 4 May 1964, 1; "Too Little, Too Late—and Inept," *Nation,* 11 May 1964, 470–71; Neuberger, House hearing, 1964, 25.

17. "Cigarette Advertising: Testimony Presented Before FTC," *Consumer Reports,* May 1964, 246–50; Maurine Christopher, "Broadcasters Ponder Ads for Cigarets, Liquor," *Advertising Age,* 6 April 1964, 1.

18. "Advertising is Scapegoat in Cigaret Controversy: AFA" *Advertising Age,* 25 January 1965, 48; "Cigarettes and the Ad Man," *New Republic,* 9 May 1964, 6.

19. House hearing, 1964, 200–76; Senate hearing, 1965, 268–381; Fritschler, 127.

20. Pertschuk, 34–35; Senators John Pastore, Sam Ervin, Thruston Morton, Senate hearing, 1965, 222, 388–91, 903; Senator Vance Hartke, *Congressional Record,* 1965, 13919.

21. Allan Brandt, "Behavior, Disease, and Health in the Twentieth-Century United States: The Moral Valance of Individual Risk," in Allan Brandt and Paul Rozin, eds., *Morality and Health* (New York: Routledge, 1997), 62; Mark Rushefsky, *Making Cancer Policy* (Albany: State University of New York Press, 1986), 6, 64, 183.

22. FTC, *Trade Regulation Rule,* 87, 105.

23. Ibid., 105.

24. Diehl, Dr. George James, Neuberger, Senate hearing, 1965, 106, 694, 908; Neuberger, House hearing, 1964, 24.

25. King, *Congressional Record,* 1965, 14419; Neuberger, *Congressional Record,* 1965.

26. House hearing, 1964, 140; Senate hearing, 1965, 246.

27. Senate hearing, 1965, 140, 125.

28. *Congressional Record,* 1965, 13902, 13908–909.

29. FTC, *Trade Regulation Rule,* 116.

30. Senate hearing, 1965, 256, 125, 140.

31. Gray, Senate hearing, 1965, 256; Kornegay, Gray, House hearing, 1964, 156, 139.

32. Bass, Pastore, Morton, Senate hearing, 1965, 561, 222, 699; Rogers, House hearing, 1965, 188.

33. Rogers, *Congressional Record,* 1965, 14413; Dr. Clarence C. Little, Bass, Senate hearing, 1965, 834, 904–905, 462; Kornegay, House hearing, 1964, 26.

34. FTC, *Trade Regulation Rule,* 115.

35. Ibid., 123; Senate hearing, 1965, 4, 101, 108, 130, 145, 151, 161, 651.

36. Moss, Neuberger, Terry, Senate hearing, 15, 20, 100; Fino, House hearing, 1964, 70–71; Robert L. Rabin and Stephen D. Sugarman, eds., *Smoking Policy: Law, Politics, and Culture* (New York: Oxford University Press, 1993), 5; Surgeon General Luther Terry, "Foreword," in Elizabeth M. Whelan, *A Smoking Gun: How the Tobacco Industry Gets Away With Murder* (Philadelphia: George F. Stickley, 1984), x.

37. FTC, *Trade Regulation Rule*, 106–13.

38. Senate hearing, 1965, 489–95.

39. Bass, Senate hearing, 1965, 98.

40. House hearing, 1964, 53, 106, 123; Mattice to Magnuson, 29 January 1965, Magnuson to Moss, 15 January 1965, and Magnuson to Bennett, 25 March 1965, NARA, RG 46, Senate Committee on Commerce, 89th Cong., S. 559, Box 6, Folder: General Correspondence. Further demonstrating how intertwined the alcohol and cigarette marketing issues were, both to constituents and to policymakers, Magnuson's Commerce Committee files on cigarettes include materials about his activities on the alcohol front without any organizational separation.

41. FTC, *Trade Regulation Rule*, 120–22.

42. Morton, Senate hearing, 1965, 16; Kornegay, House hearing, 1964, 156.

43. Pertschuk, 32–38.

44. "Digest and Comparison of S. 547 and S. 559," n.d., NARA, RG 46, Senate Committee on Commerce, 89th Cong., Box 8, S. 559, Folder: Official; "Senators Seek to Bar FTC From Cigaret Ad Rule," *Advertising Age*, 3 May 1965, 2, 93; Peter Taylor, *Smoke Ring: The Politics of Tobacco* (London: Bodley Head, 1984), 172–73.

45. U.S. House of Representatives, Committee on Interstate and Foreign Commerce, *Report on Federal Cigarette Labeling and Advertising*, 89th Cong., 1st sess., H. Rept. 449, 8 June 1965, 4–5; U.S. Senate, Committee on Interstate and Foreign Commerce, *Cigarette Labeling*, 89th Cong., 1st sess., S. Rept. 195, 19 May 1965, 5–6; Jacqueline Eagle, "Code Is Changing Face of Cigaret Ads," *Advertising Age*, 3 May 1965.

46. House, *Report on Federal Cigarette Labeling*, 19–21; Dixon to Magnuson, 13 May 1965, NARA, RG 46, Senate Committee on Commerce, 89th Cong., Box S. 559, Folder: Official; Elizabeth Brenner Drew, "The Quiet Victory of the Cigarette Lobby: How It Found the Best Filter Yet—Congress," *Atlantic Monthly*, September 1965, 76–80.

47. Kluger, 289; U.S. Congress, House and Senate Conference Report, *Federal Cigarette Labeling and Advertising Act*, H. Rept. 586, 89th Cong., 1st sess., 1 July 1965; Pertschuk to Magnuson, 29 June 1965, NARA, RG 46, Senate Committee on Commerce, 89th Cong., Pertschuk File, S. 559, Box 2, Folder 559; "Remarks of Senator Warren G. Magnuson on the Federal Cigarette Labeling Act," 16 June 1965, NARA, RG 46, Senate Committee on Commerce, 89th Cong., Box S. 559, Folder: Official.

48. *Congressional Record*, 1965, 16549.

49. Americans for Democratic Action, "Legislative Newsletter," 7 July 1965, NARA, RG 46, Senate Committee on Commerce, 89th Cong., Pertschuk File, Box 2, Folder 559; Senator John Moss to Emerson Foote, 21 July 1965, and Foote to Moss, 26 July 1965, in RFK Senate Papers, Legislative Subject File, 1965–1968, Box 14, Folder 6/65–9/65; *Congressional Record*, 1965, 13931, 14408–25, 16540–49; Neuberger, Letter to the Editor, *New York Times*, 14 July 1965, 36:5.

50. Seven members of Congress to President Johnson, 15 July 1965, RFK Senate Papers, Legislative Subject File, 1965–1968, Box 15, Folder: Statements on Bills S. 547 & 559. Americans for Democratic Action wrote a similar letter: Leon Shull, ADA National Director, to President Johnson, 24 June 1965, NARA, RG 46, Senate Committee on Commerce, 89th Cong., Box S. 559, Folder: General Correspondence.

51. *Congressional Record*, 1965, 13892–34, 15597–98; "Senate Votes to Require Warning on Cigaret Pack," *Advertising Age*, 21 June 1965, 1, 74.

52. Drew, 76–80.

53. Ibid.; "Cigarettes vs. FTC," *New York Times*, 9 July 1965, 28:1; Elman quoted

in Kluger, 291.

54. Pertschuk, 33; Pertschuk quoted in Taylor, 172–73.

55. Magnuson to William E. Nelson, 27 September 1965, NARA, RG 46, Senate Committee on Commerce, 89th Cong., Box 559, Folder: General Correspondence.

56. John F. Mahon and Richard A. McGowan, *Industry as a Player in the Political and Social Arena: Defining the Competitive Environment* (Westport, Conn.: Quorum Books, 1996), 83; Gideon Doron, *The Smoking Paradox: Public Regulation in the Cigarette Industry* (Cambridge, Mass.: Abt Books, 1979), 15; Fritschler, 132.

6–THE NEXT PUSH

1. Richard Kluger, *Ashes to Ashes: America's Hundred-Year Cigarette War, the Public Health, and the Unabashed Triumph of Philip Morris* (New York: Alfred A. Knopf, 1996), 310, 506–7.

2. U.S. Senate, Committee on Interstate and Foreign Commerce, *Cigarette Labeling*, 89th Cong., 1st sess., S. Rept. 195, 19 May 1965 (hereafter S. Rept. 195).

3. "Cigarettes vs. FTC," *New York Times*, 9 July 1965, 28:1; Magnuson to Dr. Thomas Carlile, American Cancer Society, 26 October 1965, National Archives and Records Administration (hereafter NARA), Record Group 46 (hereafter RG 46), Senate Commerce Committee Files, 89th Cong., S. 559, Box 10, also Box 2, Folder 559; Magnuson to Secretary of Agriculture Orville Freeman, 5 January 1966, NARA, RG 46, Senate Commerce Committee Files, 89th Cong., S. 559, Box 9.

4. Magnuson to J. D. Roberts, 8 November 1966, NARA, RG 46, Senate Commerce Committee, 89th Cong., S. 559, Box 8, Folder: Cigarettes. Boxes 9 and 10 contain the letters and newspaper clippings Magnuson collected applauding his efforts to keep spirits ads off the air.

5. S. Rept. 195; Magnuson to Meyner, 17 September 1965 and 30 December 1965, NARA, RG 46, Senate Commerce Committee, 89th Cong., S. 559, Box 9; "Cigaret Ads Still Run on Kids' TV, Magnuson Warns," *Advertising Age*, 27 September 1965, 1, 123; "Soft Smoke, Soft Sell," *Television Age*, 22 November 1965, 24–25.

6. Meyner to Magnuson, 23 September 1965, NARA, RG 46, Senate Commerce Committee, 89th Cong., S. 559, Box 9; "Young TV Viewers Are Big Problem in Formulating Cigaret Code: Meyner," *Advertising Age*, 22 November 1965, 3; "Soft Smoke, Soft Sell," *Television Age*, 22 November 1965; Sam Blum, "An Ode to the Cigarette Code," *Harper's*, March 1966, 60–63; Meyner to Paul Rand Dixon, 11 April 1967, Moss Papers, Special Collections, Marriott Library, University of Utah, MS 146 (hereafter Moss Papers), Box 213, Folder 1.

7. Joseph Shea, FTC, to cigarette companies, 3 November 1965, NARA, RG 46, Senate Commerce Committee, 89th Cong., S. 559, Box 9; "Cigaret Code Is Inadequate: FTC to Industry, NAB," *Advertising Age*, 8 November 1965, 1, 131; Meyner to Dixon, 11 April 1967.

8. Both quoted in Blum, "An Ode."

9. "Soft Smoke, Soft Sell," *Television Age*, 22 November 1965; Meyner to Dixon, 11 April 1967.

10. "Code Authority Minutes Show Trials, Tribulations of Industry Self Regulation," *Advertising Age*, 23 June 1969, 106.

11. Maurine Christopher, Code Board Authorizes Cigaret Ad Guidelines," *Advertising Age*, 10 October 1966, 1; "Cigaret Ads May Be Forced Off Air, Anello Says," *Advertising Age*, 6 March 1967, 1; Christopher, "NAB Code Too 'General' Says R. J. Reynolds," *Advertising Age*, 8 May 1967, 1, 142; "Code Authority Minutes," *Advertising Age*; Howard Bell to Charles Sweeny, 20 April 1967, Robert F. Kennedy Senate Papers, John F. Kennedy Presidential Library, (hereafter RFK Senate Papers), Legislative Subject File, Box 14, Folder 9/8/67.

12. Kluger, 301–2; *Congressional Record,* 1966, 172700–707.

13. Warren G. Magnuson and Jean Carper, *The Dark Side of the Marketplace: The Plight of the American Consumer* (Englewood Cliffs, N.J.: Prentice-Hall, 1968), 195; Susan Wagner, *Cigarette Country: Tobacco in American History and Politics* (New York: Praeger, 1971), 193; Federal Trade Commission, *Report to Congress, Pursuant to the Federal Cigarette Labeling and Advertising Act,* 30 June 1968, Appendix A.

14. Federal Trade Commission, "FTC Methods to Be Employed in Determining Tar and Nicotine Content, Notice of Public Hearing," *Federal Register,* 1966 (31), 14278; "Lorillard Is Early Starter in 'Tar Derby,'" *Advertising Age,* 4 April 1966, 1; Stanley Cohen, "N.Y. Cigaret Report Stirs Friends, Foes," *Advertising Age,* 5 September 1966, 1; Lois Mattox Miller and James Monahan, "To the Cigarette Makers: Just the Facts Please," *Reader's Digest,* November 1966, 61–67; Kluger, 300–301; Maurine Christopher, "Self Policing of Cigaret Ads is Hefty Effort, Says Meyner Report," *Advertising Age,* 22 July 1968, 1; Federal Trade Commission, *Report to Congress Pursuant to the Federal Cigarette Labeling and Advertising Act,* 30 June 1967, 19, 28.

15. Kennedy to Leonard Goldenson, ABC, 28 November 1967, RFK Senate Papers, Legislative Subject File, Box 15, Folder 11/1967.

16. Ibid.; *Congressional Record,* 1968, 2969.

17. FTC, *Report to Congress,* 1967, 15, 24, 28–29.

18. Ibid., "Concurring Statement of Commissioner Elman."

19. FTC, *Report to Congress,* 1968, "Concurring Statement of Commissioner Jones" and "Separate Statement of Chairman Dixon."

20. "Government Task Force Asks Strong Standards for Cigaret Advertising," *Advertising Age,* 19 August 1968, 1; American Cancer Society Resolution, 18 October 1967, Moss Papers, Box 213, Folder 2; "Smoking Foes See End of Cigaret Advertising," *Advertising Age,* 18 September 1967, 1.

21. "Tobacco Institute Attacks HEW Report on Smoking, Health," *Advertising Age,* 17 July 1967, 2; Meyner to Senate Commerce Committee, 9 August 1967, Moss Papers, Box 213, Folder 1; "FTC Seeking to Abolish Ads for Cigarets: Meyner," *Advertising Age,* 21 August 1967, 1.

22. Kennedy to Robert Walker, American Tobacco Company, 22 August 1967, RFK Senate Papers, Legislative Subject Files, Box 14, Cigarette Smoking, Folder 8/1967; *Congressional Record,* 1967, 25126–29.

23. *Congressional Record,* 1967, 26074–75; "Cigaret Conflicts Become 2-Front War," *Advertising Age,* 7 August 1967, 1, 52.

24. "Cigarette Controls: A Sick Joke So Far," *Consumer Reports,* February 1968, 97–103.

25. Elizabeth B. Drew, "The Cigarette Companies Would Rather Fight Than Switch," *New York Times Magazine,* 4 May 1969, 36–37, 129–33; "Cigaret Code's Youth TV Formula Is Inadequate: Kennedy to Tobacco Men," *Advertising Age,* 6 November 1967, 2; Kennedy to Earle Clements, 16 November 1967, RFK Senate Papers, Legislative Subject File, Box 15, Folder 11/1967; "Tobacco Men Ponder TV Use," *Advertising Age,* 25 December 1967, 1; Peter Edelman to Kennedy, RFK Senate Papers, Legislative Subject File, Box 14, Folder 10/1967.

26. Kennedy to sports teams and commissioners, 16 November 1967, Kennedy to cigarette companies and broadcast networks, 16 November 1967, and Goodman to Kennedy, 17 November 1967, all in RFK Senate Papers, Legislative Subject File, Box 15, Folder 11/67; "Kennedy Draws Diverse Replies on Cigaret Ad Ban Plan," *Advertising Age,* 11 December 1967, 115; "Tobacco Men's Letters Don't Satisfy Senators," *Advertising Age,* 12 February 1968, 1.

27. Roy Norr, U.S. House of Representatives, Subcommittee of the Committee on Government Operations, *False and Misleading Advertising (Filter-Tip Cigarettes),* 85th Cong., 1st sess, July 1957, 272–73; Maurine Neuberger, *Smoke Screen: Tobacco and the Public Welfare* (Englewood Cliffs, N.J.: Prentice-Hall, 1963), 128; Kluger, 304.

28. Reprinted in *Congressional Record,* 1966, 7006.

29. FCC, "Applicability of the Fairness Doctrine to Cigarette Advertising, Memorandum Opinion and Order," 8 September 1967, *Federal Register,* 1967, 13162–74; Kluger, 304–7.

30. "The Evolving Doctrine of Fairness," *Broadcasting,* 12 June 1967; FCC, "Applicability."

31. FCC, "Applicability."

32. *Congressional Record,* 1967, A4915, 15108, 17827–31, 17927.

33. "ANA, NAB, Nets Oppose FCC Plan to Apply Fairness Rule to Cigaret Ads," *Advertising Age,* 10 July 1967, 3; FCC, "Applicability"; "Anti-Cigarette Advertising," *America,* 21 October 1967, 433.

34. FCC, "Applicability," Loevinger's opinion.

35. Ibid.; *Congressional Record,* 1967, 15108, 17827–31.

36. FCC, "Applicability."

37. Ibid., Johnson's opinion; Ben Waple, FCC, to WCBS-TV, 2 June 1967, RFK Senate Papers, Legislative Subject File, Box 14, Folder 6/67–7/67; Thomas Whiteside, *Selling Death: Cigarette Advertising and Public Health* (New York: Liveright, 1971), 58–67; Kluger, 306–8.

38. Bazelon quoted in U.S. Senate, Consumer Subcommittee of the Committee on Commerce, *Cigarette Advertising and Labeling,* 91st Cong., 1st sess., 22 July 1969, 182 (hereafter Senate hearing, 1969); Stanley Cohen, "Cigaret 'Fairness' Decision Written to Preclude Review by Supreme Court," *Advertising Age*, 2 December 1968, 10.

39. Kluger, 309–310; *Congressional Record,* 1968, 19501–502; "Caution: This Hearing Is Hazardous," *Newsweek,* 28 April 1969, 82–83; Michael Schudson, "Symbols and Smokers: Advertising, Health Messages, and Public Policy," in Robert L. Rabin and Stephen D. Sugarman, eds., *Smoking Policy: Law, Politics, and Culture* (New York: Oxford University Press, 1993), 222; Gideon Doron, *The Smoking Paradox: Public Regulation in the Cigarette Industry* (Cambridge, Mass.: Abt Books, 1979), 86; "Regulating Television," *New Republic,* 13 July 1968, 8–9.

40. Philip J. Hilts, *Smokescreen: The Truth behind the Tobacco Industry Cover-Up* (Reading, Mass.: Addison-Wesley, 1996), 14; Kluger, 324.

41. "Dangerous Lengths: The Federal Crusade against Smoking Has Gone Too Far," *Barron's,* 2 October 1967, 1.

42. Staggers quoted in "Showdown in Marlboro Country," *Consumer Reports,* September 1969, 516–21.

43. "Caution," *Newsweek.*

44. Cohen, "Congress Cigaret Action"; Drew, "The Cigarette Companies Would Rather Fight."

45. Moss to Senators, 6 February 1969; Luther Terry to Moss, 25 February 1969, both in Moss Papers, Box 257, Folder 15; FCC, "Advertisement of Cigarettes, Notice of Proposed Rule Making," 5 Feburary 1969, FCC Docket No. 18434, *Federal Register* 1969, 1959; *Congressional Record,* 1969, 7621, 8043, 8421; David Lawrence, "Government Censorship or Freedom of the Press?" *U.S. News and World Report,* 4 August 1969, 84.

46. Drew, "Cigarette Companies"; Luther Terry, U.S. House of Representatives, Committee on Interstate and Foreign Commerce, *Cigarette Labeling and Advertising— 1969,* 91st Cong., 1st sess., 1969 (hereafter House hearing, 1969), 280; William F. Buckley, Jr., "On Not Smoking," *National Review,* 21 October 1969, 1078–79.

47. Senate hearing, 1969, 180; Moss to periodical publishers, 7 August 1969, Moss Papers, Box 257, Folder 21; and Moss to Cullman of Philip Morris, 19 May 1971, Box 339, Folder 13; *Congressional Record,* 1969, 38738.

48. "Code Authority Minutes," *Advertising Age.*

49. Ibid.; Drew, "Cigarette Companies," 37.

50. Drew, "Cigarette Companies," 132; "Caution," *Newsweek.*

51. Moss to Robert W. Ferguson, Chair, Television Code Review Board, NAB, 10 July 1969, Moss Papers, Box 257, Folder 20.

52. Doron, 96; "Showdown," *Consumer Reports.*

53. "Showdown," *Consumer Reports;* Senate hearing, 1969, 124–25; Whiteside, 92.

54. Whiteside, 96; Senate hearing, 1969, 123.

55. Michael Pertschuk, *Giant Killers* (New York: Norton, 1987), 38–39; "Cigarette Men Agree to Snuff Out Ads," *Business Week,* 26 July 1969, 29; Kluger, 333.

56. Moss to Wasilewski, 1 October 1969, Moss Papers, Box 257, Folder 23; Wasilewski, Senate hearing, 1969, 128–29; "Moss Blasts Wasilewski's Cigaret Stand," *Advertising Age,* 6 October 1969, 3; Leonard Goldenson, ABC, to Moss, 7 August 1969, Moss Papers, Box 257, Folder 21.

57. Rosel Hyde to Moss, 17 September 1969, Moss Papers, Box 257, Folder 22.

58. Wagner, 214–15; *Congressional Record,* 1969, 38732–53; "Individual Views of Mr. Moss," in *Senate Report on Public Health Cigarette Smoking Act of 1969,* Report No. 91-566, 5 December 1969.

59. *Capital Broadcasting v. United States* 333 F. Supp. 582, 1971 U.S. Dist.

60. Maurine Christopher, "Is Cigaret Companies' Success Without TV Giving Others Ideas?" *Advertising Age,* 10 May 1971, 91.

61. Dissent by Judge J. Skelly Wright, *Capital Broadcasting.*

62. Larry C. White, *Merchants of Death: The American Tobacco Industry* (New York: Beech Tree Books, 1988), 148.

63. Kluger, 465, 543–48.

64. Howard Leichter, *Free to Be Foolish: Politics and Health Promotion in the United States and Great Britain* (Princeton, N.J.: Princeton University Press, 1991), 119; "The Last Drag," *Newsweek,* 4 January 1971, 65; "Braren Asks Ban on Cigaret Ads If 'Too Successful,'" *Advertising Age,* 22 March 1971, 1; "7 Cigaret Companies to Run Health Warning in Print Ads," *Advertising Age,* 19 April 1971, 16; "Some FTC Officials Surprised by Industry Assent to Cigaret Ad Rules," *Advertising Age,* 7 February 1972, 2; Kluger, 435–39, 442–45, 491–92.

7—THE POLITICAL, LEGAL, AND SCIENTIFIC CONTEXT OF REGULATION

1. D. B. Heath, "The New Temperance Movement: Through the Looking Glass," in Edith S. Lisansky Gomberg, ed., *Current Issues in Alcohol/Drug Studies* (New York: Haworth Press, 1989), 144–52; Joseph R. Gusfield, *Contested Meanings: The Construction of Alcohol Problems* (Madison: University of Wisconsin Press, 1996), 281–82; Jack S. Blocker, Jr., *American Temperance Movements: Cycles of Reform* (Boston: Twayne, 1989), 158–60; Mark Edward Lender and James Kirby Martin, *Drinking in America: A History* (New York: Free Press, 1987), 191–204; Rebecca Murphy Marton, "The Role of Government and the Non-Profit Sector in the New Temperance Movement," <http://sunset.backbone. olemiss.edu/~phjuerg/newtemp.html>; Ruth Clifford Engs, *Clean Living Movements: American Cycles of Health Reform* (Westport, Conn.: Praeger, 2000); David Wagner, *The New Temperance: The American Obsession With Sin and Vice* (Boulder, Colo.: Westview Press, 1997); Mark Edward Lender, "A New Prohibition?: An Essay on Drinking and Smoking in America," in Jeffrey A. Schaler and Magda E. Schaler, eds., *Smoking: Who Has the Right?* (Amherst, N.Y.: Prometheus Books, 1998): 79–113.

2. "The Sobering of America: A Push to Put Drinking in its Place," *Business Week,* 25 February 1985, 112.

3. Jack S. Blocker, Jr., *American Temperance Movements: Cycles of Reform* (Boston: Twayne, 1989), 157; Robin Room, "Cultural Changes in Drinking and Trends in Alcohol Problems Indicators: Recent U.S. Experience," in Walter B. Clark and Michael E. Hilton, eds., *Alcohol in America: Drinking Practices and Problems* (Albany: State University of New York Press, 1991), 149–62; "The Sobering," *Business Week;* Jane E. Brody, "Personal Health," *New York Times,* 4 December 1985, III, 10:4; *New York Times,* 31 December 1985, 16 March 1986, and 15 March 1989.

4. Howard Leichter, *Free to Be Foolish: Politics and Health Promotion in the United*

States and Great Britain (Princeton, N.J.: Princeton University Press, 1991), 7; *Healthy People: The Surgeon General's Report on Health Promotion and Disease Prevention* (Washington, D.C.: U.S. Department of Health, Education, and Welfare, 1979).

5. Dan E. Beauchamp and Bonnie Steinbock, "Prevention and Its Limits," in Dan E. Beauchamp and Bonnie Steinbock, eds., *New Ethics for the Public's Health* (New York: Oxford University Press, 1999), 95–96; Dan E. Beauchamp, "Public Health as Social Justice," *Inquiry* 13 (1976): 1–14.

6. Beauchamp, "Public Health"; Michael Goldstein, *The Health Movement: Promoting Fitness in America* (New York: Twayne, 1992), 129, 139–43; Sylvia Noble Tesh, *Hidden Arguments: Political Ideology and Disease Prevention Policy* (New Brunswick, N.J.: Rutgers University Press, 1988), 47–48; Charles Rosenberg, "Banishing Risk," in Allan M. Brandt and Paul Rozin, eds., *Morality and Health* (New York: Routledge, 1997), 43; Allan M. Brandt, "Behavior, Disease, and Health in the Twentieth-Century United States: The Moral Valence of Individual Risk," in Brandt and Rozin, eds., 68; Leichter, 9, 95.

7. "The Worst Drug Problem," *New York Times,* 30 July 1971, 32:2; James T. Wooten, "Carter Seeks to End Marijuana Penalty for Small Amounts," *New York Times,* 3 August 1977, 1:1; Marton, "The Role of Government"; Stop Radio/TV Alcohol Pusher Ads, "Send This to Nancy Reagan," *Washington Post,* 19 August 1984.

8. William J. McCord, South Carolina Commission on Alcohol and Drug Abuse, U.S. Senate, Committee on Commerce, Subcommittee on the Consumer, *Alcohol Warning Labels,* 100th Cong., 2nd sess., 10 August 1988, 38; U.S. House of Representatives, Committee on Energy and Commerce, Subcommittee on Transportation and Hazardous Materials, *Oversight of FTC's Shared Responsibilities,* 102nd Cong., 1st sess., 21 November 1991, 128; Representative Joseph Kennedy, U.S. Senate, Committee on Commerce, Science, and Transportation, Subcommittee on the Consumer, *Alcohol Beverage Advertising Act, S. 664,* 102nd Cong., 2nd sess., 2 April 1992, 23.

9. Musto quoted in Georgia Sheron, "New 'Temperance Movement' Seen by Historian," *New York Times,* 16 March 1986, 23, 2:1; "The Worst Drug Problem," *New York Times.*

10. Richard Kluger, *Ashes to Ashes: America's Hundred-Year Cigarette War, the Public Health, and the Unabashed Triumph of Philip Morris* (New York: Alfred A. Knopf, 1996), 374–75, 502, 508–10, 538–48, 553–57, 565–67, 632, 673–76, 715; John K. Iglehart, "Smoking and Public Policy," *New England Journal of Medicine* 310 (1984): 539–44.

11. Kluger, 537, 548–52, 572–79, 620–25, 701, 705–706, 716; Ronald M. Davis, "Current Trends in Cigarette Advertising and Marketing," *New England Journal of Medicine* 316 (1987): 725–32.

12. Robin Room, "Alcohol Control and Public Health," *Annual Review of Public Health* 5 (1984), 295.

13. Author's interview with George Hacker of the Center for Science in the Public Interest, 8 October 2001; Lawrence Wallack, U.S. House of Representatives, Committee on Energy and Commerce, Subcommittee on Transportation and Hazardous Materials, *Health Warnings on Alcoholic Beverage Advertisements,* 101st Cong., 2nd sess., 18 July 1990, 268 (hereafter House hearing, 1990).

14. Morris Chafetz, *Liquor, the Servant of Man* (Boston: Little, Brown, 1965), and *Why Drinking Can Be Good for You* (Briarcliff Manor, N.Y.: Stein and Day, 1976); Blocker, 156; James Mosher and David H. Jernigan, "New Directions in Alcohol Policy," *Annual Review of Public Health* 10 (1989), 250.

15. Kettil Bruun et al., *Alcohol Control Policies in Public Health Perspective* (New Brunswick, N.J.: Rutgers University Center of Alcohol Studies, 1975), 12–13; Dan Beauchamp, *Beyond Alcoholism, Alcohol and Public Health Policy* (Philadelphia: Temple University Press, 1980), 164–82; Dean Gerstein and Mark H. Moore, eds., *Alcohol and Public Policy: Beyond the Shadow of Prohibition* (Washington, D.C.: National Academy Press, 1981).

16. Beauchamp, *Beyond Alcoholism,* 154–62, 168, 174.

17. Room, 294; Mosher and Jernigan, 252, 255; Warren Leary, "U.S. Finds Progress in Cutting Alcohol's Toll," *New York Times,* 24 December 1987, II, 9:1.

18. Mark V. Nadel, *The Politics of Consumer Protection* (Indianapolis: Bobbs-Merrill Company, 1971), 111–16; Michael Pertschuk, *Revolt Against Regulation: The Rise and Pause of the Consumer Movement* (Berkeley: University of California Press, 1982), 5–45.

19. James F. Mosher, "Alcohol Problems and the Consumer Movement," in Stephen Brobeck, ed., *Encyclopedia of the Consumer Movement* (Santa Barbara, Calif.: ABC-CLIO, 1997): 24–29.

20. Edward Cox, Robert C. Fellmeth, John E. Schulz, with preface by Ralph Nader, *The Nader Report on the Federal Trade Commission* (New York: Richard W. Baron, 1969), x, 77.

21. Philip Gold, *Advertising, Politics, and American Culture: From Salesmanship to Therapy* (New York: Paragon House, 1987), 165; Pertschuk, *Revolt,* 43.

22. FTC, *Hearings on Modern Advertising Practices* (Washington, D.C., 1971); U.S. Senate, Committee on Congress, Subcommittee on Communications, *Surgeon General's Report by the Scientific Advisory Committee on Television and Social Behavior,* 92nd Cong., 2nd sess., March 1972 (hereafter Senate hearing, 1972); Stephen Fox, *The Mirror Makers: A History of American Advertising and Its Creators* (New York: William Morrow, 1984), 318.

23. Gold, 166, 168; William MacLeod and Robert Rogowsky, "Consumer Protection at the FTC during the Reagain Administration," in Roger Meiners and Bruce Yandle, eds., *Regulation and the Reagan Era* (New York: Holmes and Meier, 1980), 78–79.

24. Leo Bogart, *The Age of Television: A Study of the Viewing Habits and the Impact of Television on American Life,* 3rd ed. (New York: Ungar, 1956, 1958, 1972); Lawrence Wallack, "Television Programming, Advertising, and the Prevention of Alcohol-Related Problems," in Dean Gerstein, ed., *Toward the Prevention of Alcohol Problems: Government, Business, and Community Action* (Washington, D.C.: National Academy Press, 1984), 87.

25. Steve Younger, U.S. House of Representatives, Committee on Energy and Commerce, Subcommittee on Telecommunications, Consumer Protection, and Finance, *Beer and Wine Advertising: Impact of Electronic Media,* 99th Cong., 1st sess., May 1985, 204–5 (hereafter House hearing, 1985); Stanley Cohen, "Congress Cigaret Action Writes Finis to Episode That Hurt All Advertising," *Advertising Age,* 9 March 1970, 16; Gold, 168.

26. Lee Loevinger, "The Politics of Advertising," in S. F. Divita, ed., *Advertising and the Public Interest* (Chicago: American Marketing Association, 1974), 10, 17, 21, 23; John Summers of the National Association Broadcasters, "The Fairness Doctrine and Counter Advertising," in idem., 215–27.

27. FCC, *Fairness Doctrine and Public Interest Standards,* 1974; Gold, 168.

28. Pertschuk, *Revolt,* 99.

29. Bernice Rothman Hasin, *Consumers, Commissions, and Congress: Law, Theory, and the Federal Trade Commission, 1968–1985* (New Brunswick, N.J.: Transaction Books, 1987), 19; Lizabeth Cohen, *A Consumers' Republic: The Politics of Mass Consumption in Postwar America* (New York: Alfred Knopf, 2003), 390–91.

30. Walter Braren, "Why the 'Truth in Advertising Act of 1971'?" in Divita, ed., *Advertising;* Martha Rogers, "Advertising Self-Regulation in the 1980s: A Review," *Current Issues and Research in Advertising* 13 (1991): 370; Harold H. Marquis, *The Changing Corporate Image* (New York: American Management Association, 1970); Fox, 305–6; Thomas Frank, *The Conquest of Cool: Business Culture, Counterculture, and the Rise of Hip Consumerism* (Chicago: University of Chicago Press, 1997).

31. Pertschuk, *Revolt,* 12, 50–68.

32. Ibid., 73, 110; Michael Pertschuk, *Giant Killers* (New York: W. W. Norton, 1986), 43–44; Hasin, 20.

33. Gary Cross, *An All-Consuming Century: Why Commercialism Won in Modern America* (New York: Columbia University Press, 2000), 203–4, 304; Rogers, 372; Matthew P. McAllister, *The Commercialization of American Culture: New Advertising, Control and Democracy* (Thousand Oaks, Calif.: Sage, 1996), 33.

34. Michael Pertschuk to FTC, 30 July 1982, and James Miller to Pertschuk, 20 September 1982, in Michael Pertschuk Papers, Library of Congress, I:44, Alcohol Advertising (hereafter Pertschuk Papers.)

35. Gold, 135; Steve Younger, "Alcoholic Beverage Advertising on the Airwaves: Alternatives to a Ban or Counteradvertising," *UCLA Law Review* 34 (1987) 1160–61; Rogers, 379; Lemuel Schofield, "First Amendment Implications of Banning Alcohol Beverage Ads on Radio & TV" *Journalism Quarterly* 62 (1985): 534.

36. Carlton Turner, deputy assistant to President Reagan, quoted in Steven Colford, "White House Offers Rx for Alcohol Ads," *Advertising Age,* 25 March 1985, 10; Colford, "Reagan Adviser Opposes Booze-Ad Ban," *Advertising Age,* 12 November 1984, 112; Dirk Olin, "This Dud's For You," *The New Republic,* 11 July 1988, 12–13; Cross, 193–207; Michael Pertschuk to Senator Packwood, 6 April 1983, and Pertschuk, Speech Before the Public Relations Society of America, "When the Cop is Off the Beat," 26 October 1983, in Pertschuk Papers, I:44, Alcohol Advertising.

37. Ronald H. Coase, "Advertising and Free Speech," in Allen Hyman and M. Bruce Johnson, eds., *Advertising and Free Speech* (Lexington, Mass: Lexington Books, 1977), 2–3, 7–8, 13–14, 25.

38. Ivan L. Preston, *The Tangled Web They Weave: Truth, Falsity, and Advertisers* (Madison: University of Wisconsin Press, 1994), 138–39; C. Edwin Baker, *Advertising and a Democratic Press* (Princeton, N.J.: Princeton University Press, 1994), 134, 138–39; *Valentine v. Chrestensen,* 316 U.S. 52 (1942); Douglas's opinion in *Cammarano v. United States,* 358 U.S. 498 (1959).

39. Baker, 136; *New York Times v. Sullivan,* 376 U.S. 254 (1964); *Bigelow v. Virginia,* 421 U.S. 809 (1975); *Virginia State Board of Pharmacy et al. v. Virginia Citizens Consumer Council, Inc., et al.,* 425 U.S. 748 (1976); *Bates v. State Bar of Arizona,* 433 U.S. 350 (1977). The first quotation comes from the decision in *Bigelow,* and the second from *Bates.*

40. Rehnquist's dissent, *Bigelow v. Virginia;* Rehnquist's dissent, *Virginia State Pharmacy v. Virginia Citizens Consumer Council.*

41. *Posadas de Puerto Rico Assoc., dba Condado Holiday Inn v. Tourism Company of Puerto Rico et al.,* 478 U.S. 328 (1986).

42. Brennan's dissent, *Posadas.*

43. 718 Federal Reporter 2nd Series, 738; "Court Ducks Liquor-ad Test of Free Speech," *Advertising Age,* 28 June 1984, 31; Schofield, 537–38; Camille P. Schuster and Christine Pacelli Powell, "Comparison of Cigarette and Alcohol Advertising Controversies," *Journal of Advertising* 16 (1987), 29. Ultimately, the Oklahoma law was shot down in 1986 when the court ruled that it discriminated against in-state operators in favor of cable operators. "Oklahoma Liquor Ads OK," *Advertising Age,* 9 June 1986, 86.

44. William W. Lowrance, *Modern Science and Human Values* (New York: Oxford University Press, 1985), 51–54. Charles Atkin and Martin Block, *Content and Effects of Alcohol Advertising* (Springfield, Va.: National Technical Information Service, 1981); W. Breed, J. De Foe, and Lawrence Wallack, "Drinking in the Mass Media: A Nine-Year Project," *Journal of Drug Issues* 14 (1984): 655–64; P. Kohn and R. Smart, "The Impact of Television Advertising on Alcohol Consumption: An Experiment," *Journal of Studies on Alcohol* 45 (1984): 295–301; Donald Strickland and David Pittman, *The Effects of Alcohol Beverage Advertising Practices and Messages on Alcohol Problems and Alcoholism in the United States: A Preliminary Report* (St. Louis: Washington University Social Science Institute, 1980); Joseph C. Fisher, *Advertising, Alcohol Consumption, and Abuse: A Worldwide Survey* (Westport, Conn.: Greenwood Press, 1993).

45. Wallack, "Television Programming," 90; David Collingridge and Colin Reeve, *Science Speaks to Power: The Role of Experts in Policy Making* (London: Frances Pinter, 1986); Mark E. Rushefsky, *Making Cancer Policy* (Albany: State University of New York Press, 1986), 23–27; Sheila Jasanoff, *Risk Management and Political Culture: A Comparative Study of Science in the Policy Context* (New York: Russell Sage Foundation, 1986).

46. Senate hearing, 1972, 26, 245.

47. Michael Jacobson, R. Atkins, and George Hacker, *The Booze Merchants: The Inebriating of America* (Washington, D.C.: Center for Science in the Public Interest, 1983), 4, 49–50; Dr. Asa Berger, U.S. Senate, Committee on Labor and Human Resources, Subcommittee on Children, Family, Drugs and Alcoholism, *Reviewing Advertisements and Television Commercials Promoting the Sale and Consumption of Alcoholic Beverages,* 99th Cong., 1st sess., 7 February 1985, 388 (hereafter Senate hearing, 1985.)

48. House hearing, 1985, 8, 477–78.

49. *Congressional Record,* 1985, 12669–70; Federal Trade Commission memo denying the Center for Science in the Public Interest's petition, printed in House hearing, 1985, 138, emphasis added; James Miller at Senate hearing, 1985, 5.

50. Leichter, 81.

51. Stephen Lambright of Anheuser-Busch, Donald Shea of United States Brewers Association, Ann Kahn of PTA, House hearing, 1985, 453, 470, 573; Jacobson, Senate hearing, 1985, 252.

52. Representative John Seiberling, Michael Jacobson, and Representative Tim Wirth, House hearing, 1985, 8–10, 487, 495–96; Joe Kennedy, House hearing, 1990, 49.

53. Project SMART only collected about 700,000 signatures. Senate hearing, 1985, 238.

54. Author interview with George Hacker.

55. Dr. Beverly R. Jackson, Director Department of Human Welfare, General Board of Church and Society of the United Methodist Church, Press Release "Alcohol Advertising," 31 November 1983, Pertschuk Papers, I:44, Alcohol Advertising; James G. Hougland, Jr., James R. Wood, and Samuel A. Mueller, "Organizational 'Goal Submergence': The Methodist Church and the Failure of the Temperance Movement," *Sociology and Social Research* 58 (July 1974): 408–15.

56. Center for Science in the Public Interest, News Release "National Organizations Launch Campaign to Restrict Broadcast Ads for Alcoholic Beverages," 25 June 1985, CSPI archives.

57. Christian Life Commission in Senate hearing, 1976, 305–13, Senate hearing 1985, 338–41, House hearing, 1990, 254; Church of Latter Day Saints in Senate hearing, 1985, 351.

58. *Congressional Record,* 1988, 1111; Mac Marshall and Alice Oleson, "In the Pink: MADD and Public Health Policy in the 1990s," *Journal of Public Health Policy* 15 (1994): 54–68.

59. Matthew L. Wald, "Saving Youth from Demon Rum: A Futile Exorcise?" *New York Times,* 29 July 1979, IV, 6:1; Felicity Barringer, "With Teens and Alcohol, It's Just Say When," *New York Times,* 23 June 1991, IV, 1:4. Robert L. Chauncey, "New Careers for Moral Entrepreneurs: Teenage Drinking," *Journal of Drug Issues* 10 (Winter 1980): 45–70; Howard Blane and Linda Hewitt, *Alcohol and Youth: An Analysis of the Literature, 1960–1975* (Washington, D.C.: NIAAA, 1977).

60. Jane E. Brody, "Doctors Find Pattern of Birth Defects Among Children of Alcoholic Mothers," *New York Times* 3 July 1973, 6:2; Joel Greenberg, "U.S. Advises Total Abstinence From Drinking For Pregnant Women," *New York Times,* 18 July 1981, 7:2; "Drinking in Pregnancy: The Danger is Disputed," *New York Times,* 10 September 1981, III, 14:3; U.S. Senate, Committee on Human Resources, Subcommittee on Alcoholism and Drug Abuse, *Alcohol Labeling and Fetal Alcohol Syndrome,* 95th Cong., 2nd sess., 31 January 1978; U.S. Senate, Committee on Labor and Human Resources, Subcommittee

on Alcoholism and Drug Abuse, *Effects of Alcohol Consumption During Pregnancy,* 97th Cong., 2nd sess., 21 September 1982; House hearing, 1990, 224, 300–301.

61. Eric Pace, "Slump Even Slows Nation's Drinking," *New York Times,* 19 January 1983, IV, 1:3; Charles G. Burck, "Changing Habits in American Drinking," *Fortune,* October 1976, 156–66; "The Liquor Industry's Aggressive New Ad Blitz," *Business Week,* 20 March 1978, 174; "Drinking in the Future: New Styles, New Tastes," *Advertising Age,* 16 February 1987, S1; Jacobson et al., *Booze Merchants,* 83–89; Richard Cowan and James F. Mosher, "Public Health Implications of Beverage Marketing: Alcohol as an Ordinary Consumer Product," *Contemporary Drug Problems* 12 (1985): 621–57.

62. George Hacker, R. Collins, and Michael Jacobson, *Selling Booze to Blacks* (Washington, D.C.: Center for Science in the Public Interest, 1987); Michael Jacobson and Bruce Maxwell, *Marketing Disease to Hispanics: The Selling of Alcohol, Tobacco, and Junk Foods* (Washington, D.C.: Center for Science in the Public Interest, 1989); "Major Effort to Woo Minorities," *Advertising Age,* 26 July 1984, 17; Jacobson et al., *Booze Merchants,* 31, 67–70.

63. Val Adams, "Channel 47 To Carry TV's First Liquor Ads Here," *New York Times,* 25 May 1966, 95:1; Philip H. Dougherty, "Advertising: TV and Liquor Commercials," *New York Times,* 16 November 1970, 60:3; Jack Gould, "TV Liquor Ads Contemplated If Economic Slump Continues," *New York Times,* 13 February 1971, 52:7; Colby Coates, "Shop Execs Air Views on Broadcast Taboos," *Advertising Age,* 10 November 1980, 78; Gay Jervey and Steven W. Colford, "Distillers Inching Toward Cable TV," *Advertising Age,* 29 October 1984, 1.

64. Joseph Winski, "Pressures Mounting to Curtail Liquor Advertising," *Advertising Age,* 18 July 1983, 1; Trish Hall, "A New Temperance is Taking Root In America," *New York Times,* 15 March 1989, I, 1:2; "Liquor Consumption in U.S. Reported at a 3-Decade Low," *New York Times,* 25 November 1989, 12:5. Ad executive quoted in "Drinks and Drivers," *New York Times,* 5 February 1984, III, 1:1.

65. Steven Colford, "U.S. Alcohol Abuse, Ads Not Linked," *Advertising Age,* 11 February 1985, 70; House hearing, 1985, 450–52.

66. Mosher and Jernigan, 260–63; P. Morgan, "Power, Politics, and Public Health: The Political Power of the Alcohol Beverage Industry," *Journal of Public Health Policy* (Summer 1988):177–97; Janet Golden, *Message in a Bottle: The Making of Fetal Alcohol Syndrome* (Cambridge, Mass.: Harvard University Press, 2005), 76–77.

8–POLICY CONTESTS

1. "Senator Raps Spuds MacKenzie Promotion," *Marketing News,* 4 December 1987, 24; "Bitching about Booze," *Economist,* 19 December 1987, 59; U.S. Senate, Committee on Commerce, Subcommittee on the Consumer, *Alcohol Warning Labels,* 100th Cong., 2nd sess., 10 August 1988, 18 (hereafter Senate hearing, 1988).

2. *Congressional Record,* 1967, 27586–88; *Congressional Record,* 1969, 5540–41.

3. *Congressional Record,* 1969, 464; *Congressional Record Index,* 1971, 39; *Congressional Record Index,* 1973, 45; *Congressional Record Index,* 1975, 30; *Congressional Record,* 1976, 6972–73.

4. *Congressional Record,* 1967, 20895–97, 33445–46; Robert D. McFadden, "Consumers Union Scores Drug Laws," *New York Times,* 29 November 1972, 1:5.

5. U.S. Senate, Committee on Labor and Public Welfare, Subcommittee on Alcoholism and Narcotics, *Media Images of Alcohol: The Effects of Advertising and Other Media on Alcohol Abuse,* 94th Cong., 2nd sess., 8 and 11 March 1976 (hereafter Senate hearing, 1976); Ardith Maney and Loree Bykerk, *Consumer Politics: Protecting Public Interests on Capitol Hill* (Westport, Conn.: Greenwood Press, 1994), 39, 45, 50.

6. Robert G. LaForge, "Misplaced Priorities: A History of Federal Alcohol Regulation and Public Health Policy" (Ph.D. diss., Johns Hopkins University, 1987), 267.

7. Leonard Slone, "Communicating Nutritional Value," *New York Times,* 7 August 1975, 49:3.

8. *Federal Register,* 1980, 40538; *Federal Register,* 1981, 55093; "Listing of Ingredients for Drinkers Rejected," *New York Times,* 8 November 1981, 60:6.

9. U.S. Senate, Committee on Human Resources, Subcommittee on Alcoholism and Drug Abuse, *Alcohol Labeling and Fetal Alcohol Syndrome,* 95th Cong., 2nd sess., 31 January 1978 (hereafter Senate hearing, 1978); Janet Golden, *Message in a Bottle: The Making of Fetal Alcohol Syndrome* (Cambridge, Mass.: Harvard University Press, 2005), 75–77.

10. *Congressional Record,* 1978, 46–47; LaForge, 370.

11. Assistant Secretary of the Treasury Richard Davis quoted in "U.S. Asks Plan to Warn Women on Alcohol Use," *New York Times,* 9 February 1979, IV, 15:2; "Alcohol Info Drive Set for Mothers-to-be," *Advertising Age,* 2 July 1979, 4; Golden, 76–81; LaForge, 374–81.

12. LaForge, 383–84; Susan Okie, "Alcohol Risks Are Termed Too Complex for Coverage on Bottle Warning Labels," *Washington Post,* 26 November 1980, A4b. U.S. Senate, Committee on Labor and Human Resources, Subcommittee on Alcoholism and Drug Abuse, *Effects of Alcohol Consumption During Pregnancy,* 97th Cong., 2nd sess., 21 September 1982.

13. *Congressional Record,* 1979, 27616.

14. Senate hearing, 1978, 8–9, 83–84; *Congressional Record,* 1977, 1028–29; *Congressional Record,* 1979, 37008.

15. *Congressional Record,* 1981, 18680–81.

16. Senate hearing, 1976, 96; Senate hearing, 1978, 84, 230–41; *Congressional Record,* 1973, 4356.

17. Senate hearing, 1978, 241, 86; *Congressional Record,* 1978, 649–50; *Congressional Record,* 1979, 37008.

18. Senate hearing, 1978, 239–41; Golden, 81.

19. Senate hearing, 1978, 239–41, 256, 285; *Congressional Record,* 1981, 18680–81.

20. Michael Jacobson, R. Atkins, and George Hacker, *The Booze Merchants: The Inebriating of America* (Washington, D.C.: Center for Science in the Public Interest, 1983); Joseph Winski, "Pressures Mounting to Curtail Liquor Advertising," *Advertising Age,* 18 July 1983, 1.

21. Center for Science in the Public Interest, "News Release," 21 November 1983, from Center for Science in the Public Interest Archives; Petition to the FTC in U.S. House of Representatives, Committee on Energy and Commerce, Subcommittee on Telecommunications, Consumer Protection, and Finance, *Beer and Wine Advertising: Impact of Electronic Media,* 99th Cong., 1st sess., 21 May 1985, 71–72 (hereafter House hearing, 1985); Richard L. Gordon, "FTC Urged to Tighten Liquor Ad Restrictions," *Advertising Age,* 28 November 1983, 14.

22. Center for Science in the Public Interest, "News Release," 25 June 1984, from Center for Science in the Public Interest Archives; "Ad Ban Drive Hits Beer, Wine," *Advertising Age,* 25 June 1984, 4; Maurine Christopher, "Alcohol-ad Fight: Remembrance of Bans Past," *Advertising Age,* 18 February 1985, 60; "Sudsless Sports?" *Fortune,* 21 January 1985, 84.

23. The video was shown at U.S. Senate, Committee on Labor and Human Resources, Subcommittee on Children, Family, Drugs and Alcoholism, *Reviewing Advertisements and Television Commercials Promoting the Sale and Consumption of Alcoholic Beverages,* 99th Cong., 1st sess., 7 February 1985, 178 (hereafter Senate hearing, 1985); Verne Gay, "TV Fights Beer Ban Talk," *Advertising Age,* 8 November 1984, 1; Idem, "Stroh to Nets: Fight Off Ad Ban," *Advertising Age,* 20 December 1984, 1; "Bursting Through the Clutter," *Advertising Age,* 26 July 1984, 15; Gay Jervey and Steven W. Colford "Distillers Inching Toward Cable TV," *Advertising Age,* 29 October 1984, 1.

24. Scott Hume, "Feds Rap Beer Promo Tactics," *Advertising Age*, 1 November 1984, 2; Idem, "Ad Ban Talk Jars Beer Meet," *Advertising Age*, 5 November 1984, 96.

25. Steven Colford, "Feds Nip at Alcohol-Ad Fight," *Advertising Age*, 24 December 1984, 39; "Make Sure the Brewery Sparkles," *Advertising Age*, 14 January 1985, 12; Steven Colford, "Alcohol-ad Fighters Find Ad-industry Ally," *Advertising Age*, 28 January 1985, 10; Idem, "Congress to Hear CSPI on Alcohol Ads," *Advertising Age* 14 January 1985, 71; "Sobering Words on Efforts to Ban Alcohol Ads," *Broadcasting*, 14 January 1985, 136; Robert Raissman, "Roone: ABC Will Fight Alcohol-ad Restraints," *Advertising Age*, 21 January 1985, 3.

26. House hearing, 1985, 71–72, 89–139; Steven Colford, "FTC Brings Cheer to Alcohol Marketers," *Advertising Age*, 22 April 1985, 14; Senate hearings, 1985, 5; Author's interview with George Hacker of the Center for Science in the Public Interest, 8 October 2001.

27. Steven Colford, "Reagan Adviser Opposes Booze-ad Ban," *Advertising Age*, 12 November 1984, 112; "Commissioners Speak Their Minds," *Broadcasting*, 14 January 1985, 134–35.

28. Senate hearing, 1985, 1.

29. Jacobson et al., *The Booze Merchants*, 141, emphasis in original; U.S. House of Representatives, Committee on Energy and Commerce, Subcommittee on Transportation and Hazardous Materials, *Health Warnings on Alcoholic Beverage Advertisements*, 101st Cong., 2nd sess., 18 July 1990, 298 (hereafter House hearing, 1990.)

30. Stephen Lambright, Senate hearing, 1985, 104, 122; Steven Colford, "Why Kennedy Wants Alcohol-ad Warnings," *Advertising Age*, 16 July 1990, 16.

31. House hearing, 1985, 297, 493; Senate hearing, 1985, 244.

32. House hearing, 1985, 209.

33. Senate hearing, 1985, 282.

34. Ibid., 102–3, 109–15, 133–38, 155; quotation from U.S. House of Representatives, Committee on Energy and Commerce, Subcommittee on Transportation and Hazardous Materials, *Oversight of FTC's Shared Responsibilities*, 102nd Cong., 1st sess., 21 November 1991, 177.

35. Jean Kilbourne, House hearing, 1990, 204, 221.

36. Jacobson et al., *The Booze Merchants*, 16, 25–27, 97–99; Senate hearing, 1985, 237.

37. Senate hearing, 1985, 301, 293.

38. Jacobson et al., *The Booze Merchants*, 47–79, 104–5, 112–13.

39. Anheuser-Busch executive quoted in "Koop Seeks Voluntary Curbs," *Advertising Age*, 5 June 1989, 6; John Calfee, U.S. House of Representatives, Select Committee on Children, Youth, and Families, *Preventing Underage Drinking: A Dialogue With the Surgeon General* 102nd Cong., 1st sess., 15 November 1991, 36–38 (hereafter House Select Committee hearing, 1991); Thomas Frank, *The Conquest of Cool: Business Culture, Counterculture, and the Rise of Hip Consumerism* (Chicago: University of Chicago Press, 1997), 118, 171.

40. Senate hearing, 1985, 107–8; House hearing, 1990, 65, 151, 175; Jacobson et al., *The Booze Merchants*, 8, 17–22.

41. House hearing, 1985, 430, 450–51; House hearing, 1990, 104; House hearing, 1991, 167; Senate hearing, 1992, 7.

42. House hearing, 1985, 208, 434–48; Senate hearing, 1985, 32–49, 77–94, 139–40, 215–25; House hearing, 1990, 109–10.

43. House hearing, 1990, 15, 30–31, 62; House hearing, 1985, 45, 53; Senate hearing, 1985, 245, 248.

44. House hearing, 1985, 8–10; House hearing, 1990, 270; Jacobson et al., *The Booze Merchants*, 11.

45. *Valentine v. Chrestensen*, 316 U.S. 52 (1942); *Central Hudson Gas v. Public Service Commission of New York*, 447 U.S. 557 (1980); House hearing, 1985, 401–5, 462; Senate hearing, 1985, 24, 57, 146, 155, 160, 167–69.

46. *Capital Broadcasting v. United States* 333 F. Supp. 582, 1971 U.S. Dist.; Senate hearings, 1985, 253.

47. Hacker, House hearings, 1990, 251; Senate hearings, 1985, 266–67. Also see House hearings, 1985, 10; House hearings, 1990, 14; and U.S. Senate, Committee on Commerce, Science, and Transportation, Subcommittee on the Consumer, *Alcohol Beverage Advertising Act S. 664,* 102nd Cong., 2nd sess., 2 April 1992, 52 (hereafter Senate hearing, 1992).

48. Christopher, "Alcohol Ad Fight;" Steven Colford, "Some Hedge on Ad Ban at Grass-roots PTA," *Advertising Age,* 4 March 1985, 100; Idem, "Higher Taxes Latest Threat in Alcohol Ad War," *Advertising Age,* 13 May 1985, 36; Brian Lowry, "California Media Wary of Ad Bans," *Advertising Age,* 5 August 1985, 66.

49. House hearing, 1985, 2, 196–205, 215, 230; Senate hearing, 1985, 164–65, 173–74.

50. *Congressional Record,* 1985, 11212.

51. Steven Colford, "House Turns Cold Shoulder to Liquor-Ad Ban," *Advertising Age,* 27 May 1985, 14; *Congressional Record,* 1985, 12669–70; Reginald Stuart, "What's Behind Those Drunken Driving Warnings?" *New York Times,* 31 December 1986, 14:3.

52. Golden, 86–87; "AMA Prescribes Strong Medicine," *Advertising Age,* 21 July 1986, S17; "60 Second Debate: Should Congress Pass Legislation to Require Warning Labels on Alcoholic Beverages?" *New York Times,* 9 July 1986, II, 5:4.

53. "60 Second Debate"; House hearing, 1990, 112.

54. "Warnings Sought on Liquor Bottles," *New York Times,* 27 December 1987, 25:1; "Beware: Labels Can Spoil Your Fun," *Economist,* 9 January 1988, 26; Patricia Taylor, "It's Time to Put Warnings on Alcohol," and James C. Sanders, "We Need Role Models, Not Labels," *New York Times,* 20 March 1988, III, 2:3; "Senator Raps," *Marketing News;* "Bitching about Booze," *Economist.*

55. Senate hearing, 1988; *Congressional Record,* 1988, 13645–46, 23411; George Hacker, R. Collins, and Michael Jacobson, *Selling Booze to Blacks* (Washington, D.C.: Center for Science in the Public Interest, 1987); Michael Jacobson and Bruce Maxwell, *Marketing Disease to Hispanics: The Selling of Alcohol, Tobacco, and Junk Foods* (Washington, D.C.: CSPI, 1989); "An Uproar Over Billboards in Poor Areas," *New York Times,* 1 May 1989, IV, 10:1.

56. Randall Rothenberg, "Koop's Idea for Alcohol Ban Debated," *New York Times,* 14 February 1990, D, 6:2.

57. *Congressional Record,* 1986, 17058–60; Stephen Barlas, "Potential Poxes and Taxes," *Beverage World,* May 1988, 104; *Congressional Record,* 1988, 111–14, 2717–20, 10662.

58. Senate hearing, 1988, 13, 17, 20, 54–75, 119, 144; Dirk Olin, "This Dud's For You," *The New Republic,* 11 July 1988, 12–13; *Congressional Record,* 1989, 21220–21; House hearing, 1990, 271.

59. Golden, 74, 92.

60. *Congressional Record,* 1989, 21220–21; House hearing, 1990, 54–61; *Federal Register,* 1989, 7160, and *Federal Register,* 1991, 5414.

61. Randall Rothenberg, "Panel Spurs Dispute over Alcohol Ads," *New York Times,* 2 December 1988, IV, 14:3; Ann Lallande, "The Liquor Law Binge," *Marketing and Media Decisions,* January 1989, 100–101; "Alcohol Ad Ban Opposed by Broadcasters, Advertisers," *Broadcasting,* 6 February 1989, 53.

62. "Koop Seeks Voluntary Curbs"; Rothenberg, "Koop's Idea." Koop did ask for warning labels on alcohol advertisements and the elimination of the tax deductibility of alcohol advertising in a lower tier of recommendations.

63. Senate hearing, 1992, 17; Lallande, "The Liquor Law."

64. *Congressional Record,* 1990, 7088–89, 8319; *Congressional Record,* 1991, 6319, 6402; *Congressional Record,* 1993, 6871, 8248.

65. Ira Teinowitz and Steven Colford, "Brewers Fight Back," *Advertising Age,* 11 November 1991, 67; "Industry Faces Ongoing Beer Ad Ban Threat," *Broadcasting,* 2 December 1991, 44; Stuart Elliott, "A Rising Tide of Rhetoric Over Warnings on Alcohol," *New York Times,* 2 April 1992, D, 18:3; House Select Committee hearing, 1991.

66. Clifford Krauss, "Liquor-Warning Bill Reflects Personal Impact on Public Policy," *New York Times,* 16 May 1993, 20:1; Steven Colford, "Doubts Greet Alcohol Ad-Label Bill," *Advertising Age,* 17 May 1993, 45; Randy Sukow, "Battling Beer-Wine Labeling," *Broadcasting,* 20 April 1992, 34–35; House hearing, 1990, 150.

67. Interview with George Hacker.

68. Solomon Katz, "Secular Morality," in Allan M. Brandt and Paul Rozin, eds., *Morality and Health* (New York: Routledge, 1997), 297–330.

CONCLUSION—THE ELUSIVE QUEST FOR RESTRAINTS

1. NBC was not the first broadcaster to air hard liquor ads, but it was the first of the major networks. Seagram's broke the voluntary ban in 1996, and some cable stations and local network affiliates aired hard liquor commercials beginning in the mid- to late 1990s.

2. Cal Thomas, "Liquor Ads Don't Belong On Television," *Columbus Dispatch,* 19 December 2001.

3. "AMA Blasts NBC for Hard-Liquor Ads," *Columbus Dispatch,* 19 December 2001; Joseph A. Califano, "NBC is Developing a Drinking Problem," *Cleveland Plain Dealer,* 24 December 2001, B7.

4. Ronald Inglehart, *The Silent Revolution: Changing Values and Political Styles Among Western Publics* (Princeton, N.J.: Princeton University Press, 1977); Samuel P. Hays, "Three Decades of Environmental Politics: The Historical Context," in Michael J. Lacey, ed., *Government and Environmental Politics: Essays on Historical Developments Since World War Two* (Washington, D.C.: Woodrow Wilson Center Press, 1989, 1991), 25; Ronald Inglehart, "The Trend Toward Postmaterialist Values Continues," in Terry Nichols Clark and Michael Remple, eds., *Citizen Politics in Post-Industrial Societies* (Boulder, Colo.: Westview Press, 1997), 58; Howard Leichter, *Free to Be Foolish: Politics and Health Promotion in the United States and Great Britain* (Princeton, N.J.: Princeton University Press, 1991), 71–75.

5. Richard A. Harris and Sidney Milkis, *The Politics of Regulatory Change: A Tale of Two Agencies,* 2nd ed. (New York: Oxford University Press, 1996), 3–10; Robert Parham, Baptist Center for Ethics, Hearing before the Subcommittee on Consumer of the Senate Committee on Commerce, Science, and Transportation, 102nd Congress, 1992, 132; Robert Kennedy, *Congressional Record,* 1966, 7462 and *Congressional Record,* 1967, 25126; Representative Joe Kennedy, Hearing before the Subcommittee on Transportation and Hazardous Materials of the House Committee on Energy and Commerce, 101st Congress, on H.R. 4493, July 18, 1990, 14.

6. Joe B. Tye, "Cigarette Marketing: Ethical Conservatism or Corporate Violence?" *New York State Journal of Medicine* 85 (July 1985): 324.

7. Lawrence Gostin, "The Legal Regulation of Smoking (and Smokers): Public Health or Secular Morality?" in Allan M. Brandt and Paul Rozin, eds., *Morality and Health* (London: Routledge, 1997), 334–37. *44 Liquormart, Inc. v. State of Rhode Island,* 517 U.S. 484 (1996); *Greater New Orleans Broadcasting Association Inc. v. U.S.,* 200 U.S. 321, 337; Tony Mauro, "Confusion Creeps Into Celebration Over Lifting of Casino Ad Ban," freedomforum.org, 15 June 1999, <http://www.freedomforum.org/templates/document.asp?documentID=10660>; *Lorillard Tobacco Co. v. Reilly.*

8. Allan M. Brandt and Lawrence O. Gostin, "Criteria for Evaluating a Ban on the Advertisement of Cigarettes," *Journal of the American Medical Association* 269 (February 17, 1993): 908.

9. *Food and Drug Administration vs. Brown and Williamson Tobacco Corporation* 120 U.S. 1291(2000); W. Kip Viscusi, *Smoke-Filled Rooms: A Postmortem on the Tobacco Deal* (Chicago: University of Chicago Press, 2002), 37–38, 129; David Kessler, *A Question of Intent: A Great American Battle with a Deadly Industry* (New York: Public Affairs, 2001); Michael Pertschuk, *Smoke In Their Eyes: Lessons in Movement Leadership from the Tobacco Wars* (Nashville: Vanderbilt University Press, 2001); Campaign for Tobacco Free Kids, "Justice Department Civil Lawsuit," 26 September 2005, <http://www.tobaccofreekids.org/reports/doj>.

10. Harvey M. Sapolsky, ed., *Consuming Fears: The Politics of Product Risks* (New York: Basic Books, 1986), 10–11. Ronald G. Walters, ed., *Scientific Authority and Twentieth-Century America* (Baltimore: Johns Hopkins University Press, 1997); Patterson, 52, 181, 254; Phillip M. Boffey, *The Brain Bank of America: An Inquiry Into the Politics of Science* (New York: McGraw-Hill, 1975); Stephen Strickland, *Politics, Science, and Dread Disease: A Short History of United States Medical Research Policy* (Cambridge, Mass.: Harvard University Press, 1972); Dean Schooler, *Science, Scientists, and Public Policy* (New York: Free Press, 1971); Don K. Price, *The Scientific Estate* (Cambridge, Mass.: Belknap Press, 1967); Ralph E. Lapp, *The New Priesthood: The Scientific Elite and the Uses of Power* (New York: Harper & Row, 1965).

11. Allan M. Brandt, "The Cigarette, Risk and American Culture," *Daedalus* 119 (1990), 156; Christopher J. Bosso, *Pesticides and Politics: The Life Cycle of a Public Issue* (Pittsburgh: University of Pittsburgh Press, 1987).

12. Mark E. Rushefsky, *Making Cancer Policy* (Albany: State University of New York Press, 1986), 5–6, 64, 183; Lawrence Gostin, "The Legal Regulation of Smoking (and Smokers): Public Health or Secular Morality?" in Brandt and Rozin, eds., *Morality and Health* (New York: Routledge, 1997), 341; Leichter, 81.

13. Brandt, "The Cigarette," 156; Rushefsky, 6; Charles Rosenberg, "Banishing Risk," in Brandt and Rozin, eds., *Morality and Health,* 49; Patterson, 216, 229; Joseph Gusfield, "The Social Symbolism of Smoking and Health," in Robert L. Rabin and Stephen D. Sugarman, eds., *Smoking Policy: Law, Politics, and Culture* (New York: Oxford University Press, 1993), 50–77; Virginia Berridge, "Science and Policy: The Case of Postwar British Smoking Policy," in S. Lock, L. A. Reynolds, and E. M. Tansey, eds., *Ashes to Ashes: The History of Smoking and Health* (Amsterdam: Editions Rodopi R.V., 1998), 143–63.

14. U.S., Congress, Senate, Committee on Commerce, *Cigarette Labeling and Advertising,* 89th Cong., 1st sess., 1965, 232.

15. Gary Cross, *An All-Consuming Century: Why Commercialism Won in Modern America* (New York: Columbia University Press, 2000), 126–28; Leo Bogart, *The Age of Television: A Study of the Viewing Habits and the Impact of Television in America,* 3rd ed. (New York: F. Ungar, 1972), 98, 184; Lynn Spigel, *Make Room for TV: Television and the Family Ideal in Postwar America* (Chicago: University of Chicago Press, 1992), 50–54; Erik Barnouw, *Tube of Plenty: The Evolution of American Television,* 2nd rev. ed. (New York: Oxford University Press, 1990).

16. Gary Cross, *The Cute and the Cool: Wondrous Innocence and Modern American Children's Culture* (New York: Oxford University Press, 2004), 164–65, 179–80, 189–90; Tom Englehardt, "Children's Television: The Shortcake Strategy," in Todd Gitlin, ed., *Watching Television: A Pantheon Guide to Popular Culture* (New York: Pantheon Books, 1986), 110; Ellen Seiter, *Sold Separately: Children and Parents in Consumer Culture* (New Brunswick, N.J.: Rutgers University Press, 1993), 38; Iain Ramsay, *Advertising, Culture, and The Law: Beyond Lies, Ignorance, and Manipulation* (London: Sweet & Maxwell, 1996), 112–18; James Gilbert, *A Cycle of Outrage: America's Reaction to the Juvenile Delinquent in the 1950s* (New York: Oxford University Press, 1986), 3–5.

17. DISCUS, "Code of Responsible Practices for Beverage Alcohol Advertising and Marketing," October 2003, <http://www.discus.org/industry/code/code.htm>; The Center for Alcohol Marketing and Youth, "Reducing Alcohol Ads Kids See Won't Cost Industry Adult Market," 5 July 2005, <http://camy.org/press/release.php?ReleaseID=28>.

18. *Reno v. American Civil Liberties Union,* 521 U.S. 844 (1997).

19. Brandt and Gostin, 908.

20. Allan M. Brandt, "Blow Some My Way: Passive Smoking, Risk, and American Culture," in Lock, Reynolds, and Tansey, eds., *Ashes to Ashes,* 164–87.

21. Pamela Pennock and K. Austin Kerr, "In the Shadow of Prohibition: Domestic American Alcohol Policy Since 1933," *Business History* 47 (July 2005): 396; The Center for Alcohol Marketing and Youth, "Alcohol Advertising and Youth," Fact Sheet, July 2005, <http://camy.org/factsheets/index.php?FactsheetID=1>; "Hearings in Order: The Alcohol Industry Should Stop Targeting Teens with Advertising," *Columbus Dispatch,* 22 April 2003, 8; S. 408, Bill on Underage Drinking, 16 February 2005, <http://frwebgate.access.gpo.gov/cgibin/getdoc.cgi?dbname=109_cong_bills&docid=f:s408is.txt.pdf>; Clifford J. Levy, "Drink, Don't Drink, Drink, Don't Drink," *New York Times,* 9 October 2005, IV, 14:1.

22. Robin Room, "Alcohol Control and Public Health," *Annual Review of Public Health* (5) 1984: 294; Timothy Egan, "A Worried Liquor Industry Readies for Birth-Defect Suit," *New York Times,* 21 April 1989, 12:5.

23. Author's interview with George Hacker of the Center for Science in the Public Interest, 8 October 2001.

24. Robin Room, "Cultural Changes in Drinking and Trends in Alcohol Problems Indicators: Recent U.S. Experience," in Walter B. Clark and Michael E. Hilton, eds., *Alcohol in America: Drinking Practices and Problems* (Albany: State University of New York Press, 1991), 156; Thomas Babor et al., *Alcohol: No Ordinary Commodity* (New York: Oxford University Press, 2003), 32; "U.S. Apparent Consumption of Alcoholic Beverages Based on State Sales, Taxation, or Receipt Data," U.S. Alcohol Epidemiologic Data Reference Manual, Vol. 1, 4th ed., June 2004, Washington, D.C.: NIH Publication No. 04-5563; Office on Smoking and Health of the Centers for Disease Control and Prevention, "Smoking Prevalence among U.S. Adults, May 2005." <http://www.cdc.gov/tobacco/research_data/adults_prev/prevali.htm>.

25. For example, Anne Underwood, "A Healthy Toast: It's Not Just Wine That Protects the Heart. All Alcohol Has Cardiac Benefits—In Moderation," *Newsweek,* 3 October 2005, 70.

26. Jane Eisner, "Treat Fat as the New Alcohol," *Detroit Free Press,* 24 November 2003, 9A; Kelly Brownell, *Food Fight* (New York: McGraw Hill, 2004); Susan Linn, *Consuming Kids: Protecting Our Children from the Onslaught of Marketing and Advertising* (New York: Anchor, 2005).

SELECTED BIBLIOGRAPHY

ARCHIVAL

National Archives. Washington, D.C.
Record Group 46, Records of the Senate Committee on Commerce.
Record Group 233, Records of the House Committee on Commerce.
William D. Hathaway Papers. Special Collections Department, Raymond H. Fogler Library, University of Maine at Orono.
John J. Hill Papers. Wisconsin Historical Society, Madison, Wisconsin.
Robert F. Kennedy Senate Papers. John F. Kennedy Presidential Library, Boston, Massachusetts.
Horace R. Kornegay Papers. Southern Historical Collection, Library of the University of North Carolina at Chapel Hill.
Senator Frank E. Moss Papers. Special Collections, Marriott Library, University of Utah, Salt Lake City, Utah.
Maurine Neuberger Papers. Special Collections, University of Oregon, Eugene, Oregon.
Michael Pertschuk Papers. Library of Congress, Washington, D.C.
Center for Science in the Public Interest Papers. Center for Science in the Public Interest, Washington, D.C.
Seagram Company Papers. Hagley Museum and Library, Wilmington, Delaware.

BOOKS AND ESSAYS

Agnew, Jean-Christophe. "Coming Up for Air: Consumer Culture in Historical Perspective." In *Consumption and the World of Goods*, edited by John Brewer and Roy Porter. London: Routledge, 1993.
Allen, Frederick Lewis. *Only Yesterday: An Informal History of the Nineteen-Twenties*. New York: Harper & Brothers, 1931.
Altman, D. "How an Unhealthy Product Is Sold: Cigarette Advertising in Magazines 1960–1985." *Journal of Communications* 37 (1987): 95–106.
Ardell, Donald. *High Level Wellness: An Alternative to Doctors, Drugs, and Disease*. Emmaus, Pa.: Rodale Press, 1977.
Atkin, Charles, and Martin Block. *Content and Effects of Alcohol Advertising*. Springfield, Va.: National Technical Information Service, 1981.
Babor, Thomas, et al. *Alcohol: No Ordinary Commodity*. New York: Oxford University Press, 2003.
Baker, C. Edwin. *Advertising and a Democratic Press*. Princeton, N.J.: Princeton University Press, 1994.

Barnouw, Erik. *Tube of Plenty: The Evolution of American Television.* 2nd rev. ed. New York: Oxford University Press, 1990.

Bauer, Raymond, and Stephen Greyser. *Advertising in America: The Consumer View.* Boston: Graduate School of Business Administration, Harvard University, 1968.

Beauchamp, Dan E. "Public Health as Social Justice." *Inquiry* 13 (1976): 1–14.

Beauchamp, Dan E. *Beyond Alcoholism: Alcohol and Public Health Policy.* Philadelphia: Temple University Press, 1980.

Beauchamp, Dan E., and Bonnie Steinbock. "Prevention and Its Limits." In *New Ethics for the Public's Health,* edited by Dan E. Beauchamp and Bonnie Steinbock. New York: Oxford University Press, 1999.

Berridge, Virginia. "Science and Policy: the Case of Postwar British Smoking Policy." In *Ashes to Ashes: The History of Smoking and Health,* edited by Stephen Lock, Lois A. Reynolds, and E. M. Tansey. Amsterdam: Editions Rodopi R.V., 1998.

Blane, Howard, and Linda Hewitt. *Alcohol and Youth. An Analysis of the Literature, 1960–1975.* Rockville, Md.: National Institute on Alcohol Abuse and Alcoholism, 1977.

Blocker, Jack S., Jr. *American Temperance Movements: Cycles of Reform.* Boston: Twayne, 1989.

Boffey, Phillip M. *The Brain Bank of America: An Inquiry Into the Politics of Science.* New York: McGraw-Hill, 1975.

Bogart, Leo. *The Age of Television: A Study of the Viewing Habits and the Impact of Television on American Life.* 3d ed. New York: Ungar, 1955, 1958, 1972.

Bordin, Ruth. *Woman and Temperance: The Quest for Power and Liberty, 1873–1900.* New Brunswick, N.J.: Rutgers University Press, 1990.

Bosso, Christopher J. *Pesticides and Politics: The Life Cycle of a Public Issue.* Pittsburgh: University of Pittsburgh Press, 1987.

Brandt, Allan M. *No Magic Bullet: A Social History of Venereal Disease in the United States Since 1880.* New York: Oxford University Press, 1985.

Brandt, Allan M. "The Cigarette, Risk, and American Culture." *Daedalus* 119 (1990): 155–76.

Brandt, Allan M. and Gostin, Lawrence. "Criteria for Evaluating a Ban on the Advertisement of Cigarettes: Balancing Public Health Benefits with Constitutional Burdens." *Journal of the American Medical Association* 269 (1993): 904–9.

Brandt, Allan M. "Behavior, Disease, and Health in the Twentieth-Century United States: The Moral Valance of Individual Risk." In *Morality and Health,* edited by Allan Brandt and Paul Rozin. New York: Routledge, 1997.

Brandt, Allan M. "Blow Some My Way: Passive Smoking, Risk, and American Culture." In *Ashes to Ashes: The History of Smoking and Health,* edited by S. Lock, L. A. Reynolds, and E. M. Tansey. Amsterdam: Editions Rodopi R.V., 1998.

Brecher, Ruth, Edward Brecher, Arthur Herzog, Walter Goodman, Gerald Walker, and the Editors of Consumer Reports. *The Consumers Union Report on Smoking and the Public Interest.* Mount Vernon, N.Y.: Consumers Union, 1963.

Breed, W., J. De Foe, and Lawrence Wallack. "Drinking in the Mass Media: A Nine-Year Project." *Journal of Drug Issues* 14 (1984): 655–64.

Bretzfield, Henry. *Liquor Marketing and Liquor Advertising: A Guide for Executives and their Staffs in Management, Sales and Advertising.* New York: Abelard-Schuman, 1955.

Brownell, Kelly. *Food Fight.* New York: McGraw-Hill, 2004.

Bruun, Kettil, et al. *Alcohol Control Policies in Public Health Perspective.* New Brunswick, N.J.: Rutgers University Center of Alcohol Studies, 1975.

Buffaloe, Neal. *What's Wrong With Smoking.* Grand Rapids, Mich.: Zondervan, 1954.

Burger, Edward J., Jr., ed. *Risk.* Ann Arbor: University of Michigan Press, 1990.

Burnham, John C. "American Physicians and Tobacco Use: Two Surgeons General, 1929 and 1964," *Bulletin History of Medicine* 63 (1989): 1–31.

Burnham, John C. *Bad Habits: Drinking, Smoking, Taking Drugs, Gambling, Sexual Misbehavior, and Swearing in American History.* New York: New York University Press, 1993.

Burns, Eric. *The Spirits of America: A Social History of Alcohol.* Philadelphia: Temple University Press, 2004.

Calfee, John E. "The Ghost of Cigarette Advertising Past." *Regulation* 10 (November/December 1986): 35–45.

Cater, Douglass. *Power in Washington: A Critical Look at Today's Struggle to Govern in the Nation's Capital*. New York: Random House, 1964.

Chafetz, Morris. *Liquor, the Servant of Man*. Boston: Little, Brown and Co., 1965.

Chafetz, Morris. *Why Drinking Can Be Good for You*. Briarcliff Manor, New York: Stein and Day, 1976.

Chauncey, Robert. "New Careers for Moral Entrepreneurs: Teenage Drinking." *Journal of Drug Issues* 10 (1980): 45–70.

Cohen, Lizabeth. *A Consumers' Republic: The Politics of Mass Consumption in Postwar America*. New York: Alfred A. Knopf, 2003.

Collingridge, David and Colin Reeve. *Science Speaks to Power: The Role of Experts in Policy Making*. London: Frances Pinter, 1986.

Coren, Robert W. *Guide to the Records of the United States Senate at the National Archives 1789–1989*. Washington, D.C.: U.S. Senate Bicentennial Publication, 1989.

Courtwright, David. "'Carry on Smoking': Public Relations and Advertising Strategies of American and British Tobacco Companies Since 1950." *Business History* 47 (July 2005): 421–32.

Cowan, Richard, and James F. Mosher. "Public Health Implications of Beverage Marketing: Alcohol as an Ordinary Consumer Product." *Contemporary Drug Problems* 12 (1985): 621–57.

Cox, Edward, Robert C. Fellmeth, and John E. Schulz. Preface by Ralph Nader. *The Nader Report on the Federal Trade Commission*. New York: Richard W. Baron, 1969.

Cross, Gary. *An All-Consuming Century: Why Commercialism Won in Modern America*. New York: Columbia University Press, 2000.

Cross, Gary. *The Cute and the Cool: Wondrous Innocence and Modern American Children's Culture*. New York: Oxford University Press, 2004.

Dannenbaum, Jed. *Drink and Disorder: Temperance Reform in Cincinnati from the Washingtonian Revival to the WCTU*. Urbana: University of Illinois Press, 1984.

Davis, Ronald M. "Current Trends in Cigarette Advertising and Marketing." *New England Journal of Medicine* 316 (1987): 725–32.

Dichter, Ernest. *The Strategy of Desire*. Garden City, N.Y.: Doubleday, 1960.

Distilled Spirits Council of the United States. "Code of Responsible Practices for Beverage Alcohol Advertising and Marketing." October 2003. <http://www.discus.org /industry/code/code.htm>.

Doll, Richard, and Bradford Hill. "Smoking and Carcinoma of the Lung. Preliminary Report." *British Medical Journal* 2 (1950): 739.

"Donovan Hits Dry Propaganda Linking Juvenile Delinquency to Drinking." *Licensed Beverage Industries Newsletter,* July-August 1954, 1.

Doron, Gideon. *The Smoking Paradox: Public Regulation in the Cigarette Industry*. Cambridge, Mass.: Abt Books, 1979.

Douglas, Mary, and Aaron Wildavsky. *Risk and Culture: An Essay on the Selection of Technical and Environmental Dangers*. Berkeley: University of California Press, 1982.

Englehardt, Tom. "Children's Television: The Shortcake Strategy." In *Watching Television: A Pantheon Guide to Popular Culture,* edited by Todd Gitlin. New York: Pantheon Books, 1986.

Fisher, Joseph C. *Advertising, Alcohol Consumption, and Abuse: A Worldwide Survey*. Westport, Conn.: Greenwood Press, 1993.

Fox, Stephen. *The Mirror Makers: A History of American Advertising and Its Creators*. New York: Morrow, 1984.

Frank, Thomas. *The Conquest of Cool: Business Culture, Counterculture, and the Rise of Hip Consumerism*. Chicago: University of Chicago Press, 1997.

Fritschler, A. Lee. *Smoking and Politics: Policymaking and the Federal Bureaucracy*. New York: Appleton-Century-Crofts, 1969.

Gallup, George. *The Gallup Poll: Public Opinion 1935–1971*. New York: Random House, 1972.

Gerstein, Dean R., and Mark H. Moore, eds. *Alcohol and Public Policy: Beyond the Shadow of Prohibition*. Washington, D.C.: National Academy Press, 1981.

Gerstein, Dean R., ed. *Toward the Prevention of Alcohol Problems: Government, Business, and Community Action*. Washington, D.C.: National Academy Press, 1984.

Gilbert, James. *A Cycle of Outrage: America's Reaction to the Juvenile Delinquent in the 1950s*. New York: Oxford University Press, 1986.

Ginzberg, Lori. *Women and the Work of Benevolence: Morality, Politics, and Class in the Nineteenth-Century United States*. New Haven, Conn.: Yale University Press, 1990.

Gold, Philip. *Advertising, Politics, and American Culture: From Salesmanship to Therapy*. New York: Paragon House, 1987.

Golden, Janet. *Message in a Bottle: The Making of Fetal Alcohol Syndrome*. (Cambridge, Mass.: Harvard University Press, 2005).

Goldstein, Michael. *The Health Movement: Promoting Fitness in America*. New York: Twayne, 1992.

Gostin, Lawrence. "The Legal Regulation of Smoking (and Smokers): Public Health or Secular Morality?" In *Morality and Health*, edited by Allan M. Brandt and Paul Rozin. New York: Routledge, 1997.

Gusfield, Joseph. "Social Structure and Moral Reform: A Study of the Woman's Christian Temperance Union." *American Journal of Sociology* 61 (November 1955): 221–32.

Gusfield, Joseph. *Symbolic Crusade: Status Politics and the American Temperance Movement*. Urbana: University of Illinois Press, 1963.

Gusfield, Joseph. "The Social Symbolism of Smoking and Health." In *Smoking: Law, Policy and Culture*, edited by Stephen Sugarman and Robert Rabin. New York: Oxford University Press, 1993.

Gusfield, Joseph R. *Contested Meanings: The Construction of Alcohol Problems*. Madison: University of Wisconsin Press, 1996.

Hacker, George, Robert Collins, and Michael Jacobson. *Selling Booze to Blacks*. Washington, D.C.: Center for Science in the Public Interest, 1987.

Hamm, Richard F. *Shaping the Eighteenth Amendment: Temperance Reform, Legal Culture, and the Polity, 1880–1920*. Chapel Hill: University of North Carolina Press, 1995.

Hammond, E. Cuyler, and Daniel Horn. "The Relationship Between Human Smoking Habits and Death Rates: A Follow-Up Study of 187,766 Men." *Journal of the American Medical Association* 154 (1954): 1316–28.

Harris, Richard A., and Sidney Milkis. *The Politics of Regulatory Change: A Tale of Two Agencies*. 2nd ed. New York: Oxford University Press, 1996.

Hasin, Bernice Rothman. *Consumers, Commissions, and Congress: Law, Theory, and the Federal Trade Commission, 1968–1985*. New Brunswick, N.J.: Transaction Books, 1987.

Hays, Samuel P. "Three Decades of Environmental Politics: The Historical Context." In *Government and Environmental Politics: Essays on Historical Developments Since World War Two*, edited by Michael J. Lacey. Washington, D.C.: Woodrow Wilson Center Press, 1989, 1991.

Heath, D. B. "The New Temperance Movement: Through the Looking Glass." In *Current Issues in Alcohol/Drug Studies*, edited by Edith S. Lisansky Gomberg. New York: Haworth Press, 1989.

Hilts, Philip J. *Smokescreen: The Truth behind the Tobacco Industry Cover-Up*. Reading, Mass.: Addison-Wesley, 1996.

Hougland, James G., Jr., James R. Wood, and Samuel A. Mueller. "Organizational 'Goal Submergence': The Methodist Church and the Failure of the Temperance Movement." *Sociology and Social Research* 58 (July 1974): 408–15.

Housman, Michael. "Smoking and Health: The 1964 U.S. Surgeon General's Report as a Turning Point in the Anti-smoking Movement." *Harvard Health Policy Review* 2 (Spring 2001): 118–26.

Hunt, Alan. *Governing Morals: A Social History of Moral Regulation.* Cambridge: Cambridge University Press, 1999.

Hyman, Allen, and M. Bruce Johnson. *Advertising and Free Speech.* Lexington: D.C. Heath, 1976.

Iglehart, John K. "Smoking and Public Policy." *New England Journal of Medicine* 310 (February 1984): 539–44.

Inglehart, Ronald. *The Silent Revolution: Changing Values and Political Styles Among Western Publics.* Princeton, N.J.: Princeton University Press, 1977.

Inglehart, Ronald. "The Trend Toward Postmaterialist Values Continues." In *Citizen Politics in Post-Industrial Societies,* edited by Terry Nichols Clark and Michael Remple. Boulder, Colo.: Westview Press, 1997.

Jacobson, Michael, R. Atkins, and George Hacker. *The Booze Merchants: The Inebriating of America.* Washington, D.C.: Center for Science in the Public Interest, 1983.

Jacobson, Michael, and Bruce Maxwell. *Marketing Disease to Hispanics: The Selling of Alcohol, Tobacco, and Junk Foods.* Washington, D.C.: Center for Science in the Public Interest, 1989.

Jasanoff, Sheila. *Risk Management and Political Culture: A Comparative Study of Science in the Policy Context.* New York: Russell Sage Foundation, 1986.

Jellinek, E. M. *The Disease Concept of Alcoholism.* New Haven, Conn.: Hillhouse Press, 1960.

Kagan, Robert A., and David Vogel. "The Politics of Smoking Regulation: Canada, France, the United States." In *Smoking Policy: Law, Politics, and Culture,* edited by Robert Rabin and Stephen Sugarman. New York: Oxford University Press, 1993.

Katz, Solomon. "Secular Morality." In *Morality and Health,* edited by Allan M. Brandt and Paul Rozin. New York: Routledge, 1997.

Kessler, David. *A Question of Intent: A Great American Battle with a Deadly Industry.* New York: Public Affairs, 2001.

Kluger, Richard. *Ashes to Ashes: America's Hundred-Year Cigarette War, the Public Health, and the Unabashed Triumph of Philip Morris.* New York: Alfred A. Knopf, 1996.

Knowles, John H. "The Responsibility of the Individual." *Daedalus* 106 (Winter 1977): 57–80.

Kohn, P. and R. Smart. "The Impact of Television Advertising on Alcohol Consumption: An Experiment." *Journal of Studies on Alcohol* 45 (1984): 295–301.

Kurtz, Ernest. *Not-God: A History of Alcoholics Anonymous.* Center City, Minn.: Hazelden, 1979.

LaForge, Robert G. "Misplaced Priorities: A History of Federal Alcohol Regulation and Public Health Policy." Ph.D. diss., Johns Hopkins University, 1987.

Lallande, Ann. "The Liquor Law Binge." *Marketing and Media Decisions,* January 1989, 100–101.

Larson, Edward. *Summer for the Gods: The Scopes Trial and America's Continuing Debate Over Science and Religion.* New York: Basic Books, 1997.

Lapp, Ralph E. *The New Priesthood: The Scientific Elite and the Uses of Power.* New York: Harper & Row, 1965.

Lears, T. J. Jackson. "From Salvation to Self-Realization: Advertising and the Therapeutic Roots of the Consumer Culture, 1880–1930." In *The Culture of Consumption: Critical Essays in American History, 1880–1980,* edited by Richard Wightman Fox and T. J. Jackson Lears. New York: Pantheon Books, 1983.

Leichter, Howard. *Free To Be Foolish: Politics and Health Promotion in the United States and Great Britain.* Princeton, N.J.: Princeton University Press, 1991.

Leichter, Howard M. "Lifestyle Correctness and the New Secular Morality." In *Morality and Health,* edited by Allan M. Brandt and Paul Rozin. New York: Routledge, 1997.

Lender, Mark Edward, and James Kirby Martin. *Drinking in America: A History.* Rev. ed. New York: Free Press, 1987.

Lender, Mark Edward. "A New Prohibition? An Essay on Drinking and Smoking in America." In *Smoking: Who Has the Right?* Edited by Jeffrey A. Schaler and Magda E. Schaler. Amherst, N.Y.: Prometheus Books, 1998.

Linn, Susan. *Consuming Kids: Protecting Our Children From the Onslaught of Marketing and Advertising*. New York: Anchor, 2005.

Loevinger, Lee. "The Politics of Advertising." In *Advertising and the Public Interest*, edited by S. F. Divita. Chicago: American Marketing Association, 1974.

MacLeod, William, and Robert Rogowsky. "Consumer Protection at the FTC during the Reagan Administration." In *Regulation and the Reagan Era: Politics, Bureaucracy, and the Public Interest*, edited by Roger Meiners and Bruce Yandle. New York: Holmes and Meier, 1989.

Magnuson, Warren. "Consumerism and the Emerging Goals of a New Society." In *Consumerism: Viewpoints from Business, Government, and the Public Interest*, edited by Ralph M. Gaedeke and Warren W. Etcheson. San Francisco: Canfield Press, 1972.

Magnuson, Warren, and Jean Carper. *The Dark Side of the Marketplace: The Plight of the American Consumer*. Englewood Cliffs, N.J.: Prentice-Hall, 1968.

Maney, Ardith, and Loree Bykerk. *Consumer Politics: Protecting Public Interests on Capitol Hill*. Westport, Conn.: Greenwood Press, 1994.

Marchand, Roland. *Advertising the American Dream: Making Way for Modernity, 1920–1940*. Berkeley: University of California Press, 1985.

Marquis, Harold H. *The Changing Corporate Image*. The American Marketing Association, 1970.

Marsden, George. *Religion and American Culture*. San Diego: Harcourt Brace Jovanovich, 1990.

Marshall, Mac, and Alice Oleson. "In the Pink: MADD and Public Health Policy in the 1990s." *Journal of Public Health Policy* 15 (1994): 54–68.

Marton, Rebecca Murphy. "The Role of Government and the Non-Profit Sector in the New Temperance Movement," <http://sunset.backbone.olemiss.edu/~phjuerg/newtemp.html>.

Mauro, Tony. "Confusion Creeps Into Celebration Over Lifting of Casino Ad Ban." freedomforum.org. 15 June 1999, <http://www.freedomforum.org/templates/document.asp?documentID=10660>.

McAllister, Matthew P. *The Commercialization of American Culture: New Advertising, Control and Democracy*. Thousand Oaks, Calif.: Sage, 1996.

McGowan, Richard, and John Mahon. "Collaborating with the Enemy: Tobacco, Alcohol, and the Public Good." *Business in the Contemporary World* 7 (1995): 69–92.

McGowan, Richard, and John Mahon. *Industry as a Player in the Political & Social Arena: Defining the Competitive Environment*. Westport, Conn.: Quorum Books, 1996.

McMannon, Timothy J. "Warren G. Magnuson and Consumer Protection." Ph.D. diss., University of Washington, 1994.

Miles, Robert. *Coffin Nails and Corporate Strategies*. Englewood Cliffs, N.J.: Prentice-Hall, 1982.

Minkler, Meredith, Lawrence Wallack, and Patricia Madden. "Alcohol and Cigarette Advertising in Ms. Magazine." *Journal of Public Health Policy* 8 (Summer 1987): 164–79.

Morgan, P. "Power, Politics, and Public Health: The Political Power of the Alcohol Beverage Industry." *Journal of Public Health Policy* (Summer 1988): 177–97.

Mosher, James F. "Alcohol Problems and the Consumer Movement." In *Encyclopedia of the Consumer Movement*, edited by Stephen Brobeck. Santa Barbara, Calif.: ABC-CLIO, 1997.

Mosher, James F., and David Jernigan. "New Directions in Alcohol Policy." *Annual Review of Public Health* 10 (1989): 245–79.

National Woman's Christian Temperance Union, *Annual Report*, 77th Annual Convention, 1951.

Neuberger, Maurine. *Smokescreen: Tobacco and the Public Welfare*. Englewood Cliffs, N.J.: Prentice-Hall, 1963.

Packard, Vance. *The Hidden Persuaders*. New York: D. McKay, 1957.

Page, Penny Booth. "E.M. Jellinek and the Evolution of Alcohol Studies: A Critical Essay." *Addiction* 92 (December 1997): 1619–37.

Parker, Alison. *Purifying America: Women, Cultural Reform, and Pro-Censorship Activism, 1873–1933*. Urbana: University of Illinois Press, 1997.

Patterson, James T. *The Dread Disease: Cancer and Modern American Culture*. Cambridge, Mass.: Harvard University Press, 1987.

Patterson, James T. *Grand Expectations: The United States, 1945–1974*. New York: Oxford University Press, 1996.

Pertschuk, Michael. *Revolt Against Regulation: The Rise and Pause of the Consumer Movement*. Berkeley: University of California Press, 1982.

Pertschuk, Michael. *Giant Killers*. New York: W. W. Norton, 1986.

Preston, Ivan. *The Tangled Web They Weave: Truth, Falsity, and Advertisers*. Madison: University of Wisconsin Press, 1994.

Price, Don K. *The Scientific Estate*. Cambridge, Mass.: Belknap Press, 1967.

Rabin, Robert L., and Stephen D. Sugarman. "Introduction." In *Smoking Policy: Law, Politics, and Culture*, edited by Robert L. Rabin and Stephen D. Sugarman. New York: Oxford University Press, 1993.

Ramsay, Iain. *Advertising, Culture, and the Law: Beyond Lies, Ignorance, and Manipulation*. London: Sweet & Maxwell, 1996.

Read, Melvyn. *The Politics of Tobacco: Policy Networks and the Cigarette Industry*. Aldershot, England: Avebury, 1996.

Reagan, Michael D. *Regulation: The Politics of Policy*. Boston: Little, Brown, 1987.

Riesman, David. *The Lonely Crowd: A Study of the Changing American Character*. New Haven, Conn.: Yale University Press, 1950.

Ripley, Randall B., and Grace Franklin. *Congress, the Bureaucracy, and Public Policy*. Pacific Grove, Calif.: Brooks/Cole, 1991.

Rogers, Martha. "Advertising Self-regulation in the 1980s: A Review." *Current Issues and Research in Advertising*, 13 (1991): 369–92.

Roizen, Ronald. "The American Discovery of Alcoholism, 1933–1939." Ph.D. diss., University of California, Berkeley, 1991.

Roizen, Ronald. "How Does the Nation's 'Alcohol Problem' Change From Era to Era? Stalking the Social Logic of Problem-Definition Transformations Since Repeal." Presented at Historical Perspectives on Alcohol and Drug Use in American Society, 1800–1997. College of Physicians of Philadelphia, 9–11 May 1997.

Room, Robin. "Alcohol Control and Public Health." *Annual Review of Public Health* 5 (1984): 293–318.

Room, Robin. "Cultural Changes in Drinking and Trends in Alcohol Problems Indicators: Recent U.S. Experience." In *Alcohol in America: Drinking Practices and Problems*, edited by Walter B. Clark and Michael E. Hilton. Albany: State University of New York Press, 1991.

Rose, Kenneth. *American Women and the Repeal of Prohibition*. New York: New York University Press, 1996.

Rosenberg, Charles. "Banishing Risk." In *Morality and Health*, edited by Allan Brandt and Paul Rozin. New York: Routledge, 1997.

Rotskoff, Lori. *Love on the Rocks: Men, Women, and Alcohol in Post-World War II America*. Chapel Hill: University of North Carolina Press, 2002.

Rubin, Jay L. "Shifting Perspectives on the Alcoholism Treatment Movement, 1940–1955." *Journal of Studies on Alcohol* 40 (1979): 376–86.

Rubin, Jay L. "The Wet War: American Liquor Control, 1941–1945." In *Alcohol, Reform, and Society: The Liquor Issue in Social Context*, edited by Jack S. Blocker, Jr. Westport, Conn.: Greenwood Press, 1979.

Rushefsky, Mark E. *Making Cancer Policy*. Albany: State University of New York Press, 1986.

Samuel, Lawrence. *Brought to You By: Postwar Television Advertising and the American Dream*. Austin: University of Texas, 2001.

Sapolsky, Harvey M., ed. *Consuming Fears: The Politics of Product Risks.* New York: Basic Books, 1986.

Scates, Shelby. *Warren G. Magnuson and the Shaping of Twentieth-Century America.* Seattle: University of Washington Press, 1997.

Schofield, Lemuel. "First Amendment Implications of Banning Alcohol Beverage Ads on Radio & TV." *Journalism Quarterly* 62 (1985): 533–39.

Schooler, Dean. *Science, Scientists, and Public Policy.* New York: Free Press, 1971.

Schudson, Michael. "Symbols and Smokers: Advertising, Health Messages, and Public Policy." In *Smoking: Law, Policy and Culture,* edited by Stephen Sugarman and Robert Rabin. New York: Oxford University Press, 1993.

Schudson, Michael. "Delectable Materialism: Second Thoughts on Consumer Culture." In *Ethics of Consumption: The Good Life, Justice, and Global Stewardship,* edited by David A. Crocker and Toby Linden. Lanham, Md.: Rowman & Littlefield, 1998.

Schuman, Leonard, M. "The Origins of the Report of the Advisory Committee on Smoking and Health to the Surgeon General." *Journal of Public Health Policy* (March 1981): 19–27.

Schuster, Camille P., and Christine Pacelli Powell. "Comparison of Cigarette and Alcohol Advertising Controversies." *Journal of Advertising* 16 (1987): 26–28.

Seiter, Ellen. *Sold Separately: Children and Parents in Consumer Culture.* New Brunswick, N.J.: Rutgers University Press, 1993.

Silk, Leonard, and David Vogel. *Ethics and Profits: The Crisis of Confidence in American Business.* New York: Simon and Schuster, 1976.

Smith, Glenn H. *Langer of North Dakota: A Study in Isolationism, 1940–1959.* New York: Garland, 1979.

Sobel, Robert. *They Satisfy: The Cigarette In American Life.* Garden City, N.Y.: Anchor Books, 1978.

Socolofsky, Homer. *Arthur Capper: Publisher, Politician, and Philanthropist.* Lawrence: University of Kansas Press, 1979.

Spigel, Lynn. *Make Room for TV: Television and the Family Ideal in Postwar America.* Chicago: University of Chicago Press, 1992.

Stearns, Peter. *The Battleground of Desire: The Struggle for Self-Control in Modern America.* New York: New York University Press, 1999.

Stone, Jon. *On the Boundaries of American Evangelicalism: The Postwar Evangelical Coalition.* New York: St. Martin's Press, 1997.

Storms, Roger. *Partisan Prophets: A History of the Prohibition Party, 1854–1972.* Denver: National Prohibition Foundation, 1972.

Strickland, Donald, and David Pittman. *The Effects of Alcohol Beverage Advertising Practices and Messages on Alcohol Problems and Alcoholism in the United States: A Preliminary Report.* St. Louis: Washington University Social Science Institute, 1980.

Strickland, Stephen. *Politics, Science, and Dread Disease: A Short History of United States Medical Research Policy.* Cambridge, Mass.: Harvard University Press, 1972.

Tate, Cassandra. *Cigarette Wars: The Triumph of 'the Little White Slaver.'* New York: Oxford University Press, 1999.

Taylor, Peter. *Smoke Ring: The Politics of Tobacco.* London: Bodley Head, 1984.

Tesh, Sylvia Noble. *Hidden Arguments: Political Ideology and Disease Prevention Policy.* New Brunswick, N.J.: Rutgers University Press, 1988.

Troyer, Ronald, and Gerald Markle. *Cigarettes: The Battle over Smoking.* New Brunswick, N.J.: Rutgers University Press, 1983.

Tye, Joe B. "Cigarette Marketing: Ethical Conservatism or Corporate Violence?" *New York State Journal of Medicine* 85 (July 1985): 324–27.

Vanderpool, Harold Y. "The Wesleyan-Methodist Tradition." In *Caring and Curing: Health and Medicine in the Western Religious Traditions,* edited by Ronald Numbers and Darrel Amundsen. New York: Macmillan, 1986.

Viscusi, W. Kip. *Smoke-Filled Rooms: A Postmortem on the Tobacco Deal.* Chicago: University of Chicago Press, 2002.

Wagner, David. *The New Temperance: The American Obsession With Sin and Vice.* Boulder, Colo.: Westview Press, 1997.

Wagner, Susan. *Cigarette Country: Tobacco in American History and Politics.* New York: Praeger, 1971.

Walters, Ronald G., ed. *Scientific Authority and Twentieth-Century America.* Baltimore: Johns Hopkins University Press, 1997.

Watts, Thomas, ed. *Social Thought on Alcoholism: A Comprehensive Review.* Malabar, Fla.: Robert E. Krieger, 1986.

Wertham, Fredric. *Seduction of the Innocent.* New York: Rinehart & Co., 1953.

Whelan, Elizabeth. *A Smoking Gun: How the Tobacco Industry Gets Away with Murder.* Edited by Stephen Barrett. Philadelphia: George F. Stickley Co., 1984.

White, Larry. *Merchants of Death: The American Tobacco Industry.* New York: Beech Tree Books, 1988.

White, William L. *Slaying the Dragon: The History of Addiction Treatment and Recovery in America.* Bloomington, Ill.: Chestnut Health Systems, 1998.

Whiteside, Thomas. *Selling Death: Cigarette Advertising and Public Health.* New York: Liveright, 1971.

Whyte, William H. *The Organization Man.* New York: Simon and Schuster, 1956.

Wilson, James Q., ed. *The Politics of Regulation.* New York: Basic Books, 1980.

Witkowski, Terrence. "Promise Them Anything: A Cultural History of Cigarette Advertising Health Claims." *Current Issues and Research in Advertising* 13 (1991): 393–409.

Wuthnow, Robert. *The Restructuring of American Religion: Society and Faith Since World War II.* Princeton, N.J.: Princeton University Press, 1988.

Wynder, E. L., and E. A. Graham. "Tobacco Smoking as a Possible Etiologic Factor in Bronchogenic Carcinoma. *Journal of the American Medical Association* 143 (1950): 329–36.

Younger, Steve. "Alcoholic Beverage Advertising on the Airwaves: Alternatives to a Ban or Counteradvertising." *UCLA Law Review* 34 (1987): 1139–93.

GOVERNMENT DOCUMENTS

Alcohol

Congressional Record.

U.S. Senate. Subcommittee of the Committee on Interstate Commerce. *To Prohibit the Advertising of Alcoholic Beverages by Radio.* 76th Cong., 1st sess. 29 and 31 March 1939.

U.S. Senate. Committee on Interstate and Foreign Commerce. *Liquor Advertising.* 80th Cong., 1st sess. 12 and 13 May 1947.

U.S. Senate. Committee on Interstate and Foreign Commerce. *Liquor Advertising.* 80th Cong., 2nd sess. 21–22 April 1948.

U.S. Senate. Committee on Interstate and Foreign Commerce. *Liquor Advertising.* 81st Cong., 2nd sess. 12–14 January 1950.

U.S. Senate. Committee on Interstate and Foreign Commerce. *Liquor Advertising Over Radio and Television.* 82nd Cong., 2nd sess. 30–31 January and 6–7 February 1952.

U.S. House of Representatives. Committee on Interstate and Foreign Commerce. *Advertising of Alcoholic Beverages.* 83rd Cong., 2nd sess. 19–21 and 24 May 1954.

U.S. House of Representatives. Committee on Interstate and Foreign Commerce. *Advertising of Alcoholic Beverages.* House Report 2670. 83rd Cong., 2nd sess. 1954.

U.S. Senate. Subcommittee of the Committee on Interstate and Foreign Commerce. *Liquor Advertising.* 83rd Cong., 2nd sess. 21, 22, and 24 June 1954.

U.S. House of Representatives. Committee on Interstate and Foreign Commerce. *Advertising of Alcoholic Beverages.* 84th Cong., 2nd sess. 16–17 February 1956.

U.S. Senate. Committee on Interstate and Foreign Commerce. *Liquor Advertising.* 84th Cong., 2nd sess. 15–17 February 1956.

U.S. Senate. Committee on Interstate and Foreign Commerce. *Alcoholic Beverage Advertising.* 85th Cong., 2nd sess. 22, 23, 29, and 30 April 1958.

U.S. Senate. Committee on Labor and Public Welfare. Subcommittee on Alcoholism and Narcotics. *Media Images of Alcohol: The Effects of Advertising and Other Media on Alcohol Abuse.* 94th Cong., 2nd sess. 8 and 11 March 1976.

U.S. Senate. Committee on Human Resources. Subcommittee on Alcoholism and Drug Abuse. *Alcohol Labeling and Fetal Alcohol Syndrome.* 95th Cong., 2nd sess. 31 January 1978.

U.S. Senate. Committee on Labor and Human Resources. Subcommittee on Alcoholism and Drug Abuse. *Effects of Alcohol Consumption During Pregnancy.* 97th Cong., 2nd sess. 21 September 1982.

U.S. Senate. Committee on Labor and Human Resources. Subcommittee on Children, Family, Drugs and Alcoholism. *Reviewing Advertisements and Television Commercials Promoting the Sale and Consumption of Alcoholic Beverages.* 99th Cong., 1st sess. 7 February 1985.

U.S. House of Representatives. Committee on Energy and Commerce. Subcommittee on Telecommunications, Consumer Protection, and Finance. *Beer and Wine Advertising: Impact of Electronic Media.* 99th Cong., 1st sess. 21 May 1985.

U.S. Senate. Committee on Commerce, Science, and Transportation. Subcommittee on the Consumer. *Alcohol Warning Labels.* 100th Cong., 2nd sess. 10 August 1988.

U.S. House of Representatives. Committee on Energy and Commerce. Subcommittee on Transportation and Hazardous Materials. *Health Warnings on Alcoholic Beverage Advertisements.* 101st Cong., 2nd sess. 18 July 1990.

U.S. House of Representatives. Select Committee on Children, Youth, and Families. *Preventing Underage Drinking: A Dialogue With the Surgeon General.* 102nd Cong., 1st sess., 15 November 1991.

U.S. House of Representatives. Committee on Energy and Commerce. Subcommittee on Transportation and Hazardous Materials. *Oversight of FTC's Shared Responsibilities.* 102nd Cong., 1st sess. 21 November 1991.

U.S. Senate. Committee on Commerce, Science, and Transportation. Subcommittee on the Consumer. *Alcohol Beverage Advertising Act, S. 664.* 102nd Cong., 2nd sess. 2 April 1992.

Cigarettes

Congressional Record.

U.S. House of Representatives. Committee on Government Operations. The Legal and Monetary Subcommittee. *False and Misleading Advertising (Filter-Tip Cigarettes).* 85th Cong., 1st sess. July 1957.

U.S. House of Representatives. Committee on Government Operations. The Legal and Monetary Subcommittee. *False and Misleading Advertising (Filter-Tip Cigarettes).* 85th Cong., 2nd Sess. H. Rept. 1372, 20 February 1958.

U.S. House of Representatives. Committee on Interstate and Foreign Commerce, *Cigarette Labeling and Advertising.* 88th Cong., 2nd sess. 1964.

Federal Trade Commission. *Trade Regulation Rule for the Prevention of Unfair or Deceptive Advertising and Labeling of Cigarettes in Relation to the Health Hazards of Smoking.* Washington, D.C., 22 June 1964.

U.S. Public Health Service. *Smoking and Health: Report of the Advisory Committee to the Surgeon General of the Public Health Service.* U.S. Department of Health, Education, and Welfare, PHS Publication No. 1103, Washington, D.C.: U.S. Government Printing Office, 1964.

U.S. House of Representatives. Committee on Interstate and Foreign Commerce. *Cigarette Labeling and Advertising—1965.* 89th Cong., 1st sess. 1965.

U.S. Senate. Committee on Commerce. *Cigarette Labeling and Advertising.* 89th Cong., 1st sess. 1965.

U.S. Senate. Committee on Interstate and Foreign Commerce. *Cigarette Labeling.* 89th Cong., 1st sess. S. Rept. 195, 19 May 1965.

U.S. House of Representatives. Committee on Interstate and Foreign Commerce. *Report on Federal Cigarette Labeling and Advertising.* 89th Cong., 1st sess. H. Rept. 449, 8 June 1965.

U.S. Congress. House and Senate Conference Report. *Federal Cigarette Labeling and Advertising Act.* 89th Cong., 1st sess. H. Rept. 586, 1 July 1965.

Federal Trade Commission. *Report to Congress, Pursuant to the Federal Cigarette Labeling and Advertising Act.* 30 June 1967.

Federal Trade Commission. *Report to Congress Pursuant to the Federal Cigarette Labeling and Advertising Act.* 30 June 1968.

U.S. Senate. Consumer Subcommittee of the Committee on Commerce. *Cigarette Advertising and Labeling.* 91st Cong., 1st sess. 22 July 1969.

U.S. House of Representatives. Committee on Interstate and Foreign Commerce. *Cigarette Labeling and Advertising—1969.* 91st Cong., 1st sess. 1969.

Other

Federal Trade Commission. *Hearings on Modern Advertising Practices.* Washington, D.C., 1971.

U.S. Senate. Committee on Congress. Subcommittee on Communications. *Surgeon General's Report by the Scientific Advisory Committee on Television and Social Behavior.* 92nd Cong., 2nd sess. March 1972.

Federal Communications Commission. *Fairness Doctrine and Public Interest Standards* 39 Fed. Reg. 26372, 1974.

Public Health Service. *Healthy People: The Surgeon General's Report on Health Promotion and Disease Prevention.* Washington, D.C.: U.S. Department of Health, Education, and Welfare, 1979.

Federal Trade Commission. *In the Matter of Children's Advertising: FTC Final Staff Report and Recommendation.* Washington, D.C., 1981.

COURT CASES

Valentine v. Chrestensen 316 U.S. 52 (1942).

New York Times v. Sullivan 376 U.S. 254 (1964).

Capital Broadcasting v. Mitchell 333 F. Supp. 582, U.S. Dist. (1971).

Bigelow v. Virginia 421 U.S. 809 (1975).

Virginia State Board of Pharmacy et al. v. Virginia Citizens Consumer Council, Inc., et al. 425 U.S. 748 (1976).

Bates v. State Bar of Arizona 433 U.S. 350 (1977).

Central Hudson Gas v. Public Service Commission of New York 447 U.S. 557 (1980).

Posadas de Puerto Rico Assoc., dba Condado Holiday Inn v. Tourism Company of Puerto Rico et al. 478 U.S. 328 (1986).

44 Liquormart, Inc. v. State of Rhode Island, 517 U.S. 484 (1996).

Reno v. American Civil Liberties Union, 521 U.S. 844 (1997).

Greater New Orleans Broadcasting Association Inc. v. U.S. 200 U.S. 321, 337 (1999).

Food and Drug Administration v. Brown and Williamson Tobacco Corporation 120 U.S. 1291(2000).

Lorillard Tobacco Company v. Reilly 533 U.S. 525 (2001).

INDEX